Agents in Early Welsh and
Early Irish

Agents in Early Welsh and Early Irish

NICOLE MÜLLER

OXFORD
UNIVERSITY PRESS

Great Clarendon Street, Oxford OX2 6DP

Oxford University Press is a department of the University of Oxford.
It furthers the University's objective of excellence in research, scholarship,
and education by publishing worldwide in

Oxford New York

Athens Auckland Bangkok Bogotá Buenos Aires Calcutta
Cape Town Chennai Dar es Salaam Delhi Florence Hong Kong Istanbul
Karachi Kuala Lumpur Madrid Melbourne Mexico City Mumbai
Nairobi Paris São Paulo Singapore Taipei Tokyo Toronto Warsaw

and associated companies in Berlin Ibadan

Oxford is a registered trade mark of Oxford University Press
in the UK and in certain other countries

Published in the United States
by Oxford University Press Inc., New York

British Library Cataloguing in Publication Data

Data available

Library of Congress Cataloging-in-Publication Data

Müller, Nicole, 1962–
Agents in early Welsh and early Irish / Nicole Müller.
p.   cm.
Includes bibliographical references (p.   ) and index.
1. Welsh language—Middle Welsh, 1100–1400—Passive voice. 2.
Irish language—Middle Irish, 1100–1550—Passive voice. 3. Welsh
language—To 1100—Passive voice. 4. Irish language—To 1100
Passive voice. 5. Welsh language—Verbals. 6. Irish
language—Verbals. 7. Agent (Philosophy) I. Title.
PB2164 .M85 1999   491.6'65—dc21   99-16107

ISBN 0–19–823587–9

10 9 8 7 6 5 4 3 2 1

Typeset by BookMan Services
Printed in Great Britain
on acid-free paper by
Bookcraft (Bath) Ltd., Midsomer Norton

To Professor D. Ellis Evans

Contents

Abbreviations   ix

1. Introduction   1
    1.1. Data orientation versus theory orientation   1
    1.2. Tools of analysis: terms and definitions   2
    1.3. Construction types   8
    1.4. The textual basis of analysis   26
    1.5. Overview   33

2. Welsh   34
    2.1. Evidence from narrative texts   34
    2.2. Evidence from law texts   63
    2.3. A Middle Welsh agentive passive? Evidence from annals   68
    2.4. Related categories: IAG, CAUSE, and INST   74

3. Irish   83
    3.1. Evidence from narrative texts: VN clauses in
         Táin Bó Cúailnge   83
    3.2. VN clauses in non-narrative texts: laws and annals   115
    3.3. The agentive passive in narrative texts: evidence from
         Táin Bó Cúailnge   140
    3.4. Full passives in laws and annals   160
    3.5. A 'noun phrase passive'?   165
    3.6. Related categories: IAG, CAUSE, and INST   170

4. Aspects of Meaning: P1 and its Markers   179
    4.1. Earlier analyses of P1 marking   180
    4.2. The genitive as P1 marker   185
    4.3. Welsh *o*: P1 as source   187
    4.4. Irish *ó*: P1 and source   188
    4.5. Irish *do*: P1 as affected entity—the low-energy P1   190
    4.6. Welsh *i*: P1 as affected entity   193
    4.7. Irish *la*: the person in charge   195
    4.8. Welsh *gan* and *y gan*: P1 as the person in charge, and
         point of departure   197

5. Summary and Concluding Remarks   201

Appendices   205
References   249
Index   259

Abbreviations

Works of reference

AC   *Annales Cambriae*, ed. J. Williams ab Ithel (London: Longman, Green, Longman & Roberts, 1860)

Acall. *Acallam na Senórach*, ed. W. Stokes (Irische Texte, 4th ser., vol. 1; Leipzig: Hirzel, 1900)

Aen.   *Imthechta Æniasa. The Irish Æneid*, ed. G. Calder (Irish Texts Society, vol. 6; London: Irish Texts Society, 1907)

AL   *Ancient Laws and Institutes of Wales*, ed. A. Owen (London: Record Commission, 1841); quoted for manuscript variants of *Cyngh.*

Arch. *Archiv für celtische Lexikographie*

AU   *The Annals of Ulster (to A.D. 1131)*, Part I: *Text and Translation*, ed. S. Mac Airt and G. Mac Niocaill (Dublin: Dublin Institute for Advanced Studies, 1983)

B.   *Branwen Uerch Lyr*, in *PKM* 29–48

BB   *Bechbretha: An Old Irish Law-Tract on Bee-Keeping*, ed. T. M. O. Charles-Edwards and F. Kelly (Early Irish Law Series, 1; Dublin: Dublin Institute for Advanced Studies, 1983)

BCr   'Bretha Crólige', ed. D. A. Binchy, *Ériu*, 12 (1938), 1–77

BDC   'Bretha Déin Chécht', ed. D. A. Binchy, *Ériu*, 20 (1966), 1–66

BR   *Breudwyt Ronabwy*, ed. M. Richards (Caerdydd: Gwasg Prifysgol Cymru, 1948)

BT(R) *Brut y Tywysogyon or the Chronicle of the Princes. Red Book of Hergest Version*, ed. T. Jones (2nd edn., Cardiff: University of Wales Press, 1973)

BT(P) *Brut y Tywysogyon. Peniarth Ms 20*, ed. T. Jones (Cardiff: University of Wales Press, 1941)

CCR   *Cath Ruis na Ríg*

CCath. *In Cath Catharda*, ed. W. Stokes (Irische Texte, 4th ser., vol. 2; Leipzig: Hirzel, 1900)

CG   *Críth Gablach*, ed. D. A. Binchy (Medieval and Modern Irish Series, 11; Dublin: Dublin Institute for Advanced Studies, 1941; repr. 1979)

ChO   *Chwedleu Odo*, ed. J. Williams (Caerdydd: Gwasg Prifysgol Cymru, 1958)

CLl   *Cyfranc Lludd a Llefelys*, ed. B. F. Roberts (Dublin: Dublin Institute for Advanced Studies, 1975)

CMT	*Cath Maige Tuired*, ed. E. Gray (Irish Texts Society, vol. 52; London: Irish Texts Society, 1982)
CO	*Culhwch ac Olwen*, ed. R. Bromwich and D. S. Evans (Caerdydd: Gwasg Prifysgol Cymru, 1988)
CRR	*Cath Ruis na Ríg* (*LL*, lines 22621–23285)
CW	*Cronica de Wallia*, in T. Jones, 'Cronica de Wallia and Other Documents from Exeter Cathedral Library Ms 3514', *Bulletin of the Board of Celtic Studies*, 12/1–2 (1946), 27–44
Cyngh.	'Llyfr Cynghawsedd', ed. A. Rhys Wiliam, *Bulletin of the Board of Celtic Studies*, 35 (1988), 73–85
DIL	(Contributions to a) *Dictionary of the Irish Language, Based Mainly on Old and Middle Irish Materials* (Dublin: Royal Irish Academy; 1913–76; compact edn., 1983)
FB	*Fled Bricrend* (*LU*, lines 8038–9219)
GMW	D. S. Evans, *A Grammar of Middle Welsh* (Dublin: Dublin Institute for Advanced Studies, 1964; repr. 1976)
GOI	R. Thurneysen, *A Grammar of Old Irish* (Dublin: Dublin Institute for Advanced Studies, 1946; repr. 1980)
GPC	*Geiriadur Prifysgol Cymru. A Dictionary of the Welsh Language* (Caerdydd: Gwasg Prifysgol Cymru, 1950–)
LL	*The Book of Leinster formerly Lebar na Núachongbála*, ed. R. I. Best, O. Bergin, M. A. O'Brien, and A. O'Sullivan (6 vols.; Dublin: Dublin Institute for Advanced Studies, 1954–83)
LU	*Lebor na Huidre*, ed. R. I. Best and O. Bergin (Dublin: Hodges, Figgis & Co. for the Royal Irish Academy, 1929)
Ma.	*Math Uab Mathonwy*, in *PKM* 67–92
Ml	'The Milan Glosses and Scholia on the Psalms', in W. Stokes and J. Strachan, *Thesaurus Palaeohibernicus*, i (Oxford: Oxford University Press, 1901; repr. Dublin: Dublin Institute for Advanced Studies, 1975), 7–483
MLl	*Manawydan Uab Llyr*, in *PKM* 49–66
Ow.	*Owein*, ed. R. L. Thomson (Dublin: Dublin Institute for Advanced Studies, 1968; repr. 1975)
P.	*Pwyll Pendeuic Dyuet*, in *PKM* 1–28
Per.	*Historia Peredur vab Efrawc*, ed. G. Goetinck (Caerdydd: Gwasg Prifysgol Cymru, 1976)
PKM	*Pedeir Keinc y Mabinogi*, ed. I. Williams (Caerdydd: Gwasg Prifysgol Cymru, 1930; repr. 1982)
RBH	*Red Book of Hergest*
RC	*Revue Celtique*
ScM	*Scéla Mucce Meic Dathó*, ed. R. Thurneysen (Mediaeval and Modern Irish Series, vol. 6; Dublin: Dublin Institute for Advanced Studies, 1935; repr. 1975)

SG	'Glosses on Priscian (St. Gall)', in W. Stokes and J. Strachan, *Thesaurus Palaeohibernicus*, ii (Oxford: Oxford University Press, 1903; repr. Dublin: Dublin Institute for Advanced Studies, 1975), 49–224
TBC	*Táin Bó Cúailnge*
TBC I	*Táin Bó Cúailnge: Recension I*, ed. C. O'Rahilly (Dublin: Dublin Institute for Advanced Studies, 1976)
TBC LL	*Táin Bó Cúalnge from the Book of Leinster*, ed. C. O'Rahilly (Dublin: Dublin Institute for Advanced Studies, 1967; repr. 1984)
TBC III	M. Nettlau, 'The Fragment of the Tain Bó Cuailnge in MS Egerton 93', *Revue Celtique*, 14 (1893), 254–66; M. Nettlau, 'The Fragment of the Tain Bó Cuailnge in MS Egerton 93', *Revue Celtique*, 15 (1894), 62–78, 198–208; R. Thurneysen, 'Táin Bó Cúailghni nach H. 2. 17', *Zeitschrift für Celtische Philologie*, 8 (1912), 525–54
TBC St.	*The Stowe Version of Táin Bó Cúailnge*, ed. C. O'Rahilly (Dublin: Dublin Institute for Advanced Studies, 1961)
TBF	*Die Romanze von Froech und Findabair. Táin Bó Froích*, ed. W. Meid (IBK Sonderheft 30; Innsbruck: Universität, 1970)
UR	*Uraicecht na Ríar: The Poetic Grades in Early Irish Law*, ed. L. Breatnach (Early Irish Law Series, 2; Dublin: Dublin Institute for Advanced Studies, 1987)
VKG	H. Pedersen, *Vergleichende Grammatik der Keltischen Sprachen*, i. *Lautlehre*; ii. *Bedeutungslehre (Wortlehre)* (Göttingen: Vandenhoeck & Ruprecht, 1909, 1913)
Wb	'The Würzburg Glosses and Scholia on the Pauline Epistles', in W. Stokes and J. Strachan, *Thesaurus Palaeohibernicus*, i (Oxford: Oxford University Press, 1901; repr. Dublin: Dublin Institute for Advanced Studies, 1975), 499–712
WBRh	*White Book of Rhydderch*
WML	A. W. Wade-Evans, *Welsh Medieval Law* (Oxford: Clarendon Press, 1909)
ZCP	*Zeitschrift für Celtische Philologie*

Grammatical glosses

COP	copula
fut	future
fut2	secondary future
gen	genitive
impers	impersonal
impf	imperfect
INT	interrogative (particle)
ipv	imperative

NEG	negative (particle)
pass	passive
pl	plural
pres	present
pret	preterite
PRO	pronoun, pronominal form
PRT	(verbal) particle
pt.sub	past subjunctive
rel	relative
sg	singular
sub	subjunctive
VN	Verbal Noun

Other abbreviations

AG	Agent
EXP	Experiencer
IAG	Indirect Agent
INST	Instrument
IPN	Irish Process Noun
LPN	Latin Process Noun
P1	Participant 1
P2	Participant 2
PN	Process Noun

1 Introduction

This book is written with readers from a variety of linguistic, philological, and literary backgrounds in mind, sharing an interest in the texts of medieval Ireland and Wales. Among its aims are the presentation of specific data sets in their context, and the analysis of specific syntactic and semantic structures within their textual environments. What ties data from texts of various genres and two languages together are two closely linked common concerns: the types and use of constructions in which the participant most usually expressed by the subject of an active, finite clause is expressed by other means—for example, a prepositional phrase.

It is hoped that readers working in different frameworks and settings, among them functional and cognitive linguists, Celtic and comparative philologists and medievalists will find the presentation of data and theory in this study manageable and valuable for their own approaches.

1.1. Data orientation versus theory orientation

The approach chosen in this book is, if not theory neutral, then data oriented rather than theory oriented. The terminology and theoretical notions employed have been chosen with data orientation in mind: they are tools to describe data (as opposed to data being selected to illustrate a specific theoretical framework). Some readers may criticize this kind of approach as too eclectic and vague, in view of the fact that there are many different theoretical approaches to the analysis of language available to the linguist. But, on the other hand, data orientation may make this study accessible to a wider variety of readers.

It has to be pointed out, though, that the analyses carried out here have benefited greatly from several theoretical frameworks—for example, Simon Dik's Functional Grammar (e.g. Dik 1989), Systemic Functional Grammar (e.g. Halliday 1985), Cognitive Grammar (e.g. Langacker 1987, 1991). However, it is not to be understood as, for example, a functional grammar treatment of medieval Irish and Welsh verbal noun (VN) constructions. Both functional and cognitive linguistic frameworks address the question 'how does the natural language user work' (Dik 1989: 1). Dik juxtaposes what he calls the 'formal paradigm' and the 'functional paradigm':

In the formal paradigm a language is regarded as an abstract formal object . . . and a grammar is conceptualized primarily as an attempt at characterizing this formal object in terms of rules of formal syntax to be applied independently of the meanings and uses of the constructions described. Syntax is thus given methodological priority over semantics and pragmatics.

> In the functional paradigm, on the other hand, a language is in the first place conceptualized as an instrument of social interaction among human beings. . . . Within this paradigm one attempts to reveal the instrumentality of language with respect to what people do and achieve with it in social interaction.   (Dik 1989: 2)

The objections of (some, if not all) cognitive linguists to the formal paradigm overlap at least partly with those voiced by Dik, and in addition particular emphasis is put on the unacceptability of the language faculty as an autonomous component of the mind.[1] A fundamental assumption of cognitive linguistics is, as Taylor (1995: 19) puts it, that 'aspects of experience and cognition are crucially implicated in the structure and functioning of language'. Functional and cognitive linguistics share as a common denominator the central importance of, in Dik's words, 'natural language users', and of language as a fundamental aspect of their functioning in interaction.

1.2. Tools of analysis: terms and definitions

1.2.1. Participants and processes

This study is, in the main, an investigation of **participants** in **processes,** and the expression of participants in certain syntactic constructions current in medieval Irish and Welsh texts. Specifically, we are concerned with the expression of what I shall call **participant 1 (P1)**, and, though to a lesser extent, with **participant 2 (P2)**. In English (and indeed medieval Irish and Welsh), P1 is typically expressed by the subject of a finite clause, and P2 as the direct object of a transitive active clause, while the process is expressed by a finite verb, as illustrated in the following examples:

(1) (*a*)   Pat kissed Hilary.

(*b*)   Pat saw Hilary.

(*c*)   Pat impressed Hilary.

(*d*)   Pat fell off the ladder.

(*e*)   Pat died.

However, there are other syntactic options for the expression of participants and processes alike. This study is mainly concerned with constructions in which P1 is *not* expressed as the subject of an active clause. Consider again the situation por-

---

[1] See Taylor (1995: 16–20) for further discussion. Langacker (1990: 1) lists the views of linguistic (chiefly syntactic) theory that he most finds fault with thus: '(i) language is a self-contained system amenable to algorithmic characterization, with sufficient autonomy to be studied in essential isolation from broader cognitive concerns; (ii) grammar (syntax in particular) is an independent aspect of linguistic structure distinct from both lexicon and semantics, and (iii) if meaning falls within the purview of linguistic analysis, it is properly described by some type of formal logic based on truth conditions.'

trayed in (1a). It is possible to encode this situation in different ways, such that P1 is not the subject of a clause, for example:

(1) (a′) Hilary was kissed by Pat.

   (a″) Hilary's kissing by Pat (caused much amusement).

   (a‴) Pat's kissing of Hilary (caused much amusement).

These different syntactic patterns may fulfil different functions in a textual environment, and different contexts make different syntactic structures appropriate. At the heart of this study are constructions in medieval Irish and Welsh where P1 is not the subject of a finite clause, but is encoded in other ways. The different constructions that are to be encountered are examined both internally and externally: the 'internal examination' looks at the construction itself. Compare the following two (constructed) Old Irish and Middle Welsh examples:[2]

(2) (a)   *Ro·cét laíd la hAilill.*
          sing_pass.pret.sg song with Ailill
          'A song was sung by Ailill.'

   (b)   *Canu can o Arthur.*
          sing_VN song from Arthur
          'Arthur sang a song.'

Sentence (2a) is an example of what is commonly called a passive (and this is also the term used here, for the sake of brevity and convenience): P1 is expressed by means of a prepositional phrase, whereas P2 fulfils the role of subject, and the finite verb has 'passive' morphology. The question whether we can speak of a passive in Irish and Welsh,[3] in the sense that, for example, Latin has a passive (i.e. a personal passive) will be considered in some detail. Other questions raised concern, for example, the prepositions that may be selected to mark P1 in different construction types.

Sentence (2b) illustrates what shall be called a **verbal noun** (VN) construction: a syntactic construction where the process content is expressed not by a finite verb, but by a non-finite verb form that functions syntactically much like any other noun. P1 and P2 may enter into various syntactic relations with the VN.

The choice of construction—i.e. the choice of any one of several ways to encode a situation—is another field of investigation considered here. Below are examples of Irish transitive VN constructions (i.e. constructions where a VN expresses a

---

[2] The glosses provided for the Welsh and Irish examples in the text are intended as a grammatical orientation for the non-specialist reader, to give an indication of the structure of the construction cited in the example. As a general rule, only the verbal noun or passive/impersonal construction itself is glossed. Where a wider context is cited in the example, this will be translated, but not glossed. The abbreviations used in glosses are listed on pp. xi–xii. The translations of prepositions in glosses are placeholders, at best indications of meaning, rather than an attempt to capture the exact meaning of the prepositions in question. Case forms of nouns are given only in cases where their omission could potentially be misleading for non-specialist readers.

[3] Unless otherwise specified, Irish used on its own shall refer to Old and Middle Irish in the context of this study, and Welsh shall refer to Middle Welsh. Wherever a more specific description is necessary, additional labels, such as Old, Middle, or Modern, will be added, as appropriate.

process in which both a P1 and a P2 are involved); the situation in (2a') to (2a''') is that already encountered in (2a):

(2) (a')   (Is dóig la Conn) *cétal laíde do Ailill.*
           sing_VN song_gen to Ailill
           'Conn thinks Ailill has recited a poem.'

    (a'') (Is dóig la Conn) *laíd do chétal do Ailill.*
           song to sing_VN to Ailill
           'Conn thinks Ailill has recited a poem.'

    (a''') (Is dóig la Conn) *Ailill do chétal laíde.*
           Ailill to sing_VN song_gen
           'Conn thinks Ailill has recited a poem.'

Including the active and passive clauses, we have thus five different ways of expressing the same situation, in which the process may be either a finite verb or a VN, and P1 and P2 may enter into various syntactic relationships with either the finite verb or the VN. The study investigates the textual functions of different construction types in Irish and Welsh—i.e. how the various types fit into their textual environments.

1.2.2. Participants and circumstances: agents, experiencers, and others

The participants in a situation enter into a variety of relations with the process, depending on the type of process. The characteristics of participants, their roles played in the situations, have been subsumed under headings such as semantic functions (cf. e.g. Dik 1989) or participant roles (Halliday 1985). While I make no claim that these terms refer to exactly the same things, it would be fair to say that, in their respective theoretical frameworks, they serve as labels for the meaning role fulfilled by participants within situations. Returning again to the examples in (1) above, we can see that P1 in (1a) *Pat kissed Hilary,* (most likely) initiates the action of kissing, and is in control over said action. In (1b), *Pat saw Hilary,* P1 can only be said to be in control of the process in so far as it is in Pat's power to close his/her eyes and thus interrupting the experience of seeing Hilary, which he/she did not consciously and voluntarily initiate. In (1c), *Pat impressed Hilary,* it is difficult to decide whether P1 has any control or initiative in the effect on Hilary; Pat may have consciously set out to make an impression through an action, or the situation of Hilary being impressed may have come about without the knowledge and conscious involvement by P1.[4] Control and volition are absent from the make-up of P1

---

[4] In Dik's Functional Grammar framework, the semantic function of the first argument of the predicate *impress* (in our terms, the role of P1 of the situation that has *impress* as its process) is labelled Positioner, defined as 'the entity controlling a Position'. This function is also illustrated by expressions such as *John (Po) kept his money in a sock,* or *John (Po) was grateful to Mary,* or *John (Po) lives in London* (Dik 1989: 103 ff.). One problem with classifying roles in situations out of context (or, in Dik's terms, semantic functions of arguments in predicate frames) is that one verb may express processes that differ according to the exact characteristics of the participants involved.

in (1d) *Pat fell off the ladder* and (1e) *Pat died*. P1 may here be described as under-going an experience which is not under his/her control.

In the following discussion, a P1 that is an animate entity exercising volitional, and prototypically total, control over a process will be labelled an **agent** (AG). AGS are prototypically[5] human and carry out actions—i.e. processes that involve a degree of energy transfer from P1 and often an effect on a second participant, P2. However, the term AG applies not only to P1 in an action encoded by a transitive verb, but also to P1 of motion processes (typically expressed by intransitive verbs) that are under P1's control; for example, *walk*, *run*, *jump* all describe motion processes that are controlled by P1, whereas *fall* does not. P1 that is principally affected by a process, as in (1d) and (1e), will be referred to as an **experiencer** (EXP). The EXP prototypic-ally is a human entity that does not have control over the process it is affected by. By this definition, the P1 of processes such as *fall*, or *die*, could be labelled a prototypical experiencer, whereas the P1 of perception processes such as *see*, or *hear*, would be more peripheral members of the same category: one may exercise some control over a process of seeing by averting or closing one's eyes, for example. P1s of perception processes are for the present purposes included under the category EXP.

The discussion in this book will largely be concerned with the types of construc-tion where a P1 is expressed by some means other than the subject of a finite verb, and the marking of P1 within these constructions. In connection with the marking of P1, more specifically when discussing the meanings of prepositions used to mark P1, we shall also have occasion to refer to the categories CAUSE, **Indirect Agent** (IAG), and **Instrument** (INST).[6] The CAUSE is defined as an influence contributing to the coming about of, or advanced by the speaker as an explanation for, a situ-ation, as in:

(3)   Pat kissed Hilary because of her overwhelming beauty.

The IAG is an entity, prototypically human, that is causally involved in a process taking place, as in:

(4)   She had a child by him.

The category IAG can thus be seen as a subcategory of CAUSE. The INST is an entity (abstract or concrete) used by an AG to carry out an action, as in:

(5)   Pat smashed the window with a brick.

---

[5] For further discussion of prototype categories, see Section 1.3.3.

[6] Note that in Dik's Functional Grammar framework, categories such as *Cause, Instrument, Manner,* etc. are treated as *satellites*, as opposed to the *arguments* of the predication: whereas arguments are required by the predicate, satellites add further, additional information (cf. Dik 1989: chs. 4, 9). In Halliday's Functional Grammar, Manner (which includes instrumentality) and Cause are treated as *circumstantial elements*, as opposed to *participants* (see Halliday 1985). Where necessary, IAG, INST, and CAUSE will be collectively referred to as circumstantial elements here (note that the definitions are not borrowed from Halliday, although the term is). However, a distinction, on the clause level, between arguments and satellites, or participants and circumstantial elements, is not of direct relevance for the purposes of this investigation, since the categories CAUSE, IAG, and INST will be considered only from the point of view of prepositional marking, in connection with the prepositional marking of *P1*.

1.2.3. Beyond the single clause: participants in context

As mentioned briefly above, it is assumed here that different textual environments make different clause structures appropriate, in other words, that the choice of, for example, a passive with an overt agent as opposed to an active clause, or the choice of a VN construction rather than a finite clause, are not random, but motivated. It is, of course, difficult to predict the motivations of speakers/writers, especially of languages where we do not have direct access to those speakers. However, what can be accomplished is the observation of patterns: do certain clause types tend to occur in conjunction with other features? The (potential) patterns observed here concern the status of the information presented by P1 and P2, the continuity of the participants P1 and P2 in VN and passive clauses, and the roles of agentive constructions in their narrative environments.

1.2.3.1. INFORMATION PACKAGING

The presentation and ordering of information may be one feature that motivates the choice of a particular clause structure. Information types have been defined and handled differently in various linguistic treatises. The definitions chosen here are related to ones found in several functional frameworks, but modified to make them suitable for the textual material under investigation here. Information as represented by P1, P2, or the process element (i.e. the finite or non-finite verbal element) is labelled given, new, or inferable.

A *given* piece of information is one that has already been mentioned; it is recoverable and uniquely identifiable as something that has already occurred in the text. An item that the reader/listener can infer from a discourse entity that has already been introduced, but that has not itself been mentioned before, is labelled *inferable*. Items that have not been mentioned before and that cannot be inferred are defined as representing *new* information.[7]

In dealing with written texts of sometimes considerable length, the problem arises whether a piece of information that does not recur within a certain span of text—that is, a certain period of reading or listening time—is lost, forgotten, by the

---

[7] This tripartite classification roughly corresponds to one proposed by Brown and Yule (1983: 183, basically following Prince 1981). Prince uses the term *evoked*, rather than *given*, which is the label used by Halliday (1967, 1985) and Chafe (1976). Chafe (1976: 30) defines *given* as 'that knowledge which the speaker assumes to be in the consciousness of the addressee at the time of utterance'. This will often be an item that has been mentioned before, but this is not necessarily the case. Participants in the conversation (*I, you*) can be assumed to be in the addressee's consciousness at any time they are mentioned, yet need not have been explicitly referred to before. Halliday (1967: 211) characterizes given information as 'recoverable either anaphorically or situationally', and uses the label *new* 'not in the sense that it has not been previously mentioned, although it is often the case that is has not been, but in the sense that the speaker presents it as not being recoverable from the preceding discourse' (1967: 204). The definitions of Given ('this is not news') and New ('attend to this; this is news') in Halliday (1985: 277) again focus on the speaker's treatment of information as either recoverable or non-recoverable. It should be noted that Halliday's classification of information structure, and what he calls the 'infomation unit', first and foremost applies to spoken, rather than written language.

reader,[8] and whether this piece of information, if it is reintroduced at a later stage, is processed as new, or as 'remembered'. In other words, does the extra effort expended on recovering the item have any effect on its salience in the context in which it occurs, and does this effect make the status of the 'remembered' item comparable to that of an inferred item? In the context of this analysis, these questions would appear to be impossible to answer with any confidence. It is not possible to establish limits after which information is lost; not only does this depend very much on the concentration span of the reader, but also to a large extent on the degree to which a reader is familiar with a text or subject matter: if a text or subject matter are familiar from many previous encounters, an effect of remembering or reestablishing, for example, the main characters of a story will take place even before the first mention of those characters. However, keeping this reservation in mind, the only possible way of assessing the novelty of information presented in our texts is by reading it from the textual surface, since neither contemporary producers nor consumers of those texts are available to us.

1.2.3.2. CONTINUITY: RESUMPTION OF INFORMATION

The term *continuity* describes the resumption of an item from a preceding clause. The continuity parameter of analysis is thus closely linked to the classification of information as new, given, or inferable. Two types of continuity are distinguished here. An item may be resumed from a preceding clause and fulfil the same participant role as in the clause from which it is resumed. Two subtypes of this type of continuity are illustrated in example (6): (6*a*) shows resumption of a subject P1 by the subject P1 of the following clause (i.e. it is resumed in the same syntactic role), and (6*b*) shows the agent phrase P1 of a passive clause resumed by the subject P1 of an active clause (i.e. it is resumed in a different syntactic role).

(6) (*a*)   Pat bought a new bicycle yesterday, and she's going to sell her old one.

    (*b*)   The president was shot by an unknown gunman. Despite massive police presence at the scene, the gunman fled.

Of course, an item may also resurface in a different participant role. In example (7), P2 of the second clause resumes P1 of the first clause.

(7)   I saw Pat yesterday, but she didn't see me.

Of particular interest in the context of this study is continuity as applied to P1 in VN and passive constructions. The use of such agentive constructions is a means of presenting the P1 of a situation (even in contexts where this is not obligatory, such as in passive clauses), while at the same time removing P1 from its prototypical slot in the clause—i.e. subject position. Thus the question arises whether the use of

---

[8] Or the listener, if the text is read aloud to an audience. For the sake of brevity, the 'user' of a written text will henceforth be referred to as reader.

agentive constructions may at least in part be motivated by the continuity factor: as a means either to maintain, or to disrupt, continuity.

Further aspects of analysis concern the role of the agentive construction within the wider narrative context. It shall be investigated whether agentive constructions can be observed to fulfil structural functions within the narrative unit, or with regard to the whole narrative; whether agentive constructions have favoured positions in texts, and whether certain stages of textual and narrative development favour the use of clusters, or high frequencies, of agentive constructions.

1.3. Construction types

The main construction types, or clause types, which form the database of this study have already been mentioned in passing: VN constructions, and so-called passive constructions in Welsh and Irish, which contain an overt marker for P1. In other words, the investigation centres around the expression of P1 by means other than the subject of a finite, active clause. It must be noted at this stage that, although this is to some extent a comparative study, dealing with similar constructions in two related languages, I do not embark upon a quest for the historical origins of the constructions involved, be it within the Celtic context, or beyond. VN and passive constructions have, over the years, been the subject of much debate. What follows here is a brief introduction to VNs and passives/impersonals in Welsh and Irish, and an overview over the constructions encountered in Chapters 2 and 3.

1.3.1. Verbal nouns

The VNs of the Celtic languages represent one of the factors (along with constituent order and initial consonant mutations) that make this language group so markedly different from other Indo-European languages. Celtic does not have an infinitive, in the sense that, for example, English, German, Latin, etc. can be said to have infinitives. The grammatical category which is closest to the infinitive of other Indo-European languages is the VN, and indeed the term infinitive has been used to label this category (see e.g. *VKG* ii, §633), which has been the subject of much scholarly attention.[9] Definitions of the VN usually stress the fact that, although formally a noun, it fulfils functions that in other languages are fulfilled by infinit-

---

[9] A useful overview of the discussion, especially in recent decades, is given in Russell (1995). Studies concerned with the syntax of the Welsh verbal noun are Lewis (1928) and Morgan (1938). A further short note on the subject is Evans (1950). Lewis (1941) and Richards (1951) deal specifically with the so-called subject of the verbal noun—i.e. the expression of P1. An early study dealing with the verbal noun in Old Irish, and especially its syntax, is Baudiš (1913). Jeffers (1978) looks at Old Irish verbal abstracts from the historical-comparative angle, examining patterns of derivations, with special reference to Indo-European infinitive formations. A more recent examination of Old Irish verbal noun morphology is Wodtko (1987). Genee's work (see e.g. 1994, 1996) investigates the structure and meaning of VN constructions and their arguments within the framework of Dik's Functional Grammar.

ives, and that the VN often carries 'verbal meaning'. Thus Pedersen (*VKG* ii, §633) points out that the 'Infinitiv' in the Celtic languages is syntactically and morphologically a noun. As regards its meaning, the 'infinitive' simply expresses the process denoted by the verb ('die einfach die Handlung des Verbums ausdrücken' (ibid.)). Morgan (1938: 195) formulates the tension[10] between verbal and nominal characteristics of the Welsh VN as follows: 'Enw yw'r berfenw yn gyntaf, heb berson nac amser wrthi; ac felly heb "ansawdd ddigwyddiadol" . . .' (the verbal noun is first a noun, without person or tense marked; and therefore without the 'nature of an incident').

A division into verbal and nominal characteristics is common in descriptions of the behaviour of Celtic VNs.[11] The nominal features are modification and syntactic behaviour also found with other nouns. Thus the VN may be modified by the article (see (8*a*) and (8*b*)); by adjectives (see (8*c*) and (8*b*)); by nouns or possessives (in Irish, nominal modification is in the genitive case) (see (8*d*) and (8*e*)). The VN may also modify a noun (see (8*f*)); it may be the complement of a preposition (see (8*h*) and (8*e*)); and it may serve (either on its own or as part of a noun phrase) as the subject or object of a verb (see (8*d*) and (8*g*)). Further nominal characteristics are that the VN is neutral as regards the distinction between active and passive (see (8*i*) and (8*j*), in which the VNs have 'passive meaning') and that, in Irish, VNs are subject to gender distinctions and nominal inflection in the same way as other nouns (see (8*e*) and (8*g*)).

(8) (*a*)   *yr hela*   (*P.* 1.9–10)   Welsh
          the hunt_VN
          'the hunt'; or: 'the hunting'

     (*b*)   *incumscugud mall*   (Wb 25d26)   Irish
          the-move_VN slow
          'the slow move(ment/ing)'

     (*c*)   *ar y gossot kyntaf*   (*P.* 5.20)   Welsh
          on the strike_VN first
          'upon the first strike'

     (*d*)   Diheu, hagen, oed *y uot ef* yno.   (*CO* 1028)   Welsh
          his be_VN he there
          'However, it was certain that he was there.'

     (*e*)   *Iar riachtain dóib in tslébe*   (*TBC* I 694)   Irish
          after reach_VN to-them the_gen mountain_gen
          'after they had reached the mountain'

---

[10] However, it is likely that this tension is in the eye of the beholder—i.e. in the consciousness of the grammarian or linguist who is trained in categories that ultimately come from a latinate tradition.

[11] This summary of the characteristics of verbal nouns is based on Russell (1995: 259 ff.). The discussion in this chapter is restricted to the syntactic properties of verbal nouns, and specifically to medieval Welsh and Irish. For a more detailed discussion that includes verbal noun morphology, verbal adjectives, and that extends beyond medieval Welsh and Irish to include Breton, and the modern Celtic languages, see Russell (1995: 258–77; ch. 8).

(f)   A bit *corn canu* da am dy uynwgyl   (*P.* 15.14)   Welsh
      horn sing_VN
      'And let a good hunting horn [i.e. one with a clear sound] be about your
      neck'

(g)   nitectat *rath denma ferte* uili   (Wb 12b21)   Irish
      grace do_VN.gen miracle_gen.pl
      'Not all have the grace of performing miracles'

(h)   a *gwedy gwelet* o Lud hynny   (*CLl* 62)   Welsh
      after see_VN
      'and when Llud had seen that'

(i)   llyma uab bychan . . . *guedy troi llenn o bali* yn y gylch.   (*P.* 22.26)   Welsh
      after wrap_VN sheet from brocade
      'there was a little boy . . . with a sheet of brocade wrapped around him.'

(j)   *as·boinn a dingbáil*   (Russell 1995: 269)   Irish
      demand_pres.3sg his remove_VN
      'he demands to be removed'

The verbal features of Celtic VNs listed by Russell (1995) are the following: the
VN may be modified by adverbs (see (9*a*) and (9*b*)); it enters into periphrastic
constructions with auxiliary verbs and occurs with aspect markers (see (9*c*) and
(9*d*)); and it may replace finite verbs, both in subordinate clauses and in series of
co-ordinated strings (see (9*g*)).[12]

(9) (a)   reit yw in *gerdet yn bryssur*.   (*Ma.* 71.1)   Welsh
          travel_VN PRT hasty
          'we must proceed with haste.'

    (b)   *áisndís* doneuch as doruid *coleir*   (Wb 14d3)   Irish
          explain_VN carefully
          'explaining carefully to everyone what is difficult'

    (c)   ac ual *yd oed* y erchwys ef *yn ymgael* ac ystlys y llannerch   (*P.* 1.15)   Welsh
          was PRT reach_VN
          'and as his pack (of hounds) was reaching the edge of the clearing'

    (d)   *ataat octimthirecht* apostolorum dei   (Wb 14a30)   Irish
          they-are at-serve_VN
          'they are serving god's apostles'

    (e)   o *gwyput lad* an tat ohonot   (*Per.* 61.1)   Welsh
          if know_impf.sub.2sg kill_VN our father from-you
          'if you knew that you had killed our father'

---

[12] This latter type of construction is very common in Middle Welsh, but does not appear to occur
frequently in Irish. Gagnepain (1963: 122) cites one possible example from SG; and makes a comparison
between this construction and the historic infinitive in Latin, Romance, and Slavonic, a comparison
later taken up by Disterheft (1980: 195–6; see also Russell 1995: 271).

(*f*) *Nocho cúalaid* Cú Culainn *deglóech nó deigfer do thiachtain* ina agaid
(*TBC I* 2881–2)   Irish
NEG hear_pret.3sg Cú Chulainn fine-warrior or fine-man to come_VN
'Cú Chulainn has not heard of any competent fighter who would come against
him'

(*g*) Riuedi mawr o sswydwyr a *gyuodassant* y uynyd, *a dechrau* llenwi y got.
(*P.* 16.19)   Welsh
rise_pret.3pl; and begin_VN
'A large number of attendants rose up, and began to fill the bag.'

Dividing the characteristics of VNs into nominal and verbal features is not unproblematic, and the question arises whether it is desirable at all to make the
attempt. This point was made by Fife (1990: 399–400), and the discussion has more
recently been taken up by Russell (1995: 271–2). The verbal features are especially
problematic: while it is true that modification by adverbs is a verbal feature, the
other so-called verbal environments either cannot or do not need to be filled by
finite verbs; for example, finite verbs may not enter into periphrastic constructions
with auxiliaries; after verbs of saying or verbs of perception, finite subordinate
clauses may occur, but, equally, the direct object slot may be filled by a noun phrase
(e.g. *he said he would be late*; *he said a prayer*). The use of the VN instead of a finite
verb in coordinated strings is what Russell describes as 'one of the most verbal
characteristics of verbal nouns'. Yet even if we assume that, in a canonical clause, we
should expect a finite verb, all we can say is that Welsh, in environments such as
(9*g*) above (and indeed in others, as we shall see below), tolerates the process element in a nominal form that in all other environments behaves, to all intents and
purposes, like any other noun. Fife (1990: 401) points out the asymmetry in the two
groups of characteristics, verbal and nominal, as listed in *GMW* (159–60), and
notes that what 'traditional grammarians' appeared to have had in mind when describing 'verbal' traits of VNs was the fact that 'the "verbal" environments, though
impossible with real verbs, seem to bring out the *verbal interpretation* of the VN
more clearly than do the nominal environments'.

For the present purposes, the working definition for a VN can be formulated as
follows: a verbal noun is a noun, usually formed from a verbal base, that expresses
a verbal, i.e. a processual content, but that does not provide the contextual information that is given by a finite verb concerning tense, mood, and aspect. Thus
the VN does not define the process with regard to its position *vis-à-vis* the context
of utterance (or written use)—i.e. of reported reality.

1.3.1.1. EXPRESSION OF P1 AND P2: THE 'SUBJECT' AND 'OBJECT' OF THE VN

P1 and P2 may be expressed in a variety of ways in VN constructions. This section
provides a short overview of the construction types encountered in our texts.

Details as to the relative frequency of their occurrence and their usage in context, and the markers of P1 and P2 and their meanings, shall be discussed in the relevant chapters below. The Welsh construction types are illustrated in (10):

(10) (*a*)   *a'e datkanu oll o Pwyll.*   (*P.* 8.13)
        and-its tell_VN all from Pwyll
        'and Pwyll told [them] everything.'

    (*b*)   *galw o Uendigeiduran y mab attaw.*   (*B.* 43.13)
        call_VN from Bendigeidfran the boy to-him
        'Bendigeidfran called the boy to him.'

    (*c*)   *Redec oheni yn eu herbyn*   (*CO* 459–60)
        run_VN from-her
        'she ran towards them'

    (*d*)   *vyn dyfot* y'r llys hon   (*Per.* 61.7)
        my come_VN
        'I shall come to this court'

    (*e*)   *dyuot y crydyon*   (*MLl* 54.23)
        come_VN the shoemakers
        'the shoemakers came'

    (*f*)   A ryuedu o Owein *y'r mackwy gyuarch gwell* idaw ef   (*BR* 12.14)
        to-the young-man greet_VN
        'And Owein was surprised that the young man greeted him'

    (*g*)   *Arthur a'e gynydyon y hely Twrch Trwyth.*   (*CO* 731)
        Arthur and-his huntsmen to hunt_VN Twrch Trwyth
        'Arthur and his huntsmen shall hunt Twrch Trwyth.'

Examples (10*a*) and (10*b*) illustrate a construction type where P1 is expressed by means of a prepositional phrase, whereas P2 is marked by what I shall call here a genitive phrase.[13] Example (10*c*) shows an example of an intransitive VN with P1 marked by a prepositional phrase. Verbal noun constructions where P1 is marked by a prepositional phrase will in the following discussion be abbreviated as $VN+PP_{P1}$. The marking of P1 by means of a genitive is illustrated in (10*d*) and (10*e*) (the shorthand for this construction will be $VN+GEN_{P1}$). P1 in the form of a genitive occurs only with intransitive VNs—i.e. with processes in which no P2 participates. Together with a transitive VN, a genitive phrase can mark only P2, but not P1.[14] The

---

[13] Admittedly, the term *genitive* is awkward in that, as far as nominal inflection is concerned, there is no productive genitive case form in Welsh, the only indication of a genitive relation being word order. The use of the term in this context is justified by the fact that the genitive or possessive form is used when the participant is marked by a pronoun. It is certainly superfluous to establish a separate category for cases such as (10*b*) as opposed to (10*a*), or (10*c*) as opposed to (10*d*) (see also *GMW* §181b, where both types are subsumed under one category, but the term 'genitive' is avoided).

[14] Note in this context Richards's (1951: 51) claim that the relation of the verbal noun with its, in Richards's term, subject, 'is always genitival, whether it be simple apposition or the addition of the genitive constructions with the prepositions *o* and *i*, as in Welsh'. This view will be reconsidered in Chapter 4, in a discussion of the meaning of the prepositional markers of P1.

construction illustrated in (10e) contains P1 as the complement of the preposition i 'to', and this prepositional phrase is followed by the VN (shorthand: i_{P1}+VN). Although this construction is very common in Modern Welsh, it is of very rare occurrence in medieval texts.[15] Another very rare construction is the one exemplified in (10f). Here, P1 precedes a prepositional phrase consisting of the preposition i and the VN (shorthand: P1+i_{VN}).

The different ways of marking P1 in Irish VN constructions are illustrated in (11). Even a cursory glance reveals that there are many structural correspondences between the Welsh and the Irish clause types.

(11) (a)   *iar mbrisiud a chind do Ḟergus*   (*TBC I* 4129–30)
            after break_VN his head_gen to Fergus
            'after Fergus had broken his head'

    (b)   Ficfit fornd *iar tiachtain dúin*   (*TBC I* 158)
            after come_VN to-us
            'They will fight against us after we have come [back]'

    (c)   Ní haccobor lem *do thecht*.   (*TBC I* 1292)
            your go_VN
            'I don't want you to go.'

    (d)   Nibo machdad *dagním do dénam do-ssom* indiu   (*TBC I* 396)
            good-deed to do_VN to-him-PRO
            'It would not be surprising if he were to perform a brave deed today'

    (e)   a tarla dona feraib, *cách díb do guin a charat*   (*TBC LL* 2457)
            each of-them to slay_VN his friend_gen
            'what happened to the men, that each of them killed his friend'

    (f)   is geiss dúib *maccáem do thíchtain* infar cluchi   (*TBC LL* 776)
            young-boy to come_VN
            'it is taboo for you that a young boy should join your game'

The marking of P1 by means of a prepositional phrase (shorthand: VN+PP$_{P1}$, as above for Welsh) is exemplified in (11a) and (11b), with a transitive and an intransitive VN, respectively. In transitive constructions of this type, a genitive phrase marks P2, and can never mark P1. P1 may also be marked by a genitive phrase (shorthand: VN+GEN$_{P1}$), as in (11c); this construction is restricted to intransitive VNs. In the construction illustrated in (11d), a prepositional phrase marking P1 follows a prepositional phrase consisting of *do* 'to' followed by the VN; this phrase in turn follows a noun phrase marking P2 (shorthand: P2+do_{VN}+P1). In (11e), P1 precedes a prepositional phrase consisting of *do* followed by the VN, and P2 is marked by a genitive phrase governed by the VN (shorthand: P1+do_{VN}(+P2)). Example (11f) illustrates the intransitive counterpart of (11e).

As pointed out above, the term *infinitive* has been used to cover certain behaviours of the VN in Celtic. The term has been applied most often to the constructions

---

[15] Cf. *GMW* §181d, S. J. Williams (1980: 115), and Thomas (1996: 471; 513–14).

P2+do_{VN} (with or without overt P1) and P1+do_{VN}(+P2) in Irish. Thus Baudiš (1913) refers to them as 'do-Infinitiv'. Baudiš also makes a distinction between abstract nouns describing processes (whether or not derived from verbal stems), which he calls 'Vorgangsnomen' ('process noun'), and verbal abstracts proper, which he labels 'Verbalnomen' ('verbal noun').[16]

Gagnepain's (1963) approach is syntactic rather than morphological: he uses the constructions P2+do_{VN} and P1+do_{VN}(+P2) as the necessary and sufficient criterion for what he calls the 'nom verbal' (VN), as opposed to the 'nom d'action' (process noun): only a 'nom d'action' that occurs in either of these constructions is also a 'nom verbal'.[17] One of the main aims of Gagnepain's study is to trace the spread of P1+do_{VN}(+P2) and P2+do_{VN} through the history of Old, Middle, and Modern Irish, the latter gaining ground at the expense of the VN followed by a genitive phrase marking P2: structures such as *tol dæ do dénam* (lit. will God_gen to do_VN) become more common, whereas structures such as *dénam tuile dæ* (lit. do_VN will_gen God_gen; both: 'to do God's will') become less frequent. Gagnepain's syntactic definition has the formal advantage that it is based on a rigorous criterion. On the other hand, this advantage contains its own potential loophole: since we are dealing with medieval rather than contemporary data, the non-occurrence of a potential *nom verbal* in the required syntactic context may be a limitation of the texts Gagnepain analysed, rather than a grammatical one.

A further contributor to the discussion how Irish VNs fit into the landscape of Indo-European infinitives is Disterheft, with her (1980) monograph, followed by several shorter publications on related topics (1981, 1982, 1984, 1985). Disterheft's syntactic investigations are directed at capturing the properties of infinitival constructions, especially the relationship between the infinitive and its subject and object (in our terms, P1 and P2). The criterion defining an infinitive construction is the treatment of its subject; the three main ways of treating the infinitive subject are equivalent noun phrase deletion, overt infinitive subject, and subject raising (see Disterheft 1980: 17 ff.).

1.3.2. Passives and impersonals

'The passive' has been a favourite topic for linguistic debate for many years. The discussion is complicated by the fact, however, that there is a wealth of different constructions in different languages that have at some point or other been labelled as passives. This is a point stressed in Siewierska's cross-linguistic study: 'the ana-

---

[16] Baudiš's study, based mainly on material from the Würzburg Glosses and the Annals of Ulster, is an examination of the syntactic environments in which VNs occur. He interprets the use of VNs as complements of prepositions (e.g. *oc* 'at', *i-n* 'in', *iar* 'after', *la* 'with'; for an example, see (11*a*) and (11*b*)) as fulfilling the function of participial constructions, specifically the *-nt*-participle, in other Indo-European languages.

[17] Gagnepain (1963: 16–19) distinguishes three 'types syntaxiques': in our terminology (1) VN+GEN$_{\text{P1}}$, (2) VN+PP$_{\text{P1}}$, and (3) P1+do_{VN}(+P2) and P2+do_{VN}+P1.

lysis of the various constructions referred to in the literature as *passive* leads to the conclusion that there is not even one single property which all these constructions have in common' (1984: 1). Siewierska's own suggestion for a definition of the passive follows semantic and syntactic criteria: (*a*) the passive has a corresponding active the subject of which does not function as the passive subject, (*b*) the event or action expressed is brought about by some person or thing that is not the passive subject, but the subject of the corresponding active, and (*c*) the person or thing if not overt is at least strongly implied (1984: 256). A definition that focuses on the encoding of agent and patient (or, in our terms, P1 and P2) is suggested by Fife (1985), in terms of what he calls a 'pre-theoretic, intuitive definition': 'A structure in which the SUBJECT (or HEAD NOUN in a nominal construction) is thought of/inter-preted as the PATIENT of a process associated with the construction (either the main verb, or a nominalized verb in the case of a nominal construction). The AGENT is (often optionally) expressed by some periphrastic means (preposition, case, etc.).' Both Siewierska's and Fife's suggestions partly overlap with Shibatani's (1985: 837) characterization of what he calls the 'passive prototype':

(*a*) Primary pragmatic function: Defocusing of agent
(*b*) Semantic properties:
     (i)   Semantic valence: Predicate (agent, patient)
     (ii) Subject is affected
(*c*) Syntactic properties:
     (i)   Syntactic encoding: agent $\rightarrow$ Ø (not encoded)
                     patient $\rightarrow$ subject
     (ii) Valence of P[redicate]: Active = P/n
                          Passive = P/n$-$1
(*d*) Morphological property: Active = P
                          Passive = P[+passive]

In Dik's Functional Grammar, voice distinctions in general and the active/passive opposition are approached in terms of subject assignment. Necessary properties of passive constructions are (*a*) that 'they are alternative expressions of a predication which can also be expressed in the active' (1989: 219–20), and (*b*) that 'in a passive construction, some non-first argument must have acquired the coding and behavioural properties which characterize the first argument in the active con-struction' (1989: 219–21). Here again is a partial overlap with other definitions—for example, the ones quoted above. Thus, should one continue the search for the common passive denominator?

Quite apart from the question whether such an exercise would be useful, other problems arise. As Andersen (who criticizes Shibatani's passive prototype as basic-ally anglo-centric) highlights, there is no consensus among linguists about what 'the passive' actually represents, and it is not clear whether, when talking about 'the passive', we talk about 'a specific construction (passive), a constellation of specific properties (passiveness), a syntactic process (passivization) or all three' (1990: 195).

The choice of properties to be included in the passive prototype is problematic, and, as theoretical treatments of passives have often focused on English,[18] it is not surprising, according to Andersen, that the passive prototype tends to be identical with the passive construction in English (1991: 142 ff.). It would lead too far from the central topic of this book to unravel the passive debate in all its complexity. The short excursion above should suffice to highlight some of the problems inherent in the subject matter. Looking at the Celtic languages, one finds a further complication added to the discussion—namely, the status of the so-called impersonal verb forms: impersonal or passive?

There are verb forms that do not co-occur with a P1 subject, and, for transitive verbs, these forms enter into constructions with nominal subjects that look, if not identical, then at least very similar to passive constructions in, for example, Latin or English. Thus the Modern Welsh sentences in (12)[19] could be interpreted as passives, corresponding to their English translations. It should be noted, however, that translation alone should never be taken as indicative of the correspondence of grammatical categories in two languages. The problem is precisely this, that the categorial framework imposed by the language into which an example is translated may mask features of the language under investigation.

(12) (a)   *Lladdwyd y ffermwr gan darw*
       kill_?pass/?impers.pres the farmer with bull
       'the farmer was killed by a bull'

    (b)   *Rhoddwyd bwyd iddynt*
       give_?pass/?impers.pret food to-them
       'food was given to them'

There is a phrase that expresses the entity carrying out the action—i.e. P1—in (12a), and (12b) provides a clue that the noun phrase (representing P2) following the verb has a status different from that of a direct object of an active verb: the latter undergoes soft mutation when it is not preceded by a determiner, whereas soft mutation is absent in the impersonal/passive.[20] In fact, the behaviour of the P2 noun phrase looks very much like that of the subject of a passive clause. Furthermore, there is a periphrastic construction, much more frequent in Modern than in medieval Welsh, that can be described as a 'passive' on the grounds that its subject is the entity affected by the process expressed by the verb, and that would be

---

[18] As pointed out in Langacker and Munro (1975: 789); but see Siewierska (1984) and Keenan (1985) for cross-linguistic studies. Studies on voice distinctions in general and passives in particular are many and varied. Apart from those already mentioned, see e.g. the contributions in Shibatani (1988) and Fox and Hopper (1993). A further angle on English passives from the point of view of Cognitive Grammar is provided by Langacker (1990; 1991: 200–7).

[19] The examples are quoted from S. J. Williams (1980: 79), and it should be noted that Williams does not treat the Modern Welsh impersonal as a passive, although he notes that 'although the Welsh verb has no passive voice, the passive can be implied when the impersonal form has an object', and that, in these cases, 'the verb may be translated into English as if it were *passive*' (ibid.).

[20] As in e.g. *rhoddaf fwyd iddynt* 'I give food to them'. See Fife (1985: 98–9) for a further discussion of this point, and Ball and Müller (1992: 136–61) for a discussion of direct object mutation.

expressed as the direct object in an active clause. Example (13) is a Modern Welsh illustration of this so-called *cael*-passive, modelled on (12*a*):

(13)   *cafodd y ffermwr ei ladd*
       get_pret.3sg the farmer his kill_VN
       'the farmer was killed' (or: 'the farmer got killed')

However, on the other hand, one of the arguments against a synthetic personal passive in Welsh, medieval or Modern, is the encoding of P2 when it is not a third person singular: there is only a single ending for each tense/mood paradigm, P2 does not show subject agreement with the verb, and the pronoun form encoding P2 is that which also occurs when P2 is the direct object of an active clause: see (14) for an illustration of the use of the first person singular 'object' pronoun with active and impersonal verbs in both colloquial (*a* and *c*) and literary Welsh.

(14) (*a*)   *Gwelir fi*
             see_impers.pres me
             'one sees me'

     (*b*)   *Fe'm gwelir*
             PRT-me see_impers.pres
             'one sees me'

     (*c*)   *Fe welaist ti fi*
             PRT see_pret.2sg you me
             'you saw me'

     (*d*)   *Fe'm gwelaist*
             PRT-me see_pret.2sg
             'you saw me'

A further objection to the label 'passive' for the class of verb forms illustrated in (14) is the fact that they are formed by intransitive as well as transitive forms: see the Modern Welsh example in (15).

(15)   *Eir i mewn*
       go_impers.pres in
       'one enters'

Impersonal/passive constructions in Modern Welsh have been the object of several studies. A review of the arguments put forward *pro* and *contra* a category passive in Modern Welsh and of relevant literature is presented in Fife (1985), and a review of recent theoretical treatments can be found in Russell (1995: 189 ff.). An agentive passive as a productive, regularly occurring category does not feature in the Welsh narratives and law texts from the medieval period analysed here. However, where what looks like an agentive passive (i.e. an impersonal verb form accompanied by a prepositional phrase), and what will be referred to as such, does occur is in annalistic texts translated from Latin, which gives rise to the consideration whether the construction may be based on a Latin model (see the discussion in Sections 2.3 and 4.8).

What has traditionally been labelled the passive form of the verb in Old and Middle Irish bears similarities (structural, etymological, and syntactic) to the synthetic impersonal, or passive, in medieval and Modern Welsh. Of particular interest to this study are the syntactic behaviour, and thus the encoding of P1 and P2.[21] As in Welsh, the same morphological markers characterize transitive and intransitive 'passive' verb forms:

(16)   *Tíagair cuccu*   (*TBF* 215)
        go_pass.pres.sg to-them
        'Someone goes to them'

With passives of transitive verbs, differences emerge in the treatment of P2, according to the person and number. Where P2 is a noun phrase, it receives nominative case marking, and shows number agreement with the verb in Old Irish,[22] as illustrated in (17a) and (17b). A third person can also be implied by the bare verb form (see (17c) and (17d)).

(17) (a)   *Ní rucfaiter na baí* tarsin slíab cen raind.   (*TBC I* 1037)
             NEG carry_pass.fut.pl the cow_nom.pl
             'The cattle won't be taken across the mountain unless they are divided (into several groups).'

      (b)   ar *ro bíth Cú Chulaind* co ndechaid a áltaib dó.   (*TBC I* 3399)
             PRT hit_pass.pret.sg Cú Chulainn nom.sg
             'since Cú Chulainn had been injured and lost much blood.'

      (c)   ⁊ is a íarthur carpait *ro lád* co n-óenláim.   (*TBC I* 349–50)
             PRT throw_pass.pret.sg
             'and it is from the back of the chariot that is was thrown with one hand.'

      (d)   *Co n-accassa* íarom isin tunidi sin.   (*TBC I* 1607)
             so-that see_pass.pret.pl
             'And they were found (lit: "seen") in that plight.'

However, the verb form we find when P2 is a third person singular is also used when P2 is any first or second person (this is, again, a parallel with Welsh, with the difference that Welsh does not have a separate passive form for the third person plural). In Old and Middle Irish, a first or second person P2 is marked by an infixed pronoun, as illustrated in (18a), the pronoun being the same as the one used to mark the direct object in an active clause (see (18b)):

---

[21] For the historical development and the structural properties of the Old Irish passive, and further references, see Russell (1995: 55–6), *GOI* (256, 328), and *VKG* (388 ff.; §§622 ff.).

[22] Note that the differentiation between nominative and accusative is not always straightforward in medieval Irish, since nominative and accusative forms are not distinct in all noun classes, and those noun classes in Old Irish that do distinguish between the two cases gradually lose this distinction. However, where a difference can be made out (taking into consideration not only the morphological case form of the noun as such, but also the morphosyntactic behaviour of the case), the encoding of P2 in a passive clause is generally nominative where P2 is a noun or noun phrase.

(18) (a)   *Rom bíth ┐ tucus leth mo bráthar ar mo muin.*   (*TBC I* 494)
PRT-PRO_1sg hit_pass.pret.sg
'I have been wounded and have brought half of my brother on my back.'

(b)   *rom bí*
PRT-PRO_1sg hit_pret.3sg
'he/she/it has hit me'

A paradigm, constructed on the basis of example (18*a*), summarizes the expression of non-nominal P2s in Old/Middle Irish passive clauses:

(19)   Non-nominal P2 in passive clauses in Old/Middle Irish:
P2 = 1sg   rom <u>bíth</u>   'I have been hit'
2sg   rot   <u>bíth</u>   'You have been hit'
3sg   ro   <u>bíth</u>   'He/she/it has been hit'
1pl   ron <u>bíth</u>   'We . . .'
2pl   rob <u>bíth</u>   'You (pl) . . .'
3pl   ro   <u>bítha</u>   'They . . .'

The Old/Middle Irish pattern sketched above undergoes considerable change over time. Gradually, independent pronouns take over the functions of infixed pronouns. Another development is that a non-nominal, third person P2 comes to be expressed by means of a pronoun, as in (20*a*) (and in line with the general development of pronominal expressions, the pronouns used are independent, rather than infixed).[23] Eventually, the third person plural of the passive loses currency, and a general purpose passive/impersonal form is used (see (20*b*)); at this stage, we have basically reached the Modern Irish state of affairs, where one *saorbhriathar* (autonomous verb form) is used in conjunction with all P2s.

(20) (a)   *Tucad i trí dabchaib úaruscib é*   (*TBC LL* 1193)
give_pass.pret.sg PRO_3sg
'He was put into three vats of cold water'

(b)   *Ro tiomsaigedh fir Erenn* lé co Cruachain   (*TBC St.* 5003–4)
PRT gather_pass.pret.sg man_nom.pl Ireland_gen.sg
'The men of Ireland were gathered by her (i.e. Medb) at Crúachu'

Most studies investigating the passive in early Irish have argued from a historical-comparative perspective, linking the Irish category with passives and impersonals in other Indo-European languages. As we might expect, there is no consensus as to whether we are dealing with a passive (in the sense of a Latin personal passive), or an impersonal—i.e. a construction where P1 has been removed from subject position, without P2 having necessarily been moved into that position. Both *VKG* and *GOI* refer to the morphological category as 'passive'. Thurneysen labels forms such as *etha*, the impersonal preterite form of *téit* 'goes' as passives of intransitives

---

[23] On the history and development of infixed and independent pronouns, see Ó Máille (1910) and Ahlqvist (1976).

'in impersonal construction' (*GOI* 328; §514). In Pedersen's view, the existence of passive forms for intransitive verbs would fit in with the 'Auffassung des Passivs als "man"-Form' (*VKG* 394–5; §624.2)—that is, with an interpretation of these forms along the lines of the German *man*-impersonal construction (as in e.g. *Das tut man nicht* 'that's not done').

Vendryes (1956) uses the label 'impersonnel' for the *r*-forms of the passive, and interprets their passive interpretation as a secondary development.[24] However, Vendryes acknowledges that the meaning of the passive preterite (e.g. *marbtha* 'was killed'), being derived from an old *-*to*-participle, has always been 'passive' in Irish (1956: 187).

Hartmann's (1954) definition of passive phenomena in Irish, which could be described as a psychological one, rather than one that relies on syntactic or morphological criteria, is rather wide, and includes all forms and expressions that describe 'das zur Wirkung Gebrachtwerden und das zur Auswirkung Gelangenlassen von Kraft durch einen Agens sowie das Betroffenwerden von einer Kraft' (1954: 13) (i.e. any expressions that describe 'bringing into effect of a force, and permitting a force to take effect, as well as the [state of] being affected by a force'). The main aim of the study appears to be to illustrate and prove the author's conception of a particular *Weltanschauung* or collective unconscious prevalent in the mind of Irish speakers through the ages—i.e. the belief in an *Allkraft* as the predominant influence on life.[25]

The question whether in Old and Middle Irish we are dealing with a genuine personal passive, an impersonal, or a 'depersonalized active' of some sort will be reconsidered at a later stage, once the behaviour of what has in the past been called the (synthetic) passive has been examined more closely, especially with regard to the marking of a potential P1. I shall use the term *passive* for the sake of convenience, to denote a class of finite verbs characterized by a certain set of endings (which have often been labelled 'passive endings'), which do not co-occur with P1 in subject position. The so-called periphrastic passive constructions of Modern Irish will not be considered here, since their occurrence is limited to texts of a later period than the ones that form the basis of analysis of this book.[26]

---

[24] Kuryłowicz (1964: 67) considers two possibilities for the development of the Old Irish passive: either the original accusative of the pronominal forms in such cases as *no-m-suidigther* 'I am being placed' 'must have undergone a reinterpretation' (as nominative) under the pressure of the nominative forms of the noun used with the passive. Or the *-ar* ending found with strong verbs (e.g. *ní canar* 'is not sung'/'one does not sing') could possibly be identical with a plural *-*ro*-ending, restricted to impersonal use. Thus the *r*-forms of the passive could be 'impersonal' in origin. An early advocate of the 'impersonal' hypothesis is Zimmer (1890).

[25] Hartmann uses examples from various Irish texts of different linguistic periods, without clearly defining the corpus underlying his study, nor systematically analysing any one text. Hartmann's interest appears not to lie with texts, and linguistic structure in context, but rather with the possible psychological background reflected in linguistic structures. Hartmann's book met with very critical reactions: see e.g. the reviews by Gonda (1956) and Wagner (1956)—the former slightly less outspoken than the latter.

[26] See Russell (1995: 101–2) for a short description of these constructions; also Ó Siadhail (1989), Wagner (1959), and Ó Sé (1992).

1.3.2.1. THE 'AGENT' OF THE PASSIVE IN IRISH: AN INTRODUCTION
TO THE PROBLEM

The possibility of expressing the agent of a passive verb—i.e. P1—usually by means of a prepositional phrase or an oblique case, features in many definitions of a passive proper.[27] In descriptions of the Irish passive, or of Irish prepositions that address the question, it is generally taken for granted that certain prepositional phrases mark the agent, or P1 of the passive verb—quite possibly because such a feature is part of the authors' definition of what a passive verb is, although this definition is not always made explicit.

However, two questions arise here. First of all, is the interpretation of certain prepositional phrases as markers of P1 based on the internal evidence of the language, or on the expectation of the analyst? To approach this question from a rather roundabout way, one can state with confidence that there is no language-internal evidence that prohibits the interpretation of prepositional phrases such as the one in (21) as P1, in the sense that the complement of the preposition fulfils all the criteria for an AG, and that there is no other possible candidate to fulfil this role, and that there are no examples where a passive verb occurs with a prepositional phrase (potentially) marking P1, plus another potential marker of the same participant.

(21)   *Ro bítha* trá uli *les-*[*sium*] ar galaib óenfir.   (*TBC I* 1560)
        PRT slay_pass.pret.sg with-him-[PRO]
        'They were all slain by him then in single combat.'

Examples like these will in the following discussion be treated as passives where P1 is marked by means of a prepositional phrase, and labelled as agentive, or full, passives. A proviso for this treatment is, however, that at a later stage in the analysis we shall return to look at the meaning of the 'passive' verb form, and consider its meaning in connection with the meanings of the markers of P1 with which it co-occurs.

The second question in this context, related to the first one, is the following: since all markers of P1 in passive constructions also mark circumstantial elements (for example, of place and origin), is every prepositional phrase that potentially marks P1 to be taken as such, or are there instances that are ambiguous, or instances where a potential P1 marker in a passive construction serves as a marker for a circumstantial element? An example of a potential problem case is given in (22).

---

[27] This possibility is used in Schwyzer's (1943) analysis as one of the main formal criteria for the classification of a verb as passive, and is used as a cut-off point by Schwyzer and others (e.g. Delbrück) working within the historical-comparative framework in tracking the development from so-called intransitive to passive constructions. From the historical-comparative point of view, an added complication in connection with the development of passives/impersonals in medieval Irish is, of course, that intransitive verbs have the same impersonal/passive morphology as transitive verbs, and that deponent verbs also have separate passive forms—e.g. *mitter* 'is judged/estimated', from the deponent verb *midithir* 'judges, estimates'. See e.g. Baudiš (1913), *GOI*, *VKG*, Vendryes (1956), and also Müller (1992) for (brief) descriptive accounts of passive morphology and prepositions used to mark agents.

The preposition *la* 'with', with a noun phrase denoting an ethnic grouping as its complement, usually marks the region, or place, in which the situation portrayed by the clause takes place. We have already seen, however, that the same preposition can mark P1 in passive constructions. Thus the sentence in (22) could, in theory, be interpreted in two ways: the prepositional phrase could mark P1, as indicated in translation (i), or it could specify the local setting of the situation described by the sentence, as indicated in translation (ii).

> (22)   *ro h-imraided la firu Érenn* ...
>   PRT debate_pass.pret.sg with man_acc.pl Ireland_gen.sg
>   (i)   'It was debated by the men of Ireland ...'
>   (ii) 'There was debating/a debate among the men of Ireland ...'

It should be noted that the question is not just one of translation: interpretation (i) says that the prepositional phrase *la firu Érenn* marks the persons who carried out the action described by the verb: they, and all of them, and no one else (we know of) debated. In contrast, interpretation (ii) says that some people, not further specified, among the group described by *la firu Érenn* had a debate; i.e. the debaters are a subset (which may or may not include all) of 'the men of Ireland'. The prepositional phrase in (ii) thus denotes the place, or environment, in which the action takes place.

The potential ambiguity between a P1/AG marker and a locative marker will resurface in the discussion of individual examples below (see Chapter 3), and also in the consideration of the semantic link between the agentive use of various prepositions and the passive verb form (see Chapter 4).

1.3.3. The marking of P1: prepositions, case forms, and their meanings

It has already been hinted at, and more or less taken for granted, that all markers of P1 under investigation here, in both Welsh and Irish, also have other uses. The analysis of P1 markers will concentrate on prepositions and their meanings, and attempt to show sense relations between different uses of the same preposition.

The meanings of prepositions have been the subject of numerous studies in cognitive linguistic circles. Using as their point of departure methods ultimately derived from cognitive psychology, scholars have developed models that show the different senses of prepositions as belonging to structured categories.[28] Central to this work have been notions such as prototypes, polysemy, and family resemblance

---

[28] Among the earliest studies presenting detailed meaning analyses of prepositions in this particular linguistic framework are Brugman (1981) and Lindner (1981). See also Lakoff (1987); Hawkins (1984, 1988) on English spatial prepositions; Taylor (1988), a contrastive analysis of English and Italian preposition; Radden (1985), on causal senses of prepositions in English, to name only a few. The prepositions Eng. *in*, Dutch *in*, German *in*, and French *dans* have attracted more attention than most: see the long list of studies cited in Vandeloise (1994). The fascination exerted by prepositions has not abated, witness in more recent years the treatments of Cuyckens (1995), Müller (1995), and Rice (1996).

structures in categories. The notion of prototype categories in language is based on the work by Rosch and others, presenting evidence that humans categorize items according to prototypes, or best examples of a category, rather than according to a set of binary features shared by all members of a category.[29]

Polysemy—i.e. the fact that a word has several senses that can, however, be perceived as related in some way—lies at the heart of many studies dealing with prepositions. Thus the numerous uses of a preposition are conceptualized not as independent from each other, but as related in a structured way. However, there has also been a lively discussion concerning the status of, for example, the many uses of prepositions; whether we are dealing with polysemy, or vagueness, in Cuyckens's words, the question is whether the different uses 'constitute different meanings or whether they are just referential distinctions (i.e. different contextualizations of a more vague, general or unspecified meaning)' (1995: 185).[30] In the discussion of the meaning of P1 markers, I shall adopt the working hypothesis that the different uses of lexical items or case forms indicate polysemy.

Models involving networks in which the different nodes of a network are related to each other through various degrees of similarity have been widely used in the semantic analysis of lexical items. The metaphor underlying such networks is that of family resemblance: members of a family may not all share one feature that makes them similar to each other, but, for example, mother and eldest daughter may have the same type of nose, eldest daughter and youngest son may share the same hair colour, youngest and middle son may both be freckled, and middle son may have the same hair colour as mother. Each member of the family may be linked on grounds of similarity with one or more others, but there is no single characteristic, or set of characteristics, that is shared by all members of the family.[31] Thus elaborate meaning networks have been established in which the different uses of lexical items such as prepositions are linked to others, and in which different uses may be derived, either immediately or via others, from one or more central uses. The attraction represented by the approach would appear to lie in the possibility of presenting detailed analyses of word meaning, and of formulating links between senses of a lexical item that may, at least in part, be intuitively perceived by language users. However, despite (or maybe because of) their great popularity,

[29] See e.g. Rosch and Mervis (1975), Rosch (1978), and Rosch and Lloyd (1978). Taylor (1995) and Ungerer and Schmid (1996) give very readable introductions to prototype theory in linguistics; Geeraerts (1989) provides an assessment of the opportunities and potential problems inherent in the prototype approach; see also Wierzbicka (1996) for a more recent critical appreciation. Prototype theory in linguistics has been applied not only to lexical meaning, but also, for example, to phonology, morphology, and syntax (see Geeraerts (1989: 591) and Taylor (1995) for further references).

[30] Cf. Geeraerts (1993) and Tuggy (1993). Geeraerts's 'inconclusive overview' states that there is, so far, no operational definition of polysemy in lexical semantics that would allow us to distinguish between polysemy and vagueness in lexical items in a consistent manner. See also Cuyckens (1995) for a further discussion of this point.

[31] See Taylor (1995: ch. 3) for an introduction to and the background to family resemblance models (Wittgenstein 1953: 66–7); Cuyckens (1995) for a shorter introduction and an application to the Dutch spatial prepositions *door* and *langs*.

approaches involving prototypes, network models, and the family resemblance metaphor have not gone uncriticized.

Sandra and Rice (1995) present a highly critical review of the network analysis of prepositional meaning. They direct their criticism at what they perceive as four fundamental weaknesses of the approach:

(*a*) *Methodological weakness.* The network structures proposed for the meanings of prepositions are very detailed and finegrained, but criteria for the selection restrictions of prepositions (for example, properties of the landmark of the preposition) are not used systematically. Different linguists are, therefore, likely to make different distinctions between usage types for the same prepositions.

(*b*) *Vagueness of representational conventions.* There appear to be, according to Sandra and Rice, 'as many types as network models as there are network modellers' (1995: 94, and 96–7 for illustrations of different network types).

(*c*) *Unclear linguistic status of prepositional network analyses.* The question that remains unanswered is whether in an analysis we are describing a lexical-semantic network—i.e. specifications of the meaning of the preposition under investigation (with the network illustrating the rich polysemy of the preposition), or whether the network describes contextual variations of a single sense, or a restricted set of senses (a position described as the 'monosemy bias') (1995: 98–9). In other words, the question is whether the many varied uses of a preposition reflect different senses of the preposition, or whether the richness in usage may at least in part be due to contextual information, both linguistic and extra-linguistic.[32]

(*d*) *Unclear cognitive status of prepositional network analyses.* Being part of the cognitive linguistic framework, network analyses should be committed to principles of human cognition and perception. However, as Sandra and Rice put it, 'it is difficult to say what aspects of cognition are modelled in the prepositional network approach' (1995: 100), or, to be more precise, whether 'the psychological commitment behind these models pertain[s] to the process(es) behind the networks, i.e. the principles governing the extension of prepositional usages from other usages', or whether it also involves 'a claim on the mental representation of the meaning of a preposition' (ibid.).

A further criticism, levelled by Rice (1996), concerns the bias towards spatial senses of prepositions as prototypes, and the common assumption that temporal relations can be analysed as straightforward extensions from spatial ones. Thus Rice would analyse the categories represented by the English prepositions *at, on,* and *in* each as having two central reference points, one spatial and one temporal.

What is the relevance of a network approach, or indeed of prototype theory, to the material in hand? It is not the concern of this book to develop fully-fledged network models of the prepositions encountered as the markers of P1. However, the general approach of a network model will be a useful tool to describe the pos-

---

[32] See also the discussion in Geeraerts (1993) on polysemy as opposed to vagueness.

sible links between the agentive function of prepositions and a central sense. In this analysis, I shall make several a priori assumptions. I shall identify a spatial sense as the central (or prototypical) sense of the prepositions that can be used to mark P1. Although made a priori, this is an assumption that is backed up by other studies investigating non-spatial uses of prepositions (*pace* Rice 1996).[33] Further, I shall make the assumption that categories such as AG are prototype categories,[34] and that different markers of P1 may reflect not only that P1 can represent different participants (for example an AG, or an EXP), but also the fact that different members of the category AG or EXP may be encoded by different markers.

The application of even a much scaled-down network model to data from two medieval languages is of course not without its complications. Most studies employing network models are based on contemporary data,[35] where the description of distinctions between the senses of lexical items can be arrived at experimentally, based on the intuition of native speakers of the language under investigation.[36] With data from earlier stages of a language, native-speaker judgements are of course not available. What we do have at our disposal are data in textual environments, and our judgements regarding distinctions of usage should, therefore, be based on differences that can be traced within textual environments, which in turn requires a close analysis of data in context. The apparently obvious answer to the requirement that one remain within the texts, as it were, in one's analysis should in theory be that a large corpus of data should at least limit the dangers of misinterpretations. But not only is there only a finite amount of data, but we are immediately faced with another problem: especially in the Celtic languages, accurate dating of texts can be very difficult indeed, and it would be virtually impossible to gather, on the one hand, data from a large corpus of texts, and, on the other hand, state with some confidence that what one is looking at is a synchronic slice of language use. The only solution—if solution it is—to this latter problem would appear to be the insight that generalizations from a close analysis of data in context will have to be made with extreme caution.

---

[33] See e.g. Radden (1985) and King (1988), who link the causal functions of English and German prepositions, respectively with their spatial senses. King formulates the centrality of spatial senses in his approach in the statement that 'semantics is topology' (1988: 585). The perception that spatial relations are central in prepositional semantics is, of course, not a discovery of modern cognitive linguistics. Several earlier studies dealing specifically with Celtic material are discussed in Chapter 4 below.

[34] An approach also reflected in the definitions of 'agent' in Givón, and Van Oosten: 'A prototypical agent is thus human, direct cause, deliberate cause, controlling cause and obvious cause' (Givón 1984: 107); 'a typically human participant instigator of the action expressed by the verb, who is responsible for the action, wills the action and is the principal energy source for the action, and who experiences the action' (Van Oosten 1984: 3).

[35] Prototype theory has, however, been applied to non-contemporary data. See e.g. Aijmer (1985) and Winters (1987).

[36] But note, in this context, Sandra and Rice's warning against replacing intuition with introspection, and basing linguistic analyses on 'an attempt to make the nature of one's tacit knowledge explicit by reliance on one's own subjective judgments of what constitutes relevant units and relations in language' (1995: 94).

1.4. The textual basis of analysis

The behaviour of agentive constructions has been analysed on the basis of a number of medieval Welsh and Irish prose texts. The greater part of these texts belongs to the genre of prose narrative; this fictional-narrative core is supplemented by law texts and annals. The bias towards narrative material is conditioned by the nature of the analysis: since a large part of the analysis concerns questions of linguistic usage—i.e. the selection of alternative construction types in context—the analysis will be facilitated if the choice of expression is not influenced by metrical rules (which may determine phrasing in poetry), or interference from another language (as might be the case in a translation, or in a corpus of glosses on a Latin base text, such as the Würzburg Glosses on the Pauline epistles).[37] Of course, it may not be possible to exclude Latin influence completely, in an environment where the creators of texts were familiar with both Latin, and Irish or Welsh: this is exactly the question that is of interest with regard to the Welsh agentive passive (see Section 1.3.2 above, and Sections 2.3 and 4.8). But the absence of an immediate model—i.e. a text to be translated or the base text of a corpus of glosses—should at least reduce the likelihood of such interferences.

I do not address the ongoing discussion concerning oral versus literary traditions and transmissions of texts, or the related controversy concerning 'native' Irish and Welsh materials and 'imported' elements. The discussion is, and has been for a long time, a lively one, and any detailed consideration that would do justice to the complexity of the materials involved would lead us too far afield. For recent work in this field and overviews of the debate, the reader is referred to Tristram (1993, 1994, 1997) and Davies (1996). The approach adopted here is to accept, first and foremost, each of the texts analysed as a creation in its own right. The compilatory nature of some texts is quite obvious (see, for example, the notes on the recensions of *Táin Bó Cúailnge*, below); but even if a narrative appears to be a homogeneous whole—and whether or not it does depends at least to some extent on the literary taste and expectation of the reader, i.e. the modern-day reader—its creator is likely to have relied, to an extent that it may be impossible to define, on earlier sources.[38] Rather than indulge in a search for original strata—however one may want to define the term 'original'—it appears to be more profitable, in an analysis such as the present one, to respect the integrity of a given text. If there are marked differences of linguistic usage from one part of a narrative to another, then questions may be asked whether, for example, this may reflect different sources. The exact dating of both Welsh and Irish texts is notoriously problematic.[39] Therefore, the

---

[37] Wb.

[38] For a criticism of the 'diachronic' approach to the analysis of medieval Welsh texts, see R. M. Jones (1986), who also discusses the danger of transferring the expectations of the twentieth-century reader to a medieval text.

[39] On the Welsh material, with further references, see e.g. Davies (1996). On the difficulties concern-

references to the suggested dating of the texts introduced below are to be taken as orientations, not the last possible word on the question.

1.4.1. The Welsh texts

1.4.1.1. NARRATIVE

The Welsh narratives analysed here are all contained in the *Red Book of Hergest* (*RBH*) (*Llyfr Coch Hergest*; date around 1400; see Huws 1991: 25), and apart from one (*Breudwyt Ronabwy*, see below) also occur either in whole or in part in the *White Book of Rhydderch* (*WBRh*) (*Llyfr Gwyn Rhydderch*, date around 1350; see Huws 1991: 2). The corpus of medieval Welsh prose narratives is often conveniently referred to as the *mabinogion*;[40] however, this is not meant to imply that we are dealing with a coherent collection of closely linked texts, either in style or in subject matter.

Culhwch ac Olwen (*CO*). Edition: Bromwich and Evans (1988) from *WBRh*, supplementing the final sections from *RBH*.

Evans would date the final redaction of *Culhwch ac Olwen* towards the end of the eleventh or the beginning of the twelfth centuries. The editors state (1988: p. xxi) that, as far as the language of the text is concerned, there is a significant gap between *Culhwch ac Olwen* and the rest of the *mabinogion*. However, the language of *Culhwch ac Olwen* does not present a unified picture, some sections being linguistically more archaic than others.[41]

Pedeir Keinc y Mabinogi (*PKM*; *P.: Pwyll Pendeuic Dyuet*; *B.: Branwen Uerch Lyr*; *MLl: Manawydan Uab Llyr*; *Ma.: Math Uab Mathonwy*). Edition: I. Williams (1930), from *WBRh*.

Date and authorship of these four narratives have been widely discussed. Dates between 1060 and the middle of the thirteenth century have been suggested for their composition. *Communis opinio* tends to ascribe the four texts to a single author.[42]

Cyfranc Lludd a Llefelys (*CLl*). Edition: Roberts (1975); from *WBRh*, which contains roughly the first fifth of the text, and *RBH*.

Cyfranc Lludd a Llefelys first appears as an insertion into the Welsh version of Geoffrey of Monmouth's *Historia Regum Brittaniae*, in a manuscript from the early thirteenth century (Llanstephan 1). Roberts (1975) suggests that the story may have

---

ing the correct dating of texts from the Middle Irish period (tenth to roughly the end of the twelfth centuries), and the dangers of circularity and the domino effect caused by dating one text in relation to another (which may have been assigned to the wrong period in the first place), see Mac Eoin (1982: esp. 113–27).

[40] See Davies (1992, 1996), Mac Cana (1992), and R. M. Jones (1986).

[41] For the dating of *CO*, see *GMW*, p. xxx; also Evans (1985: 113); see also Roberts (1991: 73–4). For a discussion of the text itself, see Davies (1992, 1996: 7–8).

[42] The various suggestions for a date of *PKM*, and the question of authorship, are discussed in Davies (1996: 7–8). Davies also presents an analysis of the narrative techniques in the *mabinogion*, including a detailed consideration of oral versus literary features in Welsh prose narrative. For an earlier, and shorter treatment of the same problem by the same author (in English), see Davies (1992).

been known in oral form as early as the late eleventh century, but that the *mabinogion* text derives from the version of the Llanstephan 1 translator, rather than from an orally transmitted version.

Breudwyt Ronabwy (*BR*). Edition: Richards (1948), from *RBH*.

It has been suggested that *Breudwyt Ronabwy* was never part of the tradition of the *cyfarwyddiaid*, nor an oral folk-tale. What distinguishes *Breudwyt Ronabwy* from the other narrative texts in the corpus analysed here is the use of the dream as a frame for the story, and the satirical approach to its subject matter. Dates as far apart as 1160 and the second half of the thirteenth century have been suggested for the composition of the text.[43]

Owein (*Ow.*). Edition: Thomson (1968); from *WBRh*; lacunae filled from *RBH*.

The editor would date the text as it is preserved now to the end of the twelfth century (Thomson 1991: 160–1). On the grounds that the *Tair Rhamant* (the Three Romances, *Owein*, *Peredur*, and *Gereint*) contain much that characterizes the continental genre of the romance, fashionable around the twelfth and thirteenth centuries, it has been suggested that the three Welsh romances represent the result of the import of a literary genre, and may have been composed around the first half of the thirteenth century.[44]

Peredur (*Per.*). Edition: Goetinck (1976), from *WBRh*.

The editor suggests that a copy of the tale was in existence around the end of the twelfth century, since the text of *Peredur* in the *White Book of Rhydderch* shows correspondences with orthographic features in the Black Book of Carmarthen (Goetinck 1976: pp. xi–xii). This manuscript has now been dated to around the middle of the thirteenth century or slightly later, not *c.*1180–1200, as accepted by Goetinck. This, of course, has implications for the dating of this text, as well as any other text for which the formerly accepted date of the Black Book of Carmarthen was used as a yardstick.[45]

1.4.1.2. LAW TEXTS AND ANNALS

Llyfr Cyfnerth. Edition: Wade-Evans (1909) (*WML*) from V (BL Harl. 4353; fourteenth century), with lacunae filled from W (BL Cotton Cleopatra A xvi; first half

---

[43] See Parry (1953: 65–7), Roberts (1976: 233 ff.), Lloyd-Morgan (1991), and Davies (1996: 14 ff.) for discussions of the text. Davies (ibid.) also discusses the various suggestions for a dating of the text. The latest date (1250 or later) is based on the dating of the *Tair Rhamant* (the three Welsh romances—i.e. *Owein*, *Peredur*, and *Geraint*; see below for the former two): if one accepts that the *Tair Rhamant* were composed in the first half of the thirteenth century, then one may argue that *Breuddwyd Rhonabwy* was composed at the end of that century, or even at the beginning of the fourteenth (Davies 1996: 15–16).

[44] See Davies (1996: 14 ff.) for further discussion and dating of the text.

[45] For the dating of the Black Book of Carmarthen, see E. D. Jones (1982). The relation between the grail legend *Per.* and the other Welsh Arthurian romances, on the one hand, and the Perceval legends, on the other hand, is examined in Goetinck (1975). A more recent study of the subject is Lovecy (1991); see also Davies (1996).

of the fourteenth century). Manuscripts V and W (as well as the Book of Taliesin) are in the same hand. This law book may in its original form go back to the last quarter of the twelfth century; the surviving redactions are at least partly of the thirteenth century (see Charles-Edwards 1989: 20). The book falls into four main parts: laws of the court, laws of the *gwlad*, triads, and a section on the 'ninth days'.

Llyfr Cynghawsedd (*Cyngh.*). Edition: Wiliam (1988); from G (Peniarth 35); late thirteenth or early fourteenth century.

The 'Book of Pleading' deals mainly with the proper procedure in connection with landsuits (some sections deal with theft). References in the text to the Books of *Colan* (probably mid-thirteenth century) and *Iorwerth* (early thirteenth century) would point to a date around the middle of the thirteenth century or slightly later for the compilation of this tract (see Charles-Edwards 1989: 59; 1986).

Brut y Tywysogyon (*BT*). Editions: T. Jones (1973) from *RBH* (*BT(R)*); and T. Jones (1941) from Peniarth MS 20 (*BT(P)*), for variant readings.

Extracts from the 'Chronicle of the Princes' have been included for the discussion of the agentive passive in medieval Welsh. The versions of *Brut y Tywysogyon* in the *Red Book of Hergest* and Peniarth MS 20 represent translations of a Latin text, compiled towards the end of the thirteenth century, that appears to have been lost; however, some sections correspond closely to parts of the texts published as *Annales Cambriae* (*AC*) (J. Williams ab Ithel 1860) and *Cronica de Wallia* (*CW*) (T. Jones 1946).

1.4.2. The Irish texts

1.4.2.1. NARRATIVE

The core of the narrative material analysed here is three recensions of *Táin Bó Cúailnge* (*TBC*), the centrepiece of the *Ulster Cycle* of tales. In the course of the discussion, data from other narrative texts will be taken into consideration, but these will not receive the same in-depth treatment as *TBC*. The three recensions are:

Táin Bó Cúailnge: Recension I (*TBC I*). Edition: O'Rahilly (1976) from *Lebor na hUidre* (late eleventh/early twelfth century; lacunae filled from later manuscripts), with an introduction to the text and manuscripts, including a synopsis of which parts of *TBC I* are contained in which manuscript.

Táin Bó Cúalnge from the Book of Leinster (*TBC LL*). Edition: O'Rahilly (1967) from *The Book of Leinster*, compiled around the end of the twelfth century).[46]

Táin Bó Cúailnge: Recension III (*TBC III*). Edition: Nettlau (1893, 1894) from

---

[46] An earlier edition of *TBC* from the Book of Leinster is Windisch (1905). Diplomatic editions of the manuscripts are: Best and Bergin (1929) for *LU*, and Best *et al.* (1954–83) for *LL*. The history and relationships between Irish manuscripts have experienced lively discussion throughout the history of Irish literary scholarship. See e.g. the contributions by O'Sullivan (1966), Ó Concheanainn (1974, 1976, 1983, 1984, 1986, 1987, 1991), Dumville (1976), West (1990), and Mac Eoin (1994).

Egerton 93 (fifteenth century) and Thurneysen (1912) from H 2.17 (fifteenth/six-teenth century).

The various versions of the 'Cattle Raid of Cooley' have been the subject of many studies, by literary scholars, archaeologists, historians, and linguists.[47] Much effort has gone into attempts at establishing the relationship between the extant texts, and between those versions of the texts that have been preserved, and others that have not. However, it would lead us too far afield to trace the progress of discussion in this field, which has been going on for something like a century. The compila-tory nature of *TBC I*, the oldest extant version, has provoked the most comment, especially in comparison with the more polished, literary appearance of *TBC LL*. However, it has been pointed out recently that *TBC LL* is not the homogeneous text that earlier scholars took it to be.[48] *TBC III*, the latest of the three texts, is frag-mentary in nature. The contents mirror to a large degree the contents of the first half of *TBC LL*. However, although there are strong similarities between *TBC LL* and *III*, and instances of the same wording, *TBC III* is a separate compilation, which has been dated to the thirteenth century.[49] There appears to be a general consensus that *TBC LL* was composed in its present form in the twelfth century. Mac Gearailt (1992) concludes that, for the more conservative parts of *TBC LL*, a *terminus ad quem* of 1106 is likely, whereas the later parts were written by the compiler of the manuscript, probably towards the end of the twelfth century.[50] As far as the language is concerned, Mac Eoin (1982) distinguishes three strata in *TBC LU*. The oldest one, restricted to formulas and rhetorical passages, can be dated to the eighth century. The main body of the work consists of a tenth-century stratum, while an eleventh-century stratum is visible in certain episodes that are later than the main text.[51] Tristram (1997) assigns the *LU Táin* along with the manuscript to the early twelfth century, by absolute dating of the manuscript.

[47] See Williams and Ní Mhuiríosa (1987) and Williams and Ford (1992) for an introduction to the subject matter, Thurneysen (1921) for an earlier monograph, and the contributions in Tristram (1993) and Mallory and Stockman (1994) for an overview of more recent research in the area.

[48] For a detailed analysis of orthographic, linguistic, and stylistic features in *TBC LL*, see Mac Gearailt (1992), who comes to the conclusion that e.g. Thurneysen's (1921) and O'Rahilly's (1967) assess-ments of *TBC LL* as a homogeneous literary creation need to be revised, and that there is evidence of various contributions made at different times.

[49] See Mac Gearailt (1994) and Ó Béarra (1994) for the relationship between *TBC LL* and *TBC III*, including the date of composition of *TBC III*, and its place in its literary and linguistic context.

[50] Mac Gearailt (1992) divides the text of *TBC LL* and *Cath Ruis na Ríg*, in the same manuscript, into six 'regions': region 1: Introduction to *TBC LL* (*LL* lines 7551–7694; 3% of the text), 'a Middle Irish composition'; region 2: from the end of *Comrád cind cherchaille* to the end of *Comrac Lóich* (*LL* lines 7695–9535; 38% of the text); region 3: *Breslech Mór* (*LL* lines 9562–9882; 6.5% of the text); region 5: *Comrac Fir Diad* (*LL* lines 10047–11037; 20% of the text); region 4: the remaining 33% of the text, follow-ing region 3, but excluding region 5 (*LL* lines 9883–10047; 11038–12415; 9536–9561); region 6: *Cath Ruis na Ríg* (1992: 173). Regions 2–3 are more conservative than regions 4, 5, and 6.

[51] The manuscript was extensively revised by a later scribe, known as 'H'. Mac Eoin (1994) suggests that H was a member of the Ua Maol Chonaire family of professional historians, scholars, and scribes in what is now Co. Roscommon, and worked in the mid- to late twelfth century (see also Mac Gearailt 1997: 494 n. 2).

For the purposes of this study, each recension of *Táin Bó Cúailnge* stands first and foremost as a text in its own right. Where there are clear overlaps in usage between recensions (such as the occurrence of parallel constructions or identical wording), due note will be taken of such facts. Conversely, variance in usage within one recension may reflect the compilatory nature of the texts.[52]

1.4.2.2. LAWS AND ANNALS

The Irish law texts analysed here belong, as do most surviving Irish legal tracts, to the Old Irish period, although the manuscripts containing them were written mainly in the fourteenth to sixteenth centuries. According to Kelly (1988: 232), most texts can, on linguistic grounds, be shown to have been written (or written down) in the seventh or eighth centuries.[53]

Críth Gablach (*CG*). Edition: Binchy (1941); see also Kelly (1988: 267).
   This is a tract on status law, from the beginning of the eighth century.

Bechbretha (*BB*). Edition: Charles-Edwards and Kelly (1983); see also Kelly (1988: 274).[54]
   This tract deals with laws connected with bee keeping (trespass by bees, bee stings, ownership of swarms), and probably dates from around the middle of the seventh century.

Bretha Crólige (*BCr*). Edition: Binchy (1938); see also Kelly (1988: 271).
   The 'judgments of blood-lying', dated by the editor to the first half of the eighth

---

[52] The so-called Stowe version of *TBC* (O'Rahilly 1961) will not be discussed in detail, apart from occasional references to the usage of a construction in the text, in comparison with the other recensions of *TBC*. Occasionally, sections of *TBC* are referred to by title. The titles (and the corresponding section numbers) are those in Windisch's (1905) edition of the *LL* recension.

[53] A feature of many legal texts, or rather of their transmission, is that they were heavily glossed and extensively commented on, glosses and commentaries often being centuries removed from the base text. I have restricted the analysis to the base texts, and refer to glosses and commentaries only as and when they are of interest in connection with data from their base texts. For information concerning the often highly intricate manuscript tradition of the legal material analysed here, the reader is referred to the editions cited, and to Kelly (1988: esp. chs. 10, 11, and app. 1). Any dates given in the description of the texts are those suggested by the editors of the tracts.

[54] Charles-Edwards (1980) cites this tract as an example of what he calls 'plain prose'. 'Plain prose' is a neutral term, characterized by the absence of features typical for 'standard Old Irish textbook prose', on the one hand, and *fénechas* on the other. 'Textbook prose' is defined by the use of 'etymology, enumeration, and a particular form of question and answer in which a question is asked by a pupil and the master replies *ní anse* (*non difficile*, OW *nit abruid*) and then expounds the answer' (1980: 147). *CG* provides the best example of this type. Features typical of *fénechas* are early metre, or condensed, allusive prose, or the text having the form of instructions of a pupil by a master (ibid.); passages of *fénechas* are often to be found within tracts otherwise in 'plain' or 'textbook' prose. Charles-Edwards regards both 'plain prose' and 'textbook prose' as literate types of composition, as opposed to the originally oral character of *fénechas*. He considers the features of the textbook style as having been derived from the schools of Latin grammarians (1980: 147). Edel (1989: 117) objects that the Latin grammarians, although they make frequent use of the stylistic features of 'textbook prose' as identified by Charles-Edwards, cannot be regarded as the first literary tradition to employ them; in other words, in Edel's view, the use of 'textbook prose' in Irish legal tracts is not necessarily based on a Latin model.

century on linguistic grounds, deal with the obligations of someone who has caused illegal injury to another person to provide sick maintenance (*othrus*) for the victim.

Bretha Déin Chécht (*BDC*). Edition: Binchy (1966); see also Kelly (1988: 271).

The subject matter of the 'judgments of Dían Cécht' are the fines for illegal injuries and the fees due to a physician, according to the injury treated and the status of the injured person. The tract differs from the other legal texts dealt with here in that it exhibits two distinct types of style. The first twenty-four sections show, in the editor's words, 'comparatively straightforward Old Irish [prose] of the eighth century' (Binchy 1966: 3) comparable to the prose of other prose texts of the *Senchas Már* collection. From section 25 onwards, the text is 'couched in obscure rhetorical language' (i.e. *fénechas*), which Binchy (ibid.) associates with the *disiecta membra* of the *Nemed* collection.[55]

Uraicecht na Ríar (*UR*). Edition: Breatnach (1987); see also Kelly (1988: 269).

The 'primer of stipulations' is concerned with the various grades of poets and their qualifications, and was composed within the Old Irish period, possibly towards the second half of the eighth century.

The Annals of Ulster (to AD 1131) (*AU*). Edition: Mac Airt and Mac Niocaill (1983).

The text of *The Annals of Ulster* is preserved in manuscripts from the fifteenth and sixteenth centuries; however, the entries are much older. The question from what time onwards we can speak of contemporary annal entries—i.e. entries that were written only shortly after the events they record—has not been completely resolved. The beginnings of contemporary recording have been variously sought around AD 550, in the 680s, while a third interpretation sees signs of extensive reworking of all annals in the eighth century, from which time onwards the entries can be described as contemporary.[56]

A prominent feature of *The Annals of Ulster*, and other Irish annals, is a high incidence of code switching between Latin and Irish: the two languages exist side by side in the same entry, and often the same clause. The tradition that annalistic writing in Ireland was based upon was a Latin-speaking (or, rather, Latin-writing) one. Irish was a medium that was only gradually adapted to the task. Different studies have resulted in different pictures of the growing use of Irish and the ratio of Irish versus Latin usage in *The Annals of Ulster*. Thus Dumville (1982) states that before the 730s,[57] the use of Irish is very limited, confined mainly to proper names

---

[55] On the *Senchas Már* and the *Nemed* 'law schools', the texts associated with these collections, and their historical background, see Kelly (1988: ch. 11, esp. 242–50).

[56] For the first view, see e.g. Dumville (1982), for the second one Hughes (1972), and the third (rejected by Dumville) Kelleher (1963, 1971). For further details, and references to this controversy, see e.g. Dumville (1982: 322 nn. 6–8).

[57] Dates of *AU* given here are 'text internal time'—i.e. the 730s refer to the entries noted down in *AU* for that decade, without any claim that the entry as it has come down to us was actually written down in exactly that form at the time of the event (or very shortly after).

and some prepositions. In the 770s the number of complete entries in Irish reaches just 10 per cent, between 811 and 940 Irish entries account for just under 20 per cent per decade, and between 941 and 1050 they average almost 53 per cent of all entries per decade. Hughes (1972) presents the following sketch: up to 810 the principal language is Latin, except for the use of Irish prepositions and the occasional noun. Between 811 and 818 there are some entries in Irish, chiefly towards the end of entries for a year. After 818 Latin and Irish are intermixed, and Irish is used for 'less conventional entries, e.g. the Viking raids' (1972: 128–9). By about 830 the proportion of Irish and Latin is roughly one to one.[58]

1.5. Overview

Chapter 2 presents the Welsh data and their analysis: independent and dependent VN constructions, a consideration of an agentive passive in medieval Welsh, and a survey of the categories IAG, CAUSE, and INST. Chapter 3 follows a similar structure: an investigation of Irish VN clauses is followed by an analysis of the full passive, and the latter by a section exploring the marking of IAG, CAUSE, and INST. Results from both chapters are taken up again in Chapter 4, which considers the semantics of P1 marking. Appendices 1 to 13 provide references to the data illustrated in Chapters 2 and 3.

---

[58] The reason for this divergence might lie in different interpretations of what exactly constitutes an Irish entry; see e.g. the following: 'Expugnatio Ratho Guali la Fiachna m. Baetain' (the storming of Ráith Guala by Fiachna son of Baetán) (*AU* 623.3).

2 Welsh

Section 1.3 briefly introduced the various Welsh constructions that involve the expression of P1 and P2 by means other than the subject and object, respectively, of a finite verb. The greater part of this chapter is devoted to verbal noun constructions, their structure and behaviour in context. As pointed out above, verbal noun constructions can be said to replace finite verb clauses, in that constructions that contain a verbal noun as process element, but no finite verbal element, are grammatical. In the following discussion, such constructions will be referred to as verbal noun clauses (or VN clauses), a clause being defined for the present purposes as a construction that contains a verbal (i.e. a process) element, either finite or non-finite. The first section (2.1) of this chapter analyses VN clauses with overt P1 in Welsh fictional narrative texts. Welsh legal material forms the basis of Section 2.2. In Section 2.3 we shall consider the question whether we can speak of a productive passive construction with overt P1 in medieval Welsh. Finally, Section 2.4 examines the expression of the categories IAG, INST, and CAUSE in medieval Welsh.[1]

2.1. Evidence from narrative texts

2.1.1. VN+PP$_{P1}$: the preposition *o* 'from'

The preposition *o* 'from' is by far the most common preposition used to mark P1 in verbal noun clauses, as illustrated in (1). The prepositions *i* 'to' and *gan* 'with' occur as well, but only very rarely (see Section 2.1.2).

(1) (a)   Ac yna, gwedy daruot y tangneued, *galw o Uendigeiduran y mab attaw.*
         (B. 43.13–14)
         call_VN from Bendigeidfran the boy to-him
         'And then, when peace had been made, Bendigeidfran called the boy to him.'

   (b)   A *gwedy menegi o Lud y vrawt ystyr y neges*, Lleuelis a dywawt . . .   (*CLl* 68)
         after tell_VN from Lludd to-his brother reason the mission
         'And when Lludd had told his brother the reason for his mission, Llefelys said
         . . .'

Overall distribution of VN+*o*$_{P1}$

Table 2.1 shows the distribution of the construction VN+*o*$_{P1}$ throughout the texts,

---

[1] Appendices 1 to 4 give listings of the attestations quoted as examples or referred to in tables.

the proportion of the AGs and EXPs marked by the preposition (i.e. the proportion of action- and experience-type processes co-occurring with o as P1 marker), and the occurrence of $VN+o_{P1}$ in syntactically independent or dependent position (i.e. as main or subordinate VN clause).[2] The table shows that P1 in the construction $VN+o_{P1}$ is more often an AG than an EXP[3]—in other words, the construction occurs more often with action-type VNs, which demand an AG as P1.

TABLE 2.1. $VN+o_{P1}$ *in narrative texts*

Text	Total	Independent		Dependent		(– human)	
		AG	EXP	AG	EXP	(AG)	(EXP)
CO	36	31	4	1		1	1
P.	9	6		2	1		
B.	9	4	2	2	1		
MLl	5	2	1	2			
Ma.	14	6	1	5	2		
CLl	7			2	5		
BR	8	3	1	3	1	2	
Ow.	7			5	2		
Per.	17	6	1	8	2		1
TOTAL	112	58	10	30	14	3	2
%	*100*	*51.8*	*8.9*	*26.8*	*12.5*		

Overall, $VN+o_{P1}$ is more often used in our texts in independent (as illustrated in (1a)) than in dependent VN clauses, the ratio being 60.71 per cent versus 39.29 per cent. However, different texts show very different preferences for either independent or dependent $VN+o_{P1}$; the most extreme examples are *CO*, with thirty-five cases of independent and only one example of dependent $VN+o_{P1}$, and *CLl*, with no independent, but seven examples of dependent $VN+o_{P1}$.

Dependent $VN+o_{P1}$: syntactic environments

In dependent position, $VN+o_{P1}$ occurs most often as a prepositional phrase, the VN clause having the function of an adverbial clause, as, for example, in (1b). Most frequently, we find VN clauses introduced by *gwedy* 'after'. Other prepositions found in this construction are *am* 'about, for' (4 times), *rac* 'lest' (5), *kyn* 'before' (2), *o achaws* 'for the reason (that)' (2); *dros* 'for, instead of', *heb* 'without', *onyt*[4] 'except',

---

[2] The figures for [–human] P1 are subsets of P1 in independent and dependent VN clauses.
[3] The ratio is 85.3% AGS versus 14.7% EXPS in independent, and 68.18% AGS and 31.82% EXPS in dependent, $VN+o_{P1}$ clauses.
[4] See *GMW* (241; §272(a)) on the use of *onyt* as preposition and conjunction.

ymlaen 'before, in front of' (but here used like *rac*), and *dan amot* 'on condition' occur once each.

VN clauses may also have the function of P2; either depending on a finite verb and thus filling the direct object slot in the clause, as in (2*a*), or on a verbal noun, as in (2*b*). Examples of this latter type are labelled P2 complements in the following discussion. In P2 position, the VN clause depends on verbs or VNs expressing mental processes (such as *adnabot* 'recognize, realize', *gwybot* 'know', *tebygu* 'think'), or on *verba dicendi* (such as *menegi* 'tell')

(2) (*a*)   kam oed it dyfot y an llys, *o gwyput lad an tat ohonot*.   (*Per.* 61.1)
             if know_impf.sub.2sg kill_VN our father from-you
             'it was wrong of you to come to our court, if you knew you had killed our
             father.'

   (*b*)   Ac yna *adnabot a oruc* y marchawc *ry gaffel dyrnawt agheuawl ohonaw*
             (*Ow.* 276)
             realize_VN PRT did . . . PRT get_VN blow deadly from-him
             'And then the knight realized he had received a deadly blow'

The construction VN+o_{P1} may also fill the subject slot in a copula construction, as illustrated in (3):

(3)   A *da yw gennyf i eu kymryt ohonaw*   (*Ow.* 635)
       good is with-me me their take_VN from-him
       'And I am pleased that he should take them'

VN+o_{P1} is comparatively rare in both subject and object (i.e. P2) position in our data; the examples are frequent enough, however, to establish the pattern (see also Table 2.2).

The only other types of dependent VN+o_{P1} in the present database are as complement of the comparative particle *no* 'than' (4*a*) and of the negative particle *na* '(n)either/nor' (4*b*), and a clause that is linked semantically to the preceding one, but which shows no syntactic connection with it (4*c*).[5]

(4) (*a*)   Only byd arnat ti gywilyd uwy *no meithryn o honaf i uab kystal a hwnn*
             (*Ma.* 73.28)
             than rear_VN from-me me boy as-good-as PRT this
             'Unless there is greater shame on you than that I have reared a boy as fine as
             this one'

   (*b*)   a heb ohir, *na chael o dyn yn y ty gauael arnaw*, yny want y mab yn wysc y benn
             yn y gynneu.   (*B.* 43.24)
             nor get_VN from man in the house grasp_VN on-him
             'and without delay, nor anybody in the house managing to grasp him, he
             thrust the boy headlong into the blaze.'

---

[5] A case could be made for counting this example as an independent VN+o_{P1} clause.

(c)   diolwch y Duw *caffael ohonoty y gydymdeithas honno*   (P. 8.14)
        get_VN from-you the fellowship that
        'thank God that you have found that fellowship'

The collection of data published by Richards (1951) bears out the pattern of usage for VN+o_{P1} encountered here: subordination of VN+o_{P1} by means of a preposition is generally the most common; object and subject clauses occur, but are much less frequent.[6] The figures for the occurrence of VN+o_{P1} in dependent constructions are listed in Table 2.2.

TABLE 2.2. *VN+o_{P1} in dependent construction*

VN+PP_{P1}=	CO	P.	B.	MLl	Ma.	CLl	BR	Ow.	Per.	Total	%
Prepositional phrase	1	2	2	2	4	7	4	3	6	31	70.45
Object					1			1	1	3	6.82
P2 complement									2	2	4.55
Subject					1			3	1	5	11.36
Other			1	1	1					3	6.82

Distribution of transitive and intransitive VN+o_{P1} clauses

Although VN+o_{P1} can contain either intransitive or transitive VNs, the construction is used more often with transitive (see e.g. the examples in (4)) than with intransitive VNs. A subclass of intransitive VNs are motion VNs (such as *mynet* 'go', *dyuot* 'come', *kyuodi* 'rise'). The distribution of transitive versus intransitive VNs in VN+o_{P1} across our texts is given in Table 2.3. The preference for transitive VNs is more clearly established with dependent VN+o_{P1} clauses; altogether, transitive VN+o_{P1} clauses account for 66.96 per cent (or 75 out of 112 examples).

In a transitive VN clause where P2 is marked by a noun phrase or independent pronoun/pronominal (such as a demonstrative), there are two variants as regards the ordering of P1 and P2: P1 may either precede, as in (5a), or follow P2, as in (5b). The statistics for the texts overall are given in Table 2.4, and, as the table shows, the order P1–P2 is the preferred sequence in dependent VN+o_{P1} clauses, whereas there is no clear preference overall in independent VN+o_{P1} clauses.

(5) (a)   A gwedy *gwelet o Leuelis hynny*   (CLl 76)
            see_VN from Llefelys that
            'And when Llefelys saw that'

---

[6] Richards's (1951: 72 ff.) category in which 'the noun clause may depend on verbs and verb nouns of imploring, beseeching, praying, promising &c . . .', and in which the VN 'is preceded by the preposition *ar*' (e.g. 'ac a wediawd y arglwyd *ar gaffael ohonaw gwelet y vab*' (lit.: on get_VN from-him see_VN his son) (and he beseeched the lord that he be allowed to see his son)) does not occur in the texts analysed here.

(b)   *Kymryt crip eur o Arthur*   (CO 164)
take_VN comb gold from Arthur
'Arthur took a golden comb'

TABLE 2.3. *VN+o_{p_1}: transitive, intransitive, and intransitive (motion) VNs*

VN type	CO	P.	B.	MLl	Ma.	CLl	BR	Ow.	Per.	Total	%
Independent											
Transitive	21	4	4	2	4		1		3	39	57.35
Intransitive	7	1	1	1	1		1		4	16	23.53
Intransitive (m.)	7	1	1		2		2			13	19.12
Dependent											
Transitive		2	2	2	6	6	3	7	8	36	81.82
Intransitive	1	1			1	1	1		1	6	13.64
Intransitive (m.)			1						1	2	4.54

TABLE 2.4. *VN+o_{p_1}: order of P1 and nominal P2*

VN	CO	P.	B.	MLl	Ma.	CLl	BR	Ow.	Per.	Total	%
Independent											
1. P2–P1	11			2	3				1	17	51.52
2. P1–P2	8	3	3		1		1			16	48.48
Dependent											
1. P2–P1				1			1		3	5	18.52
2. P1–P2		2	2		5	5	2	3	3	22	81.48

Definiteness of P1 and P2

P1 is definite[7] in the majority of examples, usually either a proper name, as in, for example, (5a) and (5b), or a pronoun suffixed to the preposition *o*, as in (4a) or (4c); the statistics are presented in Table 2.5. Altogether, there are only four instances in our database where P1 is not a definite entity,[8] one in an independent, and three in dependent VN+o_{p_1} clauses.

P2 does not present such a clear-cut distribution with regard to definiteness—

---

[7] The label 'definite' includes proper names (e.g. person and place names), noun phrases containing a definite determiner/demonstrative, and personal and demonstrative pronouns.

[8] The example cited under (4b), 'o dyn yn y ty', has been included under the label 'indefinite', although a case could be made here for restricted reference, and the fact that, therefore, *o dyn yn y ty* 'by anyone in the house' is more definite than e.g. *o neb* 'by anyone', but, on the other hand, less definite than e.g. *ohonaw* 'by him', or *o Arthur* 'by Arthur'.

see the statistics in Table 2.6. Notable is the almost complete absence of names as P2.[9] Whereas there is no clear preference for either definite or indefinite P2 in independent $\text{vn}+o_{P1}$ clauses, in dependent clauses P2 is definite in a clear majority of cases. Definiteness of P1 and P2 interacts closely with the question whether either participant represents new or given information, which will be discussed in Section 2.1.4.

TABLE 2.5. *Definiteness of P1 in* $\text{vn}+o_{P1}$

P1	CO	P.	B.	MLl	Ma.	CLl	BR	Ow.	Per.	Total	%
[+Def.]											
Pronoun	17	5	2	2	10		1	5	10	52	46.43
Name	18	3	2	2		6	2		3	36	32.14
NP	1	1	3	1	3	1	5	2	3	20	17.86
[−Def.]			2		1				1	4	3.57

TABLE 2.6. *Definiteness of P2 in* $\text{vn}+o_{P1}$

VN clause	CO	P.	B.	MLl	Ma.	CLl	BR	Ow.	Per.	Total	%
Independent											
[+def.]											
Pronoun	2	1	1						2	6	15.38
NP	6	2	2		1		1			12	30.78
TOTAL										18	46.16
[−def.]											
NP	9	1		1	3				1	15	38.46
Clause/VN	4		1	1						6	15.38
TOTAL										21	53.84
Dependent											
[+def.]											
Pronoun				1	1	1	1	3	2	9	25
NP		2	1	1	2	4	2	3	5	20	55.56
TOTAL										29	80.56
[−def.]											
NP					1			1		2	5.56
Clause/VN			1		2	1			1	5	13.89
TOTAL										7	19.44

[9] The only example of a place name that is structurally a definite NP is: 'onyt goresgyn o Gaswallawn uab Beli Ynys y Kedyrn' (lit.: except overrun_VN from Caswallawn island the strong_pl) (except the conquering by Caswallawn of the Island of the Mighty) (*B.* 45.25).

Occurrence of $VN+o_{P_1}$ *in direct speech or narrative*

The characteristics of $VN+o_{P_1}$ described thus far all concern the internal structure of the VN clause. The last parameter introduced in this section, the occurrence of the construction in dialogue or narrative, is an aspect of textual usage, and the statistics established in Table 2.7 will be taken up again in connection with the role of the $VN+o_{P_1}$ clause in the construction of the narrative (see Section 2.1.4). The term *direct speech* covers text in which one or more characters speaks. *Narrative* covers all text that is not direct speech. As can be seen from Table 2.7, $VN+o_{P_1}$ is a feature of narrative rather than direct speech, although the preference is by no means exclusive and is established more clearly for independent $VN+o_{P_1}$ clauses than for dependent ones.

TABLE 2.7. *Occurrence of* $VN+o_{P_1}$ *in direct speech or narrative*

VN clause	CO	P.	B.	MLl	Ma.	CLl	BR	Ow.	Per.	Total	%
Independent											
Direct speech		1			3				3	7	10.29
Narrative	35	5	6	3	4		4		4	61	89.71
Dependent											
Direct speech		2	1		2			5	6	16	36.36
Narrative	1	1	2	2	5	7	4	2	4	28	63.64

Summary

To sum up the basic analysis of mainly internal structural characteristics: it has emerged that $VN+o_{P_1}$ occurs more often with VNs that demand an AG as P1 than with experience-type VNs. This preference might well be due to the nature of the database, rather than the construction, since narrative texts tend to be concerned with action and persons acting, rather than with experience and persons affected by experiences. Overall, the construction occurs more frequently in independent than in dependent position, although this preference is not shared by all texts examined. Furthermore, although the use of $VN+o_{P_1}$ with intransitive VNs is well established, transitive VNs are clearly more common. As regards the order of P1 and nominal P2 in the construction, our texts show that, for dependent $VN+o_{P_1}$, the order P1 before P2 is preferred, whereas no clear preference emerges for independent $VN+o_{P_1}$. P1 is a definite entity in the large majority of cases; a preference approximated for P2 only in dependent $VN+o_{P_1}$ clauses. Finally, we have seen that $VN+o_{P_1}$ is more commonly used in narrative than in direct speech.

2.1.2. Other prepositions

There are only sporadic instances of the prepositions *i* 'to' and *gan* 'with' as potential markers of P1 in the construction VN+PP$_{P1}$. Compared with the large number of occurrences of the preposition *o*, their use is very restricted indeed, and not always unambiguous. Only two potential examples of a construction VN+*gan*$_{P1}$ occur in our data, once as an independent VN clause (6*a*), and once as an object clause (6*b*).

(6) (*a*)   *a'y tharaw gantaw allan*   (B. 36.20)
            and-her break_VN with-him out
            'and he broke through it [i.e. the wall]'

   (*b*)   *ni a gawn yn goganu gan yr unben*   (Ma. 84.26)
            our revile_VN with the chieftain
            'we shall be reviled by the chieftain'

With (6*a*) the question arises whether *gan* may denote accompaniment: he breaks the wall with him—i.e. as he tackles it.[10] The example cited in (6*b*) is described in *GMW* (p. 190) as an instance where *gan* 'denotes the agent'. The question is, however, whether *gan* actually links the VN phrase *yn goganu* with the noun phrase *yr unben* and the whole composite phrase is the object of *ni a gawn*, or whether *gan* marks the person, place, or source from whom or which something is obtained. Since *gan* is frequently used with *kaffael* in this function, the latter possibility would appear to be the more likely one.[11]

The construction VN+*i*$_{P1}$ likewise has only few attestations: our database contains four possible instances of VN+*i*$_{P1}$ in independent construction,[12] as in (7*a*), and three[13] in dependent position, all occurring in the same text (*Culhwch ac Olwen*), and all introduced by a preposition, as in (7*b*).

(7) (*a*)   *Emystynnu idaw yn y peir*, yny dyrr y peir yn pedwar dryll   (B. 44.20)
            stretch-oneself_VN to-him in the cauldron
            'He stretched himself in the cauldron, until the cauldron burst into four pieces'

---

[10] The passage reads: '. . . ac yd arhoes ef yny uyd y pleit haearn yn wenn. Ac rac diruawr wres y kyrchwys y bleit a'e yscwyd a'y tharaw gantaw allan, ac yn y ol ynteu y wreic.' (And he waited until the iron wall was white[hot]. And because of the extreme heat, he charged [against] the wall with his shoulder, and he broke through it, and his wife after him) (B. 36.19 ff.).

[11] See Section 2.4.1 on the use of *gan* and *y gan* with verbs such as *kaffael* 'get', *prynu* 'buy'. The so-called *cael*-passive, judging from the evidence of our texts, does not appear to be a frequently used construction in medieval Welsh, at least not in the literary language that has been preserved in our texts. For the *cael*-passive in Modern Welsh, see Awbery (1976), Fife (1985) with further references, and Fife (1990).

[12] Among these is included *CO* 26, an example of the aspect marker *yn* being used without co-occurring auxiliary: 'diwarnawd yn hyly yr brenhin' (lit.: day PRT hunt_VN to-the king) (one day the king was hunting).

[13] Further possible examples of *i* marking P1 are the following: ' "Beth a erchi ti?" *heb y Peredur*. "Vyg kymryt yn wr itt" ' (lit.: my take_VN prt man to-you) ('What do you ask?' said Peredur. 'That you accept me as (your) man') (*Per.* 49.28). However, it seems more likely that *itt* here marks affiliation or possession, as in e.g. 'prif lys idaw' (a chief court of his) (*P.* 1.3); ' "Ony'm llad i Duw hagen, nit hawd ·· llad i" ' ('Unless God kills me, I'm not easily killed') (*Ma.* 86.14). *Llad* could potentially be a finit⸱ ⸱⸱⸱ (pres.3sg), which would make *Duw* the subject, and *i* the 'echo pronoun' of the infixed object pro⸱⸱⸱⸱⸱. The use of infixed pronoun plus 'echo pronoun' would thus mirror the use of possessive pronoun plus 'echo pronoun' in the following clause. On the other hand, *llad* is potentially a verbal noun, which would make *'m* the possessive pronoun, and *i Duw* a prepositional phrase.

(b)   mal y keffynt llad eu llettywyr *heb wybot y'r Cawr.*   (CO 812)
        without know_VN to-the giant
        'so that they could kill their hosts without the Giant's knowing.'

The example in (8) is interpreted in *GMW* (p. 162) and *GPC*[14] as an instance of *i* expressing P1.

(8)   *Canu englyn idaw ynteu yna.*   (Ma. 90.9)
        sing_VN englyn to-him (him) then
        'He sang an englyn then.'

This interpretation would seem to be supported by the use of *i* in the same function in the preceding sentence.[15] However, it also seems possible that *i* in this example does not mark P1, but rather the addressee (i.e. 'he sang an englyn to him then').

In so far as it is useful or indeed possible to observe patterns of usage from small numbers of examples, we can say that P1 in $VN+gan_{P1}$ (if that is what the two examples are) and $VN+i_{P1}$ confirms the general tendency observed with $VN+o_{P1}$ that P1 is a definite entity.

The preposition *i* features in two other constructions marking P1, which will not be analysed further here because of the very small number of attestations. The type $P1+i_{VN}(+P2)$, illustrated in (9), occurs six times in all, and its use is, apart from one example, restricted to one section of *CO*.[16]

(9)   Arthur a'e gynydyon *y hely Twrch Trwyth.*   (CO 731)
        to hunt_VN Twrch Trwyth
        'Arthur and his huntsmen shall hunt Twrch Trwyth.'

The construction $i_{P1}+VN$ is likewise a rare phenomenon in our texts, and is restricted to object clauses (3 examples, see (10a)), and subject clauses (1 example). Lewis (1928: 183) describes the example in (10a) as 'yr unig enghraifft ddilys o'r gystrawen hon yn y Pedair Cainc' (the only certain example of this syntax in the Four Branches). There are numerous cases of *i* occurring after verbs of asking, entreating, causing (somebody to do something)—for example, *erchi* 'ask', *peri* 'cause'—where *i* denotes the person affected by the process of the main verb, which also happens to be coreferential with P1 of the VN following the preposition (see e.g. (10b)). Although the construction $i_{P1}+VN$ occurs very frequently in Modern Welsh as a complement of prepositions,[17] it is not attested in this position in our texts.

---

[14] See p. 1992, s.v. i^2, 14(a).

[15] The passage reads: 'Ac yna ymellwng idaw ynteu, yny uyd yn y geing issaf o'r pren. Canu englyn idaw ynteu yna: "Dar a dyf . . ." ' (And then he let himself go, until he was on the lowest branch of the tree. And he sang an englyn (to him) then: 'An oak grows . . .') (Ma. 90.8 ff.). In *GPC* (s.v. i^2, 2(a)), and in *GMW* (p. 197) instances of this use of *i* are included under 'denoting the indirect object'.

[16] Lines 565–758, *Ysbaddaden yn nodi'r Anoethau*. For a structural parallel, see the Irish construction $P1+do_{VN}(+P2)$, Section 3.1.3 below.

[17] As in e.g. 'cyn i mi fynd' (before I went/go); see S. J. Williams (1980: 131).

(10) (a)   *ny thebygaf i y un o hyn vynet* ar dy geuyn di.   (*P.* 25.15)
        neg. think_pres.1sg I to one from these go_VN
        'I do not think that any one of these will go on your back.'

    (b)   A minheu a *baraf idaw ef vynet . . .*   (*P.* 15.11–12)
        cause_pres.1sg to-him he go_VN
        'And I will make him go . . .'

2.1.3. VN+GEN$_{P1}$: the genitive as P1 marker

The genitive, in the form of a possessive pronoun or an adnominal noun phrase, as marker of P1 is restricted to intransitive VNs. With transitive VNs, a genitive denotes P2, whether or not P1 is also overtly marked. We have seen above (Section 2.1.1) that intransitive VNs may also co-occur with a prepositional phrase as P1 marker; thus there is a choice of construction as far as intransitive VNs are concerned, with the exception of the VN *bot* 'be', which in the present database occurs only in the construction VN+GEN$_{P1}$.[18] In this analysis, only instances of *bot* as substantive verb (11a), and as auxiliary in periphrastic constructions (11b), are included, but not the copula *bot* (11c).

(11) (a)   Diheu, hagen, oed *y uot ef yno.*   (*CO* 1028)
        his be_VN he there
        'It was obvious, however, that he was there.'

    (b)   Pan wybu Gei yn diheu *y uot ef yn kyscu*   (*CO* 970)
        his be_VN he PRT sleep_VN
        'When Kei knew without doubt that he was asleep'

    (c)   ac ef yn gwybot *y uot yn uab* y wr arall.   (*P.* 24.21)
        his be_VN PRT son
        'and he knowing that he was another man's son.'

Overall distribution of VN+GEN$_{P1}$ *in narrative texts*

Table 2.8 presents the statistics of the distribution of VN+GEN$_{P1}$ in dependent and independent construction throughout our texts, with the use of *bot* as substantive verb and auxiliary listed separately. P1s of periphrastic constructions containing the VN *bot* as auxiliary are classified as AG or EXP, depending on the main VN: for example, the P1 of *y uot ef yn kyscu* in (11b) is thus classified as an EXP.

As Table 2.8 shows, P1s in the construction VN+GEN$_{P1}$ are more often AGs than EXPs, or in other words, the construction occurs more often with VNs describing action-type VNs (the ratio being 85 versus 35 examples, or 70.59 per cent versus 29.51 per cent). Overall, VN+GEN$_{P1}$ is more frequently found in dependent constructions than as an independent VN clause (87 versus 33 examples), which m

---

[18] Morgan (1938: 197) quotes examples of *bod* with *o* marking P1, but classifies this usage as 'purely artificial'.

TABLE 2.8. *VN+GEN_PL*: overall distribution

Text	Total	Independent		Dependent		*bot* (auxiliary) Independent	*bot* (auxiliary) Dependent		*bot* (substantive verb) Independent	*bot* (substantive verb) Dependent	([-human])	
		AG	EXP	AG	EXP	AG	AG	EXP			AG	EXP
CO	35	18	2	9	2			1		3	(1)	
P.	7	1		3						3		
B.	9	4		3			1				(1)	(1)
MLl	10	2		2			3	1		2	(1)	
Ma.	12			5			2	1	1	3	(1)	(1)
CLl	6			2	3		1				(1)	
BR	10			4			5			1	(2)	
Ow.	10	1		4	1		2	1		2		
Per.	21	3		7		1	2	1		7	(3)	(1)
Total	120	29	2	39	7	1	16	4	1	21	(10)	(3)
%	100	24.17	1.67	32.5	5.83	0.83	13.3	3.33	0.83	17.5	(8.33)	(2.5)

for a marked difference of usage as compared to $VN+O_{P1}$ (see Table 2.1). *Culhwch ac Olwen* contains the highest proportion of independent $VN+GEN_{P1}$ clauses; however, even here independent $VN+GEN_{P1}$ account only for roughly half the total number of occurrences of the construction. The VN *bot* (auxiliary) accounts for roughly a quarter of all dependent $VN+GEN_{P1}$ clauses (20 attestations), as does *bot* (substantive verb) (20 attestations). VNs of motion represent a high proportion of the VNs other than *bot* occurring in $VN+GEN_{P1}$, as shown in Table 2.9.

TABLE 2.9. $VN+GEN_{P1}$: *VN types (other than bot)*

VN clause	CO	P.	B.	MLl	Ma.	CLl	BR	Ow.	Per.	Total	%
Independent											
Intransitive	2	1	1							4	3.3
Intransitive (m.)	18		3	2				1	3	27	22.5
Dependent											
Intransitive	5		2		1	2	1	1		12	10
Intransitive (m.)	6	3	2	2	4	3	3	4	7	34	28.3

Note: 100% = total *n* of $VN+GEN_{P1}$, i.e. 120.

Dependent $VN+GEN_{P1}$: syntactic environments

In dependent construction, $VN+GEN_{P1}$ occurs in the same types of clause patterns as $VN+O_{P1}$ (see Table 2.10). As complement of a preposition, $VN+GEN_{P1}$ is used most commonly with *gwedy* 'after' (17 examples), followed by *kyn* 'before' (4 examples), *erbyn* 'against' (3 examples), as in (12), and *trwy* 'through' (2 examples), with *am* 'about, for, because', *eithyr* 'except', *heb* 'without', *nes* 'until', and *o* 'from' occurring once each. $VN+GEN_{P1}$ as a prepositional complement occurs only rarely with *bot* (our texts contain one example each of $bot+GEN_{P1}$ as auxiliary and as substantive verb) as VN.

TABLE 2.10. $VN+GEN_{P1}$ *in dependent construction*

$VN+GEN_{P1}$ =	CO	P.	B.	MLl	Ma.	CLl	BR	Ow.	Per.	Total	%
Prepositional phrase	7	2	1	2	4	4	3	2	6	31	35.63
Object	4	3	2	3	3		2	4	6	27	31.03
P2 complement				3	2	2	1	1	2	11	12.64
Subject	2	1			1		3	2	3	12	13.79
Other	2		2		1		1			6	6.9

Note: 100% = total *n* of subordinate $VN+GEN_{P1}$; i.e. 87.

(12)   mi a baraf bot gwled darparedic yn barawt *erbyn dy dyuot.* (*P.* 13.9)
         against your come_VN
         'I shall have a feast prepared against your coming.'

The most frequently occurring dependent position for VN+GEN$_{P1}$ is that of filling a P2 slot, either as the direct object of a finite verb (see (11*b*) for an example), or as P2 complement in a VN construction (see (13)). The use of VN+GEN$_{P1}$ in subject position in a copula construction is illustrated in (11*a*).

(13)   ac yny doeth rybydyeu idaw, a *menegi uot y crydyon wedy duunaw ar y lad.*
         (*MLl* 58.18)
         tell_VN be_VN the shoemakers after agree_VN on their kill_VN
         'and until warnings reached them, and rumours that the shoemakers had conspired to kill them.'

A type of construction attested only comparatively rarely (labelled 'other' in Table 2.10) consists of a VN+GEN$_{P1}$ clause in parataxis to a clause, as in independent position, but qualifying a noun or noun phrase of the preceding clause, as in (14), where the VN clause qualifies the noun *chwedyl.* The semantic relation is similar to that between a main clause *verbum dicendi* (e.g. *dweud* 'say') and its object clause.

(14)   E chwedyl a doeth at Uendigeituran, *bot Matholwch yn adaw y llys*
         (*B.* 32.17)
         be_VN Matholwch PRT leave_VN the court
         'the news reached Bendigeidfran, that Matholwch was leaving the court'

Definiteness

As with VN+o_{P1}, P1 is a definite entity in a large majority of all VN+GEN$_{P1}$ clauses (see the statistics in Table 2.11). The majority is slightly smaller in dependent than in independent VN clauses, but still larger than 80 per cent of all dependent VN+GEN$_{P1}$ clauses.

Occurrence of VN+GEN$_{P1}$ in direct speech or narrative

The use of VN+GEN$_{P1}$ is preferred in narrative, rather than direct speech (see Table 2.12). Again, the tendency is established more clearly with independent VN clauses.

Summary

The construction VN+GEN$_{P1}$ confirms several tendencies shown by VN+o_{P1}. The genitive marks an AG more often than an EXP; again, this is quite possibly due to the material investigated, rather than to the construction as such. P1 tends to be a definite entity, rather than indefinite, and the VN clause is more often a feature of narrative than of dialogue. Apart from the fact that only intransitive VNs can occur in VN+GEN$_{P1}$, characteristics distinguishing the two constructions are the fact that, in the present database, the VN *bot* occurs only with a genitive as P1 marker (although other intransitive VNs may take both the genitive and the preposition *o*), and that, on the whole, the preferred use of $\text{VN+GEN}_{\text{P1}}$ is as a dependent VN clause, whereas $\text{VN+}o_{\text{P1}}$ occurs more often in independent position. If we leave aside the instances of *bot* and look at all other intransitive VNs, what emerges is not so much a preference of $\text{VN+}o_{\text{P1}}$ in independent position (the total figures are thirty-one examples of independent $\text{VN+GEN}_{\text{P1}}$, as opposed to twenty-nine of $\text{VN+}o_{\text{P1}}$), but rather a strong preference for $\text{VN+GEN}_{\text{P1}}$ in dependent position with intransitive VNs (with forty-six examples of $\text{VN+GEN}_{\text{P1}}$, but only eight of $\text{VN+}o_{\text{P1}}$).[19]

TABLE 2.11. *Definiteness of P1 in* $VN+GEN_{P1}$

VN clause	CO	P.	B.	MLl	Ma.	CLl	BR	Ow.	Per.	Total	%
Independent											
P1 [+def.]											
Pronoun	3	1			1				1	6	
Name	8		1							9	
NP	8		1	2				1	2	14	
TOTAL	(19)	(1)	(2)	(2)	(1)			(1)	(3)	29	87.88
P1 [−def.]											
NP	1		2						1	4	12.12
Dependent											
P1 [+def.]											
Pronoun	6	6	2	4	6	2	5	6	11	48	
Name	2					1				3	
NP	6		1	4	2	2	3		4	22	
TOTAL	(14)	(6)	(3)	(8)	(8)	(5)	(8)	(6)	(15)	73	83.91
P1 [−def.]											
NP	1		2	3	1	2	3		2	14	16.09

TABLE 2.12. *Occurrence of* $VN+GEN_{P1}$ *in direct speech or narrative*

VN clause	CO	P.	B.	MLl	Ma.	CLl	BR	Ow.	Per.	Total	%
Independent											
Direct speech		1	1		1			1	2	6	18.18
Narrative	20		3	2					2	27	81.82
Dependent											
Direct speech	1	5	2	2	4		3	7	8	32	36.78
Narrative	14	1	3	6	7	6	7	2	9	55	63.22

[19] Morgan (1938: 196) considers the use of *o* as P1 marker of intransitive VNs as modelled on the syntax of transitive VNs, and the genitive as the original P1 marker of intransitive VNs.

2.1.4. VN constructions in context

The characteristics of VN clauses observed so far concern, for the greater part, the internal structure of the constructions. This section turns to the behaviour of vn+o_{P1} and vn+GEN$_{P1}$ clauses in context, looking at information packaging, continuity, and the narrative environment, before moving on to a consideration of the so-called *gwneuthur*-inversion.

2.1.4.1. INFORMATION PACKAGING: NEW, INFERABLE, AND GIVEN INFORMATION

VN+o_{P1}

P1 in independent vn+o_{P1} clauses follows a clear pattern: as a rule, P1 represents given information,[20] and in most cases P1 is not only a person mentioned before, but one of the central, well-established characters of the narrative. Only three exceptions to this pattern occur in our data, one of which is quoted in (15) (the other examples are *CO* 940 and 1050; in neither instance does the character introduced as P1 recur as P1 at a later stage in the narrative). In (15), P1 is not a character participating in a specific action. Rather, the VN clause represents a timeless statement, expressing customary action.

(15)   'Moes yw genhym ni, Arglwyd,' heb y Guydyon, 'y nos gyntaf y delher at wr mawr, *dywedut o'r penkerd*. Mi a dywedaf kywarwydyd yn llawen.'
        (*Ma.* 69.11)
        speak_VN from-the chief-poet
        ' "We have a custom, Lord." said Gwydyon. "The first night one comes to a great man['s household], the chief poet speaks. I will tell a story gladly." '

The regular given status of information represented by P1 is not matched by P2, as can be seen from Table 2.13, with no clear picture emerging concerning a preference for new or given P2s. The VN usually introduces new information (see Table 2.14).

The bias towards new information represented by the VN is not surprising,

TABLE 2.13. *Independent vn+o_{P1}: given/new/inferable P2*

P2 =	CO	P.	B.	MLl	Ma.	BR	Per.	Total	%
Given	8	3	2			1	2	16	41.02
New	12	1	2	2	4		1	22	56.42
Inferable	1							1	2.56

---

[20] This is also the case in the few attestations of vn+i_{P1} and the one instance of the so-called *cael*-passive in our texts.

TABLE 2.14. *Independent* $VN+o_{p1}$: *given/inferable/new VN*

VN =	CO	P.	B.	MLl	Ma.	BR	Per.	Total	%
Given	3	1						4	5.88
New	28	3	5	1	7	5	7	55	80.88
Inferable	4	2	1	2				9	13.24

since it is the verbal element—i.e. the process element—that mainly carries new development in a narrative. As inferable I have interpreted cases such as the one quoted in (16), from *Culhwch ac Olwen*, where the action taken by Culhwch and his companions is exactly the one that is to be expected from previous developments:[21] Olwen has just told Culhwch that, in order to win her, he has to come to the castle and confront her father and fulfil whatever demands Olwen's father might impose. Culhwch declares that he is ready and willing to do so, and the narrative continues:

(16)   Kerdet a oruc hi y ystauell. *Kyuodi onadynt vynteu yn y hol hi y'r gaer*, a llad naw porthawr . . .   (*CO* 510)
        rise_VN from-them (they) after-her to-the castle
        'She went to her room. They rose up after her [and went] to the castle, and killed nine porters . . .'

A case of a VN recapitulating given information, in that the action expressed has been announced earlier in the text, is given in (17), from *Pwyll*:

(17)   A chyuodi y uynyd, a dodi y deudroet yn y got *a troi o Pwyll y got* yny uyd Guawl dros y penn yn y got ac yn gyflym caeu y got, a llad clwm ar y carryeu, a dodi llef ar y gorn.   (*P.* 16.28 ff.)
        and turn_VN from Pwyll the bag
        'And he rises up, and puts his feet into the bag, and Pwyll turns the bag over so that Gwawl is head first in the bag, and he [Pwyll] quickly closes the bag, and ties a knot in the strings, and gives a blast on his horn.'

This instance is part of a chain of events that is described at the planning stage earlier in the text, phrased very similarly, in an instruction to Pwyll: 'a phan el ef, tro ditheu y got, yny el ef dros y pen yn y got . . .' (and when he does [rise and put his feet into the bag], turn the bag over, so that he goes into the bag head first . . .) (*P.* 15.12–13).

Dependent $VN+o_{p1}$ confirms the strong tendency for P1 to represent given information (namely, in 88.9 per cent, or 40 out of 45 examples). Only in two texts do

---

[21] Note that this expectation is restricted to *kyuodi onadunt.* 'Rising up' in fact would appear to mark the fact that Culhwch and his companions, having been instructed what to do, are now taking the initiative.

$VN+o_{P1}$ clauses introduce new characters.[22] Overall, P2 also represents given more often than new information (in 70.3 per cent, or 26 out of a total of 37 transitive dependent $VN+o_{P1}$ clauses).

$VN+GEN_{P1}$

In $VN+GEN_{P1}$ clauses, P1 also tends to represent given information, namely in 81.81 per cent (or 27 out of 33 cases) in our text sample in independent clauses,[23] and 82.8 per cent (or 72 out of 87 examples) in dependent clauses. There is only one example of independent $VN+GEN_{P1}$ introducing a character who recurs with some consistency right through to the end of the narrative. But note that the first introduction, quoted in (18), does not identify the person as a character in his relation to the other members of the cast; this information (the fact that he is the son of the woman who opens the chest) is supplied later. The first encounter is, rather, a visual impression:

(18)   agori kib a oruc y wreic yn tal y pentan *a chyuodi gwas pengrych melyn* oheni. (*CO* 469)
        and rise_VN boy curly-head yellow
        'the woman opened a chest by the hearth and a boy with curly yellow hair rose out of it.'

The VN, as with $VN+o_{P1}$, tends to represent new information, in 75.76 per cent of all cases in our database (or 25 out of 33 examples).[24] Again, this tendency is probably to be expected in narrative texts, where verbal elements tend to introduce new developments.

As shown above (see Table 2.9), a large proportion of $VN+GEN_{P1}$ clauses contain VNs of motion, such as *dyuot* 'come', *mynet* 'go', and *kyuodi* 'rise'. One particular variant of $VN+GEN_{P1}$ containing *dyuot* as VN deserves further attention. The construction $dyuot+GEN_{P1}$ (occurring five times in our data) is followed by the conjunction *a(c)* 'and' and a further VN; the (implied) P1 is coreferential with that of *dyuot*, as in (19).

(19)   *Dyuot y porthawr ac agori y porth,* a dyuot Kei y mywn e hun.   (*CO* 786)
        come_VN the porter and open_VN the gate
        'The porter came and opened the gate, and Kei himself came in.'

The processual information most relevant to the development of the narrative (i.e. of the plotline) is carried by the second VN, rather than by *dyuot*: in the example in (19), the relevant development is that the porter has formerly refused to open the door to Culhwch and his company, but is told by Wrnach to let Kei enter. The

---

[22] In *BR*, three out of four dependent $VN+o_{P1}$ clauses contain a new P1, all of which are [−human]; in *B.*, one out of three.

[23] The construction occurs with new P1 in *CO* (3 ex. out of 20), *B.* (2 out of 4), and *P.* (1 out of 4).

[24] The VN in independent $VN+GEN_{P1}$ represents given information in one example, and inferable information in six examples (out of twenty) in *CO*; inferable information in one example in *Ma*.

structure *dyuot*+GEN~P1~+VN serves as a two-step procedure to present a situation and its participants. Step one (re)calls P1 onto the scene, step two presents the action that advances the narrative development. As shown above, P1 tends to represent given information. Thus, in this construction, the information structuring is different from the typical VN+GEN~P1~ clause: *dyuot*, though new, contributes little to the advancement of the narrative development; then follows the recall of a piece of given information, which in turn is followed by a process with higher relevance to narrative development, representing new information.

A construction that is comparable in structure, but has a different nuance in meaning, shows *dyuot*+GEN~P1~ followed by the preposition *i* 'to' and a second VN (see (20)). This structure has final meaning, conveying the information that the P1 called onto the scene intends to carry out the action expressed by the second VN. The actual performance is implied rather than made explicit.

(20)   *dyuot seint Iwerdon attaw i erchi nawd idaw.*   (CO 1062)
         come_VN saints Ireland towards-him to ask_VN mercy to-him
         'the saints of Ireland came to ask his mercy.'

Dyuot o (i.e. P1 expressed by means of the preposition *o*, rather than a GEN) does not occur in either of these two types of construction. Where VN+*o*~P1~ is the first in a series of VNs, it introduces a linear sequence of events on the same level of relevance to narrative development; compare (21).

(21)   Ac yna *dyuot o Idawc* ac wynteu ygyt ac ef hyt rac bronn Arthur *a chyfarch gwell idaw.*   (BR 6.20)
         come_VN from Idawc . . . and wish better to-him
         'And then Idawc, and they with him, came before Arthur and greeted him.'

2.1.4.2. CONTINUITY

The P1 of an independent VN clause is, as we saw in the previous section, usually a character who has been introduced into the narrative at some earlier stage. Now the question arises whether the presentation of P1 as an oblique phrase (i.e. as a prepositional or a genitive phrase) serves to establish, or to disrupt, continuity of characters—in other words, whether P1 in a VN clause tends to be marked when a different, though previously known, P1 enters the scene, or to mark that the same P1 is still active. Given that medieval Welsh does not require marking of P1 in a finite verbal clause by means of either a noun phrase or a pronominal form,[25] and given the widespread use of chains of VNs without P1, the former can be expected, and this expectation is indeed confirmed in the texts analysed here.

VN+o~P1~

P1 in VN+*o*~P1~ resumes a character from the preceding clause (finite or non-finite)

---

[25] A feature commonly described as 'pro-drop'.

in twenty-nine out of sixty-eight examples of independent $VN+o_{P1}$ (or 42.64 per cent). However, only in nine examples (or 4.41 per cent) does P1 resume P1 of the preceding clause: a subject P1 six times (see (22a)), and the P1 of a VN clause three times (see (22b)).

> (22) (a)   Un ol diaspat y mab, *kyrchu y drws a oruc hi*, ac ar hynny *adaw y ryw bethan*
> *ohonei*   (*Ma. 77.17*)
> make-for_VN the door PRT did she; drop_VN the thing small from-her
> 'After the boy's cry[ing out] she went towards the door, and then she dropped something small'
>
> (b)   A *chymryt y wein ohonaw*, a'r cledyf yn a llaw arall. *Dyuot ohonaw vch penn y*
> *Kawr* malpei y cledyf a dottei y wein.   (*CO 819*)
> take_VN the scabbard from_him; Come_VN from-him above the giant
> 'And he took the scabbard, and the sword into the other hand. He came [and stood] above the Giant, as if putting the sword into the scabbard.'

VN+GEN_{P1}

P1 in independent $VN+GEN_{P1}$ resumes a character from the preceding clause in thirteen out of thirty-three cases (or 39.4 per cent). P1 is resumed in six examples: (23a) illustrates the continuity of the preceding subject P1, (23b) the resumption of the P1 of an elliptic periphrastic VN clause.

> (23) (a)   *Deu uab oed im, a mynet uyn deu uab* y'r mynyd doe y hela.   (*Ow. 728*)
> two sons was to-me, and go_VN my two sons
> 'I had two sons, and my two sons went to the mountain yesterday to hunt.'
>
> (b)   . . . *yd oed kawat o eira gwedi ryuodi y nos gynt, a gwalch wyllt gwedy rylad*
> *hwyat* yn tal y kudygyl. A chan twrwf y march, *kyuodi y walch* a disgynnu bran
> ar y kic yr ederyn . . .   (*Per. 30.25*)
> and hawk wild after PRT_kill_VN . . . rise_VN the hawk
> '. . . a shower of snow had fallen during the night, and a wild hawk had killed a duck in front of the cell. And with the movement of the horse, the hawk rose up and a raven descended on the flesh of the bird . . .'

In dependent VN clauses, coreferentiality between P1 and the P1 of the head clause is more frequent than between the P1 of an independent VN clause and the preceding clause (24.4 per cent or 11 examples of $VN+o_{P1}$, and 13.8 per cent or 12 examples of $VN+GEN_{P1}$), although again coreferentiality is overall not the norm.[26]

We may conclude that the marking of P1 in independent VN clauses serves to signal a change in P1, rather than to mark the continued action of the same participant (see e.g. (19) and (17) for examples where the VN clause involves a shift in

---

[26] Note that these figures include dependent VN clauses with coreferential P1 that precede their head clause (six examples of $VN+o_{P1}$, and eight of $VN+GEN_{P1}$), as in e.g. 'A *gwedy gwelet o Lud hynny*, ef a edewis holl longeu ar y weilgi' (lit.: and after see_VN Lludd that) (And when Lludd saw that, he left all the ships on the sea). Thus the continuity established here concerns the VN clause and the clause following it (in this case the head clause), rather than the preceding clause.

P1). Where the same P1 is involved in a series of actions, these are frequently listed in a series of VNs (see again (17)).

2.1.4.3. THE NARRATIVE ENVIRONMENT

With very few exceptions, independent $vn+o_{P1}$ and $vn+gen_{P1}$ clauses tend to present information that is in the mainstream of a plotline, rather than on the sidelines; in other words, these constructions tend to present content that is necessary for the advancement of a plotline. For an example of what is here described as sideline information, see (24a): the VN clause sums up the emotional state of the previous speaker, but does not contribute to narrative development. Likewise, only few examples of VN clauses with overt P1 are used as textual organizers, such as the marker for direct speech in (24b).[27]

> (24) (a) 'Duw a dalho it; hynny a debygwn i.' Ac yna *kymryt llywenyd ac ehouyndra o'r uorwyn o achaus hynny.*   (*MLl* 57.26)
> take_VN joy and fearlessness [?] from-the girl
> ' "God reward you," she said; "that is what I thought." And the girl was cheered and took heart because of that.'
>
> (b) *Dywedut o Arthur,* 'A oes dim weithon o'r anoetheu heb gaffel?'   (*CO* 1205)
> say_VN from Arthur
> 'Arthur said, "Is there any of the wonders that has not been obtained?" '

There are passages in the texts for which the term *sideline* would be appropriate in their entirety, in that they contain subplots that may be quite separate from the main narrative development. Examples are *CO* 458–66 (Custenhin's wife meeting Culhwch and his company; see further (26)), or *B.* 47.27–48.11, which, as an afterthought to the main narrative, adds a short description of the developments in Ireland. However, within those sideline passages, independent $vn+o_{P1}$ and $vn+gen_{P1}$ tend to carry mainstream information.

Independent $vn+o_{P1}$ and $vn+gen_{P1}$ only rarely introduce narrative sections—i.e. mark a new stage in the development of the narrative (one example is (24a))—but they may indicate a change of a participant's involvement, as in (25). Note that the same pronominal form *ef* 'he' has two different referents in two subsequent sentences: once *ef* refers to the stag being thrown down by Pwyll's pack of hounds, and then to Pwyll himself. The change of syntactic construction (from periphrastic *yn*+VN construction to $vn+o_{P1}$) would appear to serve as a tool to underline the change in Pwyll's involvement: whereas the description of the appearance of the second pack of hounds, and the chase of the stag is accompanied by finite clauses describing Pwyll's perceptions (*ef a glywei* 'he heard', *ef a welei* 'he saw', in *P.* 1.13, 15, 16), now Pwyll's attention focuses, and with it that of the reader.

---

[27] The other example of an independent VN clause with organizational function is *CO* 457, where $vn+o_{P1}$ serves to separate two sections of the text dominated by dialogue, *CO* 467–75 (dealing with Custenhin's son), and *CO* 476–86 (discussing Culhwch's quest).

(25)   . . . llyma yr erchwys a oed yn y ol yn ymordiwes ac ef, ac yn y uwrw y'r llawr.
Ac yna *edrych ohonaw ef* ar liw yr erchwys . . .   (*P.* 1.20)
look_VN from-him he
'. . . and the pack that was pursuing it [the stag] caught up with it and threw it
down. And then he [Pwyll] looked at the colour of the pack . . .'

Thus the large majority of independent VN clauses tend to be part of ongoing
developments of a plotline. This leads us to the consideration of clusters of $VN+o_{P1}$
and $VN+GEN_{P1}$ clauses. A 'cluster' is here defined as two or more instances of identical VN clauses, belonging to the same chain of narrative development, and without
more than one or at most two other main clause constructions intervening. A
$VN+o_{P1}$ cluster exhibits two main characteristics: it presents a quick sequence of
actions, and tends to mark the main stages of development in a passage. The occurrence of $VN+o_{P1}$ clusters is rather limited on the whole; most examples in our texts
occur in *Culhwch ac Olwen*.[28] The example in (26) provides an illustration of both
a quick sequence of actions, and the main developmental steps presented by means
of $VN+o_{P1}$ clauses.

(26)   Kyrchu a orugant vy porth llys Custenhin heusawr. *Clybot oheni hitheu y trwst*
yn dyuot. Redec oheni yn eu herbyn o lywenyd. Goglyt a oruc Kei ym prenn o'r
glydweir, a'e dyuot hitheu yn eu herbyn y geissaw mynet dwylaw mynwgyl
udunt. *Gossot o Gei eiras kyfrwg y dwylaw. Gwascu ohonei hitheu yr eiras* hyt
pan yttoed yn vden diednedic. Amkawd Kei, 'wreic . . .'   (*CO* 458–64).
hear_VN from-her she their noise PRT come_VN; run_VN from-her towards
them; thrust_VN from Kei log between her hands; squeeze_VN from-her the
log
'They reached the gate of the shepherd Custenhin's enclosure. She heard the
noise they made on arriving. She ran towards them full of joy. Kei snatched a
piece of wood from the log pile, as she came towards them to embrace them.
Kei thrust a log between her hands. She squeezed the log into a twisted withe.
Kei said, "Woman . . ." '

The section is dominated by the actions of two characters: Kei and Custenhin's
wife. The series starts off with two introductory statements, the first one setting the
scene ('kyrchu a orugant . . .'), the second one focusing on one of the dominant
characters ('clybot oheni hitheu . . .'), who is still fresh in the reader's mind from
having played a major part in the immediately preceding paragraphs. What follows
is a rapid switching back and forth between Custenhin's wife and Kei, she acting,
he reacting, and adding an unexpected twist to the sequence ('Gossot o Gei . . .').

---

[28] *CO* 459–63, *CO* 818–19, *CO* 990–2, *CO* 1036–40, *CO* 1203–13; the only other examples are *B.*
44.1–44.2 and *Ma.* 72.22–72.24. An example of $VN+o_{P1}$ in a series of independent VNs is *P.* 16.28 (see ex.
(16) above). Up to the decisive point where Gwawl fulfils Rhiannon's request, the pace of the narrative
is considerably slower, the scene being presented largely in dialogue form, than in what follows. Once
Gwawl begins to act on Rhiannon's request, we are dealing mainly with independent VN constructions.
O Pwyll 'by Pwyll', marking the shift in P1, is the bare minimum necessary to maintain the clarity of the
scene.

Through the use of identical structures, the main elements of action in this sequence are put into relief against the rest of the section. The section portrays the
quick-fire action of the participants, with Kei having to react very quickly indeed
to avoid serious (though doubtless unintended) injury or worse. There is no time
or space for evaluation or pause for thought; evaluation happens after the danger
is past, in the form of Kei's comment on Custenhin's wife's action.

It is interesting to note the use of VN+GEN$_{P1}$ *a'e duyot hitheu*. This VN clause puts
the previous clause into context (i.e. Kei picks up the piece of wood as she is
running towards them), but does not contribute any new development (we have
already been told that she is running towards them). It does not appear too fanciful
to assume that VN+GEN$_{P1}$, rather than VN+o_{P1} was used here in order to underline
that this particular clause is outside the series of major steps in the development of
the section.

In a sequence such as *CO* 1036 ff. (example (27)), the reader does not gain the
impression that the series of actions was carried out fast or hurriedly; what is of
importance, however, is the economical, unadorned, and unelaborated presentation of the main stages of development, again characterized by the use of identical
structures, without interrupting the flow of the presentation by, for example,
evaluative statements. The instance of VN+o_{P1} closing the passage is one of the few
examples of *dyuot o*. It would appear possible that the phrase was deliberately
chosen (over the more common *dyuot* + GEN) to maintain the parallel structure of
agentive VN clauses in the passage.

(27)   *Gyrru o Arthur gennat* gwedy hynny ar Odgar uab Aed brenhin Iwerdon, y
        erchi peir Diwrnach Wydel, maer idaw. *Erchi o Otgar idaw y rodi.* Y dywawt
        Diwrnach, 'Duw a wyr . . .'. *A dyuot o gennat Arthur* a nac genthi o Iwerdon.
        (*CO* 1036 ff.)
        send_VN from Arthur messenger; ask_VN from Otgar to-him its give_VN;
        and come_VN from messenger Arthur
        'Arthur sent a messenger after that to Odgar son of Aed, king of Ireland, to ask
        for the cauldron of Diwrnach the Irishman, a steward of his. Odgar asked him
        to give it [to him]. Diwrnach said, "God knows . . .". And Arthur's messenger
        came back with a refusal from Ireland.'

There are four instances of clusters of independent VN+GEN$_{P1}$ in our texts.[29] The
economical presentation of action also comes across in *CO* 1052–3, a sequence that
contains not only a cluster of VN+GEN$_{P1}$, but also an instance of VN+o_{P1} and independent VNs.[30] The sequence of two VN+GEN$_{P1}$ constructions in *Per.* 30.25 (see

---

[29]   Three in *CO* (456, 457; 786/1, 786/2; 1052, 1053), one in *Per.* (30.25/1, 30.25/2). In addition, *CO* also
contains five examples of adverbial VN+GEN$_{P1}$ occurring with a VN clause as a head clause, as in e.g. 'A
gwedy disgynnu Arthur y'r tir, dyuot seint Iwerdon attaw' (lit.: and after descend_VN Arthur to-the
land, come_VN saints Ireland to-him) (And when Arthur had disembarked, the saints of Ireland came
to him) (*CO* 1062).
[30]   'Meglyt o Lenlleawc Wydel yg Kaletvwlch a'e ellwg ar y rot, a llad Diwrnach Wydel a'e niuer achlan.
Dyuot lluoed Iwedon ac ymlad ac wy. A gwedy ffo y lluoed achlan, mynet Arthur a'e wyr yn eu gwyd yn

(23*b*)) marks the return to 'real time' (i.e. contemporary relative to the events narrated in the passage) after a short description of anterior events.

The tendency of independent VN clauses with overt P1 to convey mainstream information (i.e. to provide essential steps in the narrative development), which becomes particularly clear where they form clusters, already implies that the constructions favour a linear temporal structure. And indeed we find that, as a rule, the situation portrayed by an independent VN clause is part of a sequence of events introduced in chronological order.[31] For minimal constructions such as $VN+o_{P1}$ and $VN+GEN_{P1}$, containing no marking of tense, aspect, or mood, to be maximally effective, the context has to supply all the information situating the content of the VN clause, a linear progression of events being the default option.

Instances that do not conform to this general tendency are generally part of direct speech. Thus (15) above is an example of a timeless statement, a general rule or custom that is independent of the temporal context in which it is uttered. A hypothetical situation is portrayed in (28*a*), a series of independent VNs containing one $VN+o_{P1}$ clause marking a change of P1:[32] from the point of view of the speaker, the situation is one to be avoided, since he is describing the conditions under which he could be killed (although dramatic necessity and the expectations of the reader demand that this be brought about at the earliest opportunity). But note that this section, although it stands apart from ongoing developments in narrated reality, is organized within itself in a linear fashion. This is also the case with (28*b*), which introduces a situation planned for the future—i.e. a situation that is posterior to narrative 'present'. An event belonging to the past, anterior relative to narrative 'now', is illustrated in (23*a*) above.

(28) (*a*)   'A dwyn bwch,' heb ef, 'a'y dodi gyr llaw y gerwyn, *a dodi ohonof uinheu y neill troet* ar geuyn y bwch   (*Ma.* 87.1)
and put_VN from-me me the one foot
' "And if one were to take a he-goat," he said, "and put it next to the tub, and if I were to put one foot on the back of the he-goat" '

(*b*)   Archaf i oet ulwydyn, hagen, hyny delwyf o'm neges ac yna, ar vyg cret, *vyn dyfot y'r llys hon*   (*Per.* 61.7–8)
my come_VN to the court this
'I ask a year's postponement, however, until I return from my quest, and then, upon my faith, I shall come to this court'

Independent VN constructions are a very economical means to present the

---

y llong . . .' (Llenlleawg the Irishman seized Caledfwlch and swung it in a round and he killed Diwrnach the Irishman and all his company. The armies of Ireland came and fought with them. And after all the armies had fled, Arthur and his men, before their eyes, boarded the ship . . .) (*CO* 1050–4).

[31] This is the case for 91.2% of $VN+o_{P1}$ clauses (63 out of 68), and for 81.8% of $VN+GEN_{P1}$ clauses (27 out of 33). Note that the narrative context as defined here does not necessarily mean the immediately preceding and following clauses, but rather describes the context of events as narrated.

[32] Cf. here Morgan's (1938) remark that VN clauses such as the one occurring in (27*a*) express the 'idea of an action'.

bare bones of a plotline, the bare minimum of information necessary to keep the narrative development on track. In three of the texts analysed here, the use of independent vn+o_{p_1} and vn+gen$_{p_1}$ is largely restricted to certain parts of the narrative. Thus *Culhwch ac Olwen* contains all but three examples of vn+o_{p_1} in two sections: the first main section of the narrative (*CO* 399–819), comprising the final preparation at Arthur's court, Culhwch's setting-out together with his companions, and the meeting with Ysbaddaden, before the listing of the tasks to be performed by Culhwch. The second part of the text rich in vn+o_{p_1} is *CO* 920–end, which belongs to a series of very loosely connected quests and adventures (beginning with *CO* 759), some of which are not developed beyond the bare skeleton of events. The distribution of vn+gen$_{p_1}$ in *Culhwch ac Olwen* is not as clear-cut as that of vn+o_{p_1}, with the exception that there are no instances of either construction in the sections *Culhwch yn aswyno ei gyfarws ar aelodau'r Llys* (*CO* 175–373; with the exception of *CO* 175, where vn+o_{p_1} introduces the section), and *Ysbaddaden yn nodi'r Anoethau* (*CO* 565–789). The first of these consists largely of a listing of names, the second is also enumerative in character, as well as highly formalized and repetitive, listing hypothetical actions. Thus neither is compatible with the typical characteristics of usage that have emerged from our analysis of vn+o_{p_1} and vn+gen$_{p_1}$.

In *Branwen*, all instances of vn+o_{p_1} and of independent vn+gen$_{p_1}$ are to be found in the last third of the text.[33] The text is building up towards the section beginning with the first example of vn+o_{p_1} (see (29)): the stage reached now is that peace has been re-established between the two parties, just before the dramatic killing of Branwen's son and the ensuing fight, which in turn leads to the death of Bendigeidfran, the depopulation of Ireland, the long road home of the seven men, and the death of Branwen on the way.

(29)   Ac yna, gwedy daruot y tangneued, *galw o Uendigeiduran y mab attaw.*
        (B. 43.13)
        call_VN from Bendigeidfran the boy to-him
        'And then, when peace had been made, Bendigeidfran called the boy to him.'

Peredur exhibits a pattern comparable to that of *Branwen*, in that the text contains no instance of independent vn+o_{p_1} in the short introductory section describing the childhood and youth of Peredur, before his arrival at Arthur's court.[34] *Cyfranc Lludd a Llefelys* shows a concentration of identical structures in a passage that is overall characterized by a repetitive organization: five of the seven instances of adverbial vn+o_{p_1} (see note 26 for an example) are contained in the short section describing Lludd setting out to meet his brother and the arrangements made to secure unhindered talks.

---

[33] On the other hand, all but one of the five subordinate vn+gen$_{p_1}$ clauses occur before the arrival of Bendigeidfran in Ireland.

[34] The first example is *Per.* 12.23. The first instance of vn+gen$_{p_1}$ is *Per.* 26.5, well into the main body of the narrative.

2.1.5. Independent VN clauses and the *gwneuthur*-inversion

The preceding sections have shown that the interaction between an independent VN clause with overt P1 and its textual environment is characterized by several tendencies: P1 is given in the large majority of cases; the constructions tend to convey mainstream information as regards the development of events in their immediate environment, and there is a clear tendency for events to be portrayed in linear temporal progression. We find clusters of $\text{VN}+o_{\text{P1}}$ that represent either the main development of events in the section containing them, or rapid sequences of actions, or both. Clusters of $\text{VN}+\text{GEN}_{\text{P1}}$ are less numerous, most likely because of the overall smaller number of instances of independent $\text{VN}+\text{GEN}_{\text{P1}}$, which in turn is conditioned by the restriction that $\text{VN}+\text{GEN}_{\text{P1}}$ can occur only with intransitive VNs. Both $\text{VN}+o_{\text{P1}}$ and $\text{VN}+\text{GEN}_{\text{P1}}$ may be used to initiate new developments, or to resume the course of narrative development in the narrative 'here and now' after static descriptive sections.[35] As far as the distribution of $\text{VN}+o_{\text{P1}}$ and $\text{VN}+\text{GEN}_{\text{P1}}$ are concerned, we have seen that only three of our texts reveal clear patterns; the other texts do not contain sufficient numbers of examples to yield evidence for a preferred position of either construction.

At this stage, the question arises whether it is possible to abstract a more general functional property of independent agentive VN clauses. To this end, a comparison with a structure that has a similar organization of its components is useful. The construction in question, illustrated in (30), will be referred to here as *gwneuthur*-inversion.[36]

(30)   *Kyrchu a orugant vy* porth lys Custenhin heusawr.   (*CO* 458)
        reach_VN PRT they-did they
        'They reached the gate of Custenhin's court.'

The VN is placed at the beginning of the clause, followed by a form of the verb *gwneuthur* 'do, make' in relative construction. The *gwneuthur*-inversion is briefly dealt with in Fife's investigation of the so-called abnormal sentence in Middle Welsh (Fife 1988: 104), where its purpose is described as 'to "spill the beans". This is because . . . all the new, communicative information comes first, leaving a content-poor pro-verb to finish the clause in an anti-climax.' The *gwneuthur*-inversion has a variant that is its exact opposite in information structuring: the sentence is introduced by *sef* 'what/that which' (a conflation of the copula *ys* and the third person singular pronoun *ef* 'he/it'), followed by a form of *gwneuthur* in relative construction, in turn followed by the VN, as in (31):

---

[35] An example is the description of a knight's appearance, in the passage preceding *BR* 6.20. See also *Per.* 30.25, quoted in (22*b*).

[36] The term *gwneuthur*-inversion is adopted, and slightly adapted to a medieval Welsh context, from Fife (1986), which presents an account of the Modern Welsh counterpart of the construction (which Fife refers to as the *gwneud*-inversion).

(31)   *Sef a wnaeth Teirnon, kyuodi* ac edrych ar prafter yr ebawl   (*P.* 22.15)
        it-is PRT did Teirnon, rise_VN
        'Teirnon rose and admired the sturdiness of the foal'

The *gwneuthur*-inversion is common in all our texts, and its frequency always exceeds the frequency of either of the two agentive VN constructions. Apart from the structural similarity of placing the VN at the beginning of the clause (or rather, taking into account those instances of VN+GEN$_{P1}$ with pronominal P1, into the first stressed position of the clause), the *gwneuthur*-inversion shows other correspondences to VN clauses with overt P1: the subject of *gwneuthur* is generally given information, whereas the object—i.e. the VN—generally represents new or inferable information. The construction can dominate whole paragraphs, presenting the main steps of development.[37] The *gwneuthur*-inversion is, however, not generally restricted to the presentation of mainstream information. It also occurs, unlike independent VN clauses, with considerable frequency in direct speech, where it is generally used to describe past events.

The abnormal sentence in general is interpreted by Fife (1988) as a focusing device, a marked order that serves to topicalize the fronted element, rather than to emphasize it.[38] Topic is here defined, with Chafe (1976: 55), as the element that provides the 'frame of discourse for the sentence', or that specifies 'what the sentence is about' (as in Fife 1988: 35). Following this interpretation of the abnormal sentence, one may regard the *gwneuthur*-inversion as a sentence pattern that topicalizes a verbal content (or, with Morgan 1938, the idea of an event, or an action, rather than a specific event or action), by fronting the verbal element. One might object that it is problematic to classify the processual element of a situation—i.e. the element that is highest in information content, as the topic in the above definition (see Poppe 1991: 191). However, it may not be necessary to regard Middle Welsh word order as topic oriented throughout. It would appear possible that amid noun phrase- or adverbial phrase-initial word orders, a sentence pattern fronting the VN marks this as the most salient information in the clause (see also Poppe, ibid.). In this context, it is important to recognize that genuinely verb-initial clauses are the exception rather than the rule in Middle Welsh. Poppe (1991) quotes figures between 9.6 per cent and 2.2 per cent of verb-initial positive main statements in five Middle Welsh prose texts.[39]

---

[37] Cf. e.g. *P.* 22.11–23.3: Teirnon watches through the night over his mare, the mysterious hand appears and seizes the newborn foal, Teirnon hacks off the hand, rushes out to pursue whatever the hand may have been attached to, comes back, and finds the child. In this passage, the *sef*-construction is used to portray Teirnon's immediate reactions to events; all his other actions are presented by means of the *gwneuthur*-inversion.

[38] On the distinction between emphasis and topicalization as types of focus, see Fife (1988: 33 ff.). Fife and King (1991) present an account of the abnormal sentence as a topicalization device, from a cross-linguistic perspective.

[39] Poppe's figures concern *CO* (9.6%), *B.* (4.4%), *MLl* (0%), *BR* (2.2%), and *Breudwyt Maxen* (I. Williams 1927) (9.1%).

As Fife (1988: 137, following Bolinger 1952) points out, the information flow in a sentence usually proceeds from given to new information. Both the *gwneuthur*-inversion and $VN+o_{P1}$ regularly violate this tendency by placing new information at the beginning of the sentence or VN clause. As far as $VN+GEN_{P1}$ is concerned, this also generally holds true, with the exception of the variant $dyuot+GEN_{P1}+a(c)+VN$, as the main verbal information is carried by the VN following P1 (and, in this respect, this structure is comparable to the *sef*-construction illustrated above); this variant is comparatively rare, however.

It seems justified to interpret the construction $VN+o_{P1}$ as a focusing device for the verbal element of a (VN) clause. This much it shares with the *gwneuthur*-inversion. There are, however, clear differences in the applicability of both constructions. Containing no overt marking of tense and aspect, $VN+o_{P1}$ is usually restricted to contexts with a clear linear ordering of events, where the reader can decode the temporal setting from the context without difficulty. On the other hand, because it is a short construction, it is particularly suitable for the purpose of presenting either a situation or a series of situations in a minimum of processing time, or even for adding dramatic effect to a passage by 'speeding up' the narrative. Focus on the verbal element, as a new element of information, is underlined by the removal of P1 from subject position.[40]

The construction $VN+GEN_{P1}$ can, with certain restrictions, be interpreted along the same lines. Section 2.1.3 showed that roughly 39 per cent of all $VN+GEN_{P1}$ clauses contain a pronominal P1. This precedes the VN, but it is not a stressed element. A slight majority of $VN+GEN_{P1}$ clauses contain proper names or definite noun phrases as P1. As far as the—admittedly rare—construction $dyuot+GEN_{P1}+a(c)+VN$ is concerned, it would appear that this type is used when the process itself and P1 are of equal relevance in their context. This variant of $VN+GEN_{P1}$ appears to occupy an intermediate position between $VN+o_{P1}$[41] and a subject-initial abnormal sentence, balancing salience between processual content and P1, but emphasizing neither.

2.1.6. Interim summary: VN clauses with overt P1 in narrative texts

The independent VN clause with overt P1 has been interpreted in this chapter as a device to focus the verbal noun. Focusing the VN means focusing a verbal, or pro-

---

[40] The temporal scene setting of an independent VN clause may be achieved by either a preceding adverbial phrase or a subordinate (adverbial) clause or VN clause. In our data, 19.1% of all $VN+o_{P1}$ clauses are preceded by a temporal adverbial phrase (such as *ar hynny* 'thereupon', *ac yna* 'and then') and 7.4% by a subordinate clause. For $VN+GEN_{P1}$, the figures are 15.2% and 18.2%, respectively. Temporal scene-setting devices are not employed to the same extent in all texts. *CO* relies largely on the VN clause alone, whereas in *Ma.* and *Per.* anchoring the VN clause in its temporal context by means of an adverb or subordinate clause is the rule rather than the exception. VN clauses with overt P1 occurring in clusters are always truly VN initial. Poppe (1991: 169) gives the following figures for the order adv.+ *y*+finite verb in five prose texts: 17.5% (*CO*), 41.2% (*B.*), 22.0% (*MLI*), 44.6% (*BR*), 42.8% (*Breudwyt Maxen*).

[41] $VN+o_{P1}$ rather than $VN+GEN_{P1}$, as $dyuot+GEN_{P1}+a(c)+VN$ is not restricted to intransitive VNs following P1.

cessual content, without at the same time focusing the relation of the process with time and reality. The identification of the process as a single, specific incident is not provided by the VN construction itself, but has to be inferred from the context. Thus the independent VN clause is a device to present the semantic core of a process and its participant(s)—namely, P1 and, in transitive constructions, P2, in a maximally economical and effective way. The VN content is the most salient piece of information of the VN clause; the bare minimum of identification (or instantiation) of the process is provided by the overt mentioning of the (typically) controlling participant.

The interpretation as a focusing device is supported by several intra-clausal, as well as contextual features. The VN is placed at the beginning of the clause or into second stressed position (after an adverbial phrase). This distinguishes the VN construction from the subject/P1-first or object/P2-first so-called abnormal sentence. It is further distinguished from the VN-first *gwneuthur*-inversion by the lack of information concerning tense, mood, and aspect, and by the expression of P1 by means of a prepositional phrase or pronoun. We have seen that, in independent VN constructions, the VN tends to contain new information, and the P1 given information. Thus these constructions regularly present a sequence of new before given information; the entity that is most easily identifiable (i.e. P1) is positioned at or towards the end of the clause. The usage of independent VN clauses with overt P1 supports this interpretation: they tend to convey mainstream information, and are used to present events in linear sequence, often representing the main building blocks of a plotline, or marking the return to narrative development after static descriptive passages.

Poppe (1991: 191) tentatively suggests that the *gwneuthur*-inversion may be a sentence pattern 'used when no sentence-constituent has to be specifically marked as topic'.[42] I would agree with this, if we define topic as the entity about which the clause makes a statement. The *gwneuthur*-inversion is also a clause type that is restricted to main clauses,[43] separating contextual information of time, aspect, and mood from the semantic core of the process by relegating it to a verb that is relatively neutral in content (*gwneuthur*), and placing it after the VN in a relative construction.

We have seen that dependent agentive VN clauses share some of the features of their independent counterparts. Most relevant appears to be the strong tendency for P1 to represent given information. It is tempting to interpret these constructions as the subordinate counterpart of the *gwneuthur*-inversion in contexts where the overt marking of P1 is necessary to guarantee a smooth flow of communication

---

[42] I would not agree with Poppe's (1991) proviso that the VN in the *gwneuthur*-inversion cannot be considered as a constituent with focus-function. There appears to be no a priori reason why a process, expressed by means of a VN, should not be the most salient piece of information of the clause.

[43] Since in finite subordinate clauses the finite verb needs to follow the conjunction/subordinating element.

by assigning a process to its principal participant (where this is not necessary, bare VNs may be used). As in independent VN clauses, the relation of the process to narrated reality is provided by the context. In dependent VN clauses with overt P1, the subordinate character of the process and its participants relative to the head clause is further underlined by the removal of P1 from subject position, leaving only one subject P1 in a complex situation described by a dependent and a head clause; the hierarchy of processes and participants is thus mirrored by syntactic hierarchy.

The use of independent VNs (what has been labelled independent VN clauses here), though not specifically of VNs with overt P1, has recently been linked with a further construction, that of the historical, or narrative present. Poppe (1995: 147) suggests that what he terms the narrative verbal noun may have displaced a narrative present. Although the narrative present is not commonly used in main clauses in Middle Welsh prose, its erstwhile currency, according to Poppe, can still be traced in Middle Welsh prose through the use of the present tense in subordinate constructions 'where a verbal noun cannot be used for syntactic reasons, i.e. in adverbial clauses introduced by conjunctions which require a finite verb' (ibid.). Examples are preposed temporal clauses, introduced by *val* 'as', *pan* 'when', or postposed temporal clauses introduced by *yny* 'until, so that'.[44]

The use of a narrative present in many languages has functional parallels to that of the historical infinitive—for example, in Latin. Dressler (1968: 145–6) notes that both share what he calls 'gipfelbildende Funktion' (climactic function), and the stylistic characteristic of intensity; Leuman *et al.* (1965) talk about a 'lebhafte Vergegenwärtigung' (vivid presentation) of processes by the historical infinitive, a feature also of the historical present. This 'vivid presentation' of processes is, as we have seen, very much a characteristic of independent VN constructions in Middle Welsh. As Poppe (1995) points out, the motivations for a possible displacement of one construction by another are difficult to assess, and unfortunately we are not in a position to chart such a development through the history of our texts. However, one may speculate that, if such a displacement did take place, the syntactically nominal nature of the Welsh VN might have something to do with making the VN the preferred option to present the semantic core of processes, without contextual information as to their time-and-reality frames. Unlike an infinitive, a VN has nominal syntax, which means that, as we have seen, the principal participants (P1 and P2) are removed from their slots as subject and direct object of a clause, and treated as oblique noun phrases. This relegation of the principal participants, especially of P1, has been interpreted here as underlining the function of the independent VN clause as a device to focus the verbal content. This function is very similar to Dressler's interpretation of the historical infinitive as having 'gipfelbildende Funktion', and of Hofmann and Szantyr's 'vivid presentation'.

---

[44] As in the following: 'Ac ual y byd yn ymwarandaw a llef yr erchwys, ef a glywei llef erchwys arall' (And as he was [lit.: 'is'] listening to the noise of the pack [of hounds], he heard the noise of another pack) (*P.* 1.11–12). For further examples, see Poppe (1995: 144–5).

Thus the syntactic character of the construction, the very fact that it places the participants and process in different syntactic slots, underscores its functional impact.

2.2. Evidence from law texts

The types of VN clauses with overt P1 in the law texts are the same as those in the other Middle Welsh texts analysed in this study. In the construction VN+PP$_{P1}$, the only preposition found marking P1 is *o* 'from', whereas, in the fictional-narrative material, sporadic instances of *gan* 'with' and *i* 'to' were encountered. The type VN+GEN$_{P1}$ is markedly less frequent than VN+PP$_{P1}$, certainly mainly because a P1 marked by a genitive (possessive) can occur only with an intransitive VN, thus restricting the applicability of the construction.

2.2.1. *Llyfr Cyfnerth*

Altogether, there are forty-seven instances of VN+o_{P1} (of which thirty-four are transitive), and nine of VN+GEN$_{P1}$ in this text. The distribution over different syntactic and supra-clausal environments is shown in Table 2.15. The majority of VN clauses with overt P1 occur in what is here labelled 'condition chains'. These are hypothetical case scenarios, typically of the following pattern: an initial condition, often but not necessarily always expressed by a finite conditional clause headed by *o(r)* 'if', introduces the scenario. One or more additional conditions are added, usually by means of VN clauses. The prescribed course of action to be taken to deal with the case is headed by a finite clause, which may again be followed by VN clauses (see the following examples).[45]

TABLE 2.15. *VN clauses with overt P1 in* Llyfr Cyfnerth

VN clause	VN+o_{P1}		VN+GEN$_{P1}$	
	n	%	*n*	%
Independent	8	*17*	1	*11.1*
Condition chain	30	*63.8*	5	*55.6*
Dependent (introduced by a preposition)	6	*12.8*	3	*33.3*
Direct object/P2 complement	3	*6.4*		
TOTAL	47	*100*	9	*100*

---

[45] Quotations are by folio and line in manuscripts V and W, following the usage in *WML*.

(32) (*a*)   *Gureic aymrotho ehunan* yn llɓyn ac ymperth ywr. *aehadaɓ or gɓr hi.*
agorderchu arall o honaɓ ae dyuot hitheu yg cɓyn at y chenedyl. ac yr dadleu. *Os*
diwat y gɓr rodet y lɓ ygloch heb tauaɓt yndi.   (*WML* W 82a5 ff.)
woman PRT-surrender_pres.sub.3sg herself; and-her-leave_VN from-the
man (she); and-connect_VN another from him; and-her come_VN (she); if
deny_pres.3sg the man
'A woman who surrenders herself to a man in bush and brake, and is aban-
doned by the man who connects himself with another woman, and she come
to complain to her kindred and to the courts; if the man deny, let him swear
on a bell without a clapper.' (Wade-Evans 1909: 241)

(*b*)   Tri dygyn goll kenedyl: vn uɓ *bot mab amheuedic* heb dɓyn a heb wadu. *Allad*
o hɓnnɓ gɓr o genedyl arall heb dylyu dim idaɓ. *Talu yr alanas honno oll adylyir.*
Ac odyna ywadu ynteu rac gɓneuthur o honaɓ yr eil gyflauan.
(*WML* V 40b1 ff.)
be_VN son doubtful; and kill_VN from that-one man from kindred other;
pay_VN the galanas that all PRT-must_impers.pres.3sg
'Three calamitous losses of kindred:— one is, that there should be a doubted
son without being affiliated and without being denied; and that such should
kill a man of another kindred without owing him anything; the whole of that
galanas is to be paid; and then he is to be denied lest he should commit a second crime.' (Wade-Evans 1909: 264)

What we find here is a parallel to the usage of syntactically independent VN
clauses in the narrative material: the processes presented form links in chains of
actions, and there is linearity in that each of the processes in the chain is a vital link
in the development of the case. The presentation of the cases (hypothetical though
they are) follows a narrative pattern, with an exposition (the introductory statement or condition), a development of action following on from it, and a conclusion (the judgment or prescribed course of action). As the cases presented in the
law book are models—i.e. generally applicable—there is no actual frame of time
and reality that can provide the context for the VNs. Therefore, not only is the use
of VNs eminently useful, underlining the timelessness of the cases presented, but
the narrative-like construction becomes something of a necessity: linearity of development has to be presupposed if there are no markers for tense/aspect.

As regards the information status of P1, the tendency already observed for P1 to
be given rather than new is visible here, although not to the same extent. However,
the labels given and new cannot be applied here in exactly the same way as in the
narrative material, since there is no continuity of individual characters in a legal
text beyond a single paradigm case. Rather, there are categories of persons (the
plaintiff, the surety, the witness, etc.) that in reality will be instantiated by different
individuals. Thus, whereas in a narrative text one particular individual may be
recalled on the scene numerous times at different stages of the narrative development, in our lawbook, a character lasts only as long as the case pattern laid out, but
the brevity of the case (i.e. the narrative unit) and the limited number of stock
characters also imply a higher continuity rate of the characters within the case.

Thus P1 in vn+o_{P1} continues a character mentioned in the preceding clause in 61.7 per cent of examples (or twenty-nine out of forty-seven; in eight instances, the character continued is the P1 of the preceding clause). In 63.8 per cent altogether, P1 can be described as given. With vn+gen$_{P1}$, P1 occurs in the preceding clause in 66.7 per cent (or six out of nine examples); in none of them as P1, however.

The construction P1+i_{vn}(+P2) can be identified, potentially, twice in a passage in manuscipt V. However, there appears to be an overlap here of potential purposive and agentive functions.[46] The two clauses occur as the two first elements of a triadic structure:

(33)   Tri gǒybydyeit yssyd am tir. *henaduryeit gǒlat yǒybot ach ac etrif* y dǒyn dyn ar dylyet otir adayar. Eil yǒ gǒr o pop rantir ortref honno yǒ *amhinogyon tir yǒybot kyfran* rwg kenedyl acharant.   (*WML* V 25b19 ff.)
        elders gwlad to-know_VN kin and descent; 'doorposts' land to-know_VN sharing
        'There are three kinds of evidences for land: elders of a gwlad for ascertaining kind and descent to establish a person in his right as to land and soil. The second is; a man from every rhandir of that trev constitutes the land borderers for ascertaining the mutual sharing between kindred and relatives.'
        (Wade-Evans 1909: 205)

The translation shows that Wade-Evans interprets the constructions as purpose clauses; the noun phrases preceding the VNs present characters whose purpose and function it is to carry out the actions presented by the VN, and this particular construction can, in a timeless setting such as the lawbook, underline this function (which, unlike an individual action, is not bounded in real or narrated time). We shall encounter a construction which is similar in content and structure in the Irish material (see Section 3.1.3), the latter providing an illustration of how the same syntactic structure can become fully 'agentive'—i.e. express the completion of a specified process by a particular individual or party in a context with a specific temporal setting.

2.2.2. *Llyfr Cynghawsedd*

The 'Book of Pleading'[47] consists largely of model cases. Charles-Edwards (1986, 1989) characterizes the model cases in *Llyfr Cynghawsedd* as 'model narratives', thus drawing attention to their mode of presentation (1986: 191). The cases are

---

[46] Manuscript W shows an example that closely resembles the second (potential) P1+i_{vn}(+P2) structure quoted in (33): 'Teir marǒ tystolyaeth yssyd. . . . Eil yǒ dynyon bonhedic o pop parth. *amhinogyon tir ygelwir yrei hynny y dosparth* trǒy ach ac eturyt . . .' (lit.: 'doorposts' land PRT-call_impers.pres those to decide_VN) (Three defunct testimonies there are . . . The second is, persons of lineage from every side who are called land borderers, to decide by kin and descent) (*WML* W 103b14–15, Wade-Evans 1909: 278).

[47] Reference to *Cyngh.* is made by paragraph and line of the printed page of Wiliam's edition; variant readings are to *AL*, and reference is made by book and paragraph (e.g. vii. 23). Variation that is purely orthographic is not taken into account.

commonly introduced by the phrase *o dderfydd*[48] 'if it happens [that]', which is followed by the outline of the case:

(34)   O deruyd e den caffel javn gan argluyd am tyr a dayar, a gomed e datleu o'r amdiffennur, *a galu o'r argluyd am vraut* e gan er ygneyt am henny, javn ev barnu idav teyrbyv camlwrv . . . (*Cyngh.* §8.32)[49]
and call_VN from-the lord about judgment
'If it so happen that a man receives the right, from a lord, to land and soil, and if the defendant refuses pleading for it, and if the lord call for a judgment concerning that from the judges, it is right to adjudge three cows fine to him . . .'

This usage of VN clauses is parallel to what we have found in *Llyfr Cyfnerth*: after stating an initial condition (here, *o deruyd*, rather than *o(r)*), further conditions are added by means of VN clauses. The use of VN clauses with overt P1 in condition chains of this type accounts for 43.3 per cent (or 26 out of 60 examples) of VN+o_{P1}, thus it is not as prominent in *Llyfr Cynghawsedd* as in *Llyfr Cyfnerth*.

The utterances appropriate for and to be expected from the plaintiff (*hawlwr*) and the defendant (*amddiffynnwr*) are presented either in direct speech, or in indirect speech (i.e. the VN clause is the P2 of a verb of speech (finite or a VN), such as *dywedyd* 'say', *ateb* 'answer' (see (35)):

(35)   [O] deruyd e den holy tyr a dayar o datanud ar ac eredic, devet ar e tyr *a dewedet e vot en eyste ef* ar e tyr hvn a'r dayar blvyden a blvydened ac ar ac eredic idau arnav, a henne drvy rod ac estyn y gan argluyt, a gwede henne er reherru en agkyfreithiaul y arnav; ac ossyt a amhevo henne bot ydau dygaun a'y guypo: '*bot en wyr a dewedys*'. Ac ena atep o'r amdiffennur: 'Dyoer', ep ef, 'o buosty ema kehyt ac a dewede dy ac o'th reherrvyt en agkyfreithiaul odema, tythev a holeyst ema o datanud ac a'y kefeyst, *a gvedy e caffael ohonauty* y'th reherruyty odema val e gerrey deledauc aneledauc o gwyr a kyfreith . . .' (*Cyngh.* §19.21–6)[50]
and say_3ipv.3sg his be_VN PRT sit_VN (he); be_VN PRT true PRT say_pret.1sg; and there answer_VN from-the defendant; and after its get_VN from-you
'If a person claims *tir a dayar* by *dadannudd* of tilth and ploughing, let him come to the land and let him say that he has been established on that land for the duration of a year, and that [there is] tilth and ploughing for him on it, and that by grant and gift from a lord, and that after that he had been unlawfully driven from it; and if there is anybody to doubt that, he has enough [witnesses] who know that "it is true what I have said". And then the defendant is to answer: "God knows", he says, "if you have been here as long as you say, and if you have been unlawfully driven away from here, you have claimed here by *dadannudd*,

---

[48] Charles-Edwards (1986: 191) points out that this is one of the features that characterizes the text as originating from Gwynedd.
[49] '. . . am uraut *ar* er egneyt am henny' (*AL* vii. 8).
[50] '. . . a dewedet er ryuot er e tyr hun en eysted bluyden a bluydyned truy rod ac estyn arglwyd, ac ar ac eredyc ydau arnau er re erru en agkyfreytyaul y arnau . . . a vypo bot en wyr a dywaut . . . yth uuryvt ty odema ual e buru dyledauc anyledauc . . .' (*AL* vii. 29).

and you have got it, and after you had received it you were driven from here as
a proprietor may drive away a non-proprietor by right and law . . ." '

The statistical distribution of VN+o_{P1} (as in *Llyfr Cyfnerth*, *o* is the only prepositional P1 marker) and VN+GEN_{P1} over different construction types and in direct or
indirect speech and narrative is charted in Table 2.16. All but two examples of
VN+o_{P1} in direct speech are subordinate constructions; therefore, the text confirms

TABLE 2.16. *VN clauses with overt P1 in* Llyfr Cynghawsedd

(*a*) VN+o_{P1}

VN clause	Direct speech	Indirect speech	Narrative	Total	%
Independent	2		5	7	11.7
Condition chain			26	26	43.3
Subordinate clause	6		2	8	13.3
P2	11	6		17	28.3
Subject			2	2	3.3

(*b*) VN+GEN_{P1}

VN clause	Direct speech	Indirect speech	Narrative	Total	%
Independent			1	1	4.5
Condition chain			2	2	9.1
Subordinate clause		3	2	5	22.7
P2	6	4	2	12	54.5
Subject			2	2	9.1

the general tendency, observed before, that independent VN+o_{P1} is mainly a feature
of narrative. In *Llyfr Cynghawsedd*, as well as in *Llyfr Cyfnerth*, the use of VN+GEN_{P1}
is comparatively rarer (see table). The dominant VN occurring is *bot* 'be', either in
periphrastic construction (see *e vot en eyste ef* 'his being established' in (35)), or in
existential and positional constructions (see (36*a*)); only seven examples contain
VNs other than *bot* 'be' (see (36*b*)):

(36) (*a*)   can dyodeveisty *ve mot y ema* kehyt a henne   (*Cyngh.* §13.13)
          my be_VN here
          'since you have tolerated my being here as long as that'

    (*b*)   Kyfreith a deweit nat kyfreithiaul *menet priodaur e ar tref y tat*
          (*Cyngh.* §10.17)
          go_VN claimant from homestead his father
          'The law says that it is not lawful for someone with a claim to land to go from
          the homestead of his father'

It appears, then, that the usage of VN clauses with overt P1 in *Llyfr Cyfnerth* and *Llyfr Cynghawsedd* does not differ widely from that in the narrative texts analysed before. We encounter the same construction types, with the same markers for P1, and the distribution of syntactically independent and dependent clauses shows clear parallels in the two genres of text, in that the independent construction is mainly characteristic of narrative passages. A feature typical of these two legal texts is the occurrence of VN clauses, chiefly $vn+o_{P1}$, in what I have labelled condition chains. This, however, is paralleled by the well-established use of VNs following a finite verb form in fictional narrative: the 'reality frame' of the series is specified by the initial element of the series. Thus, a finite verb form with past reference extends this time reference over the whole series; a conditional construction (e.g. *o dderfydd*, as in the above examples) extends a hypothetical meaning.

2.3. A Middle Welsh agentive passive? Evidence from annals

As discussed in Chapter 1, medieval Welsh and Irish (as indeed their Modern continuations) each possess a set of finite verb forms, usually labelled 'impersonal', which may be used to describe a situation when, for communicative reasons, it is not necessary or possible to encode P1 overtly. These forms, as illustrated in (37*a*), are current in all the medieval Welsh texts considered so far. What is conspicuously absent from both the narrative and the legal texts is the established use of an agentive passive—i.e. the use of a finite, non-active verb form in conjunction with a prepositional phrase marking P1, of a pattern comparable to what can be found in Modern Literary Welsh, as illustrated in (37*b*), where the marker of P1 is regularly the preposition *gan* 'with, by'.

(37) (*a*)   Yr eil ormes oed, *diaspat a dodit* pob nos Kalan Mei vch bob aelwyt yn Ynys Prydein . . . a'r holl aniueileit a'r gwyd a'r dayar a'r dyfred *a edewit yn diffrwyth*. Tryded ormes oed, yr meint uei y darmerth a'r arlyw *a barattoit* yn llyssoed y brenhin . . . *ny cheffit* vyth dim ohonaw namyn *a treulit* yr vn nos gyntaf. (*CLl* 35–44)
scream PRT put_impers.impf; PRT leave_impers.impf PRT barren; PRT prepare_impers.impf; NEG get_impers.impf; PRT consume_impers.impf
'The second plague was a scream that was raised every May-Day eve above every hearth in the Island of Britain . . . and all the animals and the trees and the earth and the waters were left barren. The third plague was that, whatever the amount of provision and food which was prepared in the courts of the king, nothing could ever be had of it other than what was consumed on the very first night.'

(*b*)   *Cyhoeddwyd argraffiad* o'r chwedleu a'r rhamantau o'r Llyfr Coch *gan John Rhŷs a J. Gwenogvryn Evans*   (Bromwich and Evans 1988: p. ix)
publish_impers.pret with John Rhŷs and J. Gwenogvryn Evans
'An edition of the tales and romances from the Red Book was published by John Rhŷs and J. Gwenogvryn Evans'

The narrative texts yield just two examples that could potentially be interpreted as agentive passives, and the two legal texts another two (see (38)). In all four instances, there is a finite, transitive verb with an impersonal ending; it would appear that P2 is the subject of the clause (in the second one, there is no nominal subject), and what looks like P1 is marked by a prepositional phrase: in (38*a*) the preposition is *gan* 'with', in (38*b*) it is *y gan* 'from', and in (38*c*) *o* 'from'; the last example, a close parallel of (38*c*), also has *o* 'from'.[51]

(38) (*a*)   Deuawt oet arnaw *ny chollet oen eiroet ganthaw*   (*CO* 419–20)
              NEG lose_pret.impers. lamb ever with-him
              'It was his way that never a lamb had been lost by him'

      (*b*)   *yd anuonet idaw* o Annwn *y gan Arawn* Urenhin Annwn.   (*Ma.* 68.22–3)
              PRT send_impers.pret to-him from Arawn
              '[the pigs] were sent to him from Annwn by (or: from?) Arawn, the king of Annwn.'

      (*c*)   O Teir fford *ygƀedir mab o genedyl.*   (*WML* V 44a17)
              PRT-disown_pres.impers son from kindred
              'Three ways whereby a son is disowned by a kindred.'
              (Wade-Evans 1909: 273)

Quite apart from what might be the most convenient (or intuitively appealing) translation of these examples into English (or any other language that has an established, productive agentive passive), there appear to be alternative interpretations for all of them. The phrase *ganthaw* in (38*a*) may be read as a locative phrase: 'with him'—i.e. 'no lamb [of those] with him was ever lost'. *Y gan* in (38*b*) may denote the source—to be more precise, the human source—rather than a local provenance: '[the pigs] were sent to him from Annwn from Arawn.' As we shall discuss further in Section 2.4.1, *y gan* is frequently used with verbs and VNs of sending, receiving, selling, and buying to denote the origin of the article in question.[52] In (38*c*) (and its parallel), the preposition *o* 'from' may very well express a local relation, too: the process of disowning removes the boy from what has hitherto been considered his kindred.

These few examples are hardly enough to establish patterns for the usage of an agentive passive in medieval Welsh prose, and it is tempting to conclude therefore that the agentive passive, as a productive category, does not figure in the syntactic and stylistic inventory of medieval Welsh writers. However, if we look at a different genre of text again, we suddenly do find agentive passives—i.e. we find clauses containing finite impersonal verb forms co-occurring with prepositional phrases marking the P1 of those verbs. In *Brut y Tywysogyon* (T. Jones 1973), an annalistic

[51] 'Pan diwatter mab o genedyl' (lit.: when deny_impers.pres.sub from kindred) (When a son is denied by a kindred) (*WML* W 107a3; Wade-Evans 1909: 277).
[52] As in the passage immediately following the one quoted in (38*b*): ' "Ie," heb ynteu, "ba furuf y keffir wy y gantaw ef?" ' (lit.: what form PRT get_impers.pres them from-him) ('Yes,' he said, 'how can they be got from him?'); here, *y gan* cannot be interpreted as P1, but is clearly the point of origin of the entity obtained.

text based on a Latin original closely related to *Annales Cambriae* (Williams ab Ithel 1860) and *Cronica de Wallia* (T. Jones 1946), agentive passives do occur. Two sections of the text have been analysed here: section A comprises the entries for AD 823 to AD 1042 (no agentive passives occur in earlier entries);[53] section B spans the entries from AD 1190 to AD 1275, to allow comparison with both *Annales Cambriae* and *Cronica de Wallia*.

Of the thirty-two agentive passives in section A, nineteen (or 59.38 per cent) have corresponding agentive passives in *Annales Cambriae*; six (18.75 per cent) have no corresponding entry in *Annales Cambriae* (neither in content nor in structure), *Annales Cambriae* has an active clause in four instances (12.5 per cent) where *Brut y Tywysogyon* section A has an agentive passive, and an agentless passive in another four instances; examples for each category are given in (39).

(39) (a) *agentive passive in section A parallelled in AC*
Ugein mlyned ac wythgant oed oet Crist *pan distrywwyt castell Deganwy y gan y Saeson.* Ac yna y duc y Saeson brenhiniaeth Powys yn eu medyant. (*BT(R)* 823)
when destroy_impers.pret castle Degannwy from the Saxons
Arcem Decantorum a Saxonibus destruitur; et regionem Poy(.)uis in sua potestate traxerunt.   (*AC* 822)
castle Degannwy_gen.pl by Saxons destroy_pass.pres
'Eight hundred and twenty years was the year of Crist when the castle of Degannwy was destroyed by the Saxons. And then the Saxons took the kingdom of Powys into their rule.'

(b) *agentive passive in section A corresponds to agentless passive in AC*
Ac yna *y llas Einawn* ap Ywein drwy dwyll *gan vchelwyr Gwent.*   (*BT(R)* 984)
PRT kill_impers.pret Einion with noblemen Gwent
Eynan filius Owini *occisus est.*   (*AC* 984)
Einion slay_part.perf be_pres.3sg
'And then Einion son of Owein was killed through treachery by the noblemen of Gwent.'

(c) *agentive passive in section A corresponds to active in AC*
Ac yna *y diffeithwyt Brecheinawc* a holl gyuoeth Einawn ap Ywein *y gan y Saesson,* ac Aluryt yn dywyssawc arnunt   (*BT(R)* 983)
PRT ravage_impers.pret Brycheiniog from the Saxons
Hoelus filius Idwal *et Alfre* dux Anglorum *vastaverunt Brecheinauc* et totam regionem Einaun filii Owini   (*AC* 983)
Hywel and Aelfhere ravage_perf.3pl
'And then Brycheiniog and the whole territory of Enion ab Owein were ravaged by the Saxons, with Aelfhere as their leader'

[53] Note that 'earlier entries' is to be understood as 'entries for earlier years'. No implication that these entries were actually, in the form in which they are preserved in *BT(R)*, composed at an earlier date is intended. The dating of entries in this discussion follows the dating of annal entries as in the editions of the texts used. Unless specified otherwise, dates for entries refer to *BT(R)*; translations are also taken from this edition. Variant readings are from *BT(P)*.

Thus a small majority of agentive passive clauses in section A have an exact parallel in *Annales Cambriae*, in both content and structure, and, where there are entries in *Annales Cambriae* corresponding to agentive passives in *Brut y Tywysogyon*, these correspondences are most often also agentive passives. In section B, the pattern is less clear, although we also find a predominance of parallel structure where there are corresponding entries: of 17 agentive passives in *Brut y Tywysogyon*, 5 (29.41 per cent) have corresponding agentive passives in *Annales Cambriae*, and 8 (47.06 per cent) in *Cronica de Wallia*. One agentive passive corresponds to an active clause in *Annales Cambriae*, one corresponds to a VN clause without overt P1 in *Cronica de Wallia*, and one to an agentless passive in the same text. The other agentive passive clauses in section B have no corresponding entries in either of the two other texts.

P1 is consistently marked by means of the preposition *y gan* 'from',[54] corresponding to Latin *a(b)* 'from' in the parallel entries in *Annales Cambriae* and *Cronica de Wallia*. The semantics of *y gan* and other prepositions will be discussed at greater length below (Section 4.8). What may be noted here, though, is that the markers of P1 in transitive VN constructions and in so-called agentive passives (the label is still one of convenience: the exact semantic structure of the construction, in Welsh and in Irish, is to be considered further later in this volume) are clearly and consistently distinct from one another. As regards the syntax of agentive passives, we find three dominant patterns:

(*a*) a temporal subordinate clause, introduced by *pan* 'when'; as in (39*a*): 6 in section A, 1 in section B;

(*b*) a main clause with a temporal adverbial phrase as a first constituent; as in (39*b*) and (39*c*): 10 in section A, 13 in section B;

(*c*) a main clause introduced by *a(c)* 'and', which links up to a previous clause introduced by a temporal adverbial; as in (40): 16 in section A and 3 in section B.

(40)   Y ulwydyn racwyneb yd aeth Oto gardinal o Loeger *ac y delit ef*, a llawer o archescyp ac abadeu ac eglwysswyr erreill y gyt ac ef, *y gann Frederic* amherawdyr   (*BT(R)* 1241)
          and PRT seize_impers.pret he . . . from Frederick
          'The following year cardinal Otto went from England and he was seized, and many archbishops and abbots and other churchmen along with him, by the emperor Frederick'

The main clauses introduced by a temporal adverbial and the subordinate clauses introduced by *pan* 'when' have in common that, in both structures, the finite verb necessarily follows the conjunction or adverbial, respectively. The agentive passives introduced by *a(c)* 'and' mirror the sequencing of participants, process, and circumstantial (i.e. time-related) information of those passive clauses that are

---

[54] In the extracts analysed here, there is also one example of *gan* 'with'. For the relation between *gan* and *y gan*, see further Section 4.8.

introduced by temporal adverbials: the temporal setting is given first, then the process, then P2, and then P1 and sometimes other circumstantial information. I interpret the $a(c)$-clauses in such a way that the temporal setting is to be read as 'during the same period' (not necessarily exactly at the same time), but during the period specified by the most recent temporal adverbial, and therefore view them as a subtype of adverbial-initial clauses.

The preponderance of adverbial-initial clauses and *pan*-clauses are conditioned by the text type: annals record sequences of events. A linear temporal sequence provides the framework for the ordering of the events to be recorded; time reference could be described as the superordinate topic of an annalistic text such as *Brut y Tywysogyon*: year X (sometimes exactly specified, as in (39*a*), sometimes defined relative to a specific figure given earlier in the text, as in (40)) is what the entry 'talks about'; thus time and event, in a recurrent pattern, provide an easy-to-use topic–comment structure: at time *X*, event *Y* takes place.

However, there still remains the question why, even though adverb-initial clauses may be a textual necessity, the composer(s) of our text used the agentive passive with such frequency, while other texts do not contain any examples at all. One motivation may be the Latin original: we have seen that, where there are directly corresponding entries to agentive passives, the Latin parallels are most often agentive passives, as well. Thus a conscious emulation of a Latin original may have been one motivation.[55] But it is unlikely that this effort to conform to a model would have been carried out as consistently as in this text, if the resulting construction had not made sense within its context, with regard to both the semantics of the P1 marker, and the structuring of information both within the clause and beyond the clause boundary.

As regards information structuring and continuity, or the resumption of information from previous clauses, only limited conclusions can be drawn from the material in this text. It is difficult to describe information as 'given' or 'new' with any confidence, in the sense of items that have or have not been mentioned in the text before. An annalistic text is not necessarily intended to be consumed or considered in its entirety (unlike, for example, a narrative); rather it is a text that is most likely to be used for reference purposes, in repeated consultation of specific sections of the text. The question what should be considered as a textual unit, or paragraph, of the text is not entirely straightforward. For the purposes of this analysis, I define as a unit the entry or entries given under a specific time reference (such as the ones in (39*a*) or (40)), rather than time references made in relation to specific ones (see e.g. (39*c*)). It is assumed that, in order to locate an event in a specific year, the passage will be read as far back as the closest specific time reference, usually the beginning year of a decade, as in (39*a*).

---

[55] Note, though, that agentive passives do not occur in all medieval Welsh texts based on Latin originals (cf. e.g. the selections from *Brut y Brenhinedd* (Roberts 1971), a text going back to Geoffrey of Monmouth's *Historia Regum Britanniae*).

The entries in section A tend to be very short, reporting events that are not directly related to each other. Thus the participants mentioned tend to represent 'new' information: all but eight P1s are new, and only one is resumed in the following clause. Of the eight P1s that are given, only one continues a participant from a preceding clause; all others resume information that is further removed in the text. All but three P2s are new; only three are resumed in the following text, but only one in the clause immediately following. The entries in section B are longer, and more detail is provided concerning many of the events reported. More of a pattern emerges here: only two out of seventeen P1s represent given information, and only one new P1 is resumed again in the following discourse. As regards P2, around half of all agentive passive clauses contain a given P2 (eight, as compared to nine that are given). Even in this small data sample, a high degree of continuity emerges: four new P2s are resumed in the following clause, three as P2, and three as subject. Of the eight given P2s, seven resume the subject P1 of the preceding clause (see (40) for an example), one the subject P1 paragraph-initial clause. Thus the use of the agentive passive could be interpreted as a continuity device,[56] maintaining the syntactic function of a participant.

A Latin original may very well have provided the model for the agentive passive, as it provided the model for the structure of the whole text of *Brut y Tywysogyon*. However, it would appear that what has here been loosely termed 'agentive passive' also fulfils a functional demand of the text. Certain syntactic patterns are favoured by the structural properties of the text, and there is at least a tendency to employ the agentive passive—that is, a construction that encodes P2 in subject position, and P1 as an oblique phrase, in a way that supports the cohesion of the text. What is noteworthy is the very rare occurrence of agentive, independent VN constructions in *Brut y Tywysogyon*. This may in part be due again to the composer(s) adhering closely to the Latin model,[57] or it may rather be due to considerations of appropriateness relative to genre: if the use of agentive VN clauses was considered a narrative device, and we have seen above that they could be used to great effect to enhance the dramatic flow of a narrative, then the more sober, reporting style of *Brut y Tywysogyon* might have been considered an inappropriate stylistic environment. On the other hand, not all narrative texts make frequent use of independent VN clauses with overt P1. They are most prominent in *Culhwch ac Olwen*, our earliest text, and quite rare in, for example, *Owein*, which is later in composition and belongs to a different type of narrative, much influenced by the

---

[56] For a further discussion of the use of agentive passives as a continuity device with reference to Irish, in comparison to a study of the Latin passive, see Section 3.3.3.2.

[57] Although the use of VNs is not unknown in the Latin annals, cf. e.g. *AC* (manuscript C), *sub anno* 1220: *Translatio Sancti Thomae martyris* (The translation of Saint Thomas the martyr['s body]); in *BT(R)*, this event is recorded by means of an agentive passive: 'pann dyrchafwyt corff Thomas verthyr y gann Ystyphan' (when the body of Thomas the martyr was raised by Stephen). In *AC* this use of VNs is very rare in comparison to the Latin entries in Irish annals (to be discussed in Section 3.2.2); whether this particular usage, however, is one which in turn is influenced by Irish syntax is another question.

continental romances.[58] Thus changing literary and stylistic tastes may have contributed to a decline in the use of independent agentive VN constructions.

2.4. Related categories: IAG, CAUSE, and INST

The categories AG, IAG, CAUSE, and INST can be seen as related in the sense that they are all involved in the bringing about of a process, with various degrees of control, autonomy, and volition. This may lead us to expect that, to an extent, the markers for these categories overlap the prepositional markers for P1, and indeed with each other. This section provides an overview over the prepositions used to denote IAG, CAUSE, and INST, establishes overlaps, and attempts to establish subcategories of, for example, CAUSES marked by different prepositions. This will then lead back to a reconsideration of P1, more specifically the semantics of prepositional P1 markers, in Chapter 4. The discussion is closely based on the texts analysed in the sections above, with occasional references to other collections of data, such as dictionaries and other relevant publications.[59]

As defined in Chapter 1, the IAG is an entity, prototypically human, that essentially contributes to a process taking place. The IAG thus exercises control over initiating a process (or enabling the process to come about), prototypically in a voluntary manner; it could be described as a voluntary, controlling point of origin, and be considered as a subcategory of CAUSE. The CAUSE was defined as an influence contributing to, or an influence advanced by the speaker as an explanation for, a situation; no question of voluntary control on the part of the CAUSE arises. The INST is a means (concrete or abstract) used by an AG to carry out an action. An abstract INST is at times not easily distinguished from the manner in which an action is carried out: thus, in a sentence such as *he solved the problem with great dedication*, the prepositional phrase may refer to the INST—i.e. it was dedication that allowed P1(AG) to solve the problem—or to the manner—i.e. the task was carried out in a dedicated fashion.

2.4.1. The IAG: *gan, y gan,* and *o*

The most common collocation in our data that contains a potential IAG (rather than a source, or point of origin not voluntarily involved in the situation) is the use

---

[58] They are also conspicuously absent from *CLl*. As mentioned above (Section 1.4), the version of the text analysed here is considered by its editor to derive from the one inserted into the Welsh translation of the *Historia Regum Britanniae*. The stylistic preferences of a translator (or re-creator of a Latin original) may well be a determining factor here.

[59] However, such reference is wherever possible kept to a minimum. The main difficulty with second-hand data, especially those from dictionaries, is that they do not give any indication as to how any given example relates to the text as a whole. And, while there is an implicit assumption that examples in, for example, dictionaries are representative, the nature of medieval Celtic material often makes it necessary to revise our views as to what is representative and what is not.

of the prepositions *gan* 'with', and *y gan* 'from', with the verb *kaffael* 'get', where the preposition marks the (potentially voluntary) giver of P2, as in (41*a*) and (41*b*).

(41) (*a*)   Ny dyry ygnat llys aryant yr pengbastrabt *pan gaffo march ygan ybrenhin.*
(*WML* V 6a16)
when get_pres.sub.3sg from the-king
'A judge of a court does not give silver to the chief groom when he shall have a horse from the king.'   (Wade-Evans 1909: 158–9)

(*b*)   *Ac ny dylyant kaffel ran otir gan eu brodyr* vn vam vn tat ac bynt.
(*WML* V 43a24)
and NEG shall_3sg.pres get part of-land with their brothers
'[and they] are not to have a share of land from their brothers of the same mother and the same father as themselves.'   (Wade-Evans 1909: 271)

The phrase *kaffael* X *gan/y gan* Y occurs most frequently in *Llyfr Cyfnerth*; with the compound preposition *y gan* clearly preferred to *gan*.[60] The only difference between the two prepositions that emerges from our texts concerns the frequency of attestation and the preference for one or the other in different texts: whereas *y gan* clearly dominates *Llyfr Cyfnerth*, *gan* is on the whole preferred in the narrative material (see the examples in Appendix 4). *Y gan* and *gan* are also used with other verbs implying an exchange or an act of taking (*prynu* 'buy', *kymryt* 'take'), a request or a demand (*keisaw* 'seek, ask'), an experience (*diodef* 'suffer, tolerate'), or an experience (*clybot* 'hear'). Furthermore, *y gan* and *gan* occur in our data with expressions of greeting (*craessaw, annerch*), with *dyuot* in *dyuot* A *y gan* B 'to come from' (where B is the person sending A), and in *bot* A *yn barawt gan* B 'B having A ready/prepared'. These expressions vary quite widely as regards the potential for conscious and voluntary control exercised by the IAG. For example, *kymryt* 'take' implies less cooperation on the part of person from whom something is taken than *kaffael* 'get' (or 'receive'), or *prynu* 'buy'. The degree of control on the part of the IAG is potentially larger in those expressions where the process does not imply control on the part of P1, as in, for example, *dyuot y gan*, or *bot yn barawt gan*,[61] where P1 is characteristically inanimate. According to Evans (1964: 201), the exact function of *y* in the combinations *y am, y ar, y gan*, etc. 'cannot be ascertained . . . they often bear the same meanings as the simple prepositions *am, ar*, etc.'.[62] The distribution of the simple and combined prepositions is not further explored.

A further preposition used to mark a SOURCE[63] or IAG is *o* 'from'. It occurs with

---

[60] The ratio in *WML* is fifty-four instances of *y gan*, versus four of *gan*. *Gan* is restricted to the latter part of the text (beginning at W 40a8).

[61] The latter is reminiscent of a possessive construction (*bot* X *gan* Y 'X having Y'), which consistently has *gan*, rather than *y gan*. It is quite possible that this factor determines the choice of *gan* here, rather than *y gan*; however, the structure only occurs twice in the present database, in *Ow*.

[62] Evans's translations of the headwords *gan* and *y gan* as 'with, by' and 'by, because' would appear to show that he perceives them to be two different prepositions, but with an overlapping range of meanings.

[63] SOURCE is here defined as 'point of origin' (which can have purely local meaning, or be a 'point of coming into existence').

kaffael, although far less frequently than *gan* and *y gan*.[64] In the narrative texts, there are two examples of *o* used with *kaffael* (*etiuet*) 'have (offspring)' (see (42*a*)). There are, in addition, another two cases where a situation can be described as originating from, or being brought about by, the person named as SOURCE/IAG (see (42*b*)).

(42) (*a*)   Darogan yw itaw kaffel ettiuet; *ohonot ti yt gaffo ef kanys gaffo o arall.* (*CO* 41)
from-you (you) PRT get_pres.sub.3sg he unless get_pres.sub.3sg from other
'It is prophesied that he will have offspring; by you he will have it, since he has not got it by anyone else.'

(*b*)   eithyr Llaesgemyn e hunan, gwr *ny hanoed well neb ohonaw.*   (*CO* 1123)
NEG be-from_impf.3sg better anyone from-him
'save only Llaesgemyn, a man for whom none was the better.'
(Jones and Jones 1989: 133)

It is tempting in these examples to regard the semantic nuance 'origin' as decisive for the selection of *o* in combination with *kaffael*, possibly predominating here over 'volition' (seeing that, in (42*a*), we are dealing with a prophecy); it is unfortunate that the evidence pointing in this direction is so meagre.

Unlike *gan* and *o*, the preposition *y wrth* 'from', in conjunction with expressions such as *kaffael chwedleu* 'receive news', as in (43), or *clybot* 'hear', marks not the IAG —i.e. the transmitter of news—but the person concerned by the news.[65]

(43)   'Yawnahaf yw hynny,' heb y Pwyll, 'kymryt enw y mab y wrth y geir a dywot y uam, *pann gauas llawen chwedyl y wrthaw.*'   (*P.* 26.19)
when get_pret.3sg happy story from-him
' "It is most proper," said Pwyll, "to take the name of the boy from the word his mother spoke when she received happy news from [i.e. concerning] him." '

2.4.2. The CAUSE: *o, am, gan*

The preposition *o* 'from' in causal function may mark both an external and an internal motivation, although the latter is more common (18 versus 31 attestations in our data). Most frequently, *o* is used with a complement describing an experience (see (44*a*)), an emotional or intellectual state (see (44*b*)), or an action or activity (see (44*c*)), all on the part of P1.

(44) (*a*)   A llidyaw a oruc Arthur *o welet y deu was hayachen wedy eu llad*   (*CO* 1217)
from see_VN his two servant nearly after their kill_VN
'And Arthur became angry, seeing his two servants nearly killed'

---

[64] There are only five instances of *o* denoting the giver with *kaffael* in *WML*.
[65] Further examples are *P.* 29.9 (*clybot*), *MLl* 55.8 (*clybot*), 56.1, 56.22. See also J. E. C. Williams (1956: 146).

(b)   Trydyd cynweissat uu hwnnw *a torres y gallon o anniuiged*   (*CLl* 137)
       PRT break_pret.3sg his heart from sorrow
       'That was one of the three chief officers who broke his heart from sorrow'

(c)   ni a gawn yn goganu gan yr unben *o'e adu y prytwn y wlat arall*, onys guahodwn
       (*Ma.* 84.27)
       from-his let the this-time to land other
       'we shall be reviled by the lord, for letting him [go] at this hour to another
       land, if we do not invite him'

Marking causal circumstances external to P1, *o* can be followed by a complement
describing an event or state (often a VN; see (45*a*)), or an action or influence of a
person other than P1 (see (45*b*)). Overall, the most prominent characteristic shared
by these uses of *o* in causal function appears to be that *o* marks the influence of a
process that results in the situation portrayed in the clause.[66]

(45) (a)   Ar tir agollo vn or rei hynny *o eisseu llʋ ereill*; enillent idaʋ   (*WML* V 24b3)
           from want_VN oath other_pl
           'and the land which any of them shall lose through lack of oath on the part of
           the rest, let them make good to him'   (Wade-Evans 1909: 201)

     (b)   canys *o drycystryw gwreic* y gwneuthum yti a wneuthum   (*Ma.* 92.12)
           from evil-scheme woman
           'Since it is through a woman's evil scheming that I did to you what I did'

It is not easy to define the causal function of *am* 'about' more specifically, as dis-
tinguishable from that of *o*. The difference most readily captured is the use of *am*
with complements describing objects or persons. This usage appears to occupy the
periphery of the category CAUSE, possibly overlapping with the IAG: the difference
is the potential for volition and control; the complement of *am* in (46*a*) does not
appear to exercise a voluntary, controlled influence on the causing of the process
described. *Am* is also found with complements describing an event (or activity on
the part of a person other than P1), as in (46*b*). The most common pattern, however, is the use of *am* with a VN or a pronoun referring back to a VN or abstract
noun describing a process, expressing an action or experience on the part of P1 (see
(46*c*)).[67]

---

[66] *O* also occurs in causal function in the fixed expression *o hynny* 'because of that, therefore',
attested four times in the data collected here. These attestations all fit in with a 'result' specification for
the causal function of *o*. Rees (1935: 80–1) lists two functions of *o* headed 'i fynegi'r canlyniad' (to show
the result), and 'i fynegi'r achos neu'r rheswm' (to show the cause or reason), but a note penned into the
typescript of the thesis (presumably by the author) under the latter heading reads 'Nid oes lawer o
wahaniaeth ystyr rhwng yr adran hon ac adran 6 uchod' (there is not much difference of meaning
between this section and section 6 [i.e. the one entitled 'to show the result'] above). *O* also occurs in our
data in the compound prepositions *o achaws* 'because of' (*passim*), and *o atlo* 'by reason of' (attested
once, *WML* V 29b18).

[67] There are fourteen examples of the latter pattern, eight with concrete complements describing
persons or objects, and six with complements describing activities on the part of persons other than P1.

(46) (a)   Ac onys rody, *dy agheu a geffy ymdanei*   (CO 533)
             your death PRT get_pres.2sg about-her
             'And if you don't give her [to us], you will get your death because of her'

     (b)   ... y erchi idaw yscar a'e wreic, *am gyflauan mor anwedus* ac ar y wnaethod
             (P. 21.13)
             about crime so outrageous
             '... to demand of him to separate from his wife, for such an outrageous crime
             as the one she had committed'

     (c)   O gwnaeth hitheu gam, kymeret *y phenyt amdanaw*.   (P. 21.18)
             her penance about-him[it]
             'If she has done wrong, let her accept the penance for it.'

The property characterizing contexts such as (46c), in our database the most
common context in which *am* occurs in causal function, is a potential for control
on the part of P1 with regard to the condition presented by the prepositional phrase.
O, on the other hand, is more frequently used with verbs of perception (e.g. *o welet*
(see (44a)) and complements not under the control of a participant. However, this
distinction appears to be not absolute, but only visible as a tendency (cf. the use of
o in (44c)).[68]

The preposition *rac* 'before' in marking the CAUSE does not occur with complements expressing or implying action, or describing concrete objects or persons.
Its context of usage is rather that of an abstract characteristic or quality, ranging
from a quality ascribed to an external entity, as in (47a) to an experience or state of
mind affecting a participant. Into the latter category belongs the use of *ofyn* 'fear'
with *rac*, rather than any other preposition (see (47c)).

(47) (a)   Ni chwyuei ulaen blewyn arnaw *rac yscawnhet tuth y gorwyd* y danaw
             (CO 80)
             before lightness trot the steed
             'Not a tip of a hair would stir on him because of the lightness of the trot of the
             steed under him'

     (b)   may ryued na thodeis yn llyn tawd *rac kywilyd gan a gefeis o vatwar* gan y gwr
             du   (Ow. 199)
             before shame with PRT get_pret.1sg from mockery
             'it is a wonder that I did not melt into a pool of lard for shame, with all the
             mockery I had from the black man'

     (c)   ... a gadu rei onadunt yn vyw y hiliaw *rac ofyn* dyuot eilweith o damwein y
             ryw ormes honno   (CLl 82)
             before fear
             '... and to keep some of them alive for fear that a plague of this sort might
             come again'

---

[68] *Am* is also, though only once, attested with *gwelet* 'see' (B. 46.4). The phrase *am hynny* 'therefore,
because of that' refers in six out of seven cases attested here to an event leading up to the situation
portrayed in the clause. In one case (Ow. 412), the phrase resumes an external circumstance, rather than
a process. There is also one instance of *y am hynny* in causal function (WML W 83a12).

Gan 'with' marks the CAUSE with a complement describing a co-occurring cir-cumstance or event, as in (48*a*); a concrete complement marks a coexisting object or substance providing the condition for a situation (see (48*b*)).[69]

(48) (*a*)   A chynnwryf mawr a uu yn yr awyr *gan asgellwrych y brein*   (*BR* 15.5)
with fluttering the ravens
'And there was a great commotion in the air because of the fluttering of the ravens'

(*b*)   Yn y lle y bei vrynn arnaw abreid y glynei dyn arnaw rac llyfnet y llawr *gan vissweil gwarthec a'e trwnc.*   (*BR* 2.13)
with dung cattle and-their urine
'Where there was a hump on it [i.e. the floor], a man could hardly stand on it because of the slipperiness of the floor with cattle dung and their urine.'

Trwy 'through' only rarely occurs as marker of the CAUSE (of the seven examples, three are virtually identical; see (49)); the complement is always an abstract noun (or VN) implying the active influence of a person other than P1.

(49)   Eil yꝺ kyn mynet eneit yn daꝺ or collir *trꝺy greulonder.*   (*WML* V 44a2)
through cruelty
'The second is, before life enters into it [i.e. the foetus], if it perish through cruelty.'   (Wade-Evans 1909: 272)

Wrth 'against' marking the CAUSE, followed by a nominal complement, is virtu-ally restricted to *Llyfr Cynghawsedd*, occurring five times with complements de-scribing processes with which the person from whose perspective the situation is portrayed is confronted (see (50*a*)).[70] The phrase *wrth hynny* 'thereat, therefore', is, all attestations taken together, the phrase most commonly used to provide a causal link between two clauses (or two larger text units) (see (50*b*)). It is especially frequent in *Llyfr Cynghawsedd* (with fourteen examples, compared to two in *Llyfr Cyfnerth* and seven altogether in the narrative texts). The common denominator of the causal uses of *wrth* is that the preposition marks a circumstance or influence external to any participant; the situation described in the clause containing the *wrth*-phrase comes about through the confrontation with this circumstance.

(50) (*a*)   ac essef achaus yd vyf y en holy: *urth vot ve ran gennyty o'r tyr hvn* ac ny wedeyst tytheu ue mot y en pryodaur . . .   (*Cyngh.* §22.28–9)
against be_VN my share with-you(-you) of-the land this
'And this is why I am claiming: because you have my share of this land and you do not deny my having a claim [to it] . . .'

<hr/>

[69] Our database contains eight examples of the former and five of the latter.
[70] There is one example in a narrative, *MLl* 56.14, where the complement describes a quality: 'wrth decket yr eur' (because of the beauty of the gold). J. E. C. Williams (1956: 143) gives examples for *wrth* 'to denote the reason and the cause', but does not elaborate further on the exact meaning expressed; neither does Rees (1935). Other prepositions than the ones dealt with here in some detail are attested too rarely to permit of any further analysis: there is one example each of *dy wrth* 'from' and of *y am* 'about', and three of *yr* 'for, since'.

(b)   y da a dewedeist arnaf y e treulau o'r tev dy myvy a teleys yty hunnv val e
       dewaut e kyfreith; ac od amhevy dy henne e mae ymy dygaun a'y gvyr bot en
       wyr henne; *ac urth henne* e dodaf i ar e kyfreith na deleaf y de atep na'th
       guarandau dy bellach am er haul honno.   (*Cyngh.* §50.39 ff.)
       and against that
       'the goods you have said I have used up of yours, I have paid for that as the law
       prescribes, and if you doubt that, I have enough [witnesses] who know that it
       is true; and therefore I put it to the law that I am not required to answer you
       nor listen to you any longer concerning this claim.'

2.4.3. The INST: *a(c)*, *o*, *trwy*

The preposition *a(c)* 'with' usually marks the concrete INST or tool, as in (51*a*). The
use of *a(c)* to mark a material or substance used to make or embellish an article
(rather than the tool used to manufacture it), as in (51*b*), is comparatively rarer.[71]

(51) (a)   . . . a'e wascu yn a pwll hyt pan daroed udunt y gnithiaw yn llwyr *a'r
            kyllellbrenneu* y uaryf.   (*CO* 974)
            with-the wooden tweezers
            '. . . and pressed him down in the pit until they had completely plucked out his
            beard with the wooden tweezers.'

(b)   A gwisc ymdan y gwr o pali coch gwedy ry wniaw *a sidann melyn*   (*BR* 5.23)
       with yellow silk
       'And the man was wearing a garment of red brocade, sewn [embroidered?]
       with yellow silk'

O 'from' marking the INST or manner is used with abstract complements, describing characteristics or qualities, or activities and actions.[72] *O* occurs less frequently with concrete complements (in nine cases altogether, where the *o*-phrase
marks the INST rather than the material); sometimes a concrete complement is
used in the same context as an abstract one (see (52*a*)). An example of *o* with a concrete complement describing a material rather than the tool used is given in (52*b*).
Expressions such as *o teir fford* 'in three ways' (see (52*c*)) would appear to overlap
the boundary between INST and manner: on the one hand, they describe 'manners'
of how actions are carried out; on the other hand, the 'manner' is an enabling
factor.[73]

---

[71] The former use has forty-eight attestations in the narrative texts, thirteen in *WML*, and none in
Cyngh.; the latter seven altogether, four of which occur in *BR*.

[72] Rees (1935: 80) interprets *o* as expressing the result in examples such as 'punt a geueis o gardotta'
(lit.: pound PRT get_pret.1sg from beg_VN) (I got a pound by begging) (*MLl* 62.10); I have classified
these instances as INST. A case could be made for either: on the one hand, having the pound results from
begging; on the other hand, it is equally possible to regard the action of begging as the means by which
the pound was earned.

[73] The status of expressions such as *holi* . . . *o datanud/o priodolder* 'demanding (e.g. land) by a
[legitimate] claim/propriety', which frequently occurs in *Cyngh.*, appears to fit into roughly the same
category as *o teir fford*, in that the complement of the preposition describes the enabling condition for

(52) (a)   A phwy bynhac a vynho ennill clot *o arueu ac o ymwan ac o ymlad* . . .
           (*Per.* 57.29)
           from arms and from jousting and from fighting
           'And whoever may wish to win fame by arms and jousting and fighting . . .'

(b)   Ac *o wydyn* y daroed idaw danwaret y kyweirdebeu a welsei . . .   (*Per.* 9.16)
           from twigs
           'And with twigs he imitated the trappings he had seen . . .'

(c)   *O teir fford* yd ymdiueicha mach: *otalu* or talaʊdyr drostaʊ. Eil yw *o rod oet* or
           haʊlʊr ar y talaʊdyr yn aʊssen y vach. Trydyd yʊ *o dʊyn gauel* or haʊlʊr ar y
           talaʊdyr heb ganhat y mach.   (*WML* V 35a12 ff.)
           from three ways; from-paying; from give_VN delay; from bring_VN distress
           'In three ways is a surety exonerated; by the debtor paying for him. The second
           is, but time being granted by the plaintiff to the debtor in the absence of the
           surety. The third is, by a distress being made by the plaintiff on the debtor
           without consent of the surety.'   (Wade-Evans 1909: 231)

The preposition *trwy* 'through' occurs in the phrase *treulaw* (*amser*) *trwy* X
'spend (time) through (doing) *X*', where the preposition marks the manner, or an
abstract means or INST. Outside this phrase, *trwy* marking the INST may occur with
both abstract and concrete complements.[74]

As we have seen in this section, there are several points of overlap between the
marking of P1, on the one hand, and of IAG, CAUSE, and INST, on the other. The
preposition *o*, the most prominent marker of P1 in VN constructions, can also encode the CAUSE; often in the sense of an action, experience, or state of mind out of
which the situation described in the clause arises. *O* only comparatively rarely
encodes the IAG; the choice of *o* over *gan/y gan* in (42a) might be motivated by a
predominance of the semantic characteristic of '(source of) origin': *etiued* 'offspring' originates with the parent; the parent is not merely the 'giver'. However, in
the absence of more evidence, this semantic specification cannot be taken any
further. In INST function, *o* most frequently occurs with abstract complements that
express or imply activity that results in the situation described.[75] The prepositions

the process of claiming. In *GPC* this technical legal expression is paraphrased as '*drwy* (*gyfrwng*)' (by
(means of)), and classified as a subsense of '*â* (yn dynodi'r offeryn; &c.)' (with (denoting the instrument etc.)) (*GPC* s.v. *o*, p. 2609).

[74] *Treulaw amser drwy* X occurs six times in the narrative material; there are altogether eleven
instances of *drwy* in INST function outside this phrase, five with concrete and six with abstract complements. In addition to *a*(*c*), *o*, and *drwy*, there are very sporadic instances of *gan*, and *ar* 'on, upon'
(marking the abstract manner; see also *GMW* 184).

[75] The implication of activity is also present with some concrete complements (see e.g (52a)), 'ennill
clot o arueu' (winning fame by arms) implies the use of weapons, rather than their mere existence or
possession. A further distinction between *o* and *a*(*c*) appears to be here that instrumental *a*(*c*) with a
concrete complement is used to describe situations where P1 exercises a direct and immediate influence
on an entity by using INST. A direct and immediate result of using *arueu* 'arms/weapons' in (52a) would
be, for example, the wounding or killing of an adversary—winning fame is an indirect effect resulting
from the former.

y gan and *gan*, which we encountered as what has (tentatively) been described as P1 with the passive, feature prominently as prepositions denoting IAG, consistently used with verbs expressing or implying an act of getting, receiving, on the part of P1. *Gan* is also to be found denoting a subtype of the CAUSE, usually a co-occurring circumstance or event, or concrete entity.

3 Irish

3.1. Evidence from narrative texts: VN clauses in *Táin Bó Cúailnge*

The different VN clause types containing an overt P1 to be found in medieval Irish texts,[1] and the structural similarities they bear to their Welsh counterparts, have been briefly introduced in Chapter 1 (Section 1.3.1, example (11)). The most common types in a narrative context are $VN+PP_{P1}$ and $VN+GEN_{P1}$ (see (1*a*) and (1*b*)), the latter being, as in Welsh, restricted to use with intransitive VNs. More rarely encountered in narrative texts are $P2+do_{VN}+P1$ and $P1+do_{VN}(+P2)$ (see (1*c*) and (1*d*)); these two structures are, however, very prominent in annalistic material (see Section 3.2.2).

(1) (*a*) $VN+PP_{P1}$
Iar riachtain dóib in tslébe, imchomarcair Cú Chulaind íarom . . .
(*TBC I* 694)
after reach_VN to-them the mountain_gen.sg
'After they had reached the mountain, then Cú Chulainn asked . . .'

 (*b*) $VN+GEN_{P1}$
Rob áil dam-sa *do dula-su* co háit a fuigbithea in córugud cétna fort
(*TBC I* 2810)
your go_VN-PRO
'I should like you to go where you will be adorned in the same way'

 (*c*) $P2+do_{VN}+P1$
Nibo machdad *dagním do dénam dó-ssom* indiu   (*TBC I* 396)
good-deed to do_VN to-him-PRO
'It would be no wonder that he should perform well today'

 (*d*) $P1+do_{VN}(+P2)$
Nocho cúalaid Cú Chulaind *deglóech nó deigfer do thiachtain* ina agaid cos inndiu for Táin Bó Cúailnge   (*TBC I* 2881–2)
good-warrior or good-man to come_VN
'Until today, Cú Chulainn never heard of a brave warrior or good man to come against him on the Cattle Raid of Cooley'

The use of each of the VN constructions illustrated here is examined with regard

---

[1] Appendix 5 lists attestations of agentive VN clauses in *TBC*, Appendix 6 those in law texts, Appendices 7–10 those in *AU*. Lists of attestations of the full passive can be found in Appendices 11 (*TBC*) and 12 (laws and *AU*).

to its syntactic environments, and patterns of information structuring and continuity. The markers of P1 are set into context in connection with the categories IAG, CAUSE, and INST (Section 3.6); the semantics of P1 marking is taken up again in Chapter 4.

3.1.1. VN+PP$_{P1}$

Markers of P1

P1 in this construction is marked in a large majority of examples from *TBC* by the preposition *do* 'to'. In most cases, the *do*-phrase indicates an AG, rather than an EXP. *La* 'with, by' and *ó* 'from' also occur, but only rarely; see Table 3.1 for the statistics.

TABLE 3.1. VN+PP$_{P1}$: *markers of P1*

Text	*do* (AG)	*do* (EXP)	*la* (AG)	*ó* (AG)	Total
TBC I	14	5	2		21
TBC LL	19	1		1	21
TBC III	9	4		1	14
TOTAL	42	10	2	2	56
%	75	17.9	3.6	3.6	100

Neither of the two examples of *la* 'with', in P1 position, both quoted in (2), is entirely unproblematic:

(2) (*a*)   *Iarfaigther* co lléir 7 *a imchomarc lat.*   (*TBC I* 1740)
           question_pass.ipv.sg and his greet_VN with-you
           'Question him thoroughly and greet him.'

     (*b*)   Buí *icá gairi la húa* hi Ráith Impail   (*TBC I* 3369)
            at-his care with-his grandson
            'He was being cared for by his (or: with his) grandson in Ráith Immail'

The unusual feature in (2*a*) is the co-occurrence of a passive verb and a VN, accompanied by a P1 marker, the VN having the function of an imperative.[2] It is likely that the scope of P1 *lat* 'by you' includes both the VN and the passive, and that *la* was selected because it is the usual marker of P1 with the passive (see Section 3.3).

   The prepositional phrase *ica gairi* in (3*b*) looks at first sight like a straightforward periphrastic verbal construction consisting of *oc* 'at' followed by the pos-

---

[2] The construction is rather reminiscent of the Welsh use of a finite verb followed by one or more VNs (see Chapter 2). However, this type of construction is rare in Irish. The VN does occasionally function as an imperative (as in 'a nguin' (kill them) (*TBC I* 162)) (cf. e.g. (3*b*)), in a manner similar to that of the German usage of the infinitive as imperative, as in *aufstehen!* 'get up!'.

sessive *a* 'his', preceding a VN.[3] However, the noun *gaire* (see *DIL* s.v. *goire*) is not a verbal abstract, but is described in *DIL* as an *iā*-stem abstract formed from the adjective *gor* 'pious, dutiful, filial', meaning 'piety, dutifulness, (familial) affection'. It is used in legal texts in the sense 'care, attendance, maintenance (of parents)', and in the latter sense also occurs in non-legal contexts. And, indeed, *goire* can be found in the syntactic context that would make it qualify, according to Gagnepain's definition of a VN, for the label *nom verbal*.[4] It is certainly possible that what we have here is an abstract noun that was interpreted as a VN, possibly via its use as a technical legal term. The next question arising is whether the preposition *la* marks P1, or the location. Certainly, as far as 'real life' is concerned, the two may very well amount to the same thing: the person who defines the location (*la húa* 'with his grandson'—i.e. 'at his grandson's household') where the process takes place (*ica gairi* 'being looked after') may very well be identical with the actant. The difficulty in this case is to delimit a potential P1, more specifically AG, from a locative relation, and to determine the motivation for the selection of the marker for this particular P1—if such it is—in this particular context (rather than the more common *do*, see note 3).

The preposition *ó* can mark the starting point of a motion or the origin of an entity. The semantic characteristic 'source', or 'origin' is visible in both examples VN+*ó* that can be interpreted as agentive VN clauses (see (3)):

(3) (*a*)   Bacheird Fer Diad clesrada ána ilerda ingantacha imda bar aird in lá sain nád róeglaind ac nech aile ríam . . . *acht a ndénum úad féin* in lá sain i n-agid Con Culaind.   (*TBC LL* 3265)
              but their make_VN from-him self
              'That day Fer Diad exhibited many wonderful and brilliant feats of arms which he had not learned from anyone before that . . . but he invented them himself on that day to oppose Cú Chulainn.'   (O'Rahilly 1967: 226)

    (*b*)   Aneoch charfus d ingenaibh righ ꝛ taisech bhfer nErenn e, *a n-idhlacadh chuigi uaibh si*   (*TBC III* 547.29)
              their send_VN to-him from-you PRO
              'Those who love him of the daughters of the kings and chiefs of the men of Ireland, send them to him.'

Dénam úad féin in (3*a*) contains a component 'source' in that the actant is also the originator, or creator. The characteristic 'origin' in the sense of a spatial *terminus a quo* is evident in (3*b*). The verb *ind-anich*, *idnaicid* 'sends, bestows' contains an element of movement. Therefore, it might be argued that the preposition *ó* denotes the source or point of departure, rather than P1/AG. On the other hand, it might be argued that *ó* is selected as marker of P1 in this case because its semantic

---

[3] Cf. e.g. ' 'gá búalad d'Ḟergus' (lit.: at-his beat_VN do-Fergus) (being beaten by Fergus) (*TBC LL* 4781) (see (9)). Note, however, that the P1 marker is again *do*, rather than *la*.
[4] The example quoted in *DIL* is 'is sí inso fedb as uisse do goiri i n-aeclis' (she is the widow whom it is proper to maintain in the church) (Wb 28d24).

make-up overlaps with that of the VN, more so than that of any other preposition that can be assigned P1 function.

Transitive and intransitive VNs

The construction VN+PP$_{P1}$ does not appear to be restricted to any type of VN. As detailed in Table 3.2, transitive VNs account for the greater part of the examples in the present database. The VN *buith* 'be' occurs only once with *do* as P1 marker, as auxiliary in a periphrastic construction.[5] The two examples classified here as transitive VNs of motion contain *ríachtain*, VN of *ro-icc* 'reaches, arrives (at)', P2 denoting the endpoint of a path.[6]

TABLE 3.2. *VN+PP$_{P1}$: transitivity of VN*

VN clause	TBC I	TBC LL	TBC III	Total	%
Transitive	9	13	4	26	46.4
Transitive (motion)	2			2	3.6
Intransitive (motion)	3	4	6	13	23.2
Intransitive	7	4	4	15	26.8

Definiteness

In all but three cases in *TBC*, P1 in VN+PP$_{P1}$ is definite (again, proper names are included under this definition), and, in the majority of examples, a suffixed pronoun (see the statistics in Table 3.3). There is one example where P1 is not a simple conjugated preposition, but consists of the prepositional phrase followed by a proper

TABLE 3.3. *VN+PP$_{P1}$: definiteness of P1*

P1	TBC I	TBC LL	TBC III	Total	%
[+Def.]					
Pronoun	14	13	10	37	66.1
Name	4	5	4	13	23.2
NP	2	1		3	5.35
[−Def.]	1	2		3	5.35

[5] The example is 'Is íarom ro indis a ara do Choin Culaind *bith do Ailill 7 do Meidb og guidhi Fergusa im thecht isin chath*' (lit.: be_VN to Ailill and to Medb at beg_VN Fergus-gen.sg) (Then his driver told Cú Chulainn that Ailill and Medb were begging Fergus to go into the fight) (*TBC I* 4003). The use of *buith* as substantive verb, rather than in periphrastic constructions, with *do* is attested in other texts, e.g. in Wb. Several examples are quoted in Fraser (1912*b*: 21).

[6] *TBC I* 694, 767. These two are the only examples of their kind in our texts, and occur in the same section of the narrative (the *Maccgnímrada* or 'Boyhood deeds of Cú Chulainn').

name in the nominative case, in Thurneysen's description as the 'second co-ordinate member after a conjugated preposition . . . where the pronoun is anticipatorily put in the plural, though the first element is singular' (*GOI* §247 (a)), where the following example is quoted:

(4)   Scíth lim namá *comrac dúib 7 Cú Chulaind.*   (*TBC I* 1293)
         encounter_VN to-you(pl) and Cú Chulainn
         'I don't like the thought of a fight (lit.: encounter [in a fight]) between you and Cú Chulainn.'

P2 also shows a tendency towards definiteness (see Table 3.4).[7] Definiteness, with regard to noun phrases that are not proper names, is closely connected with given-ness, which will be discussed further in Section 3.1.4. Examples such as the one in (5) are classified here as '-P2'—that is, transitive VNs where no overt P2 is expressed.

(5)   co térno Cú Chulaind ina chotlud *cen rathugud dó etir.*   (*TBC LL* 2165)
         without notice_VN to-him at-all
         'so that Cú Chulainn recovered in his sleep, without being aware of it at all.'

TABLE 3.4. VN+PP$_{P1}$: *definiteness of P2*

P2	*TBC I*	*TBC LL*	*TBC III*	Total	%
[+Def.]					
Pronoun	4	9	2	15	*55.6*
NP	4			4	*14.8*
[−Def.]	2	1		3	*11.1*
−P2	1	2	2	5	*18.5*

Syntactic environments and direct speech

It is generally understood that the VN in medieval Irish can function like any other noun—that is, it can assume the syntactic function of any other nominal constituent in the clause, and it can also occur as an independent nominal construction (see Section 1.3.1). As regards VN+PP$_{P1}$, although we find a variety of syntactic environments in which the VN clause occurs, our texts show clear tendencies (see Table 3.5): agentive VN clauses as predicate or subject of the copula are more common in direct speech than narrative, whereas their use following prepositions (functioning as adverbial phrases) is encountered less frequently in dialogue than

---

[7] The P1 phrase tends to follow rather than to precede a P2 phrase; however, the absolute number of attestations is too small to give a reliable indication of a more widespread tendency. The order P2–P1 occurs twice in *TBC I* with definite P2–NPs, and twice with indefinite P2–NPs, and once with an indefinite P2–NP in *TBC LL*. The sequence P1–P2 occurs twice (with indefinite P2–NPs) in *TBC I*.

in narrative.[8] The occurrence of independent agentive VN clauses is comparatively rare in our texts; three of the four instances are quoted in (2a), (3a), and (3b).[9] These examples stand out not only as regards the preposition marking P1, but also as far as their syntactic function is concerned. A VN that is formally the complement of a preposition, but where the resulting prepositional phrase functions independently, is illustrated in (6):

(6)   'Cid fa bfuilter dam-sa lib?' ar Lóch. '*Do chomrac duit fri Coin Culainn*,' ar Medhb.   (*TBC LL* 1964)
       to encounter_VN to-you against Cú Chulainn
       ' "What do you want from me?" asked Lóch. "To meet Cú Chulainn in combat," said Medb.'

This example has been included in the category 'prepositional complement' in Table 3.5 (for further examples, see (8) below). However, it differs from other VN clauses in prepositional phrases in two ways, in that it is a responsive structure

TABLE 3.5. *VN+PP_{P1}: syntactic environments and direct speech*

VN clause	TBC I	TBC LL	TBC III	Total	%
Prepositional phrase					
Direct speech	2	4	3	9	53.6
Narrative	8	6	7	21	
Subject (of copula)					
Direct speech	2	3		5	12.5
Narrative	1	1		2	
Predicate (of copula)					
Direct speech	5	1	1	7	17.9
Narrative		3		3	
Direct object[a]					
Direct speech			1	1	7.1
Narrative	2	1		3	
Main clause[b]					
Direct speech	1			1	7.1
Narrative		1	2	3	
Other					
Direct speech		1		1	1.8

[a] Including genitival P2 complement.
[b] i.e. independent VN clause.

[8] The instance listed under 'other' in Table 3.5 is 'oldás a choscursom ⁊ a chommaídim-sium dam-sa' (lit.: 'than his defeat_VN-PRO and his triumph-over_VN-PRO to-me-PRO) (than his defeat by me) (*TBC LL* 1677), where the VN construction is the complement of *oldás* 'than'; the example is an extension of *TBC LL* 1676, which is a subject clause.
[9] The fourth is *TBC III* §92.

(often elliptical in character), and in that vn+pp$_{P1}$ is the complement of the preposition *do* 'to', the function of which does not appear entirely clear here. A similar instance of *do* as the head of a vn+pp$_{P1}$ clause is (7), in an almost identical phrase but with the *do*-phrase as the subject of the copula. It appears likely that *do* 'to' has purposive or final meaning in these examples (note also that *comlann* 'fight', in parallel construction with *comrac* 'encounter' (in battle), is not a VN in the sense of being formed from a verbal stem, but is at times used 'as quasi verbal noun' (*DIL* s.v. *comlann*)).[10]

(7)   'Maith linn aile', bhur Medhbh, '*do comlann 7 do comrag duit re CoinCulainn*'
        (*TBC III* 554.5)
        to fight and to encounter_VN to-you against Cú Chulainn
        ' "We want", said Medb, "you to fight and do battle against Cú Chulainn" '

The dependent syntactic environments of vn+pp$_{P1}$ are listed in Table 3.5. A discussion of each construction type in turn follows.

vn+pp$_{P1}$ *as complement of a preposition*

This is statistically the most prominent group.[11] In most instances, the prepositional VN clause, functioning like an adverbial phrase, follows its head clause (see (8a)). There are altogether four instances where the prepositional clause precedes the head clause[12] (see (8b)). These could theoretically be interpreted as cleft sentences with copula omitted, a view that could gain support from two cases where the prepositional VN clause precedes its head clause in a cleft construction (see (8c)).[13]

(8) (a)   Dosnetarraid *oc gabáil dúnaid dóib*   (*TBC I* 1530)
            at take_VN camp to-them
            'He came upon them as they were setting up camp'   (O'Rahilly 1976: 167)

    (b)   *7 agtaidhecht atuaidh doChoinculainn* adorchair Guife les   (*TBC III* §11)
            and at-come_VN from-the-north to-Cú Chulainn
            'and (it was) as Cú Chulainn came from the north, (that) Guife fell at his hand'

    (c)   *gorub agtaidhecht atuaidh do Choinculainn* domharbhasdair-se Mac Bhuachall
            (*TBC III* §10)
            so-that_PRT_COP at-come_VN from-the-north to Cú Chulainn
            'so that it was when Cú Chulainn came from the north that he killed Mac Buachaill'

---

[10] *Do* could also be interpreted as possessive pronoun, 2sg 'your'. However, this would make P2 'your' and P1 coreferential.

[11] The prepositions encountered are: *ar* 'before, for' (1 ex.), *ar bíth* 'because, for' (1 ex.), *ar*/*iar* 'after' (8 ex.), *cen* 'without' (5 ex.), *do* 'to' (3 ex.), *fri* 'against' (1 ex.), *imm* 'about' (1 ex.), *oc* 'at' (7 ex.), *ré* 'before' (2 ex.), '*gá* (see discussion, example (9), 1 ex.).

[12] These constitute two groups of two: *TBC I* 694, 767, very similar prepositional VN clauses, and *TBC III* §§11, 12, with identical prepositional VN clauses.

[13] *TBC III* §§10, 13, in the same series as §§11, 12.

The example quoted in (2*b*) serves as what can be described as a periphrastic passive construction. The following one is similar; here, however, the 'passive' is the direct object of a finite clause, comparable to raising constructions in English, or an accusative plus infinitive in Latin.

(9)   rachúala-saide in nÓcháin Conchobuir 'gá búalad d'Ḟergus mac Róig.
        (*TBC LL* 4781)
        at?-his? beat_VN to Fergus
        'he heard the Ócháin Conchobuir [i.e. Conchobar's shield] being struck by Fergus.'

The form 'gá presents a difficulty: the Stowe manuscript of *TBC* shows *da bualadh* —i.e. the preposition *do* 'to', followed by a possessive pronoun. It seems, therefore, possible that the reading 'gá in *TBC LL* represents a phonetic spelling of the same form, if we assume that, in the writer's variety of Irish, the realizations of /d/ and /g/ (and possibly those of /ð/ and /ɣ/, as well) had merged into [g] (and [ɣ], respectively) in pre-tonic, word-initial position—compare the regular merger of *do* 'to', *de* 'from, of', and *go* 'to' in Modern Western Irish. However, it is not clear how long ago this merger took place. An example of *da* in a similar function—i.e. as a marker of a durative aspect—can be found in *TBC I* 150.[14] A further possibility is that we are dealing with the preposition *oc* 'at', which is found in the periphrastic progressive construction *attá oc* X_*VN* 'he is X_ing', followed by the possessive pronoun.

VN+PP_{P1} as subject of the copula

Several occurrences of VN+PP_{P1} in subject position are problematic, chiefly, it would appear, because of the character of the VN, rather than the syntactic structure as such. Consider the following example (quoted above in (4) and repeated here):

(10)   Scíth lim namá *comrac dúib ⁊ Cú Chulaind*.   (*TBC I* 1293)
        encounter_VN to-you(pl) and Cú Chulainn
        'I don't like the thought of a fight (lit.: encounter [in a fight]) between you and Cú Chulainn.'

Morphologically, *comrac* is clearly a nominal abstract of the verb *con-ricc* 'meet, encounter'. The meaning of *comrac* in our texts is most often '[an] encounter in combat'—that is, the fact of an encounter, rather than '[an action of] meeting'. Syntactically, there appears to be only scant evidence that *comrac* is used in so-called verbal VN environments (see *DIL* s.v. *comrac*). Thus in terms of the meaning of *comrac* in this particular context, the question is whether 'comrac dúib ⁊ Cú Chulaind' refers to a process, or a fact, or whether it is indeed possible to disambiguate in this particular instance, since the frame in which the VN clause is cast— that is, the superordinate copula construction—does indeed refer to a perception, a personal judgement on a hypothetical happening, not a process that is ongoing

---

[14] 'Ní dá tánsem dam' (lit.: NEG to-their tease_VN to-me) (I am not teasing them).

or that has already taken place. The fact that VNs that unambiguously function in verbal constructions in other contexts may occur in the construction under investigation is illustrated in (11),[15] thus the ambiguity is not due to the syntactic environment.

(11)   Ba holc la suide *tuidecht dó chuccai.*   (*TBC I* 3416)
        come_VN to-him(1) to-him(2)
        'He [i.e. Cú Chulainn] was not pleased that he [Sualtaim] should come to him.'

Problems similar to the one encountered in (10) are presented by the VNs *debaid* (*TBC LL* 1571), *coscur*, and *commaídem* (*TBC LL* 1676), in constructions similar to the one quoted here. *Debaid* (*DIL* s.v. *debuith*) 'strife, contention, fight(ing)' is a VN formation of *di-taa* 'distat, differt'. However, evidence for so-called verbal VN uses of this form is meagre; the only instance given in *DIL* is 'ic debhaid ⁊ ic cathugud' (fighting and doing battle).[16] *Coscar* 'victory, triumph, slaughter', VN of *con-scara* 'kills, destroys, slaughters', does not appear to occur either with *oc* in periphrastic verbal construction, or with *do* in the so-called *do*-infinitive (see *DIL* s.v.). The same goes for *commaídem* 'act of exulting in, boasting of, celebrating; defeating, triumph, victory'.

vn+pp$_{PI}$ *as predicate of the copula*

Moving on to the VN clause as predicate of the copula, we find a similar degree of uncertainty with respect to the verbal nature of certain forms that, morphologically, are VNs. VNs that commonly occur in verbal contexts of VN syntax do occur as predicate of the copula (see (12)).

(12) (*a*) '*In cotlad do Ailill innosa?*', or Medb   (*TBC I* 2867)
            COP_INT sleep_VN to Ailill now
            ' "Is Ailill asleep now?" asked Medb'

    (*b*)   *Tráth fo imtharrung n-étaig dóib*, no benad-som a trí choícait ndechelt díb
            (*TBC LL* 838)
            while COP pulling-off_VN clothes to-them
            'Each time they pulled each others' clothes off, he would tear their three times fifty cloaks off them'

In syntactic constructions exactly corresponding to that in (12*b*), we also find *imtrascrad* 'wrestling' (VN of *imm-tascar* 'wrestles'), and *cluchi* 'game'.[17] A purely syntactic or morphological reasoning does not yield a solution to the question whether a (in Baudiš's terms) 'Vorgangsnomen'—that is, a noun that can describe a process—actually does describe a process bounded in time, or a fact unbounded in time, in a particular context: the circumstance that a particular formation can

---

[15] See also *TBC I* 3764, and *TBC LL* 952.
[16] *CCath* 2239.
[17] *TBC LL* 840 and *TBC LL* 833, respectively. The verbal formation *cluchigidir* 'plays', is denominal, derived from *cluiche*.

occur in a 'verbal' context, to use Gagnepain's definition, does not imply that the form has 'verbal' meaning wherever it occurs. Some contexts will disambiguate, such as periphrastic verbal constructions; others appear not to, such as the ones we are dealing with here. One might argue that the syntax of copula constructions is exclusively a nominal domain; copula constructions tend to ascribe attributes to entities, therefore a 'Vorgangsnomen' presents a (potentially) processual content as an attribute to an entity, and therefore describes it as a fact, outside a particular temporal context.

VN+PP~P1~ as direct object

Of the four instances of verbs taking VN+PP~P1~ as direct objects, one is a verb of perception,[18] one expresses an emotional state,[19] two are *verba dicendi*.[20] Again, we encounter the question of whether the VN has verbal function (see (13)).

(13)   ⁊ *adagur sa tachur daib*   (*TBC III* 549.17)
           fear_pres.1sg PRO fight_VN to-you(pl)
           'and I fear there will be a fight between you'

Tachor (VN of *do-cuirethar* 'puts') is attested in verbal construction with *do* in the sense 'opposing, fighting'.[21] The situation portrayed in (13) is described as (10) in *TBC I*, and phrased in a construction similar to (10) in *TBC LL*: 'is dóig lim-sa debaid duib' (I think it's likely you'll have a fight). All three versions have in common that the scenario portrayed by the VN construction is hypothetical: the encounter feared (*adagur, scith lim*) or thought likely (*is dóig lim-sa*) has not happened, is not even about to happen, but is a likely scenario if certain conditions are given. Thus the construction expresses possibilities, rather than actual processes bounded in specific time/reality frames. From this point of view, one could argue that the constructions under investigation here then present facts, rather than processes.

It appears that, especially with respect to VN+PP~P1~ functioning as subjects and predicates of the copula, a syntactic criterion for the definition of a VN (such as the one defined by Gagnepain—i.e. the occurrence in the so-called *do*-infinitive) does not help with ambiguities concerning the verbal status of VNs in particular instances, and there is, of course, also the possibility that even those VNs that may be used in syntactically 'verbal' contexts (see e.g. (5), containing *tuidecht* 'coming') might not have verbal meaning in certain syntactic environments.

3.1.2. VN+GEN~P1~

As in Welsh, VN+GEN~P1~ in Irish is restricted to intransitive VNs; there is one poten-

---

[18] 'adcualadar' (they heard) (*TBC I* 3501).
[19] 'adagur' (I fear) (*TBC III* 549/1).
[20] 'ro indis' (he told) (*TBC I* 4003); 'arná ráditis' (that they should not say) (*TBC LL* 1605).
[21] *Acall.* 6743; see *DIL* s.v.

tial exception in our data, which is discussed below (see (14)). A large proportion, just over 40 per cent, of intransitive VNs are VNs of motion. *Buith* 'be' accompanied by a genitival P1 occurs only as substantive verb in the texts analysed here, not in periphrastic VN constructions. The genitive phrase marks the EXP (including the 'subject' of the substantive verb *buith*) more often than does a prepositional phrase (compare Table 3.7 with Table 3.1)—that is, more intransitive VNs whose P1 is an EXP occur in the construction VN+GEN$_{P1}$ than in VN+PP$_{P1}$. A comparatively large role in this distribution is played by the VN *tuitim* 'falling (in battle)' (cf. *do-tuit* 'falls'), which accounts for ten instances of VN+GEN$_{P1}$ in our texts.[22] In one example, marked as transitive in Table 3.6, we appear to have an instance of VN+GEN$_{P1}$ with a prepositional P1 that is also accompanied by a nominal P2 (see (14)):

(14)   ⁊ nírop do ḟechtnaige dó *a chétgabáil gaiscid*   (*TBC I* 724–5)
        his first-take_VN weapons_gen.sg
        'and may his first taking up of weapons not bring him success'

This exception to the general rule that only intransitive VNs occur in VN+GEN$_{P1}$ could be explained in terms of the status of *gabáil gaiscid*. Formally, *gabáil* is the VN of *gaibid* 'takes'; the whole expression is used as a loose compound, 'taking up arms', the variant *chétgabáil gaiscid* being used, among other things, in the context of a young man's introduction to warrior status. This could then in turn be interpreted in such a way that the expression *chétgabáil gaiscid*, having the status of a technical term, refers not to a specific process bound into a specific time/reality context, but rather to an institution, an occasion, which might in turn explain why its syntax does not follow the usual convention of transitive VNs.

TABLE 3.6. *VN+GEN$_{P1}$: types of VN*

VN	TBC I	TBC LL	TBC III	Total	%
Intransitive (motion)	11	11	4	26	44.1
Intransitive (other)	11	14	1	26	44.1
buith (substantive verb)	3	3		6	10.1
Transitive (?)	1			1	1.7

TABLE 3.7. *VN+GEN$_{P1}$: AG and EXP*

P1	TBC I	TBC LL	TBC III	Total	%
AG	17	16	5	38	64.4
EXP	9	12		21	35.6

[22] Four in *TBC I*, six in *TBC LL*.

Definiteness of P1

As was the case with VN+PP$_{P1}$, P1 in VN+GEN$_{P1}$ tends to be definite, and is most commonly expressed by a possessive pronoun,[23] as shown in Table 3.8.

TABLE 3.8. VN+GEN$_{P1}$: *definiteness of P1*

P1	TBC I	TBC LL	TBC III	Total	%
[+Def.]					
Pronoun	20	23	5	48	81.3
Name	2	2		4	6.8
NP	3			3	5.1
[−Def.]	1	3		4	6.8

Syntactic environments and direct speech

The syntactic contexts in which we find VN+GEN$_{P1}$ are by and large the same as the ones in which VN+PP$_{P1}$ occurs. There are differences, however, as regards the preferred contexts: VN+GEN$_{P1}$ occurs most frequently as subject in copula constructions, as illustrated in (15), and in direct speech. The occurrence of VN+GEN$_{P1}$ in other contexts is much less common, notably its use after a proposition, functioning like an adverbial clause, is rare (see Table 3.9).

(15)   *Ní haccobor lem do thecht*   (*TBC I* 1292)
        NEG-COP wish with-me your go_VN
        'I don't want you to go'

There are only few examples in our texts of independent VN+GEN$_{P1}$. In two instances, the VN clause is the complement of *acht* 'but' (here classified among 'other environments'), as in (16).

(16)   'Is maith nach cúalammar ⁊ nach fetammar,' ar Ailill, '*acht do bith-siu ar bantinchur mnáa . . .*'   (*TBC LL* 8)
        but your be_VN-PRO on woman's-share woman_gen.sg
        ' "It was a wealth that we had not heard of and did not know of," said Ailill, "but you were a woman of property . . ." '   (O'Rahilly 1967: 137)

A formally syntactically independent VN clause is the example given in (17), introduced by *ocus* 'and'; the meaning is that of a conditional clause: the VN clause presenting the condition that has to prevail for the content of the preceding clause to be realized.[24]

---

[23] In *TBC III* there is one instance of a personal name in the nominative accompanying the genitival P1 phrase: 'bha comadhais acomrag ⁊ Cúchulainn' (lit.: his fight_VN and Cú Chulainn_nom.sg.) (he and Cú Chulainn should fight) (*TBC III* §62).

[24] For the subordinating use of *ocus*, see *DIL* s.v. *ocus*, section (b), (c), and (d).

(17)   'Immarchuirther fris,' or Ailill, 'Findabair do thabairt dó 7 *a dingbáil dona*
        slógaib.'   (*TBC I* 1570)
        and his keep-away_VN from-the army_dat.pl
        ' "Let a proposal be made to him," said Ailill, "Findabair shall be given to him,
        if he keeps away from the armies." '

An example that has been classified here as syntactically independent is given in
(18), in which two VN clauses (one instance of P1+*do*$_{VN}$ and one of VN+GEN$_{P1}$) follow a copula construction, representing an elaboration of its content.

(18)   'Is bán in gleó sa . . . do Reochaid mac Fathemain, ocht cét láech lánchalma do
        thuttim trina ág ٦ trina accais 7 *a dul féin* gan fuligud gan fordergad fair.'
        (*TBC LL* 3892)
        and his go_VN self
        ' "White [i.e. bloodless] is the fight . . . for Reochad mac Fathemain: eight
        hundred brave warriors have fallen because of him, and he has escaped with-
        out wounding or shedding any of his blood." '

The other syntactic environments in which we find VN+GEN$_{P1}$ are those already
encountered with VN+PP$_{P1}$.

TABLE 3.9. *VN+GEN$_{P1}$: syntactic environments and direct speech*

VN clause	*TBC I*	*TBC LL*	*TBC III*	Total	%
Prepositional phrase					
Direct speech	2	2		4	11.9
Narrative	1	2		3	
Subject (of copula)					
Direct speech	2	13	5	30	61
Narrative	3	3		6	
Predicate (of copula)					
Narrative		3		3	5.1
Direct object[a]					
Direct speech	2			2	6.7
Narrative	1	1		2	
Apposition					
Direct speech		1		1	5.1
Narrative	1	1		2	
Main clause[b]					
Direct speech	1			1	1.7
Other					
Direct speech	2	1		3	8.5
Narrative	1	1		2	

[a]   Including genitival P2 complement.
[b]   i.e. independent VN clause.

vn+gen_{p1} as complement of a preposition

As mentioned above, this context is less prominent with vn+gen_{p1} than with vn+pp_{p1}, where it is the preferred syntactic environment. One example, containing the VN *comrac* 'encounter (in combat)', presents the problem already encountered, whether the status of the VN is purely morphological (i.e. as a verbal abstract), or whether it has verbal meaning in the sense of presenting a process, rather than a fact (see (19)). It is noteworthy that most examples that present this difficulty of classification refer to potential (including future, relative to narrated reality) situations.

> (19)   'Ní bía maith *do for comruc.*'   (*TBC I* 1295)
>   from[25] your encounter_VN
>   ' "No good will come of your encounter." '   (O'Rahilly 1976: 161)

vn+gen_{p1} as subject of the copula

This is the most common syntactic environment for vn+gen_{p1} in our texts. In (20) P1 is expressed by means of a noun phrase, as well as by a so-called proleptic pronoun. It is also an instance of the use in parallel syntactic construction of VNs proper—that is, verbal abstracts—and abstract nouns referring to events and potential processes, in this case, death or dying, or being slain, rephrased three times.[26] Thus once again the question arises whether the structure vn+gen_{p1} refers to a process, in the same way a finite verbal clause would refer to a process, or to a fact.

> (20)   'Is uissiu *a bás 7 a éc 7 a aided ind fir* congreiss in ríg samlaid,' for Cathbath
>   druí.   (*TBC LL* 4032)
>   his death and his demise and his slaying the_gen.sg man_gen.sg
>   ' "More fitting is death and destruction for the man who so incites the king," '
>   said Cathbath the druid.'   (O'Rahilly 1967: 247)

Aided 'violent death' and *éc* 'death' can both occur in the so-called *do*-infinitive and in periphrastic verbal construction with *oc*,[27] whereas *bás* is not, according to *DIL*, attested in these contexts. Thus potentially two interpretations of examples such as the one quoted here are possible: *bás* and *éc* are 'Vorgangsnomina', in Baudiš's terms, and can thus, just like the verbal abstracts proper, convey the meaning of a process or a fact. On the other hand, the occurrence of non-VNs proper in parallel construction with verbal abstracts could be taken as an indication that we are dealing here with the portrayal of facts, rather than hypothetical processes. However, a purely syntactic argument is unlikely to clarify ambiguities with regard to specific forms (nominal forms though they are) in specific contexts: even so-called verbal contexts of VNs are, purely syntactically speaking, nominal.

The greeting formula illustrated in (21), another use of vn+gen_{p1} as subject of

---

[25] I interpret *do* as a graphic variant of *de* 'from'.

[26] For other examples of the triple use of near-synonyms, see e.g. Windisch (1905: lines 429, 1237, 4271).

[27] Both appear to be restricted to late texts in these constructions, however, see *DIL* s.v. See also Section 3.2.2 for *éc* in the construction p1+*do*_{vn}.

the copula (which may be omitted), occurs, with small variations, in all three recensions of *TBC*.[28]

(21)   Is annsin tainic Fiacha roimhe co hairm a mboi Cuchulainn. '*Mochen do thecht ⁊ do thorrachtain*, a Fiacha' bur CuChulainn. 'Tairise lem sa in failti sin amh' bar Fiacha.   (*TBC III* 548.5)
welcome your go_VN and your arrive_VN
'Then Fiacha came to the place where Cú Chulainn was. "Welcome" [lit. welcome your going/coming and your arrival], said Cú Chulainn. "I trust that welcome," said Fiacha.'

Other than in copula clauses, the use of VN+GEN$_{P1}$ in subject position is rare. There is one instance of a subject of an active verb (see (22*a*)), and one example where VN+GEN$_{P1}$ functions as the subject of an impersonal verb (see (22*b*)).[29]

(22) (*a*)   Fácabar Conchobar ⁊ Cúscraid Mend Macha ⁊ sochaide mór olchena. *Dofúsci-seom a ngol.*   (*TBC I* 485)
awake_pres.3sg-PRO their groan
'Conchobar and Cúscraid Mend Macha and a large group besides were left behind. Their groaning woke him [i.e. Cú Chulainn].'

(*b*)   ar *adroas a thedacht-som* isin chath   (*TBC I* 4092)
failed_impers.sg his come_VN
'since he had been unable to come to the battle'

Example (22*a*) is another instance of a noun that expresses an activity but occurs only rarely in typical VN contexts. In this case, however, it would appear to express a process—that is, a temporally bounded activity—that is fully integrated into a linear progression of events: the warriors are left behind on the battlefield (by implication: wounded)—they groan—the boy (i.e. Sétanta, the young Cú Chulainn) awakes.

VN+GEN$_{P1}$ as predicate of the copula

Only *TBC LL* contains any instances; these three attestations are further unusual in that P1 is an indefinite NP, as in (23), making the whole VN+GEN$_{P1}$ phrase indefinite.

(23)   *Girbo chomraicthi dá šubach* sámach sobbrónach somenmnach, *rapa scarthain dá ndubach* ndobbrónach ndomenmnach a scarthain in n-aidchi sin.
(*TBC LL* 3238)
although-PRT-COP meet_VN two cheerful; PRT-COP part_VN two sad
'Though it had been a meeting of two cheerful, happy, highspirited [men], their parting that night was the parting of two sad, unhappy, dispirited ones.'

---

[28] There are two examples in *TBC I*, six in *TBC LL*, and four in *TBC III* (of altogether five instances of VN+GEN$_{P1}$ in this text), all four being virtually identical. *TBC III* favours recurrent, formula-like phrases, more so than the other recensions of *TBC*. This will also become apparent in the investigation of the agentive passive—see Chapter 4.

[29] On the use of the impersonal of *at-raí* in the sense 'it is/was impossible', see *VKG* §83.5.

vn+gen_{p1} as direct object and P2 complement

This is another context in which vn+gen_{p1} occurs only comparatively rarely in our texts. In two of the four instances classfied as 'object' in Table 3.9, the VN clause is the genitival P2 of a VN (see (24*a*)), rather than the object of a finite verb, as in (24*b*).

> (24) (*a*)   . . . co mbátar oc fáschuí ⁊ oc fásguba ás chind Con Culaind *icá innisin dó*
> madma bar Ultaib ⁊ marbtha Chonchobuir ⁊ *tuittmi Fergusa* i frithguin.
> (*TBC LL* 4599)
> at-its tell_VN to-him; fall_VN Fergus_gen.sg
> '. . . and they pretended to weep and lament over Cú Chulainn, telling him the defeat of the Ulsterman, Conchobar's killing, and Fergus falling in the fight against them.'   (cf. O'Rahilly 1967: 263)
>
> (*b*)   'Ní aniub chétus,' ol Conchobar, '*co fesadar fir hÉrend mo diuchtrad-sa* asin ches a raba.'   (*TBC I* 3510)
> until find-out_pres.sub.3pl men Ireland_gen.sg my awaken_VN-PRO
> ' "I shall not wait, indeed," said Conchobar, "until the men of Ireland learn that I have recovered from the debility in which I have been." '
> (O'Rahilly 1976: 219)

Summary

As in the Welsh data, there is potential for overlap, or alternative selection, between genitival and prepositional marking of P1, since the latter is not formally restricted to any one class of VN. There is a preference for syntactic contexts, in that vn+pp_{p1} most frequently occurs as prepositional complement, whereas vn+gen_{p1} is most often found as subject of the copula; however, there does not appear to be any factor that excludes either of the two constructions from any particular syntactic context. A question arising from this is whether there are any contextual, non-syntactic factors that favour the selection of either the prepositional or the genitival expression of P1 with intransitive VNs; whether it is possible to explain the preference of prepositional P1 in (11) above, 'Ba holc la suide tuidecht dó chuccai' (he₁ was not pleased that he₂ should come with him₁), and of the genitival P1 in (15) above, 'Ní haccobor lem do thecht' (I don't want you to go), in identical syntactic environments, and similar semantic contexts, in that both statements represent the expression of one person's attitude towards the action of another. It would appear that individual contexts will need to be examined—that is, the manner in which individual VN clauses are integrated into their narrative environments and into narrated reality. It has emerged that ambiguities as regards the verbal status of VNs and abstract nouns that potentially express processes occur most often in contexts where the potential process is hypothetical or lies in an indeterminate future; we have further seen that these ambiguities occur most frequently with vn+gen_{p1}. A tentative conclusion might therefore be that the construction vn+gen_{p1} in fact portrays not processes bounded in time, but facts as properties of persons. These considerations will be pursued further in connection with the semantic status of P1 markers and in the course of the investigation of the textual environments of agentive VN constructions.

It has become clear that a general syntactic definition or criterion, such as Gagnepain's requirement that, if an abstract noun is to deserve the label *nom verbal*, it must be able to occur in either P2+do_{VN}+P1 or P1+do_{VN}(+P2), does not help with the meaning of any abstract noun, be it de-verbal (such as e.g. *gabáil* 'taking', from *gaibid* 'takes') or not (such as *gol* 'groan(ing), cry(ing)') in any specific context. The distinction between a process and a fact as that which is bounded in time, or extended over time, as opposed to that which is a property, not bounded in time,[30] may very well be context specific, but this is not to say that different syntactic constructions may not favour one interpretation over another.

3.1.3. P2+do_{VN}+P1 and P1+do_{VN}(+P2)

As outlined briefly in Chapter 1, the use of the VN after the preposition *do* has been variably linked with infinitival constructions in other Indo-European languages.[31] This section is concerned not with *do*+VN in general, but more specifically with those instances containing an overt P1, as illustrated in (1c) and (1d). In the texts analysed here, both P2+do_{VN}+P1 and P1+do_{VN}(+P2) are firmly established, and are particularly common in annalistic usage (see Section 3.2).

P2+do_{VN}+P1: markers and definiteness

The narrative texts do not contain large numbers of attestations of P2+do_{VN}+P1. As far as any tendencies can be made out from the sixteen instances, the example in (1c) represents the typical picture in *TBC* as regards the marker of P1 and its definiteness: in all but one instance (see (25)), the marker for P1 is *do*, thus showing an affinity with P1 in VN+PP$_{P1}$. P1 is always an AG, and it is always a definite entity. P2, on the other hand, is always an indefinite noun phrase; see Table 3.10 for a summary.

TABLE 3.10. *P2+do_{VN}+P1: definiteness of P1 and P2*

Participant	TBC I	TBC LL	TBC III	Total	%
P1 [+def.]					
Pronoun	4	2	7	13	*81.25*
Name		2		2	*12.5*
NP		1		1	*6.25*
P2 [−def.]					
NP	4	5	7	16	*100*

[30] Cf. the definition of a *process* as 'a relation extended over time', in Fife (1990: 59–60).

[31] Cf. Baudiš (1913), referring back to Fraser (1912a), and *GOI* §720. A more recent treatment of *do* +VN in Old Irish (Wb), investigating the pragmatics of the construction and interpreting it as a focusing device, is Genee (1994); see also Genee (1998), on sequential complementation in Irish.

(25)   Ba hassu dó *ulcha smérthain do dénam leiss.*   (*TBC I* 1901)
        imitation beard to make_VN with_him
        'It would be better for him to put on a fake beard.'

P1+do$_{VN}$(+P2): transitivity and definiteness

In this construction type, there is again a tendency for P1 to be an AG, rather than
an EXP. Indefinite P1s are more frequent here than with other types of VN clauses.
Intransitive VNs are in the majority, and the largest proportion of these are
VNs of motion—a similar tendency as the one encountered with VN+GEN$_{P1}$ (see
Table 3.11).

TABLE 3.11. *P1+do$_{VN}$(+P2): definiteness of P1 and P2, and types of VN*

Participant and VN type	TBC I	TBC LL	TBC III	Total	%
Participant					
P1					
AG	3	14	6	23	76.7
EXP	3	2	2	7	23.3
P1 [+def.]					
Pronoun			2	2	6.7
Name	1	1	2	4	13.3
NP	4	8	3	15	50
P1 [−def.]					
NP	1	7	1	9	30
P2 [+def.]					
Pronoun			2		
Name			1		
NP	2	2			
VN					
Transitive	2	2	3	7	23.3
Intransitive (motion)	1	8	2	11	37.7
Intransitive (other)	2	6	1	9	30
buith (auxiliary)	1	1		2	6.7
buith (substantive verb)			1	1	3.35

Syntactic environments

The syntactic contexts in which P2+do$_{VN}$+P1 and P1+do$_{VN}$(+P2) occur are largely
those in which other agentive VN constructions are encountered. As with VN+GEN$_{P1}$,
occurrence in direct speech is comparatively frequent, and the preferred syntactic
role is that of the subject of the copula (see Table 3.12). Like other VN constructions
with overt P1, P2+do$_{VN}$+P1 and P1+do$_{VN}$(+P2) do not often occur as independent

TABLE 3.12. *Syntactic environments and direct speech*

(*a*) P2+do_{VN}+P1

VN clause	TBC I	TBC LL	TBC III	Total	%
Prepositional phrase					
Direct speech		1		1	6.25
Subject (of copula)					
Direct speech	1	1	5	7	50
Narrative	1			1	
Predicate (of copula)					
Direct speech	1			1	6.25
Direct object[a]					
Narrative		2		2	18.75
Main clause[b]					
Direct speech	1	1	1	3	18.75
Apposition					
Direct speech			1	1	6.25

(*b*) P1+do_{VN}(+P2)

VN clause	TBC I	TBC LL	TBC III	Total	%
Subject (of copula)					
Direct speech	2	3	3	8	50
Narrative	1	6		7	
Predicate (of copula)					
Direct speech			1	1	3.3
Direct object[a]					
Direct speech	1	1	1	3	13.3
Narrative		1		1	
Main clause[b]					
Direct speech		1	1	2	10
Narrative	1			1	
Apposition					
Direct speech	1	3		4	20
Narrative		1	1	2	
Other[c]					
Direct speech			1	1	3.3

[a] Including genitival P2 complement.
[b] i.e. independent VN clause.
[c] The one instance classified as 'other' is a complement of the conjunction *nó* 'or' (*TBC III* 553.14), and is an extension of a subject clause (*TBC III* 553.13).

VN clauses in our narrative texts (unlike in *The Annals of Ulster* (see Section 3.2)). The example of P2+do_{VN}+P1 in (26a) is part of a descriptive sequence, consisting mainly of strings of nominal expressions. The instance of independent P1+do_{VN}(+P2) in (26b) shows an implied causal link with the preceding clause, the use of the markers .i. 'id est/ed ón' in the text supplying a graphic link; the marker often precedes explanations, such as etymologies and the like.

(26) (a) Mar thairc dano in fer sin do marbad, láich eile for áth dó-som nó nechtar de *longphort 7 dúnaid do gabáil d'ḟeraib Hérend* and sin co solustrath érge arnabárach. (*TBC LL* 1554)
camp and fortification to take_VN to-man_dat.pl Ireland_gen.sg
'When he has killed that man, then, another warrior to him at the ford, or else the men of Ireland to make camp there until sunrise the next morning.'

(b) Fochertar armgrith mór leó .i. *mac sethar ind ríg do ḟolmaisiu a báis.* (*TBC I* 590)
son sister_gen.sg the_gen.sg king_gen.sg to be-on-the-point-of_VN his death_VN
'They raise a great shout then; the son of the king's sister having almost been killed.'

As shown in Table 3.12, both P1- and P2-initial *do*+VN constructions can occur in what has here been labelled apposition, with P1+do_{VN}(+P2) being found more frequently in this environment. The example in (27) has been included under 'apposition' (to the direct object, in this particular case); an alternative interpretation would be to read the P1+do_{VN}(+P2) clause as a syntactically independent VN clause. The semantic link would remain the same, in as much as the VN clause represents an elaboration of the direct object *sain* 'that'.

(27) Atchúala sain Findabair ingen Ailella ⁊ Medba *in comlín sain d'ḟeraib hErend do thuttim* . . . (*TBC LL* 3887)
the number that of-man_gen.pl Ireland_gen.sg to fall_VN
'Findabair, the daughter of Ailill and Medb, heard that; that such a large number of the men of Ireland had fallen . . .'

Do+VN as complement of a preposition

There is only one instance of P2+do_{VN}+P1 in this syntactic environment, and it involves a compound preposition:

(28) 'Mairg atber ón omm,' bar Ailill, '*ar abba dúnad 7 longphort do gabáil dóib* co hellom ⁊ co héscaid.' (*TBC LL* 332–3)
because fortification and camp to take_VN to-them
' "Shame on the one who says so," said Ailill, "just because they have set up their camp quickly and promptly." '

Do+VN as subject

In so far as the comparatively small number of attestations of P2+do_{VN}+P1 and

P1+do_{VN}(+P2) in *TBC* permits a statistical comparison with other construction types, it emerges that the preferred syntactic context is that of the subject of the copula, similar to what has been found with VN+GEN_{P1} (see (29)).[32]

(29)   Maith linn aile bhar Medb *comlonn 7 comrag dodhenum did* re Coinculainn
        (*TBC III* §21)
        fight and encounter to-do_VN to-you
        'We want you to fight and do battle against Cú Chulainn'

Do+VN as predicate of the copula

In both examples of *do*+VN in predicate position, the copula clause is introduced by a conjunction (see (30)).[33]

(30)   Madafesaind *gomadh tú dobheith ann* nírisfaighbhithea.   (*TBC III* §111)
        that-if-COP you to-be_VN there
        'If I'd known it was <u>you</u>, you wouldn't have got it.'

Do+VN as direct object and P2 complement

The only two attestations of P2+do_{VN}+P1 in direct-object positions are to be found in *TBC LL*, in the same paragraph, and are phrased virtually identically (see (31*a*)). The example quoted in (31*b*) has been interpreted as an object clause here; however, this interpretation is not without problems.

(31) (*a*)   Luid Fer Diad dochum a pupla ⁊ a muntiri ⁊ rachúaid dóib *máeth n-áraig do*
            tharrachtain do Meidb fair   (*TBC LL* 2785)
            deal to reach_VN to Medb on-him
            'Fer Diad went to his tent and his followers and told them how Medb had
            managed to make a deal with him'

    (*b*)   ... tocht do ghleo ⁊ d imrisin risin earchoin irghaile *nach ḟedaid curaidh no*
            chathmhileda do tadhall no tasgadh dho?   (*TBC III* 553.31)
            NEG can_pres.3sg warrior_pl or soldier_pl to approach_VN or resist_VN to-
            him
            '... to go to fight and do battle against the bloodhound whom warriors and
            soldiers can neither approach nor withstand?'

The interpretation of (31*b*) presents several difficulties. I am taking the form *fedaid* as a 3sg present of the verb *fétaid* 'can, is able to', in an impersonal construction—that is, with an unexpressed 'it' subject, in the sense 'it is possible', similar to a copula-construction *is éitir* + P1+do_{VN}(+P2) 'it is possible + VN clause'. With the active verb form *fedaid*, the P1+do_{VN}(+P2) clause would have to be the object of that

---

[32] This is one of three virtually identical examples in *TBC III*.

[33] A possible alternative interpretation would be to read *dobheith* as 3sg past subjunctive in a relative construction, in a late variant of an Old Irish *combad tú nobeth and* (for the use of the 3rd person singular verb form when the antecedent is subject, see *GOI* §496).

verb. This is the only instance of *fétaid* being used in this way known to me—that is, as morphologically active, subjectless, and a VN clause as object.[34]

With the exception of (31*b*), the great majority of the attestations discussed here does not pose any problems of ambiguity or interpretation. There is, however, a series of examples that deserve a closer look with regard to their status either as instances of P1+*do*$_{VN}$(+P2), or as *do*-phrases expressing a purpose. The structure of these examples, which for the present purposes have not been classified as P1+*do*$_{VN}$(+P2), illustrated in (32), is that of an interrogative relative clause introduced by *cia* 'who'.[35]

(32)   Is and sin r*a* himráided ac feraib Hérend *cia bad chóir do chomruc 7 do chomlund ra Coin Culaind* ra húair na maitne muche arnabárach.
(*TBC LL* 2533)
who COP right to encounter_VN and fight_VN against Cú Chulainn
'Then the men of Ireland debated as to whom they should send to fight and do combat with Cú Chulainn at the hour of early morning on the morrow.'
(O'Rahilly 1967: 209)

The potential ambiguity here is whether *cóir* refers to P1+*do*$_{VN}$(+P2), or to the relative interrogative only; in other words, the question is whether a corresponding statement structure would be (33*a*) or (33*b*). There does not appear to be a ready solution to this ambiguity. On the one hand, constructions such as (33*c*) appear to be grammatical, thus it is possible to extract from within P1+*do*$_{VN}$(+P2).[36] On the other hand, there are instances where *do*, following an adjective and preceding a VN, expresses purpose (see e.g. (33*d*)).[37]

(33) (*a*)   Bad chóir [*X* do chomruc fri *Y*]
COP right [*X* to encounter against *Y*]
'It is right that *X* should fight against *Y*'

---

[34] A further interpretation would be to read 'curaidh no chathmhileda' as (plural) subject of the verb *fétaid*, which would leave us with lack of concord between subject and object; however, this phenomenon is not uncommon in Middle and Early Modern Irish texts (see e.g. Dottin 1913: 243). This would make 'do tadhall na tasgadh do' the object of the clause, with the presence of *do* preceding the VNs to be explained. One could make a case for an intrusive *do* (see also *TBC LL* 1964, quoted in (6), and the use of *do* in 'Maith linn aile . . . do comlund ⁊ do comrag duit re CoinCulainn' (We want you to fight and do battle against Cú Chulainn) (*TBC III* 554) (this may be comparable to the use of *a* (from *do*) in some Modern Irish dialects with VNs of motion, e.g. *ba mhaith liom a ghoil* 'I'd like to go').

[35] *TBC LL* contains two instances of this type, plus two interrogative clauses of similar structure ('cia bad chóir d'fúapairt Con Culaind accu' (who among them should attack Cú Chulainn) (*TBC LL* 1816); 'Cia bad chóir do thecht and' (Who should go there?) (*TBC LL* 4164)). *TBC III* contains five examples of the phrasing quoted in (32).

[36] Cf. e.g. *TBC LL* 4164, and *TBC LL* 1819: 'atbertatar uile combae é Cúr mac Dá Lóth bad chóir dá fúapairt' (lit.: so-that-COP he C.m.D.L. COP right to-his attack_VN) (and all said that Cúr should attack him).

[37] Cf. also 'Ba gilla comadas or se do faire duine ríg do grés in gilla sa' (lit.: COP lad suitable . . . to guard_VN fort_gen.sg king_gen.sg) (that lad would be suitable to guard a king's fort forever, he said) (*LU* 9155). Further examples can be found in *DIL* s.v. *do*; and see Fraser (1912*b*: 24) for other instances of *irlam* 'ready' in the same construction as quoted in (33*d*).

    (*b*)   Bad chóir [*X*] [do chomruc fri *Y*]
            COP right [*X*] [to encounter_VN against *Y*]
            '*X* is the right person to against fight *Y*'

    (*c*)   *X* bad chóir do chomruc fri *Y*
            X COP right to encounter_VN against *Y*
            '*X* should fight against *Y* (and no one else)'

    (*d*)   ammi irlaim hicachláo do dul martre   (Wb 4b21)
            COP_1pl ready in-every-day to go_VN martyrdom
            'We are ready everyday to go to martyrdom'

Again we see that ambiguities, or even potential ambiguities only, are produced by specific contexts. As far as the *reality* of the situation is concerned, the reality reported in the text, no ambiguity exists; the situation encoded in *cia bad choir do chomruc . . .* is envisaged for the future, as yet un-real. The person who is right for the job will very likely be the person carrying out the job. The ambiguity for the person decoding the text from a vantage point several centuries after its creation is a question of the exact relation expressed in the construction: is it a relation between the concept of 'being right' and a process (that of a fighting encounter, specified as carried out by *X* against *Y*), or between the concept of 'being right' and *X*, in the context for the purpose of a fighting encounter with *Y*.

3.1.4. Agentive VN clauses in context

The preceding sections each have examined different constructions in their own right; this section investigates how far it might be possible to determine typical conditions for the use of different constructions, focusing on aspects of information structuring, and the role of the VN clause in its narrative context. Preferences of syntactic construction have already been noted: VN+PP$_{P1}$ occurs more often as a prepositional complement in *TBC* than in any other syntactic environment, whereas the other types investigated are found predominantly as subjects in copula constructions. However, no syntactic environment in which any one VN clause type is encountered is exclusive to that type; the syntactic contexts in which we find, for example, VN+PP$_{P1}$ are also attested with VN+GEN$_{P1}$, P2+*do*$_{VN}$+P1, and P1+*do*$_{VN}$(+P2).[38] Thus, as already briefly mentioned in Chapter 1, it should in theory

---

[38] A near-exception to this observation is the type P2+*do*$_{VN}$+P1 in the present database, and its occurrence as prepositional complement: as detailed above, there is only one example; the VN clause is the complement of a compound (i.e. denominal) preposition (ex. (28)). It is interesting here that, contrary to the general rule that the noun phrase preceding *do* has the case marking required by the syntactic environment (i.e. nominative for subject of copula, accusative for direct object), in this case, the noun phrase encoding P2, although following a compound preposition, does not show genitive case marking (according to *DIL*, s.v., *apa* can be followed by the genitive or nominative). McCloskey (1980: 92–3) makes a similar observation in his investigation of the Modern Irish reflex of *do*+VN.

be possible to express the situations that Fergus should leave, or, alternatively, do a valorous deed, in any of the ways in (34):

(34)   Bad chóir . . .

    (*a*)   imthecht do Ḟergus
            dénam dagníma do Ḟergus

    (*b*)   imthecht Fergusa

    (*c*)   dagním do dénum do Ḟergus

    (*d*)   Fergus do dénam dagníma
            Fergus do imthecht

Certain tendencies are shared by all types of agentive VN clauses analysed here: P1 is a definite entity in the large majority of attestations (although there are differences with regard to the preference of pronominal over nominal P1s). AGs are more common than EXPs; this could, on the one hand, be a feature of the texts, in that the majority of situations reported are actions, rather than events or states; on the other hand, it could mean that more situations having and AG–P1 are reported by means of agentive VN clauses.

Other characteristics can be made out as tendencies with certain construction types only. For example, whereas $VN+PP_{P1}$ shows no preference for either transitive or intransitive VNs in *TBC*, $P1+do_{VN}(+P2)$ more often occurs with intransitive than transitive VNs. Whereas $VN+PP_{P1}$ is used more often in non-dialogue, narrative contexts, the other VN constructions occur more frequently in direct speech.[39] A link can be established with preferred syntactic environments: whereas prepositional (adverbial) VN clauses occur predominantly in non-dialogue, VN clauses as subjects of the copula are to be found most often in direct speech.[40] None of the majorities is exclusive, or would appear to suffice as a criterion to determine the selection of one clause type over another.

3.1.4.1. INFORMATION PACKAGING: NEW VERSUS GIVEN INFORMATION

The general tendency for P1 to be a definite entity, and especially the preference for pronominal encoding of P1 in all construction types except $P1+do_{VN}(+P2)$ already implies that P1 usually represents given information. More specifically, the construction $VN+PP_{P1}$ occurs twice with a new P1 (both in *TBC LL*), and there is one case (in *TBC I*) where P1 is expressed by an indefinite pronominal (see (35) below),

---

[39] With $P1+do_{VN}(+P2)$ showing the smallest majority, with seventeen versus thirteen examples (or 56.7% versus 43.3%).

[40] It is, however, likely that this is not only a characteristic of VN clauses in these syntactic contexts, but concerns all types of subordinate constructions.

thus being unspecified, rather than a new, but identifiable character introduced into the narrative.

(35)   *fri gabáil ngaiscid do neoch*   (*TBC I* 623)
         against take_VN weapons to someone
         'against (the occasion of) anyone taking up arms'

In the example quoted in (20) above, the P1 phrase of a VN+GEN$_{P1}$ clause could be qualified as 'new', if we assume that the speaker is stating a general rule, or else as a paraphrase of 'given' information, if we read 'ind fir congreiss in ríg samlaid' as a description of Sualtaim, the man approaching the king and his entourage and being criticized for doing so. Neither way does the construction introduce a new character into the narrative. Two further (potential) instances of a P1 in VN+GEN$_{P1}$ do not fit a 'new-versus-given' schema (see the examples quoted in (23)), if by a 'new' P1 we understand an identifiable character who has not been mentioned before.[41] Here, VN+GEN$_{P1}$ does not present a specific, new situation so much as a characterization of a situation (which itself is presented by means of another instance of VN+GEN$_{P1}$ (*TBC LL* 3240)).

Only the construction P1+do_{VN}(+P2) shows, relative to the total number of attestations, a significant proportion of P1s that represent new information. However, these cases are still only the minority of all examples of this construction type, as shown in Table 3.13. New P1s tend to be examples for categories, rather than fully

TABLE 3.13. *P1+do_{VN}(+P2): given versus new P1*

Text	P1 given	P1 new	P1 *nech/óen*[a]
TBC I	5	1	
TBC LL	10	4	1 / 1
TBC III	6	2	
TOTAL	21	7	2
%	70	23.3	6.7

[a] *Nech* 'anyone' and *óen* 'anyone (at all)' are listed as a separate category, not fitting either into 'new' or 'given'; see (35).

specified characters that participate in the progression of the narrative. The clauses in which they occur are usually comments provoked by their contexts, as in (36),[42] where, immediately preceding the utterance quoted, the young Sétanta approaches

---

[41] Note that 'identifiable' is not necessarily to be equated with 'definite': in a sentence like 'a teacher bought the house next door', the subject is indefinite and new, but identifiable by having been involved in a specific situation.

[42] This is also true for the use of *nech* and *óen*; see *TBC LL* 508, 1717.

the boys of Ulster, 'gatecrashing' their ballgame, provoking the following comment from the group's leader:

(36)   ... ⁊ táet a bás lim dáig is geiss dúib *maccáem to thíchtain infar cluchi* can chur a faísma foraib   (*TBC LL* 776)
boy to come_VN into-your game
'... and he should die at my hands, since it is a taboo for you that a boy should join in your game without ensuring his protection from you'

In addition to the examples where P1 is new, in the sense illustrated in (36), there are instances where P1 in a P1+do_{VN}(+P2) construction paraphrases a known character; that is, the expression chosen is not the proper name of the character, but an epithet or description, drawing attention to a specific characteristic, or adding new information concerning a known person, as in (37a), where it is well known that the character in question is Cú Chulainn, but the speaker, Medb, draws attention to the fact that he is the one who has killed the addressee's brother. In three instances, the phrase encoding P1 presents a potential alternative in a hypothetical situation (see (37a)).[43]

(37) (a)   'Mór in cutbiud dait' for si, '*in fer ro marb do bráthair do bith oc díthugud ar slóig...*'   (*TBC I* 1971)[44]
the man PRT kill_pret.3sg your brother to be_VN at destroy_VN our army_gen.sg
' "It's a great shame on you," she said, "that the man who killed your brother should be destroying our army..." '

(b)   cia badh ḟerr lat sa ... *Edarcomal doma mharbadh sa no misi do marbadh Edarcomail*?   (*TBC III* 553.14, 553.13)
Etarcomol to-my kill_VN PRO or I to kill_VN Etarcomol
'Which would you have preferred ... Etarcomol killing me, or me killing Etarcomol?'

The P1 as paraphrase also occurs with VN+PP$_{P1}$ and with VN+GEN$_{P1}$ in *TBC LL*,[45] but to a lesser extent than with P1+do_{VN}(+P2), compared to the total number of attestations. Taking into consideration the relatively larger number of new P1s (which do not, however, introduce new participants into the narrative development) in the latter construction, one may draw the conclusion that the position of P1 at the beginning of the agentive VN clause favours the presentation of information that is either new or recalled with regard to a particular characteristic, and is therefore considered to be more salient than other parts of the VN clause; P1 in P1+do_{VN}(+P2), preceding the VN, can be interpreted as the focus of (new) information of the VN clause.

P2 tends to represent given rather than new information in VN+PP$_{P1}$: there is one

---

[43] See also *TBC I* 2875.
[44] See also *TBC III* §75.
[45] Cf. *TBC LL* 952, and *TBC LL* 4032, 4583, respectively.

example each of a new P2 in *TBC I* and *LL* (as opposed to eight and eleven cases respectively where transitive vn+pp$_{P1}$ contains a given P2). The preposed P2 in p2+do_{VN}+p1 represents new as often as given information, as shown in Table 3.14.

TABLE 3.14. *p2+do$_{VN}$+p1: given versus new P2*

Text	P2 given	P2 new
TBC I	1	3
TBC LL	4	1
TBC III	3	4
TOTAL	8	8
%	50	50

In one attestation in *TBC I*, P2 is a summary and interpretation on the part of one of the characters, of the previous discourse; the passage follows the recitation of a poem by another character, in which he gives expression to his anger and jealousy (see (38*a*)). The example quoted in (38*b*) is one of three instances of virtually identical content and structure in *TBC III*.[46]

(38) (*a*)   Atchúala Fergus mac Róig aní sein ⊣ ba dimbág leis *comairle braith Con Culaind do thabairt do Dubthach dona slúagaib*   (*TBC LL* 2401)[47]
counsel betrayal_gen.sg Cú Chulainn_gen.sg to give_VN to Dubthach to-the army_dat.pl
'Fergus mac Roich heard this, and he was displeased at the advice to betray Cú Chulainn that Dubthach gave to the armies'

(*b*)   Maith lind aile bhar Medb *comlonn 7 comrag dodhenum* did re Coinculainn ⊣ dadingbhail dind arath rehúair namaidni muichi amarach.   (*TBC III* §21)
fight and battle to-do_VN do-you against Cú Chulainn
' "We want", said Medb, "you to fight and do battle against Cú Chulainn, and to keep him away from us at the ford at the hour of early morning to-morrow." '

In (38*b*), and examples of the same structure, it is P2, in this case two VNs/process nouns linked by the conjunction *ocus* 'and', which determine the action of the situation described, since the VN *dénam* is comparatively unspecific in content. In *TBC III* this structure is employed in formula-like fashion, introducing the discussions between Medb and the warriors sent to fight Cú Chulainn. These examples have here been classified as containing a new P2, since each refers to a new development, a new episode of single combat. However, a strictly schematic approach to information value breaks down here: since the same phrasing is employed each

---

[46] See also *TBC III* §§34, 61.
[47] See also the parallel in *TBC III* §196.

time, in very similar narrative contexts, the degree of 'novelty' of the information for the reader or listener decreases with every repetition. What gains relevance is the function of the familiar phrase to introduce new, though similar narrative situations.[48] In fact, on encountering the familiar phrase a second and third time, the reader or listener will recall previous encounters; parallelism in structure underlines parallel situations.

The use of VNs and process nouns preceding the VN *dénam* recalls, in its content if not in its syntactic make-up, the *gwneuthur*-inversion of medieval Welsh. A prominent feature of the *gwneuthur*-inversion is its frequency in narrative texts; this is not the case with $\text{P1}+do_{\text{VN}}(+\text{P2})$ containing *dénam* as VN, and the reason may very well be that, while the *gwneuthur*-inversion appears to be a tool to bring the process element of a situation to the beginning of the clause, such a tool is not necessary in Irish, where the process element—that is, the verb—occurs clause initially (not only in terms of basic constituent order, but also in terms of usage) in a majority of statements.

P2 in $\text{P2}+do_{\text{VN}}+\text{P1}$ in our texts is always an indefinite noun phrase (see also Section 3.1.3). In most instances, it is also a complex noun phrase, consisting either of two coordinated nouns (or VNs), as in, for example, (38*b*), or of a noun further modified by, for example, an adjective or a genitive phrase (see (38*a*)). The lexical weight of the P2 phrase, especially where it is a coordinated complex noun phrase, underlines its salience, relative to other elements of the clause.[49] Thus the construction $\text{P2}+do_{\text{VN}}+\text{P1}$ can, in analogy with $\text{P1}+do_{\text{VN}}(+\text{P2})$ as a means to focus P1, be interpreted as a device to focus P2.

3.1.4.2. CONTINUITY

Continuity of P1 has, under various headings, been addressed in several studies on VN constructions in early Irish. Disterheft (1980: 142 ff.) finds that the non-expression of a coreferential agent is the norm, rather than the exception in her data; Genee (1988: 45) comes to largely the same conclusion.[50] We may therefore expect that, in general, where a VN clause embedded in a main clause exhibits an overt P1, this will not be coreferential with the P1 of the main clause. This expectation is largely borne out. Where, however, the VN clause precedes its main clause (in the construction $\text{VN}+\text{PP}_{\text{P1}}$), there is always continuity, though not always co-

---

[48] One could label P2 as inferable in the second and third instance; however, the fact remains that information value, in these cases, moves into the background as compared to textual organization.

[49] Apart from one example, *TBC LL* 332–3, all coordinated P2 phrases can be classified as 'new' information in their respective contexts.

[50] Gagnepain (1963) briefly mentions coreference in the context of the spread of the construction $\text{P2}+do_{\text{VN}}+\text{P1}$ in subject position of copula clauses. According to his data, $\text{P2}+do_{\text{VN}}+\text{P1}$ occurs in Old Irish when the (understood or expressed) agent of the VN is not coreferential with any element of the copula clause. Where there is coreference, this type does not generally occur (1963: 95–9). In Middle Irish, the use of $\text{P2}+do_{\text{VN}}+\text{P1}$ expands, although the older construction $\text{VN}+\text{GEN}_{\text{P1}}$ is still to be found, without coreference restrictions found in the Old Irish data (1963: 203–7).

reference of P1s[51] (see (8b) and (8c) for examples of P1 being coreferential with the subject P1 of the main clause and with the IAG, expressed by means of a preposi-tional phrase, respectively). Continuity is clearly not a feature pertaining to a majority of dependent VN clauses, with the construction VN+PP$_{P1}$ showing the largest proportion of clauses that show continuity. This would appear to be, at least partly, conditioned by the dominant syntactic environments in which agentive VN clauses occur: constructions other than VN+PP$_{P1}$ are most frequently found in sub-ject position in copula clauses. These are in most cases evaluations of actions or experiences by others,[52] rather than by the person making the evaluation.

3.1.4.3. AGENTIVE VN CLAUSES AND NARRATED REALITY

'Narrated reality' concerns the 'here and now' of the events related in a text, as op-posed to the 'here and now' of the reader. Anchoring a dependent VN construction in the reality of the narrative can be achieved by a variety of means, explicit or implicit. An explicit expression of how the VN construction is sequenced in its context is illustrated in (39a), where the tense of the main verb (future), and the preposition introducing the VN clause ('after') together create the time frame for the situation portrayed in the VN clause: in the future, relative to the point of utterance, and (immediately) preceding the situation of the main clause. VN+GEN$_{P1}$ in (39b) is integrated into its context not by overt means, but implicitly through natural sequencing, and inferencing: the reader is aware that the addressee, Fergus, also P1 of the VN construction, has just arrived on the scene, and is greeted by the speaker; thus the reader makes the natural inference that it is this particular arrival that is commented on by the speaker, rather than any other, previous one.

(39) (a)   'Ficfit forn iar tiachtain dúin,' ol sí, '᚛ gébtait ar tír frind.'   (TBC I 158)
            fight_fut.3sg on-us after come_VN to-us
            ' "They will fight us when we come [back]", she said, "and take our land from us." '

     (b)   'Fo chen do thíachtain, a mo phopa, a Fergais!' bar Cú Chulaind.
            (TBC LL 2723)
            welcome your come_VN
            ' "Welcome, master Fergus!" [lit.: welcome your coming] said Cú Chulainn.'

Instances such as the one in (39a), where the situation in the VN clause follows the situation of the main clause, and post-dates narrative 'here and now'—that is, the stage of development reached in the narrative at the point where the VN clause is used[53]—are classified here as 'hypothetical (posterior)' relative to narrative present

---

[51]   P1 of the VN clause is coreferential with the subject P1 of the main clause in one instance in *TBC I*, and in two in *TBC III*. P1 shows coreference with another entity in the main clause in one instance in *TBC I*, in three in *TBC LL*, and in two in *TBC III*.

[52]   See e.g. 'ní haccobor lem to thecht' (I do not want you to go) (*TBC I* 1292), quoted as ex. (15).

[53]   For convenience's and brevity's sake, this will henceforth be referred to as the point of utterance, irrespective of whether the VN clause is part of a character's utterance (i.e. direct speech) or not.

(i.e. to the point of utterance). An example such as (39*b*), in which the situation referred to in the VN clause immediately precedes the point of utterance, is classified as in linear development with its context, or, more briefly, linear.[54] For the present purposes, what is interesting is not so much how the reader (or indeed listener) establishes the link between narrated reality and the processes described in VN clauses, but rather whether the construction types investigated here show any preferences with regard to their use in specific time/reality relations to the point of utterance, and which may correlate with the preferences shown for certain syntactic positions.

One basic criterion is the complex relation that in a finite verb would be signalled by an inflectional ending—that is, the time/reality frame. The following distinctions are made: processes are characterized whether they are considered real or hypothetical by the speaker, are situated in the past (anterior) or the future (posterior), relative to the point of utterance, or take place in linear development with events at the point of utterance. A further distinction concerns the presentation of the process portrayed by the VN: a process or situation can be presented as a link in a chain of events (see (39*a*)), or as part of an evaluative statement, as in (39*b*), on the part of either a character of the narrative, or the narrator. Evaluation influences the picture the reader/listener forms of the events as they unfold in the narrative; consider the following example:

> (40)   Is and *bad dóig la Fergus bith Con Culaind i nDelga*   (*TBC I* 1247)
>   COP likely with Fergus be_VN Cú Chulainn_gen.sg in Delga
>   'And Fergus believed that Cú Chulainn was in Delga'

The evaluation adds the perspective of one character to the situation commented on (of Cú Chulainn's whereabouts), as well as an element of uncertainty, and provides yet another indication, among the many others in the text, of the close link between these two characters.[55] Had the content of the VN clause been presented at first hand (*is and boi Cú Chulainn i nDelga*), this background information would have been lost, although the time/reality frame of the VN clause—contemporary relative to narrative present—would have been identical. Evaluations such as the ones quoted here tend to be copula constructions, where the VN construction occupies the position of subject; thus an 'evaluation factor' is built into the syntactic structure.

There do not appear to be any exclusive restrictions with regard to the time/ reality contexts in which agentive VN constructions are situated. VN+PP$_{P1}$ portrays situations that are hypothetical with future time reference, in linear sequence, or anterior to the moment of utterance. The use of VN+PP$_{P1}$ in a context without specific time reference, as of an unspecifically recurring action, is illustrated in (35)

---

[54] An alternative label would be 'contemporary'; however, this can now be reserved for situations that occur in parallel with narrative present.

[55] It is significant that, if there is a doubt about Cú Chulainn's movements, it is Fergus who is asked for advice.

above. In addition, a context occurs that could be labelled as 'hypothetical with anterior time reference'—see (41), where the syntactically independent VN clause makes reference to a past event, the speaker inviting an evaluation of potential outcomes. Integration into the context and interpretation of the time/reality frame is achieved by inference and contextual knowledge only; there is no unambiguous overt marker.

(41)   'ráid dam cia de bad ḟerr lat-su, *mo choscur-sa 7 mo chommaídim-se dó-som*
        oldás a choscur-som 7 a chommaídim-sium dam-sa.   (*TBC LL* 1676–7)
        my defeat_VN-PRO and my triumph-over_VN-PRO to-him-PRO than his
        defeat_VN-PRO and his triumph-over_VN-PRO to-me-PRO
        'say which you'd prefer, then, him having defeated me, or me having defeated
        him.'

Although all these time/reality frames can and do occur, there are clear preferences. Situations in linear development with the moment of utterance, part of the immediate contemporary context, are most common with VN+PP_{P1}, followed by hypothetical situations.[56] A similar pattern emerges for $\text{VN+GEN}_{\text{P1}}$;[57] a particular variant of linear or contemporary processes portrayed within an evaluation context is the greeting formula illustrated in (39a); this formula is exclusive to $\text{VN+GEN}_{\text{P1}}$. Both $\text{P2+}do_{\text{VN}}\text{+P1}$ and $\text{P1+}do_{\text{VN}}\text{(+P2)}$ show a preference for hypothetical contexts[58] over linear developments.[59] As regards the selection of intransitive VN+PP_{P1} as opposed to $\text{VN+GEN}_{\text{P1}}$, the time/reality frame does not appear to be a decisive criterion; what appears to be more relevant is the 'evaluation factor', which, as mentioned above, generally correlates with the syntactic context. Where the VN construction is couched in an evaluative context and the situation evaluated is expressed by an intransitive VN, $\text{VN+GEN}_{\text{P1}}$ tends to be used. Where the VN is transitive, $\text{P2+}do_{\text{VN}}\text{+P1}$ is favoured. Where, on the other hand, the process as process, either its development over time, or a particular stage of the development (the beginning or the endpoint, for example), is the most salient element of the situation, it appears that VN+PP_{P1} is the favoured construction (compare (42a) with (42b)):

(42) (a)   is *agtaidecht atuaidh do Coinculainn* tarla Buidhi mac Bain Bhlai dho
           (*TBC III* §13)
           at-come_VN from-the-north to Cú Chulainn
           'it was when Cú Chulainn was coming from the north that he met Buidi mac
           Báin Blai'

     (b)   'Ní haccobor lem do thecht,' or Fergus   (*TBC I* 1292)
           NEG-COP wish with-me your go_VN
           ' "I do not want you to go," said Fergus'

The situations portrayed in the VN clauses in (42a) and (42b) are both part of the

---

[56]   At 44.6% and 30.4% of attestations, respectively.
[57]   At 42.4% and 35.6% of attestations, respectively.
[58] $\text{P2+}do_{\text{VN}}\text{+P1}$: 62.5%; $\text{P1+}do_{\text{VN}}\text{(+P2)}$: 70%.
[59] $\text{P2+}do_{\text{VN}}\text{+P1}$: 18.75%; $\text{P1+}do_{\text{VN}}\text{(+P2)}$: 16.7%.

immediate context of the situation described in their main clauses—that is, contemporary developments. The difference appears to lie in the relevance of the process as process, and of the exact temporal relation between the VN clause and its context: in (42a) the process described in the VN clause provides the time frame for the main clause; while one process unfolds, another takes place. In (42b) an action (in this case, movement) is evaluated as a whole, and as a property of a character, rather than as a development over time. The process starts (i.e. the addressee's accompanying Fergus, which is met with a negative evaluation) just before the evaluation is made, and continues into the future, but this aspect is not given prominence. What is relevant is the speaker's attitude to the situation as a whole—that is, to the combination of the participant (the addressee) and the process (going). In the present data, VN+GEN$_{P1}$ is not used to portray situations that themselves provide the background setting against which another situation takes place.

3.1.5. Agentive VN constructions in *Táin Bó Cúailnge*: summary

A conclusion from this and the preceding sections may thus be formulated: transitivity and the time/reality frame of the situation portrayed do not provide decisive criteria for the selection of one VN construction over another. Although VN+GEN$_{P1}$ is restricted to intransitive VNs, the use of intransitive VNs is also well established with the construction VN+PP$_{P1}$, and both constructions show a preferred use with processes that are part of the immediate context of the situation portrayed in the main clause.

The strongest criterion that has emerged from the present data is the syntactic environment, and thereby, implicitly, the relevance attached to the process of the situation described as process. The preferred context for VN+PP$_{P1}$ is that of a prepositional phrase, the function of which is similar to that of a finite adverbial clause. It seems relevant here that, in this type of complex situation, two processes enter into a relation with each other. This is not the case where a situation is evaluated or commented upon. We have seen that evaluative statements of the type illustrated in (42b) represent the favoured context of VN+GEN$_{P1}$. In such a statement, a situation is commented upon, thus related to a person, rather than to another situation. I would suggest that in this context, the processual element—that is, the boundedness in time—of the situation is less relevant than the elements making up the situation—that is, the type of process (rather than its actual development over time) and the participant. If this is the case, then we can establish a link between the selection of a VN construction and the prominence that the process as process has in the context in which the construction is used: a relatively higher salience of the processual character would favour the use of VN+PP$_{P1}$, whereas, in a context where the processual development has less salience, other VN constructions would be employed.

There is an obvious asymmetry, due to the restriction of VN+GEN$_{P1}$ to intransitive VNs. However, we have seen that P2+*do*$_{VN}$+P1 or P1+*do*$_{VN}$(+P2) are used to present

P2 or P1, respectively, as focus of information, in much the same preferred syntactic environment as $VN+GEN_{P1}$. Tentatively, we may conclude that $P2+do_{VN}$, with or without a P1 phrase, functions as the transitive near-equivalent of a $VN+GEN_{P1}$ clause. By focusing one participant in the situation (i.e. P2), the prominence of the process as process is reduced.

What has been suggested here differs from the results of Gagnepain's study. He states that in Old Irish, where the *nom verbal* occurs as the subject of the copula, and is accompanied by an agent, 'la structure ne peut être que celle que nous avons définie comme caractéristique du type 2' (Gagnepain 1963: 101)—that is, the type $VN+PP_{P1}$.[60] The agent, or in our terms P1, is in Gagnepain's data always expressed by a pronoun, and he observes that the occurrence of an agent with a VN is only rarely to be encountered. He further notes that in Middle Irish, because of a conflation of two construction types, $VN+PP_{P1}$ and $P1+do_{VN}(+P2)$, a new type arises—namely, $P2+do_{VN}+P1$, initially with pronominal agents only, while nominal agents are found with $VN+PP_{P1}$ (1963: 207–8). Gagnepain thus expresses usage in terms of historical development, and as correlations between construction types and the status (morphological, but to an extent also informational, since a participant expressed by means of a pronoun generally tends to resume given information) of the agent. As we have seen from the various recensions of *TBC*, the different constructions analysed are all well established. The semantic nuance that appears to emerge from the usage of different constructions may very well be a development that emerged only once the historical development Gagnepain mentions had led to the establishment of $P2+do_{VN}+P1$.

3.2. VN clauses in non-narrative texts: laws and annals

3.2.1. Law texts

VN constructions with overt P1 are not a prominent feature in the law texts analysed here. Attestations are few and far between; too sparse to allow any observations concerning the usage of the different construction types in comparison with their counterparts in *TBC*. The constructions encountered are of the same types as in *TBC*. What is (in some examples potentially) P1 is marked by *la* 'with', *do* 'to', or *ó* 'from' (see (43a)–(43c)).

(43) (a)   gniitt, cumala caínógat a ngnímu, a folog *foa mbíathad lia flaith*   (CG 485)
            under-their feed_VN with-their lord
            'Manservants and bondwomen who fulfil their services well, their sick-maintenance according to their feeding by their lord'[61]

---

[60] As opposed to $P2+do_{VN}+P1$ and $P1+do_{VN}(+P2)$; Gagnepain does not include the type $VN+GEN_{P1}$ in his analysis.

[61] This translation follows Binchy's interpretation of the passage (see Binchy 1941: 36 n. and glossary s.v. *la*).

(b)   Dligid fer dota-etet bes bunadach doib trian a toraid co cenn téora mblíadnae
       acht is ónd nemud a n-imchomét . . .   (*BB* §37)
       but COP from-the dignitary their look-after_VN
       'The man who tracks them and who is their original owner is entitled to one
       third of their produce for three years, but they are looked after by the digni-
       tary . . .'   (Charles-Edwards and Kelly 1983: 83)

(c)   Ocus fer do chlaind filed do-gní frithgnum *íar scarad frie día athair 7 día*
       šenathair cid grad do-berar dó?   (*UR* §9)
       after part_VN against-it to-his father and to-his grandfather
       'As for a man from a family of poets who attends a course of study after his
       father and his grandfather have parted from it, what grade is conferred on
       him?'   (Breatnach 1987: 107)

Even from these three examples, it becomes obvious that the material is not entirely unambiguous. *La* in (43*a*) might be interpreted as marking a spatial relation:
'in the vicinity of their lord'—that is, in practice, 'in the service of their lord'.
Whether the dignitary (*nemed*) in (43*b*) looks after the bees himself, or is rather the
person arranging for someone else to do the job—that is, *ó* marking the IAG or
source—is not entirely clear. The texts do not yield enough potential examples and
counter-examples to establish patterns for the distribution of P1 markers and
markers for related categories.

Constructions of the same structure as VN+GEN$_{P1}$—that is, VNs accompanied by
a genitive phrase denoting an animate (human) entity capable of being a P1—generally do not express individual processes; altogether, only three VN+GEN constructions can be interpreted as agentive VN clauses. There are examples of what are
formally verbal abstracts, accompanied by genitive phrases; however, the abstract
nouns do not have 'verbal' function since they do not express individual processes,
bounded in time, but rather properties associated with persons, as in (44*a*), and
often an original VN has acquired a specific technical meaning—for example,
naidm in (44*b*) (note here also the use of verbal abstracts and other abstract nouns
in parallel construction).

(44) (a)   *Án a airchetal, án a frithgnum.*   (*UR* §12)
            splendid his compose_VN, splendid his practice_VN
            'Splendid is his poetry, splendid is his attendance at his study.'
            (Breatnach 1987: 109)

     (b)   Lóg a enech, is ed im[m]atuing, *téit fora naidm* ⁊ a ráith ⁊ a aitiri ⁊ a fiadnaise.
            (*CG* 127)
            goes on-his bind_VN
            'His honourprice, it is what [i.e. the amount] he swears about, it goes in
            his suretyship, and his guarantee, and his personal suretyship and his evid-
            ence.'

If uttered while observing a poet diligently at work, (44*a*) could conceivably
mean 'splendid is his (current) composing and his studying'. In the present con-

text, however, it is clear that 'airchetal' and 'frithgnum' do not refer to identifiable processes, but are properties characterizing a particular type of person—that is, a class of poet, the *ánruth*, using the device of etymology to explain the label.

There is only sporadic evidence for potential attestation of P1+do_{VN}(+P2),[62] and each of the six examples could also be interpreted as a purpose clause. The ambiguity is the same as the one already encountered in *TBC* (see (45)):

(45) (a)   *Cia as choir 7 as téchtae do dénum biid ríg?*   (*CG* 553)
            INT COP_rel right and COP_rel proper to do_VN food_gen.sg king_gen.sg
            'Who is right and proper to prepare a king's food?'

    (b)   *Cléirig do dénum it(i)gi a thige.*   (*CG* 572)
            cleric_nom.pl to do_VN prayer_gen.pl his house_gen.sg
            'Clerics make [recite] the prayers of his house.'

The example quoted in (45*a*) recalls the recurrent structure *cia bad choir do chomrac...* (who should fight...) in *TBC*. The problem encountered was whether the clause should be interpreted as an agentive construction—that is, as a relative variant of P1+do_{VN}(+P2)—or as a purpose clause. The same question arises with (45*a*), and similar examples (see also *CG* 584). Mac Néill interprets the clause in (45*b*) as a purpose clause, rather than as an agentive construction, and translates 'there are clerics for making the prayers of his house' (1923: 305). The difficulty of interpretation on the part of the modern-day analyst (without access to 'native speaker intuition' as regards the texts under investigation) may again lie in the fact that all the instances that present this ambiguity describe situations that can be described by both a purpose clause, or by a P1+do_{VN}(+P2) clause, since they all refer to hypothetical scenarios: in *TBC*, the recurrent *cia bad chóir do chomrac...* always makes reference to bouts of single combat at the planning stage; (45*a*) does not enquire about a particular person preparing food for a particular king, but is a question of general, timeless applicability; similarly, in (45*b*) there are always clerics who recite the prayers in the house: it is their function, and the process they carry out habitually. A purpose clause matches a potential AG with a process: in (45*a*) the right type of person for the purpose of preparing the king's food, in (45*b*) the right type of person to recite the prayers. The ambiguity, in these particular examples, arises out of the general applicability (rather than out of hypothetical-future time reference, as in *cia bad chóir to chomrac...* in *TBC*). As we shall see in the next section, this contrasts strongly with the prevalent use of P1+do_{VN}(+P2), as in (45*b*) (and also of P2+do_{VN}+P1), in contexts where a specific time frame in an annalistic text (i.e. a date) provides a unique temporal reference for the reader, and the basis for an interpretation of the construction as an assertion that the situation described has actually taken place.

---

[62] The construction P2+do_{VN}+P1 is not attested in the law texts analysed here.

3.2.2. *The Annals of Ulster*: post-Patrician text to AD 1131

The Annals of Ulster represents a genre of text which is quite distinct from both fictional narrative and legal material, with its own distinctive style and conventions. Caution is in order when it comes to the dating of linguistic phenomena according to their occurrence in the annals: although at least part of *The Annals of Ulster* can with some confidence be described as 'contemporary' with its dating in the text, the time when a certain linguistic phenomenon finds its way into a written text of a certain type does not necessarily coincide with its development, or spread, in the language as a whole. We do not have, at this stage, sufficient information concerning the linguistic register employed by annalistic writers, and how it relates, for example, to other registers, spoken and written, whether it represents conservative or innovative usage relative to the development of the language. This section concentrates in the main on the Irish entries in *The Annals of Ulster*. There will be occasion to make reference to features of Latin usage in the text, but these references will by necessity be restricted to cases relevant to Irish usage. A full analysis of the use of both Latin and Irish in the annals still awaits.

It has emerged from Section 3.1 that, as far as narrative texts, exemplified by three recensions of *TBC*, are concerned, the principal marker of P1 in $VN+PP_{P1}$ and $P2+do_{VN}+P1$ is the preposition *do*, while *la* and *ó* are of marginal occurrence only. Furthermore, agentive VN constructions tend to occur in syntactically dependent position, rather than, as is common in medieval Welsh, as independent VN clauses. The legal material analysed here neither confirms nor contradicts these observations, since the evidence is too thin on the ground. As we shall observe in this section, the material from *The Annals of Ulster* follows different patterns:[63] there is greater variety with regard to the use of the prepositions *do*, *la*, and *ó*, and the favoured syntactic environment for agentive VN constructions is that of the syntactically independent nominal clause.

Another prominent characteristic of *The Annals of Ulster* is the frequent use of abstract nouns denoting activities, such as *slógad* 'military expedition', *crech* 'plundering expedition, raid', *cath* 'battle, fight', which are not derived from verbal bases, referring to specific processes with identifiable time reference, in other words, in the same function and construction as VNs proper. Such instances have been included under the heading of VN clauses for the present purposes; where a distinction is necessary, the term process noun[64] is used to refer to a non-VN referring to a process, and VN for a verbal noun proper. Baudiš (1913: 382, 398) draws attention to these constructions; he does not, however, analyse them any further in comparison with constructions employing VNs proper. The VN con-

---

[63] Entries from *AU* are throughout quoted according to the uncorrected year dating, for consistency's sake, although entries before 1013 are overall a year behind 'real time'. Examples are quoted by the year of the entry, thus *AU* 913 refers to the entry for the year 913; *AU* 851.3 refers to the third section of the entry for the year 851. The translations given are those of the editor (to be found on the facing page in the edition), unless otherwise indicated.

[64] Cf. Gagnepain's usage of *nom d'action*, and Baudiš's term *Vorgangsnomen*.

structions encountered in *The Annals of Ulster* are those also found in the narrative texts: VN+PP$_{P1}$ (with the variant PN+PP$_{P1}$, where PN is a process noun), VN+GEN$_{P1}$, P2+*do*$_{VN}$+P1, and P1+*do*$_{VN}$(+P2).

3.2.2.1. VN+GEN$_{P1}$

Verbal nouns (i.e. verbal abstracts) accompanied by a genitive P1 phrase are very rare in this text: there are five attestations altogether; four of these have a pro-nominal P1, which is coreferential with a person named in a preceding clause, as in (46*a*); (46*b*) is the only exception to this rule; it is also the earliest example.[65]

> (46) (*a*)   Fir Mhaigi Itha . . . do ghabail taighi for righ Fer Manach ⁊ *a thuitim leó*
> (*AU* 1128.1)
> and his fall_VN with-them
> 'The men of Magh Itha . . . stormed a house against the king of Fir Manach . . . and he fell by them'
>
> (*b*)   *Tetact Dubgennti du Ath Cliath* co ralsat ár mór du Ḟinngallaibh . . .
> (*AU* 851.3)
> come_VN black-heathens to Áth Cliath
> 'The dark heathens came to Áth Cliath, made a great slaughter of the fair-haired foreigners . . .'

Process nouns with a genitive denoting P1 are likewise rare, considering the length of the text: there are instances (twelve altogether) of *brat* 'plundering', *bellum* 'war', *slógad* 'military expedition', *éc* 'death',[66] but, as we shall see below, these nouns are constructed much more frequently with prepositional P1s, or as preposed P1s in P1+*do*$_{VN}$(+P2). The almost complete absence of VNs of motion in construction with a genitive P1 is one aspect where usage in *The Annals of Ulster* differs markedly from that in narrative texts. Where VNs of motion occur, they are generally encountered in P1+*do*$_{VN}$(+P2). Without pre-empting too much of the analysis of this construction in the context of *The Annals of Ulster* (see Section 3.2.2.4), it would appear likely that the latter construction is favoured with VNs of motion in this text, since processes such as 'going' and 'coming' are, in the context of a text that tends to record momentous events, comparatively un-momentous, and that where, for example, the going of a person is recorded, it is more generally the person who is the focus of information of that clause, and therefore a construction is used that underlines this informational status, whereas the momentous process recorded in a following clause is cast in different syntactic construction (compare also the Welsh construction *dyuot + P1 + VN*, which was interpreted as a two-stage device to (re-)present a P1, and a process).

---

[65]   The other four occur between AD 924 and 1128.

[66]   There are also instances of Latin nouns with genitive phrases denoting the EXP; this usage is largely restricted to expressions such as *mors* X '[the] death of X', *quies* X '[the] repose of X'. There is one attestation of *bellum* 'war' with a genitive AG.

3.2.2.2. VN+PP$_{P1}$

Prepositional phrases denoting P1 (always an AG, rather than an EXP) in constructions of the type VN+PP$_{P1}$ occur in *The Annals of Ulster* with VNs (47*a*); with process nouns (47*b*);[67] and with Latin process nouns (47*c*). The distribution of P1 markers is listed in Table 3.15.

(47) (*a*)   *Loscadh Beithre la Feidlimidh*   (*AU* 826)
        burn_VN Beithre with Feidlimid
        'The burning of [Delbna] Beithre by Feidlimid'

    (*b*)   *Sloghadh la Niall co lLaighniu* coro digestar ri foraibh   (*AU* 835.1)
        military expedition with Niall to Laigin
        'Niall led an army to Laigin and he set up a king over the Laigin'

    (*c*)   *Uastatio Midi la Aedh* m. Neill   (*AU* 797)
        devastation Mide_gen.sg with Aed mac Neill
        'The devastation of Mide by Aed mac Neill'

The numerical distribution of P1 markers with VNs (as opposed to both Irish and Latin process nouns) is strikingly different from that found in the three recensions in *TBC*; with process nouns, the difference is even more pronounced: clearly, *la* is a favoured marker for P1, with *do* being used only relatively rarely, and less frequently than *ó*. If we assume that the choice of P1 marker is not in free variation, different characteristics of the constructions encountered in the different texts should be detectable. The determining criteria could lie in the type of process portrayed by the VN, or in the specifics of P1, or diachronic factors might be responsible.

TABLE 3.15. *VN+PP$_{P1}$: marking of P1 in* The Annals of Ulster

P1 marker	VN		IPN		LPN		Total	
	n	%	*n*	%	*n*	%	*n*	%
la	43	*43.4*	188	*98.4*	43	*81.1*	274	*79.9*
ó	37	*37.4*	2	*1.1*	9	*17*	48	*14*
do	19	*19.2*	1	*0.5*	1	*1.9*	21	*6.1*
TOTAL	99	*100*	191	*100*	53	*100*	343	*100*

[67] A fixed expression, which will not further enter into the discussion here, is the following construction: 'Cathc(h)oscradh re nDonnchad … for Aedh nIngor …' (lit.: battle-overthrow before Donnchad on Aed Ingor) (A battle-overthrow was inflicted … by Donnchad on Aed Ingor …) (*AU* 791.5). The *for*-phrase, naming the defeated party, may precede or follow the *re*-phrase (naming the victorious party), or be omitted altogether. The process noun involved is always a noun from the semantic field 'battle, war', e.g. *cath* 'war, battle', *bellum*, *roíniud* 'defeat(ing), routing', *maidm* 'defeat, rout', etc. The expression appears to be a variation on *maidm (catha) re* X *for* Y (lit.: break_VN (battle-gen.sg) before X on Y), 'X defeats Y'.

We find that the three prepositions are not evenly distributed as regards their use with different VNs. *Do* occurs with eleven different VNs, but with only three of them more often than twice (*orgain* 'destruction' is attested five times, and *foirtbe* 'slaying, slaughter' three times). The use of *ó* appears more specialized: it occurs with eight different VNs, most frequently with *orgain*, *loscad* 'burning', and *innrad* 'invading, invasion' (eighteen, eight, and four attestations, respectively). *La*, the most common P1 marker, occurs with eighteen different VNs, and is most frequently combined with *innred* (12 times), *sárugud* 'violating, violation' (5 times), *orgain* (5 times) and *loscad* (4 times). The three most frequent VNs (*innred*, *orgain*, *loscad*) are used with all three P1 markers in VN+PP$_{P1}$ clauses.[68] We may, therefore, conclude that the motivation for the choice of P1 marker does not lie with the VN, or with the VN alone, although the frequency of *orgain* combined with *ó*, and of *innred* with *la*, does look noteworthy.

The construction VN+PP$_{P1}$, involving VNs proper, is used in entries between AD 721 and 1129. *La* and *do* appear as P1 markers for the first time in AD 721 and 733, respectively, the last entries being AD 1127 and 1129, respectively. The use of *ó* is more restricted: the first entry is AD 795, the last one AD 1052. The greatest concentration of VN+PP$_{P1}$ clauses occurs in the entries between AD 809 and 870. In this period, *The Annals of Ulster* shows twenty-four instances of VN+*la*, nine of VN+*do*, and twenty-five of VN+*ó*. Within this period, there is another peak of usage to be observed between AD 820 and 839: here, VN+*la* occurs fifteen times, VN+*do* four times, and VN+*ó* eighteen times.[69]

With Irish process nouns (IPNs), the preposition denoting P1 of the implied process is almost invariably *la*, as shown in Table 3.15. In this group, two recurrent constructions account for a large majority of the attestations: 110 out of 191 (or 57.6 per cent) IPN clauses are instances of *slógad la* (see (47b)); the second most frequent IPN is *crech* 'plundering, raid' (38 examples, or 19.9 per cent) (see (48)).[70]

(48)   *Crech la Flaithbertach* m. Conchobair, la righ nAiligh, *i nDal nAraide* cor inder
        Condire . . .   (*AU* 962.1)
        raid with Flaithbertach into Dál Araidi
        'Flaithbertach son of Conchobor, king of Ailech, made a raid in Dál Araidi
        and plundered Condaire . . .'

[68] The recurrence of a comparatively small number of VNs as such is no more than one would expect in a text that records events considered as important: invasions (*innred*), the destruction (*orgain*) or burning-down (*loscad*) of a settlement, and the violation of sanctuaries or dishonouring of persons of high rank (*sárugud*) are certainly among the more momentous events in the history of a country or region, and would therefore merit listing in the eyes of the chroniclers.

[69] In order to facilitate the 'diachronic' distribution of different construction types, the text has been divided into segments at twenty-year intervals—for example one segment comprising the entries from AD 800 to AD 819. It should not be assumed, however, that an entry listed for example for the year 800 was necessarily written, in the form in which the text now stands, at that time. Diachrony as observable here is as much a matter of the internal organization of the text (i.e. earlier or later in the text) as of real time.

[70] There are a further six instances of the compound *crechsluagad* 'plundering expedition'; the next most common IPN is *ár* 'slaughter'.

The bulk of the attestations of IPN+PP$_{P1}$ occurs in entries after AD 900. Specifically, the periods AD 1000–19 (29 examples), AD 1020–9 (17 examples), 1100–19 (22 examples), and AD 1120–31 (16 examples) show high concentrations of this construction type—for the greater part, instances of *slógad*, *crech*, *crechsluagad la* X. The construction begins to appear regularly after AD 740,[71] about the same time as the use of VNs proper with prepositional P1 markers.

Agentive noun clauses containing Latin process nouns (LPNs) and Irish prepositions, as in (47c), also show a clear preference for *la*. The distribution of expressions is not quite as polarized as with IPNs; of the fourteen different expressions, six occur three times or more with *la*, and one more than three times with *ó*. The most common expressions are *lex* '(promulgation of) law' (9 attestations with *la*), *occisio* 'killing, slaying (6 *la*, 1 *ó*), *uastatio* 'devastation' (5 *la*, 1 *ó*).

The earliest attestations of this subtype of N+PP$_{P1}$ are to be found in entries for AD 454 and 504 (in the hand of the main scribe), and for AD 482 (with *la*-phrase added by H[1]). The greatest proportion of examples occurs between AD 740 and 839 (twenty-eight, four of which contain *ó*, and twenty-four *la*). Even during this period, the highest density of occurrences is only eight for a twenty-year period (AD 780–99). However, we can note that the construction was most commonly used in entries slightly earlier than those that show the highest concentration of Irish VNs in VN+PP$_{P1}$. The last two examples are noted under AD 852 and 903; thus this type gradually fades out of use by the time Irish and Latin are represented in *The Annals of Ulster* at about equal proportions, according to Hughes (1972: 128–9), *c.*830.

One might expect, then, that around this time Latin expressions such as *occisio*, *uastatio*, and so on are replaced by Irish ones (*marbad*, *orcain*). This is only partly the case: although *orcain la* is one of the more common VN constructions, *marbad* 'killing', which would be a rough equivalent of *occisio* and *iugulatio*, is rare in the construction VN+PP$_{P1}$. The turn of phrase that typically contains *marbad* is P2+*do*$_{VN}$+P1 (see below).[72]

The feature common to the three subtypes of VN+PP$_{P1}$ illustrated in (47) is thus that, in all three, the preferred marker of P1 is *la*. The use of *ó* is well established with LPNs as well as Irish VNs, whereas *do* is used with some regularity only with VNs proper.

Since we are dealing here with a bilingual text, the original elements and the final compilation of which were written by authors familiar with both Latin and Irish, and which ultimately goes back to a Latin written tradition, Latin influence on Irish phrasing is a possibility to be considered. The difficulty is that it would be

---

[71] The earliest occurrences, in entries for AD 469 and 470, are clearly non-contemporary.

[72] The comparison between *occisio/iugulatio* and *marbad* is comparatively easy, since the killing of single persons is one type of process that keeps recurring throughout the text. Others, such as the burning-down of settlements (*combustio* vs. *loscad*), or the promulgation or enforcement of laws (*lex* vs. *forus cána*) are overall much less frequent, and thus the potential replacement of one expression by another is difficult to pinpoint.

very problematic, if possible at all, to quantify such influence. One transfer phenomenon that might be expected is the proliferation of the preposition *ó*, which is
semantically closer to Latin *ab* 'from' (the dominant preposition used in agentive
function in Latin) than either *la* or *do*. However, this does not happen, and even in
the variant of vn+pp$_{P1}$ that contains LPNs, and in clauses that are surrounded by
Latin entries, the favoured preposition is *la* rather than *ó*. This does not negate any
influence of Latin on the usage of Irish, but a direct, lexical calquing of Irish
prepositional expressions does not appear to have happened.[73]

Although there are concentrations of the use of one preposition rather than
another with certain VNs or PNs, there are no exclusive patterns. Thus, it does not
appear to be the specific semantic content of any one VN or PN that determines
the selection of P1 markers. It is, however, possible that some more general feature
of the situation described in the VN/PN clause influences the selection.

Part of the semantic make-up of an agentive expression is what shall here be
referred to as the 'number factor': an action such as the burning-down of a house
may be carried out by a single individual, by a group acting together without any
individual being marked as more prominent than any of the others, or by an individual in charge of or directing a group. It is usually the case that the addressee is
able to interpret the particular nuance using both the information provided in the
clause, and knowledge of the world. In a sentence such as *this garden shed was built
by my grandfather*, the grandfather in question was quite likely the person who did
the actual physical work of erecting the garden shed, thus the by-phrase expresses
a sole agent. This is rather less likely in, for example, *the courthouse was built by my
grandfather*; the addressee will interpret the by-phrase as an 'agent in charge': the
person financing the building, or providing the plans, or the person in charge of
the building firm carrying out the building; in short, the person responsible for
and initiating the process described, and, from the speaker's perspective, the most
relevant person involved. In cases such as these, P1 combines characteristics of an
AG proper and an IAG: s/he is both an AG in his/her own right, and the initiator of,
and responsible for, action carried out by others.

Whether a single person named in a P1 phrase is also a sole AG can sometimes be
determined by the content of the process element; to return to Irish examples, we
can note that it would take more than one person to invade a territory (*innred*),
very likely more than one to destroy or plunder a settlement (*orgain, crech*), or to
burn it down (*loscad*). Other processes can conceivably be carried out either by a
sole individual, or by an individual aided by or leading a group; examples are

---

[73] A similar expectation—namely, that the preposition that is overall semantically closest to the
Latin model (i.e. *ab* 'from') would fulfil P1 function—could be held with regard to the Welsh annals
considered in Chapter 2 with specific reference to a Welsh agentive passive. There, we encountered a
subtler type of potential influence, in that it was not prototypical senses of prepositions that appeared
to have been mapped onto one another, but specific subsenses, which resulted in the use of *y gan* and
gan, in accordance with their use as denoting the spatial reference point of origin with verbs of getting,
obtaining, buying, etc.

sárugud 'violation (of a sanctuary), dishonouring (of a person)', *marbad* 'killing' (depending on the numbers killed), and *guin* 'slaying (by wounding)'. The attestations in *The Annals of Ulster* of vn+pp$_{P1}$ (for VNs, IPNs, and LPNs) have been analysed according to whether the P1 phrase describes:

α a sole AG[74]—i.e. a single person acting on his/her own, as in (49a);
β a plural AG—i.e. a group acting together, as in (49b);
γ an individual in charge, acting with the assistance of a group, as in (49c).

The application of this criterion to VNs proper results in the distribution shown in Table 3.16.

(49) (a)   M. na hAidhchi H. Ruairc . . . *a marbad do Diarmait* h Cuinn . . .   (*AU* 1053.1)
           his kill_VN to Diarmait ua Cuinn
           'Mac na hAidhchi ua Ruairc . . . he was killed by Diarmait ua Cuinn . . .'

     (b)   *Orgain Cluana Cremha . . . do feraib Breibne 7 do Śil Cathail*   (*AU* 815.7)
           destroy_VN Cluain Crema to man_dat.pl Bréfne and to Síl Cathail
           'Cluain Crema was plundered . . . by the men of Bréfne and the Síl Cathail'

     (c)   *Indredh Liphi la Concobar*   (*AU* 831.11)
           invade_VN Life with Conchobar
           'The plundering of Life by Conchobar'

TABLE 3.16. *P1 types in* vn+pp$_{P1}$ *in* The Annals of Ulster

P1 type	*la*		*ó*		*do*	
	n	*%*	*n*	*%*	*n*	*%*
α	6	*13.9*	2	*5.4*	2	*10.5*
β	7	*16.3*	31	*83.8*	13	*68.4*
γ	27	*62.8*	4	*10.8*	4	*21.1*
α/γ	3	*7*				
TOTAL	43	*100*	37	*100*	19	*100*

A tendency appears for the preposition *la* to mark a P1 of type γ, whereas both *ó* and *do* most often express plural (i.e. type β) P1s. In some cases, the interpretation is not entirely unproblematical. Thus, a few instances that have here been interpreted as type α could conceivably be of type γ, as in (50a): the text gives no indication whether the 'killing/murdering' was carried out by a single individual or by several persons under the named individual's leadership. As regards (50b), it is more likely that the named person had help in the abduction and gave orders to

---

[74] In principle, each of the subtypes of the AG described here could have its EXP counterpart. However, prepositional P1s that are EXPs rather than AGs do not figure in *AU*.

have his victim blinded (if we read the *la*-phrase as referring to both *tabairt amach* and *dalladh*), rather than acting on his own.

(50) (*a*)   *Orggain Donnchadha* m. Ḟollomain ⁊ *Flainn* m. Mael Ruanaig *la Mael Sechnaill* m. Mael Ruanaidh.   (*AU* 845.7)
destroy_VN Donnchad_gen.sg and Flann_gen.sg with Mael Sechnaill
'Donnchad . . . and Flann . . . were killed by Mael Sechnaill.'

(*b*)   Scanlain H. Dungalain . . . sarugad Duin fair ⁊ *atabairt amach* ⁊ *a dalladh* a Finnabhair *la Niall* m. Duibh Tuinne   (*AU* 1010.6; add. H¹)
his-take_VN out and his blind_VN with Niall
'Scanlán . . . was outraged in Dún [Lethglaisi], abducted and blinded in Finnubair, by Niall son of Dub Tuinne'

A notable feature among the preponderance of type β P1s marked by *ó* is the frequency of the phrase *ó genntib* 'by the heathens', which accounts for twenty-two out of thirty-one instances where *ó* marks a plural P1. In addition, there are five instances of the phrase *ó Gallaib* 'by the foreigners' (both phrases referring to the Norsemen, or Vikings) (see (51*a*) and (51*b*)):

(51) (*a*)   *Orggan Etir o genntibh*   (*AU* 821.3)
destroy_VN Étar from heathen_dat.pl
'Étar was plundered by the heathens'

(*b*)   *Orggain Droma hIung o Gallaibh*   (*AU* 835.12)
destroy_VN Druim Ing from foreigner_dat.pl
'The foreigners plundered Druim Ing'

In addition, *ó*+3pl in one instance refers back to *Gaill* 'foreigners' of a preceding clause, in another example to *genti* 'heathens'.[75] Up to and including the entry in *AU* 896.6, *ó* in vn+PP$_{P1}$ combines only with *genntaib*, and three times with *Gallaib*. *Do* also combines with *genntaib* and *Gallaib*, but less frequently (four times and once, respectively). In one case, a *do*-phrase takes up *ó genntaib* from a preceding clause, in another, *o Gallaibh Atha Cliath*.[76] A possible reason why *genntaib* combines more readily with *ó* than *do* may be that the phrase was modelled on the Latin *a gentibus*, with *ó* being semantically closer to Latin *a* than *do*. However, as we have seen before, such a direct modelling of prepositional phrases does not appear to be a prominent feature of our text.

The construction IPN+PP$_{P1}$ reveals a similar pattern to the one just described; with Latin process nouns, the distribution is not quite as clear-cut (see Tables 3.17*a* and 3.17*b*).[77] Thus the tendency for *la* to be used to mark a type γ P1 is visible with

---

[75]   *AU* 951.7, 921.8.
[76]   *AU* 798.2 and 936.2, respectively.
[77]   The same difficulties of interpretation are encountered as with VNs proper. I have classified instances of *occisio* (as in e.g. 'Occisio Cuinn . . . la Flann m. Congalaigh' (The slaying of Conn . . . by Flann . . .) (*AU* 795.2)) as sole agents, wherever the text gives no indication whether the person named in the P1 phrase acts as a single individual or as a person in charge of a group.

TABLE 3.17. *P1 types with process nouns in* The Annals of Ulster

(*a*) IPN+PP$_{P1}$

P1 type	la		slógad la		crech la		ó		do	
	n	%	*n*	%	*n*	%	*n*	%	*n*	%
α	2	1.1								
β	21	11.2	[3	1.6]	[8	4.3]	2	100	1	100
γ	165	87.8	[107	56.9]	[30	15.6]				
TOTAL	188	100					2	100	1	100

(*b*) VN+PP$_{P1}$

P1 type	la		ó		do	
	n	%	*n*	%	*n*	%
α	8	18.6	4	44.4		
β	7	16.3	5	55.6		
γ	27	62.8			1	100
α/γ	1	2.3				
TOTAL	43	100	9	100	1	100

all subtypes of VN+PP$_{P1}$, and it is also apparent throughout the text (wherever there are enough examples in any one time-interval to warrant a comparison). The predominant use of *ó* with VNs proper, with a type β P1 is heavily biased by the frequency of the phrase *ó genntaib*/*ó Gallaib*. This may, on the one hand, suggest a Latin model; on the other hand, it may mean no more than that, frequently, Viking raids were carried out by groups whose leaders were either not known, or irrelevant as far as the writer was concerned. The pattern of distribution is consistent as a tendency, but as a tendency only; the 'number factor' is not an absolute condition for the selection of a P1 marker in VN+PP$_{P1}$ clauses.

3.2.2.3. P2+do_{VN}+P1

This is the most common type of agentive VN clause in *The Annals of Ulster*, with 333 instances altogether.[78] *La, do,* and *ó* occur regularly as P1 markers; in addition, there is one instance where *oc* 'at' appears to fulfil agentive function:

---

[78] As compared to 343 attestations of VN/IPN/LPN+PP$_{P1}$, and 164 of P1+do_{VN}(+P2).

(52)   Concobur m. Flannacan ... do orcain fri daigidh i Cluain Fota; m̃. Fini do
         sarughadh isin eclais ⁊ minna Finnia do sarugad oco ⁊ do loscadh.   (AU 891.2)
         community? Finnia to violate_VN ... and holy-objects Finnia to violate_VN
         at-him and to burn_VN
         'Conchobor ... was destroyed by fire in Cluain Fhata. The community (?) of
         Finnia was outraged in the church and Finnia's halidoms were profaned by
         him and burned.'

There are no other instances of oc 'at' marking a P1 in *The Annals of Ulster*.[79] The
agentive function of oc appears otherwise to be restricted to late Middle or early
Modern Irish texts (see *DIL* s.v. oc). It is, therefore, tempting to consider the phrase
'⁊ minna Finnia do saruguad oco ⁊ do loscadh' as a later addition. It is in the hand
of the main scribe (H) of manuscript H.1.8; this was, however, written in the late
fifteenth century. But this cannot be supported by any evidence other than the
isolated use of an unusual P1 marker, which, moreover, has considerable semantic
affinity with *la*.

The earliest example of $P2+do_{VN}+P1$ is contained in the entry for AD 553. From
AD 798 onwards, the construction occurs with some regularity. The frequency of
occurrence is markedly higher in the later sections of the text: from AD 1000 onwards, only one twenty-year interval contains less than thirty instances,[80] whereas
before AD 1000 there are only two twenty-year intervals containing twenty attestations or more.[81] Both *la* and *do* occur throughout the text, from the entry for AD 789
onwards. The usage of *ó* is more restricted diachronically: the earliest attestation
is in the entry for AD 837, the latest one AD 1094. The higher concentration of
$P2+do_{VN}+P1$ after AD 1000 affects all three prepositions. The distribution of P1
markers and AG types[82] is listed in Table 3.18. The correlations between P1 types and

TABLE 3.18. *P1 types in* $P2+do_{VN}+P1$ *in* The Annals of Ulster

P1 type	la		ó		do	
	n	%	n	%	n	%
α	46	41.1	3	8.6	37	19.9
[α, marbad]	[43	38.4]	[3	8.9]	[33	17.7]
β	22	19.6	28	80	130	69.9
γ	36	32.1	1	2.9	16	8.6
α/γ	8	7.1	3	8.6	3	3
TOTAL	112	100	35	100	186	100

[79] As discussed in Section 3.3, oc does, however, occur in agentive function with the passive in *TBC
LL* and *III*.
[80] AD 1080–99: 29 examples.
[81] AD 940–59: 26 attestations, and AD 980–99: 20 attestations.
[82] As with VN+PP$_{P1}$, P1 in $P2+do_{VN}+P1$ always marks an AG, rather than an EXP, in this text.

prepositions is slightly different here from what emerged with vn+pp$_{P1}$: although *la* is again the most commonly used preposition with type γ, and shows the highest proportion of use with type γ as compared to the other two prepositions (at 32.1 per cent, as opposed to 2.9 per cent and 8.6 per cent), in absolute terms, *la* is used more frequently to mark P1s of type α—i.e. sole AGs. Both *ó* and *do* again most often mark P1s of type β.

As specified in Table 3.18, the largest proportion of what has here been interpreted as a preposition denoting a sole AG involves the VN *marbad*. All three markers can occur in close proximity to each other, as shown in (53), which shows *do*, *la*, and *ó* in the entries for a single year, AD 1007.

(53) (*a*)   *Mael Ruanaidh* m. Ardghair *do marbad o Matudhan* m. Domnaill. (*AU* 1007.1)
        Mael Ruanaid to kill_VN from Matudán
        'Mael Ruanaid . . . was killed by Matudán son of Domnall.'

    (*b*)   *Motadhan* m. Domnaill, ri Ulad, *do marbad don* d[*T*]*urc* i n-ecluis Brigte for lar Duin da Lethglas.   (*AU* 1007.4)
        Matudán to kill_VN to-the boar
        'Matudán was killed by the "Torc" in Brigit's church in the middle of Dún dá Lethglas.'

    (*c*)   *Cu Connacht* m. Dunadaigh, toisech Sil nAnmchada *do marbad la Brian* per dolum {H¹: alias la Murchad m. Bria<in ⁊> H. Dungalaig . . .}
        (*AU* 1007.5)
        Cú Chonnacht, to kill_VN with Brian
        'Cú Chonnacht, chief of Síl Anmchada was treacherously killed by Brian . . .'

    (*d*)   *In Torc*, rí Ulad, *do marbad do Muiredach* m. Motodhan i ndighail a athar tri nert Dé ⁊ Patraicc.   (*AU* 1007.8)
        the boar to kill_VN to Muiredach
        'The "Torc", king of Ulaid, was killed through the power of God and Patrick by Muiredach son of Matudán in revenge for his father.'

The revenge killing, apparently sanctioned by God and Patrick, in (53*d*) would suggest that we are dealing here with a sole AG—that is, Muiredach personally killing the 'Torc'. The reason for this particular killing is given in (53*b*); may we again assume that the action was carried out by a sole AG—that is, by the 'Torc'? This action in turn is a reaction to yet another killing, presented in (53*a*); here we have a different P1 marker, *ó*. Are we to conclude that the relation between P1, P2, and the process is of a different nature? In (53*c*) the addition in hand H¹ suggests that maybe Brian acted with assistance, or that there is doubt as to who actually carried out the deed, and the P1 marker is different again, this time *la*. However, this cannot be inferred from the original entry alone.

Examples where the text does not give any indication that the named person in the P1 phrase acted in charge of a group have been interpreted here as type α—that is, sole AGs. The difficulty of interpretation and possible ambiguity is the same as

the one already encountered with *iugulatio, occisio* 'killing' in the construction
LPN+PP$_{P1}$, and it is not entirely clear whether we are simply dealing here with a
problem of decoding. As we have seen, VNs or PNs describing processes that involve typically more than one person as agents, even if only one person is named,
most often combine with *la* when the person named is the person in charge (in the
construction VN+PP$_{P1}$ and its variants). It would, therefore, be tempting to assume
that the attribute 'AG in charge' is the decisive criterion for the selection of *la* (as
opposed to, for example, *do*) with the VN *marbad*, even where there are no other
explicit indications to this effect in the text. However, tempting though it may be,
the conclusion that any P1 phrase marked by *la* and naming one person, in combination with *marbad*, represents a type γ AG appears somewhat premature. On the
other hand, the possibility that the figures in Table 3.18, presenting a high proportion of sole AGs marked by *la*, are the result of interpretive caution cannot be
ignored, either.

What can be observed, though, is that the marking of what is clearly a type γ P1
by means of *do* is comparatively rare (and even rarer with *ó*), and in particular in
combination with *marbad*. But to conclude from this that, therefore, *la* marks an
'AG in charge' as the default option would be, though convenient and neat, a conclusion *e silentio*. Although we have seen above that, with both *do* and *ó*, type γ
P1s are rare in the construction VN+PP$_{P1}$, the type is attested. One might speculate
that we might be dealing with a question of diachronic development, whereby the
agentive function of *do* and *ó* gradually widened to cover all three AG types. This,
however, cannot be convincingly demonstrated by the evidence of our text; AGs of
type γ marked by *do* and *ó* appear with a noticeable frequency around the same
time, which also shows a marked increase in the number of type α and type β AGs.
There is, conversely, theoretically the possibility that the agentive function of *la* has
experienced, over time, a broadening of its definition (or a weakening of its speci-
ficity); if we take the distribution emerging from VN+PP$_{P1}$ as an indication that the
prototypical P1 marked by *la* is an AG in charge, such a widening of definition
would lead to a more frequent use of the same marker with type α and type β AGs.
The problem again is that this hypothesis cannot be convincingly proved using the
data at our disposal. With the construction P2+*do*$_{VN}$+P1, the subcategory 'sole
AG'—that is, type α—is clearly dominated by one recurring phrase (*marbad la*);[83]
therefore, any patterns emerging will be skewed by any difficulties of interpretation
arising from this one recurring phrase. Taking the evidence of VN/IPN/LPN+PP$_{P1}$
and P2+*do*$_{VN}$+P1 together, we have to bear in mind that the construction types are
not evenly distributed over time: the majority of examples of VN+PP$_{P1}$ occurs in
entries dated between AD 809 and AD 870, the majority of Latin process nouns
in the same construction somewhat earlier (AD 740 to 839), and the mass of Irish

---

[83] Also, in the construction VN+PP$_{P1}$ by the phrases *occisio la, iugulatio la*, to a lesser extent; the
difficulties have been dealt with above and should not be ignored when looking at the diachronic
distribution.

process nouns, as well as of $P2+do_{VN}+P1$, after AD 1000. To an extent, this means that, as far as entries after AD 970 are concerned (which is when the VN *marbad* begins to account for the majority of examples of $P2+do_{VN}+P1$), one is trading one common phrase against another: *slógad/crech la* X against Y *do marbad la* X; and the former one has a heavier influence on the count, simply because it occurs more frequently. Thus it is not surprising that across constructions, from AD 740 onwards (earlier entries do not provide enough examples for comparison), *la* is to be found most commonly with type γ AGs; at no period is the number of occurrences higher for type α than for type γ.[84]

One might argue that, once phrases such as *slógad la*, *crech la*, and so on become fixed, they are used as units, without a speaker making an effort of composition, or combination of the elements concerned, and therefore without renewed matching up of the semantic make-up of the component elements—in this case, a process noun and a preposition. This means that such phrases may survive intact even though one or more of their constituent elements might undergo semantic shifts or modifications in other environments.[85] However fixed, well-established expressions do not arise out of thin air. We may assume that the combination of linguistic elements, such as a process noun and a preposition, happens on the basis of optimal compatibility of their semantic make-up. In this particular case, this means that phrases such as *slógad la*, *crech la*, considering the fact that these process nouns are not used with any other prepositions denoting a principal AG,[86] provide a strong hint that the meaning 'AG in charge' is one facet that distinguishes the agentive function of *la* from that of other prepositions—at a time when the phrase is coined and becomes established.

The tendency for *do* and *ó* to combine with type β AGs noted for $VN+PP_{P1}$ is also visible for $P2+do_{VN}+P1$, though it is less pronounced (see again Table 3.18). The preposition *ó* is much less specialized with regard to the type of P1 in this construction. Whereas with $VN+PP_{P1}$ the phrases *ó genntaib/ó Gallaib* account for the majority of attestations of this syntactic type, there are only eight instances of *ó genntaib/Gallaib* to be found with $P2+do_{VN}+P1$, as compared to twenty-five attestations containing *do*. This could be interpreted as pointing towards a tendency for Irish usage to become more independent from the Latin of the earlier part of the text, if we assume that the *ó genntaib* in $VN+PP_{P1}$ is modelled on a Latin *a gentibus*, since most instances of *do genntaib/Gallaib* occur later than the bulk of the type $VN+ó$ *genntaib/Gallaib*.

[84] The distribution is as follows (740 etc. marks the beginning of a twenty-year interval), AD (α/γ): 740 (0/7); 760 (0/5); 780 (4/5); 800 (0/11); 820 (1/20); 840 (2/7); 860 (1/5); 880 (0/2); 900 (0/13); 920 (1/6); 940 (1/11); 960 (3/9); 980 (2/9); 1000 (10/13); 1020 (5/21); 1040 (7/10); 1060 (9/9); 1080 (5/14); 1100 (2/24); 1120 (0/19).

[85] In terms of Langacker's approach (e.g. 1987; see also the discussion in Fife 1990: 36 ff.), phrases such as *slógad la*, *crech la*, may very well have acquired 'unit status' for medieval Irish annalists.

[86] This is true not only for *AU*, but also for the *Annals of Inisfallen* (Mac Airt 1944).

3.2.2.4. P1+do_{VN}(+P2)

The earliest attestation of P1+do_{VN}(+P2) in *The Annals of Ulster* occurs in the entry
for AD 817. The majority of instances are to be found in entries after AD 1000: from
then onwards, no single twenty-year period contains less than twelve examples of
the construction; the highest density being twenty-four instances (AD 1020–39).[87]
The intransitive variant of the construction, illustrated in (54*a*), is considerably
more frequent than the transitive variant (see (54*b*))—the ratio being 127 versus 37
examples, or 77.4 per cent versus 22.6 per cent.

(54) (*a*)   *Ceile*, commarba Comgaill . . . *do dul* i n-ailithri.   (*AU* 928.7)
    Céile to go_VN
    'Céile, successor of Comgall . . . went on pilgrimage.'

(*b*)   *Gothfrith* h. Imhair co nGallaib Atha Cliath *do thoghail Dercca Ferna*
    (*AU* 930.1)
    Gothfrith to destroy_VN Derc Ferna
    'Gothfrith, grandson of Ímar, with the foreigners of Áth Cliath, razed Derc
    Ferna'

Transitive P1+do_{VN}(+P2) clauses are not only overall less frequent, but also comparatively rarer in the later parts in the text; roughly half occur in entries up to AD 1013
(19 examples), as compared to slightly less than a third (39 examples) of the intransitive clauses. This correlates with the fact that, from around the same entry
dates onwards (i.e. around AD 1000), we encounter a growing number of preposed
EXPs, as opposed to AGs: seventy-eight in total[88] (47.6 per cent of the total of 164 attestations of P1+do_{VN}(+P2)), virtually all co-occurring with intransitive VNs/PNs.[89]
Two recurring VNs/PNs with their variants, *éc* and *écaib*[90] 'death', and *(com)tuitim*
'falling (in combat or battle) (at each other's hands)', account for almost the total
number of P1+do_{VN}(+P2) clauses containing EXPs as P1; seventy-five altogether; see
(55), in which the earliest attestations of these expressions are quoted:

(55) (*a*)   *Mael Sechlainn* m. Mael Ruanaidh, ridomna Ailigh, *do éc* do fesaigi
    (*AU* 997.2)
    Mael Sechlainn to death
    'Mael Sechlainn . . . died of a *fesaigi*'

---

[87] Compare to this the highest concentration before AD 1000, nine examples within a twenty-year
interval (AD 900–19).

[88] All but five of these occur in entries dated after AD 1000.

[89] The exception is 'Mael Achidh . . . do dul martrai la Delmnai' (lit.: Mael Achidh to go_VN martyr-
dom_gen.sg with Delbna) (Mael Achidh . . . suffered a violent death at the hands of the Delbna) (*AU*
896.8). But note that this example does not contain a prototypical transitive action-VN, but rather a VN
of motion with the endpoint of the motion expressed in transitive construction.

[90] The use of a dative plural in this construction is curious. There does not appear to be any identifiable difference in meaning. *DIL* (s.v. *éc*) gives examples of a construction *téit do écaib* 'dies' (lit.: goes
to deaths), besides *téit éc* and *téit do éc*, but without further comment as to a semantic distinction. It
might be possible to interpret the use of *écaib* (and indeed of the singular *éc*) in P1+do_{VN}(+P2) as an
elliptical version of this phrase—i.e. of X *do dul/thecht to écaib*; however, this does not elucidate further
the use of the dative plural.

(b)   *Mathgamain* m. Conaing m. Duinn Cuan, ridomna Mumain, *do ecaibh*.
       (*AU* 1019.6)
       Mathgamain to death_dat.pl
       'Mathgamain . . . heir designate of Mumu, died.'

(c)   *Alene*, rí Mugdorn Magen ⁊ Mugdorn Bregh, 7 *Indergi* m. Mochain *do toitim* a
       llurg Congalaigh i Connachtu.   (*AU* 955.2)
       Aléne and Innéirge to fall_VN
       'Aléne, king of Mugdorna Maigen and Mugdorna of Brega, and Innéirge, son
       of Mochán, fell on Congalach's march into Connacht.'

Intransitive P1+*do*$_{\text{VN}}$(+P2) clauses with AGS as P1 contain VNs of motion, such as
techt, dul 'going', *tiachtu, tuidecht* 'coming'. These occur throughout the text. However, EXP constructions become more frequent in the later part, as we have seen.
This could point to a shift in 'reporting policy' on the part of the annalists, in that
more deaths of prominent personages are now reported from the perspective of
the victim, as it were. We further find that, after AD 1020, the variety of transitive
expressions is more restricted than before; now, only five transitive VNs occur, and
only one of those more often than once.[91] Before AD 1020, P1+*do*$_{\text{VN}}$(+P2) occurs
with nine transitive VNs, four of which occur twice or more.[92]

Taking into consideration the large number of clauses containing *éc*(*aib*) and
(*com*)*tuitim*, we can note a tendency towards a growing lexical specialization of the
construction P1+*do*$_{\text{VN}}$(+P2) in *The Annals of Ulster* over time. A similar trend has
already emerged from the distribution of VNs and with P2+*do*$_{\text{VN}}$+P1 (for the use of
marbad), and IPNs in VN/PN+PP$_{\text{P1}}$ (*slógad/crech la*). What we might be observing
here is the development of a specialized annalistic register, or rather phraseology,
in which certain types of events are expressed with increasing consistency by
specific, fixed expressions. The difference in onset time for different constructions
could have several reasons, and the following scenario offers one possible explanation.

The phrase *slógad la* X 'a military expedition by *X*' occurs with considerable
consistency from the eighth century onwards, a century before Irish becomes as
prominent as Latin in our text. On the other hand, there is no concise Latin
nominal expression in *The Annals of Ulster* that could be roughly equated with
slógad la[93] (compare, in contrast, the pairs *combustio* versus *loscad* 'burning',
occisio/iugulatio versus *marbad* '(violent) killing'). Though it could be argued that
'military expeditions' or 'hostings' were not among the events commonly noted
down before the middle of the eighth century (which is true, although battles/wars
(*bella*), sieges (*obsessiones*), and the like were), one should have expected an annalist around the middle of the eighth century to choose a Latin phrase, if a suitably

---

[91] *Gabáil* 'taking', in the sense of taking over an office, or of storming a fortification (14 ex.).
[92] *Innred* 'invading', *gabáil* 'taking', *dergiu* 'leaving, abandoning', *orcain* 'destroying'.
[93] There is one instance only of *periculum*, with a genitive expressing the AG in charge: 'Primum
periculum Uloth in Eufonia' (The first expedition of the Ulaid to Man (?)) (*AU* 577.5). This would be
roughly equivalent to a *slógad Ulad*.

concise one had come to mind (unless we assume, of course, that all notices of the type *slógad la* X are later additions, which seems unlikely).[94]

The expressions Y *do marbad la/do/ó* X, and X *do éc(aib)* do not appear regularly until around the middle and the end of the tenth century, respectively. The reasons for this may be, first, that there were concise Latin nominal expressions to portray both situations (*occisio/iugulatio* Y, and *mors/quies* X), and, secondly, that the syntactic structure of the Irish phrases is further removed from the Latin of the earlier text, which could potentially have been a deterrent against their usage in a Latin-based genre. That *do*+VN, with or without a P1 phrase, was in use during the Old Irish period has been demonstrated, from texts other than *The Annals of Ulster*, by Fraser (1912a) and Gagnepain (1963: part 1). However, it appears possible that a phrase of the type Y *do marbad do/la/ó* X would become part of an accepted annalistic register only after it was part of common usage,[95] and indeed after the Latin expressions conventionally employed in the earlier part of the annals would have seemed out of date with contemporary usage.

This leads us on to the question why different syntactic structures are chosen to portray different types of situations. Describing a situation in which person *Y* is killed by person *X* as Y *do marbad do* X, rather than *marbad* Y *do* X, or X *do marbad* Y, is a matter of perspective, or focus. We have already noted above that the constructions P2+do_{VN}+P1 and P1+do_{VN}(+P2) appear to be used in contexts where focus on P2 and P1, respectively, makes sense in the context. In those Irish expressions describing 'the killing of person(s) *Y* by person *X*' and 'the dying/death of person(s) *Y*' that become dominant usage in *The Annals of Ulster*, the victim is put into focus by being placed at the beginning of the clause,[96] and by being encoded as a nominative rather than oblique noun phrase.

It appears that focus is not assigned on the basis of informational salience in the context of the individual annal entry, but that a more general principle, a type of animacy hierarchy, is operative. Such a mechanism would favour the focusing of an animate entity (other than P1) over an inanimate one. In more concrete terms, it seems that, in Irish annalistic usage as manifested in *The Annals of Ulster*, a tendency developed towards placing an animate, or, more specifically, an individualized human, P2 and EXP-P1 at the beginning of the clause[97]—see Table 3.19

[94] There are, on the other hand, Latin constructions in *AU* that appear to follow an Irish pattern, such as 'Obsesio Aberte *apud* Selbachum' (the siege of Aberte by Selbach) (*AU* 712.5), where the use of *apud* (rather than the expected *ab*) is reminiscent of an Irish *la*. There are altogether eleven examples of *apud* 'with, among' being used to denote P1, six of which, of the type illustrated here, combine with a noun, and five with a passive verb (for further detail, see Section 3.4.2).

[95] And note here Gagnepain's claim that the construction P2+do_{VN}+P1 was a conflation of P1+do_{VN}(+P2) and P2+do_{VN}, and gained currency later than either of the latter constructions.

[96] Although the question has not been researched here in detail, it appears, on an impressionistic level, that focus by means of word order also plays a role in the Latin usage of *AU*. But rather than a variation between nominal expressions, we find a choice between nominal and finite verbal phrases: *iugulatio* X, *mors* X thus contrast with X *iugulatus est/iugulatur*, X *moritur*, etc.

[97] As far as its relation with the process is concerned, an EXP corresponds to an animate P2—i.e. the EXP is the entity primarily affected by a process, with the difference that no AG is involved in the process.

for a listing of the different construction types and the proportion of human P2s.[98]

The high count of animate P2s with $p2+do_{VN}+p1$ is linked with the frequency of the VN *marbad*, which accounts for 209 examples. Among the five most common VNs in this clause type, three demand an animate P2.[99] The fact that any of these can occur with other VN constructions points to a deliberate choice of this clause type where an animate P2 is involved in the situation to be portrayed. Both $p1+do_{VN}(+p2)$ and $VN+PP_{P1}$ are favoured when P2 is [−human].[100] In other words, we may deduce that from around the middle of the tenth century (from which time[101] onwards, as has been pointed out, the type Y *do marbad la/do/ó* X occurs regularly), annalists involved in what later became *The Annals of Ulster*, when reporting a situation that affected a single individual, or individuals (generally adversely, as, for example, the killing, wounding, blinding of the person(s) in question), chose a syntactic construction that gave the affected person(s) prominence over the process and P1.

TABLE 3.19. *[human] P2s in agentive VN clauses in* The Annals of Ulster

P1 type	$p2+do_{VN}+p1$		$p1+do_{VN}+p2$		$VN+PP_{P1}$	
	n	%	*n*	%	*n*	%
[+human]	264	79	4	10.8	25	26.6
[−human]	69	21	33	89.2	69	73.4
TOTAL	333	100	37	100	94	100

Note: The transitive variants of $p1+do_{VN}(+p2)$ and $VN+PP_{P1}$ are taken as 100%, rather than the total number of attestations.

3.2.2.5. AGENTIVE VN CONSTRUCTIONS, INFORMATION, AND TEXTUAL STRUCTURING IN *THE ANNALS OF ULSTER*

Baudiš (1913: 382, 410) comments briefly on the use of syntactically independent constructions as statements introducing paragraphs in *The Annals of Ulster*. He views the syntactically independent VN clause as 'Existentialsatz' (existential sen-

---

[98] $VN+PP_{P1}$ in Table 3.19 involves only VNs proper. The tendency towards inanimate P2s is not apparent with LPNs, since three of the more common 'transitive' expressions demand an animate P2 (*iugulatio*, 11 ex.; *occisio*, 7 ex.; *strages* 'slaughter', 3 ex.). As regards IPNs, there are too few 'transitive' examples to allow for a comparison.

[99] Apart from *marbad* 'killing', these are *dallad* 'blinding' (17 ex.), and *guin* 'killing (by wounding)' (10 ex.), *orgain* 'destroying' (26 ex.), and *loscad* 'burning' (13 ex.).

[100] The highest concentration of examples of the latter construction, and the strongest tendency to use it where P2 is inanimate, occurs between AD 800 and 840: 34 versus 7 examples.

[101] In 'intra-textual', if not necessarily 'real', time.

tence), which can serve to introduce the 'Thema' (theme). He does not explicitly define the term 'Thema', but evidently views it as 'what the statement or discourse is about'.[102] Baudiš remarks that a VN clause at the beginning of an entry or a paragraph introduces 'ein neues Faktum', and further, that 'das, was man zu dem Faktum als Bemerkung hinzufügen will, oder was nur das Faktum weiter erklären oder schildern soll, wird im Verbalsatz weiter hinzugefügt' (A new fact, and that which is added to the fact, or which is intended to further explain or describe the fact, is added by means of a [finite] verbal sentence.)[103]

What Baudiš describes as introducing 'a new fact', which is then elaborated upon in the following discourse, corresponds to what Dik, following Hannay (1985: 108 ff.), calls the 'presentative function' of an argument. Dik's discussion of the phenomenon (1989: 178 ff.) is centred around locative and existential constructions, and the role of pragmatic functions therein. According to Hannay (1985: 171), a term has 'presentative function' if it 'refers to an entity which the speaker by means of the associated predication wishes to explicitly introduce into the world of discourse' (Dik uses the technical term New Topic to refer to an argument with 'presentative function').

Baudiš does not analyse the selection of contruction types in the position he defines as 'themaartig'[104] (theme-like). In the context of Baudiš's analysis, the relevant point is the fact that, at the beginning of many entries in *The Annals of Ulster*, we find VN constructions more often than finite clauses, since the main argument of his paper is that Irish has a marked preference for nominal over verbal expressions.[105] His statement that the function of these clauses is to introduce the 'theme' of the entry does not take into consideration that the three construction types we are dealing with present their information in quite different ways, since the participants and the process involved in the situation portrayed are ordered differently. The following discussion is intended to take Baudiš's general observation that VN

[102] Cf. e.g. the definition of *topic* in Fife (1988: 35): 'it is generally taken that topics either *set the frame of discourse for the sentence or specify "what the sentence is about"*'. In analogy, a discourse topic can be seen to set the frame for the discourse.

[103] Note that Baudiš's use of the term *Faktum* (and its translation as 'fact') does not stand in contrast with the term *process* as it is used here.

[104] Neither does Gagnepain, who merely states that, in the annals, both the *do*+VN (his 'type 3') and the type VN+PP$_{P1}$ occur, and that the former is more frequent (1963: 229).

[105] The use of *do*+VN as independent noun clause and as apposition (with evidence for the former gathered mainly from *AU*, for the latter from Wb, Sg, and Ml) is Baudiš's main argument against Fraser's attempt to link *do*+VN with the historical infinitive of Latin (see Fraser 1912*a*). This latter construction occurs, according to Baudiš (1913: 412), chiefly in dynamic narrative (see also the discussion in Chapter 2 on the Welsh independent VN). Gagnepain (1963: 229) describes the use of VN clauses in the annals as 'cette formulation propre aux Annales . . . qui consiste à réduire le texte, correspondant à chaque date à ce qu'on pourrait appeler son minimum catégoriel' (that formulation proper to the Annals . . . which consists of reducing the text, corresponding to each date, to what one might call its categorical minimum). He concludes from Baudiš's presentation of the data (which does not include details concerning the distribution of P1 markers) that 'en ce qui concerne la marque de l'agent, *ó* et *la* se trouvaient aussi souvent que *do*' (as regards the marking of the agent, *ó* and *la* were encountered as often as *do*) (1963: 230). This, as we have seen from the discussion in this section, is somewhat oversimplified.

clauses present the 'theme' of the following discourse further by looking in more detail at the presentation of information in the three types of agentive VN clauses, in order to determine whether any specific patterns emerge in how their information is resumed in the following discourse.

At this stage, the term 'following discourse' needs to be put into its context. By no means all VN clauses with overt P1 are integrated into a further context (except, of course, the context of the text as a whole). As regards the type $VN+PP_{P1}$, we find that 40 of 99 instances (or 41 per cent) containing VNs proper are isolated clauses —that is, the entry or section of the entry for the year contains only the VN clause, and if the year entry contains further sections, they are not linked in subject matter. For LPNs in the same construction, the proportion is even higher, 37 out of 53 examples (69.8 per cent). The same type containing IPNs shows a much lower ratio of isolated instances, 25 of 192 attestations or 13.1 per cent.

In part, the fact that many entries are isolated instances is a function of the textual genre, a genre in which many events are simply listed as bare-bones entries, without any further elaboration. This is more prominent in the earlier (by entry dates) parts of the text, and there is a gradual development of the annals from consisting largely of isolated statements that are not further commented on to the, albeit at times very short, narratives we find in the entries of the later tenth, eleventh, and twelfth centuries. This development is partly reflected in the ratio of VN constructions that stand alone. As above, a higher proportion of $LPN+PP_{P1}$ clauses stands alone than of $IPN+PP_{P1}$, which correlates with the fact that the former type is chiefly used and 'peaks' in an earlier section of *The Annals of Ulster*. But, on the other hand, both $P2+do_{VN}+P1$ and $P1+do_{VN}(+P2)$ show a high proportion of isolated clauses, 257 (77 per cent) and 91 (55 per cent) respectively, and, as we have seen above, the highest concentration of either type is to be found in entries dated later than the second half of the tenth century.

A large proportion of VN clauses integrated into a further context within an entry does indeed occur in section-initial or paragraph-initial position, and the following discussion concentrates on these examples—that is, section-initial agentive VN clauses. With $VN+PP_{P1}$ containing VNs proper, the ratio is 39.4 per cent, or 39 out of 99 attestations altogether. P1 is resumed in the following clause (finite or VN) in around a third of these. P1 is coreferential most commonly with the overt or implied P1 of the following clause (for examples, see the discussion of the type $IPN+PP_{P1}$); but no single category shows a majority of preference.[106] Of the 191 instances of $IPN+PP_{P1}$, 144 (75.4 per cent) occur in section-initial position. Here, a clearer tendency of resumption of P1 emerges, in that an overall majority of section-initial $IPN+PP_{P1}$ show resumption of their P1 as overt P1 in the second

---

[106] Coreferentiality between P1 of the section initial $VN+PP_{P1}$ is found in twelve out of thirty-nine clauses, or 30.8%. Overt P1s account for eight of these (3 subject P1s, 5 P1s in VN constructions), or 20.5%. In addition, section-initial P1 is coreferential with four implied P1s in the following clause. The resumption of P2 in the second clause occurs six times; no pattern or tendency emerges. The resumption of either P1 or P2 at a later stage in the entry (i.e in the third or fourth clauses) is negligible.

clause, and of those a majority are resumed as subject P1.[107] The examples in (56) illustrate the resumption of P1 by a subject P1 (*a*), by a prepositional P1 of a passive clause (*b*), and by an implied coreferential P1 (*c*).[108]

(56) (*a*)   *Slogad la Flaithbertach* m. Muirchertaich, la righ nAiligh, i Cinel Conaill *co roacht* Magh Cetne co tuc boghabhail moir ⁊ co tainic imslan. *Slogad la Flaithbertach* doridhisi i Ceinel Conaill *co roact* Druim Cliabh ⁊ Tracht nEothaili coro marbsat m. Gilla Patraicc m. Fergaile . . . *co tucsat* maidm for Mail Ruanaidh H. Mael Doraidh, acht ni fargbadh nech ann. *Slogad* caleic tara n-eisi *la Mael Sechlainn* i Tir nEogain co Magh da Ghabhul *coro loiscset* a crecha Telaigh nOóc co ruc gabhail. *Slogad la Flaitbertach* bes co rici Aird Ulad *coro ort* in Aird ⁊ co tuc gabhala is moamh tuc ri riam eter brait ⁊ innile, ce nach n-arimter.
(*AU* 1012.2)
1. hosting with Flaithbertach; so-that reach_3sg.pret; 2. hosting with Flaithbertach; so-that reach_pret.3sg; so-that give_pret.3pl; 3. hosting with Mael Sechnaill; so-that-PRT burn_pret.3pl; 4. hosting with **Flaithbertach**; so-that-PRT destroy_pret.3sg
'Flaithbertach . . . led an army into Cenél Conaill and came as far as Mag Cétne, took a great spoil of cows and returned safe. Flaithbertach again led an army into Cenél Conaill as far as Cruim Cliab and Trácht Eóthaile, and they slew the son of Gilla Pátraic . . . and inflicted a defeat on Mael Ruanaid . . . but no one was lost there. Mael Sechnaill meanwhile in their absence led an army into Tír Eógain to Mag Da Gabul, and their raiding parties burned Tulach Óc and took spoil. Flaithbertach also led an army into Ard Ulad, plundered the Ard, and took the greatest spoils, both in captives and cattle, that a king ever took, though they are not counted.'

(*b*)   *Slogadh la Flann* m. Mail Sechlainn co firu Muman *cor innredh leis* o Gabhran co lLuimnech.   (*AU* 906.3)
hosting with Flann; so-that-PRT invade_pass.pret.sg with-him
'An expedition by Flann against the people of Mumu, and he harried from Gabrán to Luimnech.'

(*c*)   *Aenach Carmain la Donnchad* mc. Gilla Patraicc *iar ngabail* righi Laigen.
(*AU* 1033.4)
fair Carman_gen.sg with Donnchad; after take_VN
'The fair of Carman was held by Donnchad . . . after he had taken the kingship of Laigen.'

---

[107]   The figures are as follows: P1 is resumed as subject P1 in ninety-one (63.2%), and as P1 in a VN clause in five (3.5%) cases. In addition, there is coreferentiality between P1 and an implied P1 in the second clause in five (3.5%) clauses.

[108]   One might dispute whether it really makes sense to distinguish a coreferential subject P1 that is only expressed by a verb ending, but not individualized overtly from an implied P1 in a VN construction. The identification of the third person singular with a given character is due to the reader's interpretation of the text, and the same could be claimed for the P1 of the VN. However, there is a difference that could be regarded as one of degree, on a scale of individualization: a general 3sg is identified as a single person, thus narrowing down the scope for identification, which is not the case with the VN. However, the mechanisms of cohesion, especially in connection with non-individualized P1s and their indentification in their contexts in Old and Middle Irish, await further study.

The passage quoted in (56*a*) represents probably the best example in *The Annals of Ulster* of the use of agentive VN clauses in presentative function, or, in Baudiš's terms, to present 'new facts' (or rather, situations). The main headlines, as it were, are presented by the structure *slogad la*, and are then fleshed out by means of finite clauses, the subject P1 of which is coreferential with the P1 of the VN clause. Note that, in three cases, the AG in charge of the VN clause is then resumed and subsumed in the group he leads (*coro marbsat* 'and they killed', *co tucsat maidm* 'and they inflicted defeat', *coro loiscset* 'and they burned'). That two of the three entries quoted here contain *slógad la* reflects the prominence of this expression in the evidence for continuity of P1, and this may well be another reason why the structure IPN+PP$_{P1}$ is so often followed by statements providing further details concerning the event, since leading an army (into foreign territory) tends to be the beginning of a development, rather than a self-contained event. It would also seem that in these cases, where one initial situation marks the beginning of a series of events, it is the process noun that presents the most salient piece of information, rather than the responsible party (i.e P1), or the affected party, if mentioned (i.e. P2). The process noun situates P1 in a context, a starting point as it were, and P1 is resumed as a given agent, quite literally, in the following discourse. It seems that this was what Baudiš had in mind when stating that VN clauses of the type illustrated in (56) present 'a new fact', which is then further developed in following finite clauses.

As mentioned above, continuity between section-initial VN+PP$_{P1}$/PN+PP$_{P1}$ is not universal, but, even where it does not occur, the following discourse generally provides a comment on the initial VN clause, including, for example, consequent developments; see (57), which illustrates the use of code switching within an entry:

(57)   *Ar nUmill la gennti ubi ceciderunt Coscrach* m. Flaindabrat ⅂ Dunadhach rex
       Humill.   (*AU* 813.4)
       slaughter Umall_gen.sg with heathens where fall_perf.3pl
       'The slaughter of Umall by the heathens in which fell Coscrach son of Flannabra and Dúnadach, king of Umall.'

If we compare now the construction P2+*do*$_{VN}$+P1, we find a higher rate of resumption of P2 than of P1 in the following discourse. Of fifty-five section-initial P2+*do*$_{VN}$+P1 clauses, twenty-four (or 43.6 per cent) have P2 resumed in the second clause, as compared to fourteen instances (or 25.5 per cent) of resumption of P1. P2 is resumed as P2 in ten cases (18.2 per cent) (see (58)),[109] P1 as P1 in seven instances (12.7 per cent).[110]

(58)   *Broen* m. Murcadha, rí Laigen, *do ergabhail do Ghallaib* 7 *a marbad* iarum.
       (*AU* 980.8)
       Braen to seize_VN to foreigner_dat.pl and his kill_VN
       'Braen . . . king of Laigin, was taken prisoner by the foreigners and afterwards put to death.'

---

[109] As object P2 once, as P2 in a VN construction seven times, and as subject P2 in a passive clause twice.

[110] As subject P1 in three, as an oblique P1 in four examples.

The fact that the preposed P2 of a section-initial P2+do_{VN}+P1 clause shows a higher degree of resumption in the following discourse can be interpreted as additional evidence that, in this construction, P2 is of greater salience than P1. The reason why a comparatively large number of P2+do_{VN}+P1 clauses are isolated entries without any further elaboration is linked with the frequent occurrence of *marbad* 'killing' in this construction. Unlike *slógad*, discussed above, *marbad* 'killing' describes a situation that is to a high degree self-contained, not necessarily leading on to a further development in which P2, which is focused on in a construction preposing this participant, is prominently involved.

As regards the type P1+do_{VN}(+P2), we find that it occurs more often as isolated clauses than integrated in a further context, 91 out of a total 164 attestations (or 55.5 per cent), compared to 54 instances (32.9 per cent) of clauses in section-initial position. The proportion of isolated clauses is higher in the later parts of the text, correlating with the high frequency of the expressions X *do éc*(*aib*) and X *do* (*chom*) *thuitim*, most of which occur in entries dated after AD 1000; these statements are self-contained in the same way as P2+do_{VN}+P1 containing *marbad*. Of thirty-two instances that show continuity, P1 is resumed as P1 in twenty-two cases (40.7 per cent),[111] more frequently than in any other role. Additionally, there are thirteen instances where P1 of the section-initial clause is coreferential with an implied P1 of a following VN.

With this construction type, we do not find a comparable number of series of 'headlines', elaborated upon by means of finite clauses (as illustrated in (56a) above) as encountered with IPN+PP$_{P1}$. There are some instances, though, where a non-initial P1+do_{VN}(+P2) clause presents P1 as the focus of new information, as in (59):

(59)   Mael Patraicc H. Bileóce, airdfer leiginn Aird Macha, ꝛ sui crabuid ꝛ na oighi, in senectute bona quieuit. *Dub da Leithe* m. Mael Muire *do gabail na firusa leighinn.*   (*AU* 1046.5)
Dub dá Leithe to take_VN the_gen.sg lectorship_gen.sg
'Mael Patraicc . . . chief lector of Ard Macha, and one eminent for piety and chastity, rested at a ripe old age. Dub dá Leithe son of Mael Muire took the lectorship.'

Overall, the resumption rate of any participant of a section-initial P1+do_{VN}(+P2) clause in the second clause can be compared to that of IPN+PP$_{P1}$ (83.4 per cent versus 84 per cent, including the cases where P1 is coreferential with P1 of a following VN). A difference with regard to the usage of both constructions is illustrated by the examples in (56a) and in (59): the processes presented in (56a) by means of *slógad la* are of at least the same salience as the P1s; the four examples of *slógad la* represent the main stages of development of the 'narrative', the processes being the starting point of further developments. In (59), the most salient point

---

[111] In fourteen cases (25.9%) as subject P1, in eight as P1 in a VN construction; this compares with five examples of P1 being resumed as P2 (9.3%). Continuity of the P2 of the section initial P1+do_{VN}(+P2) in the second clause is very rare (four instances occur altogether).

of information is clearly P1, the process being to a certain extent predictable: after the death of the former lector, the salient point is not the fact that someone did take over the vacant office, but rather who the successor was.

3.3. The agentive passive in narrative texts: evidence from *Táin Bó Cúailnge*

3.3.1. Markers of P1, and clause types

As discussed above (Section 1.3.2), so-called passive, or impersonal, forms in Irish, as in Welsh, may be either transitive or intransitive. However, clauses that can be interpreted as agentive passives all involve transitive verbs. There are five potential markers of P1 (not all examples, nor indeed markers, being equally unambiguous) attested in the three recensions of *TBC*, in descending order of frequency, they are *la* 'with', *ó* 'from', *oc* 'at', *do* 'to', and, very sporadic, *ra/re* (an amalgamation of Old Irish *la* and *fri* 'against, towards'). The passive accompanied by a P1 phrase is overall not a very common phenomenon. The distribution of the different markers in the texts is listed in Table 3.20.

Table 3.20 contains not only unambiguous examples of passive clauses with P1 markers (indeed, one of the concerns of this section, and of Chapter 4 will be whether there is such a thing as an unambiguous agentive passive in medieval Irish), but also doubtful and borderline cases. Thus the figures in the table cannot stand alone, but should be seen in conjunction with the discussion in this section, and with reference to the examples in the text.[112] Doubtful attestations are included here because they may provide the links between different functions of the prepositions under investigation. A discussion of ambiguous cases follows.

Passive + la

The chief difficulty with *la* as P1 marker is the relatively frequent possibility of interpreting the prepositional phrase as denoting a locative relation. This is most often the case when the complement of the preposition is a plural noun or plural suffixed pronoun, as illustrated in example (22) in Chapter 1, or when there is a complex noun phrase, as in (60):[113]

(60)   *Alta-som* ém . . . *la máthair 7 la athair* ocond Airgdig i mMaig Murthemne.
        (*TBC I* 399)
        rear_pass.pret.sg-PRO with-his mother and with-his father
        'He was reared by his father and mother at the Airgtech in Mag Muirthemne.'
        (O'Rahilly 1976: 136)

O'Rahilly, as indicated in the translation, clearly interprets 'la máthair ⁊ la athair' as

---

[112] Listings of the attestations can be found in Appendix 11.
[113] Cf. a similar difficulty in the use of *la* as P1 with VNs, Section 3.1.1.

TABLE 3.20. *P1 markers in passive clauses in TBC, and syntactic environments*

Passive clause	Main clause				Interrogative clause				Relative clause				Subordinate clause[a]				Total			
	I	LL	III	Total	I	LL	III	Total	I	LL	III	Total	I	LL	III	Total	I	LL	III	Total
+ la	11	14	4	29		1		1	2	2	1	5			1	1	13	17	6	36
%																				46.6
+ ó	5	5		10	1			1	1	4	3	8	2			2	8	10	3	21
%																				27.3
+ oc		5	7	12														5	7	12
%																				15.6
+ do	2	2	1	5											1[b]	1	2	2	2	6
%																				7.8
+ ra/re		1		1							1	1						1	1	2
%																				2.6
TOTAL				57				2				14				4				77
%				72.7				2.6				18.9				5.2				100

[a] Introduced by a conjunction.

[b] 'Doigh' in *TBC III* 545.32, 'doigh nisribloingesdair do beth 'na f(h)arrad' (for likely translation and literal gloss, see ex. (67b)) is interpreted here as a variant of the conjunction *dáig* 'since, for'.

a P1 phrase. However, it is equally clear that, in this case, the function of *la* marking P1 overlaps with the spatial sense of the preposition: the person defining the spatial setting is also an actant. The other recensions of *TBC* containing this passage show a different phrasing, which avoids a possible ambiguity: *TBC LL* 740: 'Dáig alta in mac sin i tig a athar ┐ a máthar'; *TBC St.* 765: 'Ro hoiledh tra an mac sin . . . i ttig a athar ┐ a mathar' (for the boy was reared at his father's and mother's house). However, it would be premature to conclude on this basis that this is also necessarily the intended reading in *TBC I*.[114]

Passive + ó

Except for three instances,[115] all passives followed by an *ó*-phrase interpretable as P1 are either verbs of 'giving' (e.g. *do-beir* 'gives', *berid* 'carries (to)', *ind-anich* 'gives, bestows, delivers'), as in (61*a*), or of speaking (in the wider sense, including *ad-gládathar* 'addresses', *guidid* 'prays') (see (61*b*)).

> (61) (*a*)   *da idnaicthea comraind úad díb*   (*TBC LL* 3130)
>   if send_pass.pret.sg equal share from-him of-them
>   'if an equal share of them was sent from him'
>
>   (*b*)   *Acaltar úait Cú Chulaind,* a Ḟerguis   (*TBC LL* 1429)
>   address_sg.pass.ipv from-you Cú Chulainn
>   'You speak to Cú Chulainn, Fergus'

In some instances, the preposition *ó* is possibly to be interpreted as the source (or the IAG), rather than as P1, since the context does not show whether there is contact between giver and receiver, or whether the person named in the prepositional phrase is the origin, whereas the act of giving is carried out by someone else.[116] It is interesting in this context that O'Rahilly's translation of *TBC LL* 3130, quoted above in (61*a*), as 'an equal portion was sent from him' is not consistent with her translation of the other occurrences of this phrase (*TBC LL* 3127, 3170, 3173), where the prepositional phrase is rendered as 'by him'. This may be a simple inconsistency of translation, or it may, on the other hand, reflect the fact that the preposition *ó* can denote both the origin/source, and P1—i.e. an AG. The choice of the verb 'send', rather than 'give', though, would indicate that the editor interprets the situation portrayed as one where there is no direct contact between giver (origin) and receiver, and that the source and the person handing over the gift are not identical.[117] This semantic nuance of distance between giver and receiver is not encountered

---

[114] Other instances of *la*-phrases that could be interpreted as either P1 or locative are *TBC I* 1, 2568; *TBC LL* 114.

[115] 'nár millter' (let not be violated) (*TBC I* 1567); 'forróeglass' (who were (lit.: was) chosen) (*TBC LL* 3745); 'adchota' (might be found) (*TBC I* 1543) (following the editor's interpretation of the form as the reflex of an Old Irish *adcotae*; MSS Y and C read *adcotad*).

[116] See *TBC I* 216, 2234, 3885; *TBC III* §§135, 140; *TBC LL* 2261, 3127, 3130, 3170, 3172; the last four being virtually identical.

[117] Windisch regularly translates the sentence as 'wurde von ihm aus überbracht'—i.e. 'was delivered from him (or even: 'at his behest')' (cf. the translations of lines 3591, 3595, and 3641 in Windisch (1905)).

with all examples where *ó* can be interpreted as P1; see again (61*b*), and also (62), where we can assume immediate contact between giver and receiver:

(62)   (brat) . . . *dobrethea oChonchobur do Choinchulainn*   (*TBC III* §135)
         give_pass.pret.sg from-Conchobor to Cú Chulainn
         '(a cloak) . . . which was given by Conchobor to Cú Chulainn'

Verbs of saying, speaking, addressing, and so on also contain a characteristic of 'transfer' or 'giving', such that the speaker transfers words, a proposal, a request, a prayer, or the like to the addressee, who is also a receiver (compare here the commonly used sender–receiver metaphor in communication theory). Thus the question arises whether, in the cases discussed here, the choice of *ó*, which can mark the source or origin (whether in a local sense or one of creation) as well as an AG, is, in the cases attested here, determined by the semantic make-up of the verb it accompanies. If this is the case, then this would be further evidence that the selection of a preposition to express P1 is not random among a number of prepositions that can fulfil this function, but that there is a close link between the type of situation portrayed, and the type of P1 that is part of this situation, on the one hand, and the semantic make-up of the preposition selected, on the other.

Passive + oc

This construction does not occur at all in *TBC I*, and it is tempting to explain its complete absence from this text as due to diachronic reasons.[118] *Oc* 'at' is less common in *TBC LL* than *la* in passive clauses. Of the five attestations with *oc*, two are identical examples of the sentence shown in (63*a*), and, in one instance, *oc* and *la* are used side by side, and would appear to have the same function (see (63*b*)):

(63) (*a*)   Is and sin *ra himráided ac feraib Hérend* . . .   (*TBC LL* 2531)
             PRT debate_pass.pret.sg at man_dat.pl Ireland_gen.sg
             'Then the men of Ireland debated . . .'

     (*b*)   *Ra cruthaiged comairle occu* . . . *Ocus ba sed a comairle ra cruthaiged leó* . . .
             (*TBC LL* 587, 589)
             PRT shape_pass.pret.sg counsel at-them; the counsel PRT shape_pass.pret.sg
             with-them
             'They held counsel . . . and that was the counsel that was decided by them . . .'

Of the seven attestations of passive + *oc* in *TBC III*, six are virtually identical examples of the sentence quoted in (63*a*). It is used as a formula to introduce narrative passages, describing, in five out of six cases, Cú Chulainn's single combats.[119]

---

[118] The earliest instances of passive + *oc* quoted in *DIL* (s.v. *oc*) are from *TBC LL* (587), and from *Arch.* iii. 225.23: 'ro benait na cluic ac na cleirchib' (the bells were rung by the clerics); note the late passive form *benait*, in contrast to an earlier form *ro bitha*.

[119] These sentences are the same as the ones containing the purpose clauses ('cia bad chóir do chomlonn . . .' (who should/would be the right one to fight . . .)) discussed in Section 3.1.3. *La* also occurs in this environment: 'Is andsin ro himráided leó-som íarom cia fer bad túalaing dingbáil Con Culaind díb' (then they debated as to who would be capable of repelling Cú Chulainn) (*TBC I* 2568; introducing *Comrac Fir Diad*).

Thus, although the number of occurrences of *oc* and *la* in passive clauses is nearly the same in this text, the latter structure has the wider range of use, whereas the former is largely repetitive.

Example (63*a*) shows that passive + *oc* presents the same ambiguities as passive + *la*—that is, between locative or agentive function of the prepositional phrase, where the preposition has a plural complement. *DIL* claims that, in combination with a passive or a verbal noun, 'strictly, *oc* indicates, not the agent, but the quarter, group or individuals, etc. in which the action takes place or has its origin'. However, one may add that the 'group in which the action takes place' and the actual actants may very well be identical; in other words, what we are dealing with may be not so much an ambiguity between two functions (that is, a difficulty of decoding), but an overlap, in cases such as (63*b*) or (64):

> (64)   'daria Cethern mac Fintain . . . agus *frithálter acaib é*.'   (*TBC LL* 3792–3)
> expect_pass.ipv.sg at-you him
> 'Cethern mac Fintain will come . . . and you must expect [and be ready to deal with] him.'

Passive + do

Do is only rarely used with the passive verb in what can be interpreted as agentive function, whereas, as we have seen, it is the most common P1 marker in VN constructions. The two instances in *TBC I* both contain the verb *guidid* 'prays, entreats, asks for', but in different construction types: whereas, in (65*a*), the addressee of *guidid* is marked by a prepositional phrase and the direct object marks the entity asked for, in (65*b*) the addressee of *guidid* is the direct object and the entity asked for is marked by a prepositional phrase. The *do*-phrase in (65*a*) is interpreted by the editor as expressing the beneficiary, rather than P1 (see the translation). This is supported by the context, as it transpires that neither of the speakers, but a third person, carries out the action demanded. In the same text,[120] the verb *guidid* in a syntactic construction parallel to (65*a*) also occurs with the preposition *ó*, interpretable as P1, see (65*c*), and translated as such by the editor.

> (65) (*a*)   '*Guitter* dano *cairdi chlaidib dún* for Con Culaind' for Ailill ⁊ Medb.
> (*TBC I* 1686)
> pray_pass.ipv.sg truce to-us
> ' "Let Cú Chulainn be asked for a truce for us," said Ailill and Medb.'
> (O'Rahilly 1976: 172)
>
> (*b*)   *Guitter* dano *Cúr* mac Da Láth *dóib* im dula for cend Con Culaind.
> (*TBC I* 1695)
> pray_pass.pres.sg Cú Chulainn to-them
> 'Then Cúr was asked by them to encounter Cú Chulainn.'
> (O'Rahilly 1976: 172)

---

[120] Also the same section in hand H.

(c)   'Guitter cardi chlaidib úand for Coin Culaind,' or Ailill.   (TBC I 1545)
        pray_pass.ipv.sg truce from-us
        ' "Let us ask Cú Chulainn for a truce," said Ailill.'   (O'Rahilly 1976: 168)

Unfortunately, there are not enough attestations to establish any clear pattern of use for *do* as P1 marker in passive clauses, as opposed to any other preposition. The two examples of a passive verb followed by a *do*-phrase in *TBC LL* (1302 and 4872) are nearly identical, and it seems likely that one is an echo of the other (see (66)). The explanation of the passive clause, introduced by 'is inund són' (this is the same as) invites speculation whether the writer felt it necessary to elaborate on an unusual phrase, which might very well be the use of *do* with a passive.

(66)   *foclassa búrach dó*, is inund són ⁊ focheird úir dá lúib taris   (TBC LL 1302)
        dig_pass.pret.sg-his/its (or: pass.pret.pl) to-him
        'and the earth was pawed up by him, that is, he cast the turf over him with his
        heels'   (O'Rahilly 1976: 174)

The two instances of a *do*-phrase accompanying what might be an impersonal or passive verb form in the prose of *TBC III* are, if anything, even less straightforward than the ones discussed above (see (67)):

(67) (a)   ⁊ mad fírlaech é, *nirisriblaingesdair do* a fhaisgin   (TBC III 538.19)
            ?tolerate_pass.pres.sub.sg to-him
            'and if he is a true warrior, he will not tolerate the sight of it'

    (b)   *doigh nis ribloingesdair do beth 'na fharradh*   (TBC III 545.32)
            for ?NEG-PRO3_sg PRT-tolerate_pass.pret.sg to-him
            'for he could not bear to be near him'

Windisch (1905) translates the form *nis-ribloingesdair, ni ris-/rosriblaingesdair* with 'er ertrug es nicht', 'er hielt es nicht aus' (he did not/could not bear/tolerate it); however he does not analyse the form itself. What we have here looks potentially like an s-preterite (*ro*-preterite) deponent formation of the verb *fo-loing* 'suffers, tolerates', with the nasal of the present stem, the form in *TBC III* 538.19 like an s-subjunctive with an additional particle *ro*. The use of a *do*-phrase with these forms may indicate a reinterpretation as passives. There is one instance of a form comparable to the ones in (67), but without a *do*-phrase and used as a deponent form, in *TBC III*:

(68)   *nírasribhlainngesdair Cúchulainn* bheith mábhráthbhemeandaibh
        (*TBC III* §88)
        ?NEG-PRT-PRO_3sg-PRT-tolerate_pret.3sg Cú Chulainn
        'Cú Chulainn could not tolerate to be subjected to the destructive blows'
        (cf. Windisch 1905: 317: 'daß Cú Chulainn es nicht aushielt')

It seems realistic to add these forms to the list of 'artificial' preterite formations of the verb *fo-loing* 'bears, tolerates, suffers' discussed by Mac Gearailt (1989: 24–5). He quotes 'ni forulngither dósom' (*LL* 23007), 'nir barulngither da ngillaib óca' (*LL* 23095), 'nir brulngither do Chairpre Nia Fer' (*LL* 23173), and 'nir borulngither dó' (*LL* 23192), all occurring in the text *Cath Ruis na Ríg* (*CCR*). Mac Gearailt also quotes instances of the usual Middle Irish preterite *farlangair* used both with *do* (*LL* 32390, *Aen.* 2144) and without (*TBC LL* 3342).

If the forms quoted in (67), as well as those listed by Mac Gearailt and cited above are to be interpreted as passives, there remains the question why those who used them as such chose as P1 marker the preposition whose agentive function is the least well established in use with passive verbs. Mac Gearailt (1989: 23–4) mentions another 'artificial' form from *Cath Ruis na Ríg* (*LL* 22858), *barroeblangair dósom* (from *for-ling* 'jumps, leaps over'), as well as an instance of the Old Irish preterite of the same verb, also 'mit einer konjugierten Präposition, deren Bedeutung nicht klar ist' (with a conjugated preposition, the meaning of which is not clear): *nach faroeblangatar . . . díb* 'they jumped' (Mac Gearailt 1989: 23–4). One is tempted to conclude that the choice of preposition is consciously vague, and a feature of a deliberately obscure, and maybe archaizing style. However, the motivation for the choice of a deliberately obscure expression is far from obvious, in the context of otherwise perfectly straightforward narrative passages.

Passive + ra/re

The form *ra*, *re* occurs frequently in Middle Irish texts in place of Old Irish *la*,[121] and *ra* and *re* in the following examples are interpreted as such:

(69) (*a*)   Araí sen *ragníad ra Meidb* dunibúali ursloicthi ar cind Chonchobuir
(*TBC LL* 4269)
PRT-make_pass.pret.sg with Medb
'Nevertheless Medb drew up a hollow array to face Conchobar'
(O'Rahilly 1967: 253)

(*b*)   dóigh robo chiamair dho chrú ⁊ d'fuil icon ar *laighter re Coinculainn*.[122]
(*TBC III* §103)
let_pass.pres.sg(rel) with Cú Chulainn
'since it [the stream] was murky with the gore and the blood shed during the slaughter by Cú Chulainn.'

Although the use of the forms *re/ra* is by no means uncommon in *TBC LL* and *III*, there is no noticeable tendency for them to replace *la* as P1 marker. Rather, the tendency appears to be that *oc* gains ground in this function in these recensions.

3.3.2. Internal structure of full passive clauses

Clause types, tense/mood, direct speech, and narrative

The sentence types in which full passives (and 'potential' full passives) occur in our texts are listed in Table 3.20. Main clauses are on the whole dominant, and a sub-

---

[121]   Cf. e.g. the instances listed by Windisch in the wordlist for *TBC*, s.v.
[122]   This example follows the word division in Windisch (1905: 337 n. 3), which appears to make more sense than the one given by Nettlau: 'dho chrú ⁊ dfhuil i conarlaighter ré Coinculainn'.

group of these are passive imperatives, as illustrated in (61*b*), (64), and (65). The passive imperative with overt P1 is not a very common construction in *TBC*: there are no instances at all in *TBC III* (possibly because of the relative shortness of the text); four occurrences in *TBC I* can be interpreted as full passive imperatives, and *TBC LL* contains seven imperatives accompanied by a P1 phrase, three of which occur in sequence, in one utterance of one of the main characters, Ailill, at the outset of the campaign:

(70)   '*Sáditer sosta 7 pupaill lind*', ar Ailill, '*7 déntar urgnam bíd 7 lenna lind 7 cantar*
         ceóil 7 airfiti lind 7 [déntar] praind 7 tomaltus.'   (*TBC LL* 685–6)
         set-up_pass.ipv camps and pavilions with-us; make_pass.ipv preparation
         food_gen.sg and drink_gen.sg with-us; sing_pass.ipv music and entertain-
         ment
         ' "Let us set up camp and tents", said Ailill, "and let us prepare food and drink,
         let us play music and entertain [ourselves], and let us eat and drink." '

The carefully constructed syntactic structure where each verb form is accompanied by a complex noun phrase combining two elements of related meaning is reused twice: a few lines further on (*TBC LL* 689–90), preterite passives report that Ailill's order has been carried out, and that all is in good order in the warcamp.[123] The structure is echoed once more (*TBC LL* 1465–6); this time verb forms are negated.[124] It seems a deliberate move to recall to the reader's mind the undisturbed, well-ordered setting-up of the camp, virtually at the outset of the campaign, before any direct confrontation of the main adversaries, at a point where the element of well-orderedness has given way to threat and destruction: during the three nights when the army camps at Druim Én, Cú Chulainn kills 100 warriors each night.

Interrogative clauses containing full passives are rare; our data contain only two instances, both in *TBC LL*. Likewise, there is a marked reluctance to use the full passive in subordinate clauses introduced by a conjunction; only four examples occur (two in *TBC I* and two in *TBC III*). Relative clauses containing full passives in our texts all have P2 as the antecedent (i.e. as subject of the passive verb), as illustrated in (71).[125]

(71)   ar ba aincís mór lei *an ro bíth leis dia slógaib*   (*TBC I* 1919)
         that-which PRT beat_pass.pret.sg with-him of-her army_dat.pl
         'for the number of her army that was killed by him caused her great worry'

As regards the occurrence of full passives in direct speech or narrative, and tense and mood of the passive verb, we can observe that roughly one-third of all instances in our texts (including, as before, potentially ambiguous examples) occur in direct speech. As might be expected in narrative texts, full passives in narrative

---

[123] 'ra sádit a sosta 7 ra suidigit a pupla. Darónad urgnam bíd 7 lenna leó . . .' (their camp was made and their tents set up; preparations of food and drink were made . . .) (*TBC LL* 689–90).
[124] 'Acht níro sádit sosta nó pupla 7 ní dernad praind nó tomaltas leó . . .' (but no camp or tents were built, no meals nor food were made by them . . .) (*TBC LL* 1465–6).
[125] This example from *TBC I* has its exact parallel in *TBC III* §73.

passages tend to contain the verb in the *ro*-preterite or the preterite, whereas other tenses and moods tend to occur in direct speech; the figures are given in Table 3.21.

TABLE 3.21. *Full passives in* TBC: *tense/mood, direct speech, and narrative*

Tense/mood	TBC I	TBC LL	TBC III	Total	%
Preterite					
Direct speech	1	1	1	3	62.3
Narrative	11	21	13	45	
Present					
Direct speech	1	3		4	11.7
Narrative	4		1	5	
Imperative					
Direct speech	4	7	2	13	16.9
Future					
Direct speech	1	2		3	3.9
Secondary future					
Direct speech		1		1	1.3
Present subjunctive					
Direct speech			2	2	2.6
Past subjunctive					
Narrative	1			1	1.3
TOTAL					
Direct speech	7	14	5	26	100
Narrative	16	21	13	51	

Definiteness

The P1 of a full passive in our texts is always a definite entity, and in the majority of instances what we find is a pronoun suffixed to the prepositional P1 marker (see Table 3.22). Thus the type, common in English, of full passives with indefinite overt P1, as in, for example, *the burglars were surprised by a neighbour* does not have an equivalent in the current database. P2, on the other hand, is more often an indefinite noun phrase than a definite entity (see Table 3.22); the figures do not include relative passive clauses). We can also note that it is comparatively rare for P2 not to be marked lexically, or to be marked only by an enclitic pronominal form such as -*som*, or -*side*.

Ordering of P1 and P2

As regards the sequence of P1 and P2, a full passive in early Irish with a nominal or stressed pronominal P2 may follow two patterns:

type 1: (*X*) V(erb) P2 P1
type 2: (*X*) V(erb) P1 P2

(*X* indicates any entity that may precede the verb, such as an adverbial expression, or a copula followed by an adverbial expression.)

The distribution of the two types in main clauses across the texts analysed here is shown in Table 3.23. As mentioned above, agentive passive relative clauses have P2 as antecedent; other sentence types are too marginal in occurrence to permit a valid analysis. Passive sentences containing clauses as P2/subject always follow type 2. Of the thirteen instances of type 2*a*, nine are accounted for by the introductory formula already mentioned, and illustrated again in (72). The entity preceding the verb in this opening formula is always the temporal adverbial expression *annsin/andsin* 'there, then', with or without the copula *is*.

(72)   *Is and sin ra imráided oc feraib Hérend cia bad chóir* do chomlond ⅂ do chomrac ra Coin Culaind ra húair na maitni muchi arnabárach
(*TBC LL* 2607)
COP there PRT debate_pass.pret.sg at man_dat.pl Ireland_gen.sg who COP right
'Then the men of Ireland debated who would be right to fight and do battle against Cú Chulainn in the early hour of the next morning'

TABLE 3.22. *Definiteness of P1 and P2*

Participant	TBC I	TBC LL	TBC III	Total	%
P1 [+def.]					
Pronoun	12	26	9	47	61
Name	6	5	4	15	19.5
NP	5	4	6	15	19.5
P2 [+def.]					
Pronoun		3	5	8	12.9
Name	1	2	1	4	6.5
NP	2	1		3	4.8
Enclitic	2	1		3	4.8
–P2	2	1		3	4.8
P2 [–def.]					
NP	11	18		29	62.9
(VN) clause	2	2	8	12	19.4

TABLE 3.23. *Sequence of P1 and P2 in passive main clauses*

Type	TBC I	TBC LL	TBC III	Total	%
1: V P2 P1	10	16		26	45.6
1a: X V P2 P1	1			1	1.8
2: V P1 P2	2	5	4	11	19.3
2a: X V P1 P2	1	4	8	13	22.8

Where P2 is a stressed personal pronoun,[126] it follows the P1 phrase. It would therefore seem that a pronominal P2 in a passive clause in our data occupies the position in the clause regularly occupied by a (non-contrastive, non-emphatic) pronominal P2 in Modern Irish clauses, generally at the very end of the clause.[127] Definite noun phrases or proper names as P2 occur only comparatively rarely; therefore no valid conclusions as regards their preferred position in the full passive clause can be established. Indefinite noun phrases, on the other hand, show a tendency to precede rather than follow the P1 phrase (the ratio being 26 to 3 cases).

3.3.3. Agentive passives in context

This section looks at the behaviour of full passive clauses in their textual environments. The structuring of information is assessed, then we turn to the question whether the full passive can be said to be a device either to disrupt or to maintain continuity, and then we move on to the role of the full passive in its narrative context.

3.3.3.1. INFORMATION PACKAGING: NEW, INFERABLE, AND GIVEN INFORMATION

As with Welsh and Irish VN constructions, information is classified as new, inferable (entities that the hearer or reader can infer from an entity already mentioned), or given (entities that have already been mentioned). One question that arises in this context concerns the status of the well-known characters of our texts, and whether they can or should realistically be classified as new information, or whether, for instance, the opening sentence of *TBC I* (see (74)) evokes the main characters in the mind of the addressee, all lined up and waiting for their cues, as it were. A similar question would seem to arise concerning characters who very often occur together, as, for example, Cú Chulainn and his charioteer. Thus the only definition of new information that approaches objectivity (and testability) is one that classifies entities as new that have not been mentioned in the preceding text—that is, entities that are introduced for the first time in a given context. This also leaves leeway for the assumption that any new reading or hearing of even a well-known text, or any first encounter with well-known characters in a new text, is for the listener or reader truly a new experience and therefore a new encounter with the characters (or settings) in question. The distribution of new, inferable, and given P1s and P2s is listed in Table 3.24.[128]

---

[126] The texts contain seven instances of *é* 'he' and one of *iat* 'they'.

[127] For Modern Irish, see Ó Siadhail (1989: 207–8). Using data from Strachan (1904), Ahlqvist (1976: 173) notes that the position of the object pronoun (i.e. P2 in active clauses) in Middle Irish is more variable than in Modern Irish, and that no strict rules emerge for his corpus of data at least.

[128] Relative clauses (and the interrogative relative in *TBC LL*) are not included in the count for P2, since the antecedent P2 is given information as far as the relative clause is concerned. One exception is the following example: 'Ocus ba sed a comairle ra cruthaiged leó, Cormac . . . do lécud úadib' (And this was the counsel that was taken by them, to send Cormac . . .) (*TBC LL* 589).

As Table 3.24 shows, P1 tends to represent given information in the greater part of our data; this fact is already implied by the observation made above (see Table 3.22) that, in the majority of all attestations, P1 is expressed by means of a suffixed pronoun, which, unless it refers to a discourse participant (first or second person), has to have a referent that is given. However, not only pronominal P1s represent given information.

TABLE 3.24. *Given, new, and inferable P1 and P2 in agentive passive clauses*

Text	P1		P2		
	New	Given	New	Given	Inferable
TBC I	4	19	12	6	2
TBC LL	1	34	14	10	5
TBC III	2	17	9	5	
TOTAL	7	70	35	21	7
%	*9.1*	*90.9*	*55.6*	*33.3*	*11.1*

Of the seven instances of new P1s, four occur in relative clauses of the type illustrated in (73). The relative clause serves to add descriptive information concerning the antecedent noun, rather than information that is of relevance to advance the plotline. This sentence type, a full passive relative clause with new P1, describing an antecedent that is the subject of the relative clause, does not occur outside chapter xvii, section 3, *In Carpat Serda* (in Windisch's (1905) numbering), in the different recensions of *TBC*.[129] This chapter is in the main a long descriptive sequence, giving details concerning Cú Chulainn's and his charioteer's battle equipment, and Cú Chulainn's distortion in preparation for the battle. The clauses in question all contain *ó* as P1 marker, which is, as discussed in Section 3.1.1, not entirely unambiguous as regards its status as P1 marker.

(73)   . . . don tlachtdíllat Tíre Tairngire *dobretha dó ó Manannán mac Lir* . . .
          (*TBC LL* 2261)
          give_pass.pret.pl to-him from Manannán mac Lir
          '. . . of the garment of the Promised Land, given to him by Manannán mac Lir
          . . .'[130]

Of the three remaining examples of new P1s in passive clauses, one is a doubtful instance of *ó* as P1 marker.[131] The second, *TBC I* 399, stands at the beginning of a

---

[129] See *TBC I* 2243, *TBC III* §§135, 140.

[130] Note that O'Rahilly (1967: 201) translates 'of garment . . . brought to him from Manannán mac Lir', thus interpreting the preposition *ó* as marking the source or origin, rather than P1.

[131] 'Dobreth biad dó óna bri[u]gadaib' (give_pass.pret.sg food to-him from-the hosteller_dat.pl) (food was brought to him from/by the hostellers) (*TBC I* 3885). See also example (73), and n. 130 for another example of the use of *ó* in what could be either P1 function, or the marker of the source or origin.

chapter (vii, *Macgnímrada*), and the third, example (74), is the opening sentence of the narrative in *TBC I*, and is a good illustration of the question whether any character of the 'inner circle' can really be classified as 'new' information in the sense of 'unknown': any reader or listener reasonably familiar with the heroes of Ulster tales who is about to experience a rendering of *TBC* would very probably expect the narrative to start with a statement concerning one or more of the main characters —that is, infer their presence.

> (74)   *Tarcomlad slóiged mór la Connachtu, .i. la hAilill ⁊ la Meidb,* ⁊ hetha úaidib cossna trí chóiced aili. Ocus fóite techta ó Ailill co secht maccu Mágach . . . (*TBC I* 1 ff.)
> assemble_pass.pret.sg muster great with Connachtman_acc.pl .i. with Ailill and with Medb
> 'A great army was mustered by the Connachtmen, that is, by Ailill and Medb, and word went from them to the three other provinces. And Ailill sent messengers to the seven sons of Mágu . . .'   (O'Rahilly 1976: 125)[132]

P2 represents new information in the majority of all cases; the majority is smaller in *TBC LL* than in *TBC I* and *III*; again see Table 3.24. P2s that are clauses or VNs, as in (75), always represent new information.

> (75)   *Guitter ón tslóg forro bith 'na tost*   (*TBC I* 1622)
> pray_pass.pres.sg from-the army on-them be_VN in-their rest
> 'They were begged by the army to leave off'

Clausal subjects in the introductory formula (see (72) for an example) have also been classified as new; the clause represents new information by virtue of the interrogative pronoun *cia* 'who', referring to an as yet unspecified person. Arguably, the subject clause might be labelled inferable, in all instances but the first occurrence of the formula in each text. It has already been pointed out that the main textual function of these recurring constructions is to serve as an introduction to the following narrative section. The most relevant new element of information is the person to be introduced, and the way for the introduction is prepared by a formulaic expression.

A subject P2 that is unambiguously inferable is contained in the clause quoted in (76a); the passage follows the pattern of *TBC LL* 1302 so closely that it could be described (and is doubtless intended to be) its echo (see (66)). More problematic is the series of four examples that begins with *TBC LL* 3127 (see (76b)).[133]

---

[132] In spite of O'Rahilly's interpretation, it seems possible to take 'la Connachtu' as a locative phrase ('in Connacht') and to look only at 'la hAilill ⁊ la Meidb' as the actual P1 phrase. This may be a case of different degrees of involvement of several potential candidates for the role of P1: it is hardly possible for the king and queen of Connacht to assemble an army in the region without the involvement of those who actually make up the army—i.e. the Connachtmen themselves. However, the highest degree of control is doubtless exercised by the king and queen, who may thus qualify for the role of P1.

[133] See also *TBC LL* 3130, 3170, 3172.

(76) (*a*)   Atchonnaic cách a chéile dina tarbaib ⁊ *foclassa búrach dóib* and ⁊ fócerddetar
in n-úir thairsiu.   (*TBC LL* 4872)
dig_pass.pret.sg-his/its (or: pass.prct.pl) pit to-thcm
'Each of the bulls caught sight of the other and they pawed the ground and
cast the earth over them'   (O'Rahilly 1967: 271)

   (*b*)   Cach luib ⁊ cach lossa ícci ⁊ slánsén raberthea ra cnedaib . . . Con Culaind, *ra
idnaicthea comraind úad díb* dar áth siar d'Ḟir Diad   (*TBC LL* 3127)
PRT send_pass.pret.pl equal-shares from-him of-them
'Every herb and every healing plant and cure that was put on the wounds . . .
of Cú Chulainn, an equal amount of them was sent by him west across the
ford to Fer Diad'

The instance quoted in (76*b*) is classified as inferable: the reader can infer from the
structure of the preceding clause that the information contained there will be followed up on; the antecedent of the relative clause is a noun clause (not containing
a verbal element), not bound into a sentence structure, and it refers back to the
object of the preceding clause.[134] This rather elaborate recapitulation of a complex
unit already mentioned would plainly not be necessary if there were not another
element, linked to that unit, to be introduced, and the repetition of the phrase
prepares the way for this information. In other words, as the series 'cách luíb ⁊ cach
lossa ícci . . .' is reiterated (with the slight modification of having *cach* 'each' added
to each of its elements), the reader certainly comes to expect another piece of information closely linked with this series. This should justify the classification of
TBC LL 3127 as inferable, if we understand inferable in such a way that the reader
comes to expect the information.

Another problem posed by what I have called the series *TBC LL* 3127, 3130, 3170,
3172 lies mainly in the repetitive nature of these attestations; indeed the whole narrative passage (chapter xx, *Comrac Fir Diad*), after the initial meeting of the pro-
tagonists and the exchange of greetings and challenges, follows a repetitive pattern.
The basic structure is as follows. The two heroes fight; at the end of the first day
their charioteers make camp together. Healers look after them; Cú Chulainn sends
an equal portion of every medicine to Fer Diad (*TBC LL* 3127–8, example (76*b*)
above); Fer Diad sends an equal portion of every sort of food or drink to Cú
Chulainn (*TBC LL* 3130–1; the clause structure is identical to that of 3127). This pattern is repeated to relate the events of the second day, and again we find the same
clause structure and indeed virtually the same content in *TBC LL* 3170 and 3172 as
we find in 3127 and 3130.[135] These instances have here been classified as inferable
with regard to the information content of their subjects (i.e. P2), reserving the term
'given' for information that has actually been mentioned previously. The question

---

[134] '. . . ⁊ focherdetar lubi ⁊ lossa ícci ⁊ slánsén ⁊ ra cnedaib ⁊ ra créchtaib, ra n-áltaib ⁊ ra n-ilgonaib'
(*TBC LL* 3124 ff.) (and they put herbs and healing plants and a curing charm into their wounds and cuts,
their gashes and many stabs) (O'Rahilly 1967: 223).

[135] The only difference being that, in 3170, the medical aids are 'cach iptha ⁊ gach éle ⁊ gach orthana'
(all the spells, incantations and charms . . .) (O'Rahilly 1967: 224).

remains, however, whether the function of repetitive or formulaic structure of the type just discussed is in the main informational, or organizational.

There appears to be no immediate simple connection between the ordering of P1 and P2 and the informational content they represent. All clausal subjects, presenting new information, follow the P1 phrase. So do pronominal P2s, which, however, always represent given information. Where P2 is an indefinite noun phrase, it usually precedes the P1 phrase. Of those indefinite P2s that precede P1, eight are new, and two inferable in *TBC I*, nine are new, and two given in *TBC LL*. There appears a preference, then, to place a new P2 in a passive clause before the P1 phrase, unless it is a clausal subject. Placing a long, structurally complex expression between verb and P1 phrase would seriously disrupt the information flow in the sentence, and, given that P1 is a prepositional phrase, be a source of potential ambiguity as to the referendum of the prepositional phrase.

3.3.3.2. CONTINUITY

Resumption of P1 and P2 is considered from two angles: the occurrence in the preceding main clause of the entity encoded as P1 or P2 in the passive clause, and the semantic and syntactic role fulfilled by those entities. P2 was not taken into consideration in the investigation of VN constructions; the reason being the nature of the constructions under investigation: whereas, in a VN clause, both P1 and P2 are encoded as oblique noun phrases, in a passive clause there is a two-way effect, in that the choice of a passive clause implies not only relegation of P1 to an oblique noun phrase, but also the promotion of a nominal P2 to subject role.[136]

The specified syntactic and semantic functions in the following discussion are those of subject and object, and P1 and P2. The heading 'subject' also includes the subject of copula constructions; all other roles (for example, temporal, local, or modal adjuncts, indirect objects on the syntactic, and beneficiaries, IAG, CAUSE, etc. on the semantic level) are subsumed under 'other'. In Tables 3.25a and b, 'retrospective' refers to continuity from the clause preceding the passive construction and 'prospective' refers to continuity in the following clause (the reference point for comparison (100 per cent) is the total number of full passive main clauses; *TBC I*: 18, *TBC LL*: 27, *TBC III*: 12).

Looking first at *TBC I*, we find that the proportion of passive main clauses showing continuity of either P1 or P2, retro- or prospective, is less than half the number of all occurrences of full passives in our text.[137] Among the four cases

---

[136] The question still remains whether we claim the same for third person singular P2 that is not lexicalized, or, in other words, whether forms such as *marbthair* (sg.pass.pres of *marbaid* 'kills') express, or only imply, P2. The discussion will return to this question further below.

[137] Identifier tags, such as 'ol in gilla' (said the boy) (*TBC I* 589), which interrupt the flow of direct speech to identify the speaker, have been left out of consideration. If we were to count them along with the rest of the data, *TBC I* 589 would be another instance of a subject P1 being resumed as P1 of a passive clause, and recurring as subject of the following clause. An instance where a following identifier tag is identical with the P1 of the preceding passive clause is *TBC I* 1686.

TABLE 3.25. *Continuity of P1 and P2 in passive main clauses*

(a) Continuity of P1

P1 =	Retrospective					Prospective				
	TBC I	*TBC LL*	*TBC III*	Total	%	*TBC I*	*TBC LL*	*TBC III*	Total	%
Subject, P1	4	5	2	11	*19.3*	3	8	8	19	*33.3*
Other, P1		4		4	*7*		5	1	6	*10.5*
Subject, other						1	1		2	*3.5*
Other	2	8	2	12	*21.1*	2	6		8	*14*
TOTAL	6	17	4			6	20	9		
%	*33.3*	*63*	*33.3*			*33.3*	*74.1*	*75*		

(b) Continuity of P2

P2 =	Retrospective					Prospective				
	TBC I	*TBC LL*	*TBC III*	Total	%	*TBC I*	*TBC LL*	*TBC III*	Total	%
Subject, P1	1	2		3	*5.3*	1			1	*1.8*
Subject, other		2		2	*3.5*					
Object, P2	1	1		2	*3.5*	2	1		3	*5.3*
Subject of pass. clause, P2	1		1	2	*3.5*			3	3	*5.3*
Other	1	2	1	4	*7*	1	3		4	*7*
TOTAL	4	7	2			4	4	3		
%	*22.2*	*25.9*	*16.7*			*22.2*	*14.8*	*25*		

where the P1 of the passive clause resumes the subject P1 of the preceding main clause, there is one where P1 is also the subject and addressee of an imperative; see (2a), repeated here as (77):

(77)   'Collaa dún, a popa Loíg . . . *co n-airlither Lugaid* . . . dús cía dotháet . . .
Iarfaigther co lléir 7 a imchomarc lat.' Rosoich iarom Láeg.   (*TBC I* 1740)
so-that consult_pres.sub.2sg L; question_pass.ipv.sg and his greet_VN with-you
' "Go for me, friend Láeg . . . and consult Lugaid and find out who is coming
. . . Question him closely and greet him." Láeg went off then.'
(O'Rahilly 1976: 173)

The P1 of a passive clause is resumed three times as P1 in the following clause in *TBC I*, out of six instances altogether in which P1 recurs. There is one instance where P1 of the passive clause continues the subject P1 of the preceding clause, and is identical with the speaker of the following direct speech, thus representing continuity not on the syntactic, but on the discourse level.[138] P2 is resumed four times from the preceding clause, once as the object P2 of the preceding main clause, co-referential with the subject P1 of an intervening subordinate clause (see (78)). Note that, here, P2 of the passive clause is expressed by means of an enclitic pronoun. Of the four cases in which P2 is resumed in the main clause following the passive clause, the coreferential entity is the object P2 in two.

(78)   In fer déidenach níndránic acht ind mbéimme conid corastair i mmúaidhi.
Anachtai-side la Coin Culaind íarom.   (*TBC I* 3187)
rescue_pass.pret.sg.-PRO with Cú Chulainn
'The last man, he only received a glance of a blow, so that he fell into a swoon.
He was rescued by Cú Chulainn later.'

At first sight, continuity of P1 is more common in *TBC LL* than in *TBC I*: in the former, P1 in the passive clause resumes a subject P1 in five instances, and the P1 of a passive clause in four. It is coreferential with the subject P1 of the following main clause in eight cases, and with the P1 of a passive clause in five. However, what accounts for these comparatively higher figures is the repetitive structure of certain passages: the three series of 'sáditer sosta ┐ pupaill lind . . .' (let us make camp and set up tents . . .)[139] and its variations account for four instances of P1 of a passive clause resuming another one, and in turn being coreferential to the P1 of the following passive clause. The repetitive section beginning with *TBC LL* 3127 (see (76b) and the discussion of this series) accounts for several of the unspecified occurrences of P1, in a syntactic and semantic role other than P1 or P2. Another example of recurring structures are the introductory formulas, in both *TBC LL* and *TBC III*, where P1 of the passive clause is resumed as subject P1.[140] With only very minor

---

[138] 'Tic Nad Crantail fo šodain. Hi fénai bretha arm la suide. "Cate Cú Chulaind?" ol sé' (Then Nad Crantail arrived. In a cart he brought his weapons along. 'Where is Cú Chulainn?', he asked) (*TBC I* 1443).
[139] *TBC I* 681/1, 681/2, 681/3; 690/1, 690/2; 1465/1, 1465/2.
[140] See e.g. 'Is and sin ra himráided ac feraib Hérend . . . Iss ed ra ráidsetar uile . . .' (Then the men of Ireland debated . . . This is what they all said . . .) (*TBC LL* 2531–2).

variations, every attestation in *TBC LL* and *TBC III* of this formula follows the pattern of resuming P1 of the passive clause as subject P1 in the following main clause, which accounts for five of eight instances of the resumption of a passive P1 by a subject P1 in the following clause. Thus the tendency that here is a higher degree of coreferentiality of a passive P1 with another P1, rather than with any other participant or entity visible in our texts, is to an extent conditioned by repetitive constructions.

The fact that repetitive or strongly patterned sections of narrative skew statistical counts does not mean they should necessarily be kept apart from the rest of the data. However, one needs to register that these sections do have structures that distinguish them from the rest of the narrative. Is is equally obvious that such repetitive constructions as are to be encountered in *TBC LL* and *III* partly maintain the continuity of the narrative in that a recurrence of a familiar sentence will re-evoke the section or sections in which it was used before.

As regards the continuity of syntactic structures, we can note that agentive passives do not occur in passive clusters[141] in the majority of cases. Altogether, clusters account for less than half of all full passive constructions: nine examples in *TBC I* (39.1%), seventeen in *TBC LL* (48.6%), and four examples (21.1%) in *TBC III*. One of the instances in *TBC I* is the opening of the narrative (see (74)). Of the seventeen instances in *TBC LL*, eleven are to be found in the repetitive structures already discussed above.[142]

3.3.3.3. AGENTIVE PASSIVES IN THEIR NARRATIVE ENVIRONMENTS

Agentive passive main clauses tend to convey mainstream information—that is, core developments of the narrative section in which they occur. An example of what is understood here as non-mainstream, or sideline information, is given in (78). Although the participant introduced here as P2 does return at a later stage of the narrative (he is the one who carries the warning of Cethern's approach), the fact that he had been rescued by Cú Chulainn is not mentioned again, and not developed any further. As we have seen, our texts contain examples of full passives that, through their repetitive and therefore immediately recognizable structure, contribute to the organization of the narrative—for example, the formula introducing the narrative sections presenting Cú Chulainn's single combats (see e.g. (72)). These are here categorized as 'organizational'.[143]

---

[141] A passive cluster is defined as the occurrence of two or more passive clauses, without other syntactic constructions intervening. Clusters that cross chapter boundaries, three altogether in *TBC I*, are included in this definition.

[142] 'sáditer sosta ┐ pupaill lind . . .' (let us make camp and set up tents) (*TBC LL* 685 ff., 690 ff., 1456 ff.); 'cach bíad . . . daberthea ó fheraib Hérend . . .' (every food which was brought by/from the men of Ireland) (3130 ff., 3172 ff.).

[143] Mainstream developments account for 70.2% (or 40 attestations) of all full passive main clauses, sideline developments for 11.5% (7 examples), and organizational use of full passives for 17.5% (10 examples). *TBC III* has the highest proportion of the organizational use of full passives (6 examples, 50%).

As regards the temporal structure of the narrative, we find that most agentive passive main clauses are used to portray linear developments—in other words, the sequence of situations introduced in the narrative corresponds to the sequence of the events reported. Much less frequently, we find the use of full passives to describe situations that lie in the future relative to the narrative development—for example, situations that are announced by means of a full passive. The passive imperatives discussed above, example (70), have been classified as 'posterior' relative to their occurrence in the narrative development, as the situations they describe are, as it were, at the planning stage. Example (78) is an instance of a full passive main clause presenting a situation posterior to its temporal context.[144] Having classified the instances of the introductory formula as having a clearly organizational function, the question arises how to categorize other repetitive structures already discussed, such as the sequence beginning with *TBC LL* 690/1:

(79)   *Darónad urgnam bíd 7 lenna leó 7 ra canait ceóil 7 airfiti leó ⅂ darónad* praind
         ⅂ tomaltus.   (*TBC LL* 690/1, 690/2)
         make_pass.pret.sg preparation food_gen.sg and drink_gen.sg with them and
         PRT sing_pass.pret.sg music and entertainment with-them
         'Food and drink was prepared by them, and music and entertainment performed by them, and a meal and repast taken.'

As mentioned above (see (70)), lexically and structurally very similar sequences occur in *TBC LL* 685 (passive imperatives), and 1465 (negated preterite forms). Each of these sequences is part of the mainstream development of the text and is here classified as such; however, one should not lose sight of the fact that these repetitive series, as pointed out already, also serve an organizational function in that they recall previous encounters of similar sequences, and thereby previous episodes of the narrative, to the reader's mind. A similar dual function is served by the recurrent constructions introduced with *TBC LL* 3127 (see again (76*b*)): because of their repetitive structure, series of lexically and structurally similar constructions stand out from their context, they are easily recalled, and they can thus be used to maintain links between episodes.

Subordinate full passive clauses present a different distribution of temporal relations between the clause and its context, in that situations in linear development with their context account for less than half of the attestations—a circumstance that is, of course, closely linked with a function of subordinate clauses—that is, that of contributing circumstantial information, including information concerning events preceding and following the point reached in the development of the narrative.[145] A relation between the passive clause and its environment that

---

[144] 71.9% (or 41 examples) of full agentive passives portray developments contemporary relative to their temporal environments, and 24.8% (15 examples) are classified as 'posterior'. There is one example categorized as 'hypothetical' (*TBC LL* 4708).

[145] Altogether, 40% (or 8 ex.) represent situations in linear development with their context, 45% (9 attestations) situations that are anterior, and 15% (3 ex.) situations that are posterior to their contexts.

does not occur with main clauses in our texts is that of the subordinate passive clause presenting a situation anterior to the narrative 'here and now', illustrated in (80):

(80)   Días sain de fénnedaib na hIrúade *forróeglass d'óentoisc ó Ailill 7 ó Meidb* ar
        dáig do gona-su . . .   (*TBC LL* 3745)
        choose_pass.pret.sg especially from Ailill and from Medb
        'These are two warriors from Iruath who were chosen especially by Ailill and
        Medb in order to kill you . . .'

3.3.4. Interlude: full passives in *Táin Bó Cúailnge* and other narrative texts

Several tendencies have emerged from the preceding sections: the most common marker of P1 in passive clauses is the preposition *la* 'with, by'. The relatively frequent occurrence of *oc* 'at' in *TBC III* may be due to the later date of the text; but, equally, the frequent repetitions of one formulaic expression needs to be kept in mind when considering the statistics. P1 in passive clauses is expressed by definite noun phrases or pronouns suffixed to the preposition, and represents given information in a majority of the attestations in our texts. There is no clear preference for P2 to represent new, given, or inferable information.[146] As regards the sequence of P1 and P2, we have seen that pronominal as well as clausal P2s follow the P1 phrase, whereas an indefinite nominal subject P2 tends to precede the P1 phrase. Overall, the agentive passive is a feature of narrative, rather than dialogue, presenting situations that are in linear development with their narrative contexts. Continuity of P1 or P2 is not realized in a majority of cases; where there is continuity, we can observe that P1 tends to be coreferential with another P1 rather than with any other entity, and P2 with another P2.

The question arises whether any of the tendencies can be taken as reliable, since they are derived from a comparatively small number of attestations. The agentive passive is on the whole a rare construction, and thus even long narrative texts such as *Táin Bó Cúailnge* show only a comparatively small number of attestations. This characteristic, as well as other features of the agentive passive, is mirrored in other texts. Four other narratives examined here, *Fled Bricrend* (*LU* lines 8038–9219), *Scéla Mucce Meic Dathó* (Thurneysen 1935), *Táin Bó Fraích* (Meid 1970), and *Cath Maige Tuired* (Gray 1982) yield altogether fourteen agentive passives. P1 is marked by *la* in thirteen examples (92.8 per cent), and once by *ó*. In all except this latter case, given in (81), P1 is a definite entity, and represents given information. The one example containing *ó* as P1 marker is exceptional in other respects as well, in that it is a subordinate clause, presenting an author- (or narrator-) comment, and in that the passive verb is in the imperfect tense (which is a further indication that the clause stands outside the main narrative development).

[146] Although there is an overall slight majority for P2 to introduce new information (58.1%).

(81)   Is aire immorro nolabraidis demna d'armaib isan aimsir-sin *ar noadraddis airm ó daínib isin ré-sin*   (*CMT* 783)
because PRT-worship_pass.impf.pl weapon_nom.pl from person_dat.pl. in-the time-that
'This is why demons used to speak from weapons then, because weapons used to be worshipped by people at that time'

P2 in these examples is represented by an indefinite noun phrase in eight cases (57.1 per cent), and the indefinite P2 is always new and precedes the P1 phrase. Altogether, P2 precedes P1 in ten examples; in a further two attestations, a nominal, given P2 follows the P1 phrase, and two clauses do not contain a lexically marked P2. Only three of the fourteen examples occur in direct speech, and all examples but one are main clauses. Nine of these present developments that are in linear sequence with their contexts, three portray anterior, and one posterior developments. This additional database, though small, supports the main findings for the full passive in *TBC*. In the next section, data from other text types are examined, before we return to a more general consideration of the full passive, and passive and impersonal characteristics of this construction type.

3.4. Full passives in laws and annals

3.4.1. Law texts

The agentive passive is not a construction greatly favoured by composers of early Irish legal material: of the five texts analysed here, only *Críth Gablach* and *Bechbretha* contain any instances, one and two examples, respectively. The P1 markers used are the prepositions *ó* and *la*. The three examples are given below.[147] The interpretation of *CG* 28, example (82a), follows Mac Néill (1923: 83).[148] Binchy reads *la* as expressing accompaniment in this instance ('along with' (1941: 59)).

(82) (a)   Snádid a chomgrád tara thúaith fadesin ⁊ *bía(d)tair leis* co ndíched tar crích. (*CG* 28)
feed_pass.pres.sg with-him
'He₁ protects his₁ equal in rank across (or: beyond?) his₁ own *túath* and he₂ is fed by him₁ until he₂ crosses the border.'

(b)   To-bert a chin forsin fer batar beich noch is sí breth inso *brethae la Ultu* ⁊ *Féniu imbi*.   (*BB* §33)
bear_pass.pret.sg.rel with Ulsterman_acc.pl and Féni_acc.pl about-it
'He charged the man who owned the bees with its offence and this is the judgment which was passed by the *Ulaid* and the *Féni* about it.'
(Charles-Edwards and Kelly 1983: 71)

---

[147] The translation of the quote from *CG* is my own, and has been kept as literal as possible; translations of examples from *BB* are the renderings provided by the editors.

[148] Mac Néill (1923: 83) translates 'he protects his equal in grade over his own *túath* and he (the protégé) is fed by him until he goes over the border'.

(c)   Air iss i suidiu ar-tét sochaide cinaid n-óenḟir nad forúachtatar uili la Féniu
. . . no [amal] fer gonar a ucht ṡlúaig máir nadid-lamethar airthech na fortach
for nech sainredach dib. *Di-renar in fer úadaib uilib* no do-rochratar uili i
ndílsi.   (*BB* §35)
pay_pass.pres.sg the man from-them all_dat.pl
'For it is in this case in Irish law that a multitude is liable for the offence of one,
[an offence] which they have not all committed . . . or a man who is killed in
the midst of a great crowd, and no one ventures a vicarious oath or an oath
fixing guilt on anyone of them in particular. Compensation for the man is
paid by them all, or they have all become forfeit.'
(Charles-Edwards and Kelly 1983: 73)

Unlike the other two examples quoted here, *BB* §33 is linked with a specific historical event,[149] rather than stating a general rule independent of time. A gloss in the
hand of the main glossator of manuscript A of *Bechbretha*, who worked in the first
half of the fourteenth century, gives a rendering of the second half of §33 (see (83)).
Note that the glossator uses the preposition *ag* (Old Irish: *oc*) rather than *la*, to
mark P1—a usage already encountered in *TBC LL* and *III*, but not in *TBC I*.

(83)   .i. seichim conad i seo breath *rugadh ag ultaib*   (*BB* §33, gloss b)
bear_pass.pret.sg at Ulsterman_dat.pl
'i.e. "I say" that this is the judgment which was passed by the Ulstermen about
it'   (Charles-Edwards and Kelly 1983: 71)

BB §35 (82*c*) is an instance of a verb expressing 'giving' (in the widest sense) being
accompanied by the P1 marker *ó*, a pattern that also occurs in *TBC*. However, as the
verb *biadaid* 'feeds' (see (82*a*)), can also be said to contain the semantic component of 'giving' (food, in this case), and the preposition chosen to express P1 in this
example is *la*, this criterion cannot be taken as a generally applicable principle for
the selection of *ó* versus *la* in agentive function.

It is hardly possible to deduce patterns of usage from a total of three instances
of a construction in a body of texts. It can be noted, however, that these three
examples follow the general tendency that P1 is definite and represents given information.

3.4.2. *The Annals of Ulster* (post-Patrician text to AD 1131)

The earliest instance of an Irish full passive in *The Annals of Ulster* is 804.8, the last

---

[149] The incident referred to is the blinding of Congal Cáech by a bee, and is integrated into the text
as follows: 'Mad súil rocháecha iss i suidiu áilid cocrann forsin lestrai n-uili; cip lestar día toth dib ar-tét
a ḟiach' (If it be an eye which it has blinded, it is then that it (the injury) requires the casting of lots on
all the hives: whichever of the hives it fall upon is forfeit for its (the bee's) offence) (*BB* §30); 'Air is sí
cétnae breth inso ceta-rucad im chinta bech for Congail Cháech cáechsite beich' (For this is the first
judgment which was passed with regard to the offences of bees on Congal the One-eyed, whom bees
blinded in one eye) (*BB* §31); 'Ba-ch rí Temro conid-tubart assa ḟlaith' (And he was king of Tara until
[this] put him from his kingship) (*BB* §32).

one 1128.5; altogether, there are thirteen examples in the text up to AD 1131; in eleven, P1 is marked by *la*, and in two instances by *ó*. The very first instance, 804.8, could conceivably be an interpolation, since it is in a hand different from that of the main scribe,[150] and added in the margin. The second full passive occurs in the entry for AD 850. Thus this syntactic structure makes its appearance around the time by which Irish attains the same significance as Latin in this text as a medium to record history. As mentioned in connection with agentive VN constructions in *The Annals of Ulster*, the use of Latin *apud* 'with, among' to mark P1 is reminiscent of Irish *la*. As well as with Latin process nouns, *apud* occurs in passive clauses, six times in the former, and five times in the latter construction.[151] Nine of these eleven potential *apud*-P1s ocur in entries between *AU* 695 and 731. It is possible that, in these nine cases, we are witnessing the work of one or several subsequent annalists whose Latin acquired a particular Irish flavour, modelling the use of *apud* on *la*. On the other hand, it may be that what we see is rather a usage similar to that described by Graur (1933: 231–47) for Gaulish Latin, where *apud*, as well as *ab* 'from', and *cum* 'with', are employed as agent markers, without the assumption of any necessary substrate influence.

Judging from the textual evidence, we have so far seen that the full passive is mainly a feature of dynamic narrative: its occurrence is most common in passages that serve to advance the development of the narrative (compare the characteristics noted above, notably the mainly linear temporal organization of situations portrayed in full passive clauses relative to their contexts). We might expect, then, that the full passive in the annals represents not mere listings of events, but a certain 'narrative' development. Looking at all the instances of this construction in *The Annals of Ulster*, we find that the full passive is the first clause of an entry in only two cases: 804.8, a main clause introduced by a temporal adverbial phrase, and 1126.11, which is a relative clause, embedded in a verbal noun clause of the form $P2+do_{VN}+P1$, with the subject of the passive as antecedent (the passive clause is therefore not the initial main clause of the paragraph, although the first verbal element is the passive verb). All full passives, with the exception of these two instances, occur in paragraphs introduced by VN or process-noun clauses, either following these directly, as in (84*a*), or following intervening finite clauses, as in (84*b*).[152]

(84) (*a*)   Slogad la Cenel nEogain, .i. la Domnall m. Aedho ⁊ la Niall m. Aedho *co rolscath leo Tlachtgha.*   (*AU* 908.1)
         so-that PRT-burn_pass.pret.sg with-them Tlachtga
         'An expedition by the Cenél Eógain, i.e. by Domnall son of Aed, and by Niall son of Aed, and Tlachtga was burned by them.'

---

[150] Mac Niocaill's H², as opposed to the main hand H.
[151] LPNs: *AU* 454, 701.8, 711.3, 712.5, 731.4, 804.5; passives: *AU* 695.1, 713.7, 714.2, 714.8, 726.1.
[152] The translations given are those of Mac Niocaill's edition of the text.

(b)   Cinaedh m. Conaing . . . du frithtuidecht Mail Sechnaill . . . ⁊ cor[o] ort innsi
       Locha Gabur dolose corbo comardd fria lar, ⁊ *coro loscad leis derthach Treoit* ⊐
       tri xx.it dec di doinibh ann.   (*AU* 850.3)
       so-that-PRT burn_pass.pret.sg with-him oratory T.
       'Cinaed son of Conaing . . . rebelled against Mail Sechnaill . . . and he deceit-
       fully sacked the Island of Loch Gabor, levelling it to the ground, and the ora-
       tory of Treóit, with seventy people in it, was burned by him.'

Clauses introduced by *co^n*, such as the ones quoted in (84), are classified as main
clauses here, since the function of *co^n* as used here is coordinating rather than
subordinating. However, *co^n* cannot be equated with *ocus*, as there is always an
interdependence between the introductory clause (often a VN or a noun clause)
and the *co^n*-clause, of a temporal and sometimes also a causal nature: the situation
portrayed in the *co^n*-clause always follows, in real time, that of the introductory
clause, and it can be a (logical) consequence of the latter.[153] *Ocus* can express this
relation, but does not invariably do so. There is in *The Annals of Ulster* a group of
five instances that correspond in structure to the examples quoted in (84). P1 is
always identical with that of the introductory nominal clause, and, in all cases, the
P1 marker *la* immediately follows the passive verb—that is, it precedes the subject
P2 (word-order type 2—see Sections 3.3.2 and 3.3.3) in four of the cases; one does
not contain an overt P2 (see (85)).

(85)   Slogad la Flann m. Mael Sechlainn co firu Muman *cor innredh leis o Ghabran
        co lLuimnech.*   (*AU* 906.3)
        so-that-PRT invade_pass.pret.sg with-him from Gabrán to Luimnech
        'An Expedition by Flann son of Mael Sechnaill against the people of Mumu,
        and he harried from Gabrán to Luimnech.'

In all these cases, the full passive portrays a situation that is the last in a series of
actions and events carried out or dominated and controlled by the P1 of the passive
(which is, as mentioned above, also the character introduced in an initial VN or
noun clause). This is also true for an additional instance, where P1, however, is reintroduced as the subject P1 of an active clause preceding the full passive (see (86)).
Note that, here, the full passive follows word-order pattern 1 (V P2 P1), as opposed
to pattern 2 (V P1 P2) in the other instances of the full passive introduced by *co^n* in
The Annals of Ulster.

(86)   Slogad la Brian, ri Caisil . . . co tangadur Gaill Atha Cliath dia fuabairt . . . co
        remaidh forro ⊐ coro ladh a n-ár . . . Do-luidh Brian iar sin i nAth Cliath *coro
        ort Ath Cliath leis.*   (*AU* 999.8)
        so-that_PRT destroy_pass.pret.sg Áth Cliath with-him
        'Brian . . . led an army . . . and the foreigners of Áth Cliath . . . came to attack
        him. And they were defeated and a slaughter was inflicted on them . . . Brian
        afterwards entered Áth Cliath, and Áth Cliath was destroyed by him.'

[153]   For the functions of *co^n* in the Old Irish glosses, see *GOI* §896.

In altogether nine of the thirteen instances of Irish full passives in *The Annals of Ulster*, the passive clause is the last clause of the section of the entry in which it occurs. Keeping in mind that the absolute number of instances in this text is quite small, we can still note that the full passive tends to end a paragraph—in other words, to form the conclusion of the minimalist narratives that the sections represent. The only case of a full passive being the first clause of a section is *AU* 804.8. This untypical behaviour might be another point in favour of the argument that this example is a later interpolation into this section. The tendency of full passives to conclude sections is not limited to the group of *co*ⁿ-passives. An impressionistic interpretation, admittedly resting on a small database, is that the full passive in *The Annals of Ulster* serves to present a situation that represents the endpoint, temporally and logically, of the developments of action established earlier in the section. There are aspects of textual organization that back up this view. In all but one paragraph-final full passive, the situation presented is in linear temporal organization with respect to its context. The one exception here is *AU* 1004.5, one of the two cleft sentences containing the full passive in *The Annals of Ulster* (see (87)).[154] The construction in question is an object clause that partly rephrases, and gives an alternative view of, a situation that has been presented before in the section. Note also that, untypically, the P1 marker is *ó*, rather than *la*.

(87)   Cath Craibe Telcha eter Ultu ⁊ Cenel nEogain . . . Do-rochair ann dono Aedh
         m. Domhnaill H. Neill, rí Ailigh . . . acht as-berat Cenel nEogain *is uadhibh*
         fein ro marbad.   (*AU* 1004.5)
         COP from-them self PRT kill_pass.pret.sg
         'The battle of Craeb Tulcha between the Ulaid and the Cenél Eógain . . .
         Moreover, Aed son of Domnall ua Néill, king of Ailech, fell there . . . but the
         Cenél Eógain claim that he was killed by themselves.'

The full passive in *The Annals of Ulster* shows tendencies of information structuring similar to those found in the narrative texts. P1 tends to be given rather than new; the ratio being eight given versus five new P1s. With the exception of one, all section-final full passives contain given P1s (this group includes all *co*ⁿ-passives). The subject P2 represents new information in nine cases, as opposed to four examples where P2 resumes given information. As before, 'given' is defined for *The Annals of Ulster* as 'having been mentioned in the entry for the same year'. Although this seems at first sight to presuppose a very short attention span on the part of the reader, one has to keep in mind that the annals were not necessarily read, or indeed intended to be read, as a continuous text. There is a high rate of P1 continuity, already implicit in the short interval of resumption of information. Seven out of eight passive clauses containing given P1s resume P1 of the preceding clause or VN clause. The exception is *AU* 850.3 (see (84*b*)), where a copula clause intervenes. The sequence of given and new information in full passive clauses in *TBC* tends to be 'new before given', where P2 is expressed by a noun phrase. This pattern does not

---

[154] The other example is *AU* 1013.4.

emerge from *The Annals of Ulster*, where word-order type 2 is slightly more frequent than type 1.[155]

To an extent, the fact that P1 of the full passive (and indeed of other constructions) in *The Annals of Ulster* is in all cases but one a definite entity—that is, an individual or named group—can be explained through the nature of the text, which deals in the main with situations brought about or experienced by named individuals or groups.[156] This further parallel to the characteristics of the passive in *TBC* should therefore not be overvalued. The characteristic 'definite' may be seen to be implied by the characteristic 'given', which it is in many cases, since given information is usually referred to by definite noun phrases, or pronominal expressions. The term 'individualized' is possibly more appropriate. An entry such as *Orggain la díberga co loscad leó tech n-óil* 'a plundering by marauders, and they burned down a pub' would be conceivable (in structure, if not in content), where P1 of the passive clause, though definite by virtue of being expressed by means of a prepositional pronoun, is not individualized. However, this structure does not commonly occur. The—partial—exception to the tendency that P1 is an individualized person or group is *AU* 1128.5:

(88)   Gním granna anaithnigh aniarmartach . . . do dhenamh do Thigernan
        H. Ruairc ⁊ do hUi[b] Briuin .i. . . . . Ise imorro an iarmuirt do fhass don
        mhignimsa conach fuil in Erinn comuirce is tairisi do dhuine fodhesta *no curo
        dhighailter o Dia ⁊ o dhoeinibh in t-olc-sa.*   (*AU* 1128.5)
        but until-PRT avenge-pass.pres.sub.sg from God and from person_dat.pl the
        evil-that
        'A detestable and unprecedented deed of evil consequence . . . was committed
        by Tigernán ua Ruairc and the Uí Briúin, .i. . . . . The aftermath that came of
        that misdeed is that there exists in Ireland no protection that is secure for
        anyone henceforth until that evil deed is avenged by God and men.'

Unlike the sober, quite unemotional entries that are the norm in *The Annals of Ulster*, this paragraph clearly mirrors the just anger of the annalist at the crime committed (i.e. the party of the successor of Patrick having been robbed). The clause 'no curo dhighailter o Dhia ⁊ o dhoeinibh' is to be understood as a demand for action concerning the grievance reported; the use of an unspecific 'o dhoeinibh' (on the face of it both unindividualized and indefinite) is addressed to 'everyone', and thus a degree of definiteness on a semantic level is maintained.

3.5. A 'noun phrase passive'?

As mentioned in the introductory chapter, passive constructions are among the more thoroughly researched structures, cross-linguistically. How, then, does what

---

[155] There are five instances of type 2, as opposed to four of type 1, and four where the parameter is not applicable.
[156] This would also explain why P2 tends to be definite, rather than indefinite (as seen in *TBC*).

is here labelled the medieval Irish full passive compare to full passives in other languages? As regards the participants in situations portrayed by means of passive clauses, the strongest tendency observed is the status of P1, which is usually a definite, given entity. According to Pinkster's (1985) study of the passive in classical Latin,[157] P1 (Pinkster uses the term agent) represents given information in 62 per cent of all cases in his database. Thus givenness of P1 is not as strong a characteristic in Pinkster's Latin data as it is in our texts.[158] Conversely, the degree of givenness of the subject P2 is higher in Pinkster's texts than in *TBC* (53 per cent in Cicero). His figures for the continuity of the agent with respect to the preceding clause are higher (38 per cent) than what we have found in our data, with the exception of *The Annals of Ulster*, which, because of the nature of the text, shows a high degree of continuity. He states further that the subject of the full passive tends to resume the subject of the preceding clause (in 23 per cent of all full passives in Cicero), rather than any other constituent (1985: 113). Looking at the realization of continuity in the Irish data, one has to agree with Pinkster's statement that 'the answer whether passivisation is a continuity or a discontinuity device must be that it is both' (1985: 114). This emerges especially clearly when comparing *TBC* with *The Annals of Ulster*, the latter showing continuity as a regular feature.

As Pinkster notes, his findings with respect to givenness of P1 and the subject of the full passive do not correspond to studies on the German passive, which show that P1 tends to represent new, and the subject P2 given, information.[159] This tendency for P1 to represent new information has also been noted for English passives, from both fictional and non-fictional texts, by Givón (1979: 30), who finds that the majority of P1s in full passive clauses is indefinite, and that P1 is always the focus of new information (with approximately 10 per cent of all passive clauses containing overtly marked P1s). On the other hand, Van Oosten's (1984) research, based on American English data, finds a distribution that is biased towards givenness of P1 in full passive clauses, but, nevertheless, a large proportion of P1s represent new information: in her data, 63 per cent of all passive clauses ($n = 74$) contained a given P1 (this figure includes inferable P1s, 27 per cent of the total number), new P1s account for 37 per cent of all cases.

Andersen (1985), analysing Vedic passive construction and using data from Jamison (see Jamison 1979*a*, *b*), also finds that P1 is regularly new, and thus the focus of new information. P2, on the other hand, is generally a given entity, and definite (1985: 51). Siewierska (1984) generalizes on the status of the agent, or P1, in passive clauses and draws the conclusion that, as 'the agent tends to be both new and generally less inherently topical than the patient, it is the agent and not the subject/topic which constitutes the information focus' (1984: 236).[160] The primary

---

[157] Pinkster uses data from Cicero, *De Republica*, and Plautus, *Mostellaria*.

[158] Pinkster's definition of agent does not exclude the inanimate agent; his category 'agent' is thus not directly compatible with the P1 of the passive as investigated here.

[159] See Schoenthal (1976: 115) and Pape-Müller (1980: 124).

[160] Siewierska defines the topic as the initial constituent of a clause, usually representing given

function of the full passive is, according to Siewierska, the maintaining of the unmarked given-before-new distribution of information in the clause (1984: 222).

As we have had ample opportunity to observe, the data analysed here do not fit with this generalization, nor do they agree with the language-specific studies quoted above. The givenness, and definiteness, of P1 in full passives, as indeed in VN constructions, is the strongest overall tendency to emerge from the texts analysed in detail, and, as the spot checks across other texts quoted above (Section 3.3.4) reveal, this appears to be a regular feature of full passives. The status of P1 is, however, only one characteristic that distinguishes medieval Irish passives from canonical personal passives in other languages (such as Latin, or Sanskrit, or German). The encoding of P2 is another. As outlined in Chapter 1, P2 in medieval Irish passives is encoded as the nominative subject only if it is expressed by means of a noun phrase. If it is a first or second person, the encoding is the same as for a direct object of an active clause; if it is a third person singular, the conventional interpretation is that the Old Irish passive verbal ending encodes the subject P2, an interpretation supported by the existence of a separate form for the third person plural. The question arises, is there a link between the information status of P1 in full passives, and the encoding of P2, and if so, what is the link?

The notions of backgrounding and foregrounding passives as used by Keenan (1985), and of a pragmatic pivot (Foley and Van Valin 1985) are useful in this context. Backgrounding in passive clauses concerns P1, which is either expressed by means of an oblique noun phrase or eliminated altogether. Conversely, P2, the object of the active clause, is foregrounded by promoting it to the status of subject in the passive clause. Foley and Van Valin (1985: 322) define foregrounding passives as 'passives which serve to permit a non-actor to occur as pragmatic pivot'; the pivot is the particular noun phrase that controls a large proportion of the language's syntax (such as, for example, subject–verb agreement). Where the choice of pivot is at least in part determined by discourse requirements, it is called a 'pragmatic pivot', and this is the type of pivot that is found, for example, in English, and indeed in early Irish passives with nominal P2s.

An interpretation of the medieval Irish passive as a backgrounding device for P1 of a situation, and a foregrounding strategy for nominal P2s, can account both for the particularities of P1 in full passives, and for the subject/object-like split in the encoding of P2.[161] Motivations either for removing P1 from view entirely, or for moving it to a marginal position in the clause (i.e. into the role of an oblique noun phrase), can vary. For example, it may not be possible, or indeed vital in the context of the situation to be portrayed, to identify P1 exactly, and thus it will not be overtly encoded. In other cases, P1 may very well be known, and discourse requirements may make it necessary to recall P1 to the reader's mind. And indeed we have seen

---

information. In an unmarked structure, the information focus, representing new information, follows the given topic (see 1984: 218–19).

[161] See also Müller (1994).

that P1s in full passive clauses generally are not only given information, but well-established, central characters of the narrative. Thus we can think of the full passive as a device that maintains the continued presence of a character in the reader's mind, albeit in the background of the situation portrayed.

As regards the foregrounding properties of the medieval Irish passive, in principle two interpretations are possible: the passive in early Irish foregrounds a P2 either if and only if that P2 is a third person, or if and only if that P2 is a noun phrase. The difference between these two possibilities lies in the interpretation of the passive verb form. If the first hypothesis is adopted, it is necessary to read the passive verb form, whether singular or plural, as expressing the third person subject P2, just as, for example, *as-beir* 'he/she/it says' expresses a third person subject P1. Thus one would interpret, for example, *canir* as 'it is sung', and *benair Fergus* as 'Fergus is struck'. In this interpretation, there is no problem with the plural verb form: since the subject controls verb agreement, a plural subject requires plural marking on the verb. A difficulty lies in the treatment of the first and second persons: if the verb form actually expresses a third person subject P2, then the use of the same verb form in cases where P2 is a first or second person, and marking it like a direct object, appears unfelicitous. A further point hard to reconcile with this interpretation is the historical development of pronominal, third person P2s. Once these come to be marked analytically, they are invariably marked as 'objects', rather than 'subjects'—that is, the marking of P2 in active and passive clauses is the same, and differs from P1 marking in active clauses.

The second interpretation, that P2 is encoded as pivot (subject) only if it is a noun phrase, does not pose this particular problem, although it is not without difficulties of its own. According to this view of the passive clause, where P2 is a third person, but not specified by means of a noun phrase, it is to be inferred from the context, rather than expressed by the verb form itself. This interpretation is backed up by data, in that a large majority of implied P2s occur in the close preceding context of the clause, and that there never appear to be potential sources of ambiguity.[162] And indeed, leaving P2 to be inferred from context is not confined to passive clauses, as (89) shows, where the clause '⁊ tuc Ailill i lláim Ḟergusa' does not contain an overt P2, the identity of the implied P2 being known in the context.

(89)   Tánic Fer Loga reime ⁊ *tuc in claideb* laiss . . . *tucad in claideb* i lláim Ailella ⁊ *tuc Ailill* i lláim Ḟergusa.   (*TBC LL* 4717–19)
        bring_pret.3sg the sword; give_pass.pret.sg the sword; and give_pret.3sg Ailill
        'Fer Loga came and brought the sword . . . and it was put into Ailill's hand, and Ailill placed [it] into Fergus's hand.'

---

[162] Although immediate continuity (either syntactically or semantically) between P2 and an entity of the immediately preceding clause is not given in a majority of full passive clauses, an examination of all passive clauses shows that, in *TBC I*, 97.9 per cent of all implied P2s in passive clauses occur within the two preceding clauses (though not necessarily as P2); the figure for *TBC LL* is 89.4 per cent.

When P2 is a noun phrase, it is encoded as subject, or pivot. What we may see at work here is a mechanism that does not cast P2 as pivot unless that P2 is to receive special focus in the clause (recall that the prototypical pivot is P1, as the prototypical subject of a transitive clause). One of the motivations for focusing a P2 is that it constitutes new information that advances the development, and becomes the New Topic of the following discourse, as in (90). Note also that, in this example, the overt P1 maintains continuity of that participant in the context, facilitating its recovery where it recurs in the next clause.

(90)   *Ebéltair culén* din chúani chétna *lem-sa* duit, ꟼ biam cú-sa do imdegail do chethra . . . *cor ása in cú hísin* ꟼ corop ingníma.   (*TBC I* 598 ff.)
raise_sg.pass.fut whelp with-me; until_PRT grow_pres.sub.3sg the hound that
'A whelp from the same litter will be raised by me for you, and I will be a hound protecting your cattle . . . until that hound has grown up and is ready for action.'

However, not all nominal P2s are new. This is true for full passives, as well as for passives without overt P1, where generally around half of all nominal P2s represent new information. And, although there is some tendency for a new nominal P2 to precede P1, this is not an absolute pattern. A given P2 may be referred to by means of a pronoun (a usage attested in our database in *TBC LL* and *III*, but not in *TBC I*) or left to be inferred from the context, or else it may be referred to by a noun phrase. Entities that can sensibly be referred to by means of pronouns, or indeed can be left to be inferred by the reader from the context, have by default and definition a high inherent salience—that is, they are immediately accessible and identifiable. This includes discourse participants—that is, first and second persons (both on an intra-textual level—for example, characters of a narrative—and on the level of writer/narrator and reader)—but also third persons mentioned in the immediately preceding context. It is not necessary to make a special effort to recall them to the reader's mind, since they are already present in short-term memory. Thus a violation of the unmarked, normally preferred pattern of not casting P2 as pivot is not necessary, and, moreover, it is uneconomical as regards the preferred flow of information in the clause. If discourse requirements make the removal of P1 from pivot position necessary, this can be done without automatically promoting P2 to pivot.

   If, however, an entity representing given information is recalled by means of a noun phrase, this can be read as an indication that its salience in the clause needs to be enhanced: either it needs to be recalled into the hearer's mind (i.e. P2 may represent information previously introduced, but this information may by now be dormant and not accessible without some effort), or attention is drawn to a particular feature of P2, or P2 is to serve as topic for the following discourse. In any of these cases, the pragmatically marked casting of P2 as pivot is justified as a means of adding salience. Example (91) illustrates the highlighting of a particular feature of P2:

(91)   And sain *ro irgabad in mac bec* isin charput. *Tucad* i trí dabchaib úaruscib *é* do díbdud a ḟerge. Ocus in chétna dabach i *tucad in mac bec* . . .
(*TBC LL* 1192–4)
PRT seize_pass.pret.sg the boy small; put_pass.pret.sg him; put_pass.pret.sg the boy small
'The little boy was seized in the chariot. He was put into three vats of cold water to extinguish his rage. And the first vat into which the little boy was put . . .'

Here, P2 would be clearly identifiable from the context as Sétanta (the young Cú Chulainn). By using the term *in mac becc*, rather than, for example, the boy's name, the writer highlights the fact that it is a child we are dealing with here, which makes the events related in this section of the narrative (the *Maccgnímrada*, or 'Boyhood deeds of Cú Chulainn') all the more unusual.[163]

This interpretation of the passive as promoting noun phrases, and noun phrases only to subject pivot in medieval Irish, is not without difficulties. In particular, the existence of the third person plural passive verb form is a problem. I would suggest that this arises out of the requirement that a verb agrees with a plural subject in number, and that its use is extended by semantic analogy to refer to any third person plural P2 with which the 'passive' verb form co-occurs. Although this is not an entirely satisfactory explanation, it may be noted here that the plural passive verb form is not a stable entity, and that its disappearance is one of the changes the passive undergoes over time. Thus it appears justified to interpret the passive in medieval Irish as a 'personal NP passive', whereas when P2 is not a noun phrase, this verbal category functions more strictly speaking like an impersonal: the difference is largely one of varying degrees of focus on, or salience of, P2.

3.6. Related categories: IAG, CAUSE, and INST

3.6.1. The IAG: *la/ra, oc, fri,* and *tre*

There are two recurrent, lexically fixed constructions containing a preposition marking the IAG. The first is the phrase *do-tuit* X *la/ra/oc* Y 'X falls (i.e. dies) at the hands of Y' (see (92a)); the second involves the substantive verb *attá* 'is' with infixed pronoun (expressing possession), followed by a prepositional phrase (see (92b)).

---

[163] The frequent use of *in macc becc* to refer to the youthful hero is not confined to passive clauses in this section of the text, but is a habitually used phrase.

(92) (a)   dáig níbam béo *meni thaeth cara nó náma limm* d'feraib Hérend innocht.
            (*TBC LL* 557)
            if-not fall_fut.3sg friend or enemy with-me
            'For I shall not live if a friend or foe among the men of Ireland fall not by my
            hand tonight.' (O'Rahilly 1967: 153)

     (b)   'Atbirt frim trá', or in Mórrígan, '*ním bíad íc lat* co bráth.'   (*TBC I* 2051)
            not-PRO-1sg be_fut2.3sg healing with-you
            ' "But you told me", said the Mórrígan, "that I should never get healing from
            you." ' (O'Rahilly 1976: 182)

There is some variation with regard to the preposition marking the IAG in the
construction illustrated in (92a) in *TBC LL* and *III*. The former text shows one
instance each of *fri* and *ra*, as well as two of *ac* (a variant of *oc*). The preposition
usually found with the phrase is *la*.[164] I would attribute the use of *ra/re* to the
gradual merging of *fri* 'against' and *la*, rather than to a fully fledged IAG function of
fri, since the variant found is more often the hybrid form *ra/re* than *fri*, and since *fri*
is used only once in IAG function outside the construction *do-tuit* X *la/re* Y. The
possessive construction exemplified in (92b) is, in the present database, restricted
to *TBC I*.[165] The preposition marking the giver is usually *la*; there is one instance of
ó (*DIL*, col. 473 41–2, quotes one further instance).

On the whole, *la* is the most frequently occurring preposition in IAG function.
The IAG does not normally co-occur with a prepositional P1. Where examples containing *la* are doubtful, the ambiguity is between locative and IAG function, as, for
example, in (93).[166]

(93)   Ní fail ní *itágammar-ne la Ultu.*   (*TBC LL* 207)
        fear_pres.1pl-PRO with Ulsterman_acc.pl
        'There is nothing we fear from the Ulstermen.' (O'Rahilly 1967: 143); or:
        'there is nothing we fear in Ulster.'

Apart from the possessive construction illustrated in (92b) above, the domain of
warlike pursuits (killing and bloodshed, and the like) accounts for a large proportion of instances in which *la* is used as IAG marker. In fact, *TBC I* shows only eight
examples that do not contain an expression for killing; of these, two refer to bloodshed (*ardáilfe fuil* 'blood will be spilled'), two to the defeat of an army (containing
maidid 'breaks, is defeated'), one indirectly to the killing of men (*beitis lir cenda
fer . . .* 'men's heads will be as numerous . . .' (*TBC I* 4007)). *TBC LL* contains one

---

[164] *La* occurs ten times in *TBC I*, thirty times in *TBC LL*, fifteen times each in *TBC III* and in *AU*. *AU*
also shows two instances of the phrase *(bellum) . . . in quo cecidit/ceciderunt* X *la* Y '(the battle of) . . . in
which X fell at the hands of Y' (*AU* 632.2 and 703.2; in the latter, the *la*-phrase is added in hand H²).
There is also one instance of *apud* used in this construction (*AU* 714.5); this occurs in the same period
(*AU* 695–731) as the majority of examples for the agentive use of *apud* (see Section 3.4).
[165] Other texts that contain this construction are e.g. Wb (2 instances), *Bethu Brigte* (Ó hAodha 1978)
(3), *ScM* (1); see also Müller (1992).
[166] Similarly, *TBC LL* 4715 and *TBC I* 1054 (these examples are parallel), and *TBC I* 4019 are ambiguous.

example where *la* marks the IAG, outside the 'killing/dying' domain, *TBC III* and *The Annals of Ulster* none.

Other prepositions used to denote the IAG are found less frequently than *la*. The rarity of *fri* has already been noted.[167] *Oc*, or *ac*, is restricted to *TBC LL* and *III*. There is some further overlap between the use of *la* and *oc*: one example in *TBC LL* (4710) and one in *TBC III* (538.1) are parallelled by the use of *la* in *TBC I* (4019 and 1054; 804 and 809, respectively). As with *la*, the demarcation between a local sense of the preposition *oc* and its use as IAG marker can be difficult, as in example (94), where *oc* can be interpreted as marking a locative relation, or an IAG, or indeed as covering aspects of both.

> (94)   ... focheird clesrada ána ilerda ingantacha imda bar aird in lá sain *nád róeglaind ac neoch aile ríam*, ac Scáthaig ná ac Úathaig ná ac Aífe.
> (*TBC LL* 3277 ff.)
> NEG-REL PRT-learn_pret.3sg at anyone else ever
> '... and [he] performed that day many brilliant, wonderful feats which he had not learned from any other, not from Scáthach nor from Úathach nor from Aífe.' (O'Rahilly 1967: 227)

The use of *ó* in what can be described as the function of IAG generally shows close affinity to that of a SOURCE. The dividing line between an (animate) entity denoting the starting point of a movement or exchange, and the person portrayed as responsible for the situation, is at times difficult to draw (see (95)). In all cases attested in *TBC*, the verbal element implies an exchange or an act of giving or receiving.[168]

> (95)   Ni derntar isin cath ... *ní nád fesur úaid*.   (*TBC I* 3991)
> something NEG-REL know_pres.sub.1sg/_fut.1sg
> 'Let nothing happen in the battle ... that I do not learn about from you.'

Tre 'through' as simple preposition marking the IAG occurs only in isolated instances in our texts.[169] There are also a few cases of *tre* forming compound pre-

---

[167] 'Atbath cét n-ánrod friss' (a hundred warriors died at his hand) (*TBC I* 1012) is conceivably an instance of *fri* for *la*, or an indication that these two prepositions are overlapping more and more closely in certain functions (note also that *la* is used in l. 1013: 'Cethri ríg ar secht fichtib ríg atbath laiss' (One hundred and forty-four kings died at his hand)). J. E. C. Williams (1956) does not include an IAG function in his description of *fri*, neither are there any certain examples quoted in *DIL*. However, the interpretation of an example of *do-tuit fri* as 'fall by [fighting against]', while descriptively quite adequate, may very well be a *post hoc* attempt at uniting an unusual construction with the more common usage 'against' of the preposition *fri*.

[168] The two instances of *ó* marking the IAG in *AU* are both from the domain otherwise dominated by *la* ('killing/dying'). Since in one case the process is expressed by a Latin noun (*mors* 'death' (*AU* 883.4)), in the other by a Latin loanword (*martre* 'martyrdom' (*AU* 825.16)), Latin influence in the choice of preposition is, while not a necessity, a possibility.

[169] There is one instance in *TBC I*, and a further one in *AU*, combining a Latin expression with the Irish preposition *tre*: 'sed míserabile pietate misertus est tria Niall ...' (but was compassionated with a wonderful (translating: *mirabile*) kindness through Niall ...) (*AU* 964.6). Again, Latin influence is possible, if not necessarily present. The patterns (syntactic and semantic) of code switching in medieval Irish texts await further study.

positions with *ág* 'cause, reason', *accais* 'cause, reason', and *fochonn* 'cause, occasion'. In our texts, the three variants occur in corresponding passages of *TBC I* and *LL* (a variant reading of *TBC I* in manuscript C shows *triana bithin* 'because of her'); *TBC St.*, on the other hand, has the simple preposition:

(96) (a)   Atchúala sain Findabair . . . in comlín sain d'feraib Hérend *do thuttim trena ág*
            7 trena accais   (*TBC LL* 3887)
            to fall_VN through-her cause and through-her reason
            'Findabair . . . heard that this number of the men of Ireland had fallen because
            of her and on account of her'   (O'Rahilly 1967: 243)

     (b)   . . . .i. *apthain na secht cét triana fochann*   (*TBC I* 3364)
            die_VN the_gen.pl seven hundred through-her cause
            '. . . that seven hundred men had died because of her'   (O'Rahilly 1976: 215)

     (c)   . . . na sect cet laoch lancalma sin *do thuitim trithe fen*.   (*TBC St.* 3833)
            to fall_VN through-her self
            '. . . that those seven hundred brave warriors had fallen because of her.'

3.6.2. The CAUSE: *la/ra, ar,* and *de*

The preposition *la* occurs as marker of the CAUSE only in *TBC I*. In seven out of eight instances in this text, it is followed by a complement denoting what can be described as an external motivation; external in the sense that it does not pertain to the entity from whose perspective the situation is presented (see (97a)). In one case, *la* marks an internal motivation, where the complement of the preposition describes a state of mind, or emotional state.

(97) (a)   Nírbo hí sin adaig ropa sám dóib *lasin snechta*   (*TBC I* 311)
            with-the snow
            'That had not been a night that had been quiet for them because of (or: what
            with) the snow'

     (b)   '*La mméit inna feirgi 7 ind lúthbasa* inddar leó ní tairset itir'   (*TBC I* 3578)
            with amount the_gen.sg anger and the_gen.sg excitement
            'Because of the strength of their anger and excitement, it seems to them that
            they will never arrive'

Re/ra in causal function in *TBC I* is restricted to the passage *In Carpat Serda*, which may be interpreted as one indication that this section of the text is of a later date than the main body of the text. In all three recensions of *TBC, re/ra* is used to mark external motivations. The evidence for *fri* marking the CAUSE is sparse. There are no examples in *The Annals of Ulster* (nor of *ra/re*), and only sporadic attestations in *TBC* and the law texts.[170] Judging from these, it appears that *fri*, like *la* and *ra/re*, tend to mark external motivations rather than internal causes. Thus they

---

[170] Two instances in *TBC I*, one in *TBC LL* co-occurring with causal *re* in the same line, and one in *TBC III*; further, there is one possible instance in the law texts (see Appendix 13).

appear as a functional unit as regards the marking of the CAUSE.[171] It is likely that the evidence we are seeing in *TBC* is an indication of a partial functional merger of *la* and *fri*, in the course of the progressing neutralization of the phonological distinction between the two prepositions, with *ra/re* being a variant illustrating this process.

The preposition *ar* 'before, for' does not present a clear-cut pattern as regards the specification of its causal function. At first sight, there appears to be a preference for complements expressing an internal motivation, such as an emotional state or experience. There is, however, a number of lexically fixed, recurring phrases which influence the count, and we find that in *TBC I*, thirteen instances of causal *ar* followed by a nominal complement include four cases of *ar omun* 'for fear' (see (98)), and two of *ar úathbás* 'for horror'.[172] Of the seventeen examples of causal *ar* in *TBC LL*, three are instances of *ar uaman*, and three of *ar ecla* 'for fear'. However, *ar* can also mark an external motivation, as in two examples in *TBC I* and one in *TBC LL*. Only two attestations of causal *ar* occur in *TBC III*.[173]

(98)   acht boí fo damdabaig scíath *ar omon Con Culaind*   (*TBC I* 2369)
        for fear Cú Chulainn_gen.sg
        'but [she] was under a shelter of shields for fear of Cú Chulainn'

The evidence for causal *ar* from the law texts is sparse, with the exception of a recurrent pattern in *Críth Gablach*, which involves the use of the question *Cid ara n-eperr X* 'why is X said', usually followed by a clause introduced by the causal conjunction *ar* 'because', or a nominal construction introduced by the preposition *ar* in causal function. The complement of *ar* in this pattern is typically a characteristic of the subject P2 of the question, and an expression of the tendency for etymological definitions common in the text.

(99)   *Cid ara n-eper[r]* ócaire? *Ar oítiu* a airechsa cedacht   (*CG* 87–8)
        what for_REL say_pass.pres.sg; for juniority
        'Why does one say *ócaire*? Because of the juniority of his *aire*-status'

J. E. C. Williams (1954: 315) defines the causal function of *ar* as 'of the cause or reason preceding the action, "because, on account of, under the influence of" '. As regards the case form following *ar*, Williams's observation (ibid.) that *ar*-phrases

---

[171] The tendency for *la* to mark an external motivation is not restricted to *TBC I*, but is also paralleled in other texts, as analysed in Müller (1988). J. E. C. Williams (1956), who draws most of his examples from Wb and Ml, does not include a causal function among the uses of *fri*; neither does Fraser (1912*b*). The evidence quoted in *DIL* (s.v. *fri*) under the heading 'on account of' come from later texts than those analysed by Williams and Fraser.

[172] For a similar collocation in Welsh, compare *rac ofn* 'for (lit.: before) fear'.

[173] Another use of causal *ar* is the phrase *is aire* + clause, usually rendered as 'therefore + clause'. In five out of the twelve examples in the present collection, the expression is followed by *at-berar* 'is said', or a similar passive form of a *verbum dicendi*. The function of the expression is very similar to that of *is de atá* and *is uime aderar*, for which see e.g. (100*a*) and (102). In the only example from a legal text (*BCr* §27), *is aire* appears to have purposive function.

are often 'inconclusive as to the case which follows *ar*' can also be applied to our data.[174]

The preposition *de* 'of, from' in what can be described as a causal function occurs, in the narrative material, most often in the fixed phrase *is de atá*, followed by a place name, whereby a present (relative to the narrator) place name is explained as having arisen as the result of events presented in the preceding discourse, as illustrated in (100*a*) below. The sense of *de* in this expression can thus be further specified as resultative, rather than describing either a concomitant external circumstance, or an internal motivation. The use of *de* marking the CAUSE outside the phrase *is de atá*, and outside the narrative texts, is comparatively rare. The specification 'resultative' covers most of these instances, as well: typically, the pronominal complement of the preposition either refers back to a causal condition or event presented in the previous discourse, or the prepositional phrase expresses an event, injury, affliction, disease, or the like, resulting in the situation (for example, a death) portrayed in the clause (see (100*b*)).

(100) (*a*)   Báite dano Reúin ina loch. *Is de atá Loch Reóin.*   (*TBC I* 928)
        COP of-it lake Reúin_gen.sg
        'Then Reúin was drowned in his lake; hence the name Loch Reóin.'
        (O'Rahilly 1967: 151).

    (*b*)   Cathusach H. Tuamman ri H. mBriuin Archaille do ghuin do Uib Cremthainn
        co nderbailt de.   (*AU* 1107.5)
        so-that die_pret.3sg of-it
        'Cathusach . . . was wounded by the Uí Cremthainn and died of it.'

There are instances of what is formally the preposition *do* 'to' marking the CAUSE (see (101)), and a further few where the preposition could be either *de* or *do*, owing to the fact either that the vowel is elided before a complement beginning with a vowel (as in e.g. *d'íttaid* 'from thirst' (*TBC LL* 2107)), or that the preposition is followed by the possessive particle 3sg (as in e.g. *dia athiusc* 'as a result of his manner'). In most of these instances, the preposition again has a resultative sense.

(101)   co n-erbaltatár cét láech díb *do úathbas 7 cridenes*   (*TBC I* 2086)
        of fright and terror
        'so that a hundred warriors among them fell dead of fright and terror'
        (O'Rahilly 1976: 183)

I interpret examples such as (101) as containing *de*, rather than *do*, and as instances

---

[174] Fraser (1912*b*: 6) assigns the causal sense of *ar* to *ar* followed by the accusative, on the basis of data from Wb; Binchy (1941) includes the meaning 'for, on account of, because of' under *ar* followed by the dative. On the borderline between a causal and benefactive sense are cases where the complement of the preposition *ar* is a person 'for the sake of' whom an action is carried out. Fraser (1912*b*: 6) refers to 'the use of *ar* to denote the person in whose interest the action takes place', noting the difficulty to draw a sharp distinction between this and a causal sense; see also J. E. C. Williams (1954: 316).

of a neutralization of the two vowels in pre-tonic position, or, in other words, spellings that may very well reflect the actual pronunciation of the vowels.[175] The form *do* occurs only in pre-nominal position; there are no examples of *do*+3sg neuter suffixed pronoun (usually *dó*), corresponding to *de*+3sg neuter in (100*a*) and (100*b*).

The prepositions *tre* 'through' and *ó* 'from' as markers of the CAUSE are very thinly spread across the texts and thus do not permit any further specfication of their use. *Imm* 'around, about' occurs in a structure fulfilling a function similar to that of *is de atá*. *Is uime aderar* X 'It is because of this that X is said' is the favoured phrase in *TBC III* to introduce a narrator comment explaining a place name, as in (102); the explanation is usually given in the following context.

> (102)   Botha ainm eile dhó dō. Doigh *is uime iderar Botha ris* oir do·rinnedar fir
> Erenn botha ⁊ bélsgalána ann.   (*TBC III* 544.5)
> COP around-it say_pass.pres.sg Botha against-it
> 'Botha is another name for it. Apparently it is called Botha because the men of
> Ireland built huts and shelters there.'

3.6.3. The INSTrument: *coⁿ* and *de*

The prepositions *coⁿ* and *de/do* are the most commonly found markers of the INST in the texts analysed here. *Coⁿ* is largely restricted to *TBC I* (with twenty-two examples, as compared to two in *TBC LL*, and none in any of the other texts), and occurs only with complements denoting concrete instruments, such as tools or weapons, but also parts of the body (see (103*a*)). This restriction would appear to be a feature of this particular text, since elsewhere *coⁿ* marks the concrete or abstract instrument, as well as the manner, with an abstract complement.[176] The distribution of *de/do* is the reverse of that of *coⁿ*: comparatively rare in *TBC I* (seven instances), it is the most common marker of both the concrete and abstract INST in *TBC LL*, illustrated in (103*b*) and (103*c*), and the only one in *TBC III*.[177]

> (103) (*a*)   La sodain fónérig Cú Chulaind ⁊ *benaid a c*[*h*]*end de cosind luirg áne*
> (*TBC I* 501)
> strike_3sg.pres. his head of-him with-the stick drive_VN_gen.sg
> 'Then Cú Chulainn gets to his feet and strikes his head off with the hurley'
>
>   (*b*)   ... ⁊ dobretha *tathulbéim do chlaidiub Conchobuir* dó   (*TBC LL* 1144)
> violent-blow of sword Conchobuir_gen.sg
> 'and he gave him a violent blow with Conchobuir's sword'

---

[175] The complete neutralization of the vowels in *de* and *do* has taken place in some Modern Irish varieties, e.g. Western (Connemara) Irish.

[176] See Müller (1992), as well as *DIL*, s.v. *coⁿ*.

[177] There are seven instances of *de/do* in *TBC I*, thirty-two in *TBC LL* (of which six mark an abstract INST), and ten in *TBC III* (one of which has an abstract complement).

(c) Luid Cú Chulaind fón fid and sain . . . ⁊ *tópacht gabail cethri ṁbend* bun barr
d'óenbéim.   (*TBC LL* 562)
cut_pret.3sg fork four end_gen.pl of one-blow
'Then Cú Chulainn went into the wood . . . and cut a forked pole of four
prongs, whole and entire, with one stroke.'   (O'Rahilly 1967: 153)

Examples (103*a*) and (103*b*) illustrate a difference in the use of *co^n* and *de*/*do* that is
typical for the majority of instances: whereas the *co^n*-phrase can be described as
depending directly on the verb (and thus directly qualifying a process), the *de*/*do*-
phrase typically depends on a noun phrase, syntactically the direct object or the
genitive complement of a VN. Thus as far as the evidence from *TBC* is concerned,
it would appear that *de*/*do* is selected where the construction calls for a qualifier of
a noun phrase expressing an action (most often *béim* 'stroke', or semantically related expressions). A counter-example is provided in (103). Neither *The Annals of
Ulster* nor the law texts contribute any further clues as to a possible distribution
pattern of *co^n* and *de*/*do*.

As with the marking of the CAUSE, I am assuming that the pre-nominal forms *de*
and *do* (as well as the ambiguous forms, *d'* and *dia*) are instances of *de* 'of', rather
than *do* 'to'. Although one might argue that, at the time our texts were composed,
the forms *de* and *do* had effectively become homonyms in pre-nominal position
and preceding the possessive particles (3sg and 3pl), as indicated by the frequency
of, for example, the spelling *do*, this does not entail a semantic merger. The general
tendency of the phonological/phonetic merger is for the non-palatal initial consonant to become dominant in pre-tonic position, with a concomitant backing of
the short, unstressed vowel, rather than for the palatal initial consonant to replace
the non-palatal one. Therefore the presence of the form *de* points to an original *de*
as marker of the INST, rather than to *do*, which is also the tacit assumption in Fraser
(1912*b*) and *DIL*, neither of which mentions an instrumental or modal function
for *do*.

The use of other prepositions in the present database to mark an instrumental
relation or modal relation is exceedingly rare. *Tre* 'through', *ar* 'before, for', and *a*
'out of' occur sporadically. *La* very occasionally marks the INST: the one example
in *TBC I* is parallelled by the use of *co^n* in *TBC LL*.[178] *Ra* occurs once, in *TBC LL*.
The Annals of Ulster shows one example of *la* in the phrase *orcain la daigid* 'destroying by fire', parelleled by four occurrences of *orcain fri daigid* 'id.' The preposition *ó* as marker of the INST is absent from my data; Fraser (1912*b*: 54) lists a few
examples from Wb.

A further marker of the INST occasionally encountered in our texts is the prepositionless dative. All but two examples are to be found in the law texts, and the
construction is more often used to denote abstract than concrete means. Three
examples of the prepositionless dative denoting the manner, rather than an INST,

---

[178] The rare use of *la* to mark the INST is not only a feature of the texts analysed here. In the data on
which Müller (1988) is based (see also Müller 1992), *la* occurs only twice in this function.

occur in *TBC I*. There are three occurrences of the expression *óenbéimm(im)* 'with one blow', all contained within forty lines of one section of the text. Two of the examples are paralleled by the use of *de/do* in *TBC LL* (cf. (104) and (103c)).

(104)   Benaid gabail i sudiu *óenbéim cona c[h]laidiub*   (*TBC I* 331)
         one-blow_dat.sg with-his sword
         'There he cut down a forked branch with one blow of his sword'
         (O'Rahilly 1976: 134)

3.6.4. Interim summary: markers of P1 and markers of related categories

The markers of the 'related categories' IAG, CAUSE, and INST overlap to very varying degrees with the markers of P1. *La*, the most common marker of P1 with the passive, and of the 'agent in charge' in *The Annals of Ulster*, is also the most commonly found preposition marking the IAG (although it has to be stressed that IAGs chiefly occur in two lexically fixed constructions). When used in causal function, *la* (as well as *ra/re*) tends to mark an external influence or circumstance (in this, and the use as IAG marker, it is paralleled by MW *gan*). *La* is not commonly found in instrumental function. The chief marker of P1 in VN constructions, *do*, does not come into the picture here: the graphic representation <do> has been analysed as a form of *de* 'of', occurring in pre-nominal, pre-tonic position.

4 Aspects of Meaning: P1 and its Markers

The previous chapters have established patterns of usage for various constructions involving a non-subject P1. Here, we shall explore aspects of the semantics underlying the selection of the markers of P1. The discussion follows on from the theoretical framework sketched in Chapter 1: it is assumed that prepositions are polysemous lexical items, and that prepositions, as well as participants in situations, can be described in terms of prototype categories. Furthermore, it is assumed that, usually, a spatial sense can be identified as a prototypical use of a preposition, and that agentive uses can be described as extensions of more concrete, usually spatial senses.

One of the features shared by many earlier studies of prepositions and case forms in Welsh and Irish (discussed below) is the attempt, whether made explicit or not, to establish a diachronic hierarchy, in other words, to distinguish earlier from later uses of, for example, a preposition, or a syntactic construction—an approach that usually also implies the assumption that later uses can be etymologically linked with earlier ones. While there can be no doubt that the uses of lexical categories change over time, and that certain senses of a preposition may go back in time less far than others, while others may die out, this is not a concern that is central to this book—although the texts analysed do not represent a synchronic slice of the Welsh and Irish language use, respectively, and therefore diachronic factors are potentially encapsulated in our material.

In theory, it is possible and indeed very interesting to document the history of the marking of different subcategories of P1, of AG and EXP, in a language over a certain timespan, given sufficient textual evidence. However, how different uses of a lexical item relate to one another diachronically is a question quite different from that of how different senses of, for example, a preposition may relate to one another synchronically. It is yet another question whether one can extrapolate backwards in time from attested uses and reconstruct, for unattested stages of a language or language families, common ancestors for the expression of categories such as the 'agent' of the passive, or other syntactic constructions.

What the analysis in this book hopes to achieve is some elucidation of possible links between uses of lexical categories and case forms (or rather, one case form, the genitive), with the role of P1 marker as a point of departure. What this also involves is a reconsideration of how P1 relates to its process, and of different types of

P1, such as the different types of AG identified in *The Annals of Ulster* (see Section 3.2.2).

4.1. Earlier analyses of P1 marking

As mentioned above, the analysis of the various uses of case forms and prepositions in Welsh and Irish in the past has usually had a strong historical orientation. Interpretations usually also include the underlying assumption that certain senses of prepositions can be viewed as extensions of other senses, often more concrete ones. What can also be observed is the attempt to link syntactic requirements of the constructions under investigation (for example, VN clauses, which show nominal syntax) with the sense of prepositional P1 markers and the fact that VN constructions express processes, on the one hand, and the qualities of subject and object (generally seen as prototypical agents and patients) of finite verbs and infinitives, on the other hand. Thus Morgan (1938: 195–6) interprets the different ways of expressing P1 (and P2) in Middle Welsh VN constructions as different types of genitival expressions: the VN being a noun, it combines with other nouns and pronouns in the same way as any other noun—that is, by means of genitival constructions. With transitive verbs, two participant parties can be identified, the object (in our terms, P2), and, though less essentially, the subject (or P1).[1] Two devices, each with its own syntax, are required to link the two parties with the action of the verb. P2, the 'patient', is put in the position of the (adnominal) genitive ('genidol normal'), and a different genitive construction ('cystrawen enidol arall') is employed to join P1 with the action—namely, the preposition *o*. According to Morgan, the preposition *o* specifically expresses a partitive genitive relation ('genidol cyfrannol').[2] With intransitive verbs, only one person is part of the process—that is, the subject (P1) of the VN. Therefore, P1 comes to take the position of the 'genidol normal'. Morgan regards this as the original syntax of intransitive VNs, and the use of *o* in intransitive VN clauses as modelled on the syntax of transitive constructions.

Morgan appears to analyse the use of the term 'genidol normal' as a label for what is the 'more essential' entity pertaining to the process described by the VN— that is, for P1 with intransitive VNs, and P2 with transitive ones. It is significant that he interprets the preposition *o* when accompanying a VN as the marker of a genitive relation, more specifically of a partitive relation in which the first noun denotes a part of the second one, and the second one the sum total of inseparable parts.[3]

---

[1] That the latter is a less essential, in Morgan's terms, element can be deduced from the fact that it may be omitted, as in e.g. *torri'r goeden* 'the felling of the tree'.

[2] Morgan (1938) also mentions the use of *i* in various VN constructions.

[3] Morgan (1938: 195): 'yr enw cyntaf yn rhan o'r ail, a'r ail yn gyfanswm o'r rhannau diwahaniaeth'. Morgan's study is, in part, a reaction to Lewis (1928). Lewis mentions that *o* is the most common marker

Evans (1950) discusses the relation between *i* and *o* from a historical perspective. He interprets the use of *i* in the construction VN+PP$_{P1}$ as old, gradually ousted by the use of *o*.[4] He also (1948, 1950) interprets the use of *i* in the construction P1+*i*$_{VN}$(+P2) (for which there is, however, only little evidence in Middle Welsh (see Section 2.1.2, examples (9) and (10*d*)) as representing an old structure, basing his judgement on a comparison with Irish, in which the type P1+*do*$_{VN}$(+P2) is of very common occurrence. Evans (1948) views the use of the genitive as P1 marker with intransitive VNs not as a partitive genitive, but rather as a subjective genitive ('genidol goddrychol'), having the same function as the genitive depending on abstract nouns containing a verbal element; thus 'bydd "dyfodiad y dyn" a "dyfod y dyn" . . . yn cyfateb o ran ystyr a chystrawen'[5] (1948: 259). He largely agrees with Morgan's interpretation that the preposition *o* marks a genitival relation.[6]

The prepositions *gan* and *y gan*, which we have encountered as markers of P1 with the passive in the Welsh annals, are only very rarely found with VNs. Thus it is only to be expected that considerations of genitival relations do not figure in interpretations of the agentive functions of either. *Gan* is used in Modern Welsh to denote the agent with the so-called *cael*-passive, and with the synthetic passive/impersonal (see Chapter 1). One question that arises out of the considerable semantic overlap between *gan* and *y gan* is the semantic contribution, if any, made by the element *y*. Lewis (1937: 298) assumes that the agentive use of Modern Welsh *gan* originates with *y gan*—literally, 'from with' (*y* < **dē*). J. E. C. Williams (1948: 8) considers a possible influence of *y gan* on *gan*, but refers to the use of *gan* to mark instrument or manner, and the cause, as having had a role in establishing its use as agent marker (but note that, in our data, *gan* marks the IAG rather than the CAUSE or manner; this discrepancy may, however, be due to different definitions of the categories in question). The historical influence of *y gan* on *gan* seems to be taken as read by Fife (1990: 478), who interprets Modern Welsh *gan* as having two basic senses, one spatial (which is closely linked with the use of this preposition to mark possession), and a path specification 'from', with the agentive use falling under the second basic sense, where *gan* expresses an abstract path, 'from x as the source of action'.

A marked reluctance to ascribe the subject and object relations found with

of the subject of the VN (i.e. P1); he also quotes three examples for the use of *i* in the construction VN+PP$_{P1}$, and one of *gan* with the so-called *cael*-passive, but does not further comment on the choice of different P1 markers. A view similar to Morgan's is expressed by Richards (1951: 51), who states that the relation between the VN and the (pro)nouns denoting P1 and P2 'is always genitival, whether it be simple apposition or the addition with the prepositions *o* and *i*'.

 4 According to Evans, *i* in P1 position was still used in the late 1940s in the construction *heb wybod i* X 'without *X*'s knowing', having disappeared outside this phrase centuries before. For an example of this expression from the present database, see (9*d*).

 5 '*Dyfodiad y dyn* [lit.: arrival the man] and *dyfod y dyn* [lit.: come_VN the man] . . . correspond as regards meaning and syntax.'

 6 He notes, however, that, in the data underlying his study, *o* is not used to mark the subjective genitive when it depends on a noun (1948: 260), the same being the case for *i* (ibid. 260).

infinitives to the VN in Irish is expressed by Windisch (1877), based on the syntactic —that is, nominal—behaviour of the VN; he does, however, use the label 'Infinitiv'. Windisch perceives an affinity between the constructions P2+do_{VN}+P1 and VN+PP$_{P1}$ as regards the relation established by the preposition *do*: in both constructions, the second element is to be interpreted as being in a predicative or predicative-attributive relation with the first element, and thus the two types share what Windisch calls a 'grammatisches Schema' (grammatical schema).[7] A different interpretation of the role of *do* as P1 marker is provided by Fraser (1912*b*), who compares the agentive dative in Latin and Greek. He sees the agentive use of *do* as an extension of the '*dativus commodi*, and whether or not it has the force of the "dative of the agent" depends on the nature of the verb' (1912*b*: 21); Fraser also, however, perceives an overlap of the agentive and possessive functions of *do*. Baudiš (1913: 400), on the other hand, criticizes Fraser for seeing the *dativus commodi* everywhere. Neither does he agree with the interpretation of *do* as basically having possessive function, which he sees underlying Windisch's (1877) interpretation, also expressed by Havers (1911: 241). Baudiš interprets the possessive use of *do*[8] as an extension of the same wider sense of the dative case, and of *do*, which also underlies the use of *do* as marker of the agent. He links the latter use with the occurrence of *do* in constructions such as illustrated in (1).[9]

(1) (*a*)   *deiudeib dobarnaib digeintib dothit*
             of-Jew_dat.pl to-Barnabas of-gentile_dat.pl to-Titus
             'Barnabas was a Jew, Titus a gentile'

    (*b*)   *Fecht do Patraic 7 dia fiair . . . ic ingaire caorach*
             occasion to Patrick and to-his sister . . . at herd_VN sheep_gen.pl
             'Once Patrick and his sister . . . were herding sheep'

    (*c*)   *ar nar bo do Ulltaib do*
             since NEG-PRT COP_3.sg.pret to/of Ulsterman_dat.pl to-him
             'since he was not an Ulsterman'

    (*d*)   *doatrob do dia and*
             to-dwell_VN to God in-it
             'that God may dwell therein'

The important characteristic common to these constructions is, according to Baudiš, what he calls 'Impersonalität' (impersonal perspective), and he interprets VN constructions with overt P1 as portraying the agent as the goal, or endpoint, of the process.[10] Gagnepain's (1963) interpretation of *do* in VN+PP$_{P1}$ seems to hover

---

[7] Windisch illustrates this by his paraphrases of *in bolc do blith* (the sack to grind_VN) as 'der Sack (ist) zu mahlen', and of *marbad do* Y (kill_VN to Y) as 'Tödten ist ihm, kommt ihm zu'.

[8] As in e.g. *mac do* X (son to X) 'a son of X's'. This structure is used where the possessee is an indefinite entity and the possessor definite; *mac* X_*gen* would always convey the meaning 'the son of X'.

[9] Examples (1*a*)–(1*c*) (from Baudiš 1913: 401–2) illustrate so-called impersonal construction types.

[10] 'daß das Irische bei den Vorgangsnominibus das Agens als Ziel der Handlung darstellt, und daß solche Ausdrücke zu den Impersonal-konstruktionen in engerer Beziehung stehen' (Baudiš 1913: 403).

between the possessive/ergative view and that of Baudiš, in that he states that *do* following a VN is more often possessive than 'ergative' in the narrow sense; on the other hand, he also mentions a possible link between the impersonal constructions involving *do*, and the agentive use of the preposition (1963: 17–18).

A different variant of the 'possessive as agent' explanation is offered by Greene (1967). Whereas Windisch, Havers, Baudiš, and Gagnepain consider *do* to be, most likely, the original agent marker with the VN (or at least as contemporary with other markers, but numerically predominant), Greene views the use of *do* as an innovation, gradually ousting *la*, which he interprets as the preposition originally found in this function. *Do* can replace *la* by virtue of its ability to express a genitive relationship (see note 8). *La* accompanying a VN or a process noun marks a genitival relation, that of the subjective genitive (see also Morgan's interpretation of Welsh *o* as marking the subjective genitive). One factor contributing to the gradual replacement of *la* by *do* in construction with transitive VNs in Old Irish was the 'increasing specialisation of *la* to indicate ownership . . . as well as opinion' (Greene 1967: 172).[11] Once the use of *do* was established with transitive VNs, it began to encroach onto the use of possessive pronouns with intransitive VNs, leading to VN clauses such as 'buith domsa iniriss' (my being in the faith) (Wb 5b20) (lit.: be_VN to-me in-faith). Greene interprets the absence of *la* in this construction as a 'clear indication of the chronology of these events' (1967: 172). However, the use of *la* as P1 marker with the passive is in Greene's view an innovation, *ó* being the original marker, used by virtue of its semantic proximity to Latin *ab* 'of, from', the agentive passive a construction based on Latin influence, and the use of *la* possible in analogy to its agentive function in VN clauses.

Greene's interpretation presents several problems. One is clearly his database, consisting of a few examples from *The Annals of Ulster* and Wb. Even in these texts, there is no evidence that *ó* is the 'oldest' marker of P1 in passive clauses; this conclusion is based purely on the view that we are dealing with a construction modelled on Latin.[12] However, even if this were the case (as it may very well be in Welsh), the modelling of a syntactic construction on one in another language, or maybe rather the reinterpretation of an existing one according to a foreign language model, does not necessarily imply that the semantic links between the components will end up the same as in the language providing the model. In other words, the interpretation or metaphor establishing the link between the preposition *ab* in Latin with a passive verb need not be the same as the one linking a passive (or indeed impersonal) verb in Irish with a preposition. Similarly, the conclusion that *la* represents the

---

[11] As in *is limm-sa a tech* (COP with-me-PRO the house) 'the house is mine', and *is maith limm a tech* (COP good with-me the house) 'I like the house'.

[12] Wb contains three passives with *la* and three with *ó* as P1 marker. Of thirteen VNs/process nouns accompanied by *la*, three contain the noun *peccad* 'sin', and five the noun *serc* 'love'. *Do* accompanying a VN occurs twelve times, *ó* twice (these figures are based on Müller 1988). The slight majority for *la* is quite possibly influenced by lexically fixed phrases (especially *serc* X *la* Y '*Y*'s love for *X*'). For the distribution of P1 markers in *AU*, see Section 3.4.2.

'original' device for marking P1 in VN clauses is not supported by data, and it is even doubtful whether one could ever convincingly demonstrate this. Rather, it is based on an interpretation of what is in reality a grammaticalized function of the preposition *la*, the possessive construction with the copula.

A further difficulty lies in the reading of *la* as a 'subjective genitive'; genitives are confined to nominal environments and should not be expected to spread to verbal contexts—unless Greene assumes that the extension of the 'genitive' use really concerns the 'subjective' sense, in other words, the preposition becomes a marker of P1 by virtue of signalling a relation between a VN or process noun and the complement of a preposition that is canonically expressed, at least with intransitive VNs, by an adnominal genitive. He refers to a possessive-agentive parallel in Modern Irish to support his interpretation: *cad tá agat* 'what have you (got)' versus *cad tá á rá agat* 'what are you saying' (lit: 'what is at-you' versus 'what is to-its say_VN at-you'). This comparison is not entirely unproblematic: the structure *cad tá á rá agat* is a relatively recent (Modern Irish) development; secondly, although there are clear overlaps between *la* and *ag* (Old/Middle Irish *oc*), a comparison across lexical categories does not prove the point intended. Furthermore, the syntactic structures are quite different.

In other analyses of the agentive use of *la*, its locative function and etymology figure to varying extents. Thus Fraser (1912*b*: 47 ff.) identifies a use 'indicating the sphere of action in the widest sense' (as well as the use 'indicating possession like the dative with *esse* in Latin') as a subsense of the local sense of *la*, and sees the agentive use (with both VNs and passives) as developing out of the local sense. Based on the etymology deriving *la* from the noun *leth* (u,n) 'side', Baudiš (1913: 400) considers the primary function of the preposition to have been sociative (i.e. expressing accompaniment), approximating to German *mit*. Out of this sense arose the marking of the instrument, the cause, and then that of the agent. Baudiš may have been influenced in his analysis by a commonly encountered phenomenon in Indo-European languages whereby the case form and/or preposition marking the instrument is also used to denote P1 in passives or other non-subject P1 constructions (for example, Latin). As far as early Irish is concerned, INST and P1, or in Baudiš's terms the agent, overlap only rarely; what we typically observe is that the INST, especially the concrete tool, is marked by *co[n]*, rather than *la*, the use of which in this function becomes more frequent only in later Middle and Modern Irish (where *co[n]* virtually disappears). Hartmann (1954), also using the etymology of *la* as his point of departure and positing a local sense as basic to the preposition, likewise links the marking of P1 with that of the INST; the fact that the same preposition marks both categories shows, according to Hartmann's argument, that agents in Irish perceive themselves essentially as instruments through which certain processes are carried out. This argument, however, ignores Hartmann's own observation—namely, that the use of *la* (later *le*) to mark the INST is mainly a feature of Middle Irish and later texts.

The use of *ó* to mark P1 is generally seen as an extension of its use to denote the source or origin, as in Fraser (1912*b*), Baudiš (1913), and also Gagnepain (1963); Hartmann (1954) observes that *ó* as agent marker occurs mainly with verbs of 'giving' or 'taking'. Gagnepain sees the motivation for the use of *ó* with VNs of *verbes d'attribution* in the avoidance of ambiguity: whereas *do* is the usual marker of the agent with VNs, its use with, for example, *tabairt* 'giving' would lead to confusion between the source of the action (i.e. the giver) and the receiver. As mentioned above, Greene (1967) attributes the use of *ó* with passives to a modelling of the structure on Latin usage, *ó* being the Irish preposition most compatible with Latin *ab*.

4.2. The genitive as P1 marker

As we have seen, most prepositional P1 markers in Welsh and Irish (namely, Welsh *o* and *i*, Irish *do* and *la*) have been analysed as representing a 'genitive' of some sort or other. Therefore, before embarking on an analysis of the semantic properties of these prepositions in P1 function, a discussion of the characteristics of the genitive as P1 marker with VNs in Welsh and Irish will be useful. As before, the term genitive, unless otherwise specified, covers possessive pronouns in both Welsh and Irish, the genitive case in Irish, and the use of the adnominal 'genitive' noun phrase in Welsh.

Genitives have, compared to prepositional phrases, clearly defined syntactic and semantic relations: a genitive phrase in Irish and Welsh is syntactically linked to its head noun, and its semantic scope is limited to the head noun.[13] Its consistent use with the VN to mark P2 is one of the indications that the VN is indeed syntactically a noun, as opposed to an infinitive (comparable to the infinitive in, for example, Latin or German), the traditional definition of which is that it exhibits verbal behaviour—i.e. that P2 is encoded as in a finite active clause, usually by means of the accusative case. One aspect of the nominal syntax of genitives in Celtic is the fact that a definite genitive renders its head noun (and thereby the whole noun phrase) definite. A phrase of the type *mab y brenhin* in Welsh or *macc in ríg* in Irish (lit.: son the king) is always interpreted as definite—i.e. 'the king's son' (rather than 'a son of the king'). In the present database, a genitive P1 is generally expressed by means of either a definite personal pronoun (i.e. a possessive pronoun) or a definite noun phrase (including personal names). Thus, VN+GEN$_{P1}$ clauses of the type 'dyuot y porthawr' (the porter arrived) (*CO* 786) represent, syntactically, definite noun phrases, whereas those of the type 'codi gwas pengrych . . .' (a curly-haired lad rose . . .) (*CO* 469) are syntactically indefinite. Whether the opposition definite versus indefinite has any influence on the use of a genitival or prepositional

---

[13] There are exceptions to this general rule in Irish, where the genitive can occur in certain clearly defined syntactic contexts without an antecedent noun (see *GOI* §250). These do not, however, affect the present argument.

P1 marker is at this stage unclear. However, the fact that the attribute definite spreads, as it were, from the genitive to the head noun may be interpreted as an indication that the genitive establishes a close conceptual link between the entities represented.

This, in turn, may be a reason why, in transitive VN constructions, it is P2 that is regularly marked in Welsh and Irish by a genitive, whereas P1, if it is overtly expressed, is indicated by means of a prepositional phrase (see also Morgan 1938). A transitive construction that does not indicate P2 is perceived as incomplete. Thus, within a situation that involves a process, an AG-type P1 and a patient-type P2, process and P2 appear to be conceptually more closely linked than process and P1. This leads on to the question whether there is a link between the use of the genitive to denote P2 in transitive, and P1 in intransitive constructions, other than that each contextualizes the process by assigning it to its one necessary participant. Transitive processes typically involve scenarios where P2 is affected in some way by the process, which in turn is under the control of P1; the effort and energy expended by P1 are directed at P2.[14] This is not the case in intransitive processes: where there is effort, or a discharge of energy, it is undirected (or self-directed)—as, for example, the effort, and control, necessary to sustain self-propelled voluntary motion. The identical marking of P1 in an intransitive process, and P2 in a transitive process, may thus be an indication that the former is conceptualized as on the same level of voluntary effort, energy expenditure, and control as the latter—i.e. as affected by the process in question. As we have seen, P1 of intransitive VNs is not exclusively marked by means of a genitive. Even so, several characteristics of P1 markers in both the Welsh and Irish data would seem to support the suggestion that the 'energy factor' (involving effort, control, and the expenditure of energy) has a bearing on the choice of P1 marker.

In the Welsh material, the large majority of intransitive VNs occurring in the construction $VN+PP_{P1}$ are VNs requiring an AG as P1—i.e. a P1 exercising voluntary control and effort, such as VNs of motion (such as *dyuot* 'come', *kyuodi* 'rise'), or action without a specified P2 (such as *bwyta* 'eat'), or VNs where the direction of the action is specified by a prepositional phrase (such as *galw ar* 'call on s.b.', as opposed to *galw* 'call s.b.'). All these involve a conscious effort and exercise of control by an AG. In our data, the VN *bot* 'be' never occurs with a prepositional P1.[15] A similar distribution can be observed in the Irish data: the preposition *do* following a VN tends to mark an AG, rather than an EXP, although overall the proportions of EXPs in intransitive VN+*do* clauses are higher than in the Welsh data (see Table

---

[14] An exception to this tendency are processes of perception described by transitive VNs, such as Welsh *clybot* 'hear', or *gwelet* 'see'. However, these represent only a minority of VN constructions with overt P1, and need not affect the present argument.

[15] The collection of material in Richards (1951) supports the observation that, generally, only P1s of 'energetic' and controlled intransitive processes are expressed by means of the preposition *o*. Evans (1948) finds one instance of *bod+o* in his database, a construction that is considered as artificial and restricted to literary usage by Morgan (1938).

3.1). This may indicate that the semantic opposition genitive versus *do* in Irish is not perceived to be as great as that of genitive versus *o* in Welsh. This leaves us with the question how 'non-energetic' transitive VNs (such as VNs of perception, or of involuntary processes, such as Irish *fagbáil* 'find, come across, get') fit into the picture. One may look at these from the point of view that the situation dictates the potential syntactic possibilities: the processes involve two participants, which cannot be encoded by the same marker. Therefore a hierarchy of effort and control comes to be applied, and the participant with the least degree of effort and control —i.e. P2—is encoded as the genitive, whereas the participant exhibiting the relatively higher degree of effort and control is encoded as the prepositional phrase (one may end a process of 'hearing' by stopping one's ears and thus influence the process, and one has to be awake and mentally alert to hear anything).

4.3. Welsh *o*: P1 as source

The Welsh texts show a remarkably consistent, almost exclusive, use of the preposition *o* as P1 marker. In a local sense, the preposition *o* denotes the point of origin, either as the point of departure of movement (2*a*), or as the locality from which the referendum originates (2*b*) (the latter may be interpreted as an extension of the former).

(2) (*a*)   Ac ef a *gychwynnwys* y nos honno *o Arberth*   (P. 1.6)
              start_pret.3sg from Arberth
              'And he set out that night from Arberth'

      (*b*)   'a pha wlat *yd hanwyt titheu oheni?*' 'O Annwuyn', heb ynteu.   (P. 2.25)
              PRT originate_pres.2sg you from-her; from Annwn
              ' "and which country are you from?" "From Annwn," he said.'

We may assume that the sense 'point of departure' is central to the senses of *o*. In a situation such as the one illustrated in (2*a*), the complement of *o* marks the beginning of a path along which the referendum travels. In example (2*b*), there is no motion through space. The relation described by *o* can be seen as transferred from a spatial to an abstract domain: the point of origin, in this case the birthplace or home of a person, is conceptualized as the point of departure for a 'journey through life and time'.[16] The agentive use of *o* can be linked with the sense 'point of departure' such that the AG is seen as the point of origin, and (from an even more locally oriented point of view) the point of departure along which the energy expended in an action, directed at P2, travels. King (1988) interprets the agentive function of German *von* 'from, of' along these lines, interpreting an agent as a 'point-source of energy within an event-space' (the event, in turn, is described as an 'extended

---

[16] Note that *o* also has a temporal sense, marking the beginning of a timespan.

space', and an action as an 'event-space within which an agent produces energy') (1988: 581). If there is a patient, in our terms P2, the energy is transferred from the agent to the patient.

If we assume that P1 as marked by *o* is conceptualized as the 'point of origin of energy expended', which is either transferred to P2 (as with transitive verbs), or undirected (as with intransitive verbs), the tendency of *o* to occur preferably with VNs requiring an AG as P1 is not surprising. The complement of *o* as the 'source of energy' is at first sight hard to reconcile with its occurrence with transitive VNs of perception, such as *clybot* 'hear', or *gwelet* 'see'. As mentioned above, a continuum, a hierarchy of control and effort, may come into operation, in that the P1 of a VN of perception, although possessing less control over the process than the P1 of a VN of action (e.g. *lladd* 'kill', or *adeiladu* 'build'), but more than P2. On the other hand, the diachronic development assumed by Evans (1948, 1950) may be worth recalling—namely, that *o* has replaced an 'older' marker, *i* 'to'. Although this as-sumption appears to be based largely on comparative evidence from Irish, it may very well be that *i* did at some stage have wider currency; the difficulty is that we cannot read this off the available textual evidence. We shall return to the use of *i* as P1 marker below.

4.4. Irish *ó*: P1 and source

The use of Irish *ó* as P1 marker can be linked with its spatial sense in a way similar to that applied above to the Welsh preposition *o*. However, there are some interest-ing distinctions regarding the further application of the sense 'point of departure/ origin'. The spatial sense of Irish *ó* can be described as defining the point of depart-ure on a path, as in (3a). Note that, in the second clause, the person who marks the point of departure for the messengers sent can also be interpreted as the sender, and thus as P1. If the point of departure, the place of origin, is conceptualized as a bounded area (such as a country or region), rather than a point, the relation is usually described by *a(ss)* 'out of', as in (3b).

(3) (*a*)   ⌐ *hetha húaidib* cossna trí chóiced aili. Ocus *foíte techta ó Ailill* co secht maccu Mágach   (*TBC I* 2–3)
go_pass.pret.sg from-them; send_pass.pret.pl messenger_nom.pl from Ailill
'and word went from them to the three other provinces. And Ailill sent mes-sengers to the seven sons of Mágu'   (O'Rahilly 1976: 125)

(*b*)   'Can dothéig?' '*A hAlbain iar foglaim filidechta*'   (*TBC I* 42–3)
out-of Britain after learn_VN poetry_gen.sg
' "Where do you come from?" "From Britain, after learning the seer's art" '

Ó also marks the origin with verbs of giving or receiving (see (4)); the giver can be seen as the point where the gift originates, and begins its path towards the re-ceiver.

(4)   Ógfritecht for rátha *mani éta nech a frepaid ó fiur chinad*   (*CG* 59–60)
           unless obtain_3sg.pres.sub anyone his cure from man_dat.sg guilt_gen.sg
           'The full (amount of their) warranty (falls) on the sureties if someone does
           not obtain his cure from the guilty party'[17]

As we have seen, the use of *ó* to mark what is potentially P1 is quite restricted in the
Irish material, especially in comparison with the dominance of Welsh *o*. In passive
clauses containing *ó*, the verb is usually one of giving or sending, as in (3*a*)—i.e. a
verb that includes an element of 'abstract motion from a point of origin' in its
semantic make-up. The use of *ó* in VN clauses in the narrative material is of almost
negligible frequency (see Appendix 5), with two instances in *TBC*, both ambiguous
as to the exact relation portrayed by the preposition. However, a curious feature in
The Annals of Ulster is the almost exclusive use of *ó* in combination with a plural
complement (and especially in the phrases *ó genntaib* and *ó gallaib* 'from/by the
gentiles/foreigners', both of which apply to Viking raiders), whereas the preposition occurs only rarely with a noun phrase or personal name identifying a single
individual.

We may conclude that *ó* describes a relation between a process and its point of
origin, but the point of origin and the AG are not necessarily identical. In a clause
such as 'dobreth biad dó óna briugaidaib' (food was brought to him from the
hospitallers) (*TBC I* 3885), it is quite possible, maybe even likely, that the point
where the action of 'bringing' originated, the hospitallers, is not identical with the
persons carrying out the action: the hospitallers may provide the food, or have it
taken to Cú Chulainn by unspecified messengers. Similarly, the VN clause 'Orggain
Droma hIung o Gallaibh' (Druim Ing was plundered by the foreigners) (*AU* 835.12)
indicates that a 'foreign raid' took place, but does not necessarily identify the
specific group of individuals who carried out the raid. One may further speculate
whether *ó* was perceived as appropriate to mark the point of origin of the Viking
raids, because these typically did involve a force moving towards the location of the
raid from outside. Thus it appears that a potential P1 in Irish marked by *ó* does not
necessarily imply the identification of the 'point source of energy' (in King's sense)
with the 'point of departure' of a process, unlike in Welsh, where the identification
is complete. This is illustrated by VN clauses containing VNs of motion (e.g. *dyuot
o gennat Arthur* 'Arthur's messenger arrived'), where *o* does not mark the locality
where the movement starts, but the moving entity, the messenger. To this we can
compare the first clause in (3*a*), 'hetha úaidib' (people went) (employing the im-
personal/passive form *etha*), where *ó* defines the sender, rather than the person
going.[18]

---

[17] This translation follows Binchy (1941: 26).

[18] Any potential ambiguity is also avoided by the fact that there appears to be a constraint against the
use of P1 markers with intransitive impersonal verbs. Note that in 'foíte techta ó Aillill' (3*a*), the ambiguity between P1 and point of origin does exist.

4.5. Irish *do*: P1 as affected entity—the low-energy P1

Baudiš (1913) suggested that the use of *do* to mark an agent is an indication that the agent is understood as an energyless entity. This interpretation is directly derived from the local sense of *do*, that of defining the endpoint of a path, as in (5*a*). The use of *do* to mark the receiver, with verbs of giving, as in (5*b*), can be interpreted as a subsense of the local sense. The endpoint of a path can also be marked by the preposition *co* (c.acc.) 'to, as far as' (see (5*c*)). This appears to be the more common usage where a purely local sense is to be conveyed.

(5) (*a*)   fo bésad fir *téte do chath*   (Wb 9a3)
go_pres.sg.rel to battle
'after the manner of a man going to battle'

(*b*)   *Dobeir gaí 7 scíath dó*   (*TBC I* 621)
give_pres.3sg spear and shield to-him
'He gives spear and shield to him'

(*c*)   *Do-thét-side co Conchobar* co n-epert fris . . .   (*TBC I* 646)
come_pres.3sg-PRO to Conchobar
'He comes to Conchobar and said to him . . .'

A difference between the spatial senses of *co* (c.acc.) and *do* emerges: whereas *co* appears to have a purely local sense (where the endpoint of the path indicated is, for example, a place or a person), the use of *do* implies that the entity at the end of the path travelled by the referendum is also in some way affected by it. As illustrated in (5*a*), a man going to battle expects to fight in it; the battle does not just mark the end of his path. Another instance is 'tair lem don fleid dia tíagom' (come with me to the feast to which we are going) (*TBC I* 564): the person going to the feast intends to participate in it. Note also that only *co* (c.acc.) has a temporal sense (marking the end of a timespan, as in *co matain* 'until morning'), whereas only *do* can indicate the receiver—that is, the person affected by the process of giving or sending.

One may summarize the two salient attributes of the spatial sense of *do* as 'motion to', and 'effect', such that the endpoint of the motion is affected by the process. This provides a further link with the receiver-sense of *do*, in that the receiver of a gift or delivery is not only the endpoint of the entity given or sent, but is also affected by, or involved in, the process by accepting the entity. It is this attribute 'effect' (i.e. 'being affected', on the part of the complement of the preposition) that enables the preposition *do* to mark P1 in VN constructions.[19] In a clause such as example (6), it is obvious that the relation described by *do* has been completely

---

[19] The use of *do* in 'impersonal construction, especially compounds with *imm-* denoting reciprocal action' (*DIL* s.v. *do*; see also Vendryes 1956: 192) also appears to be based on this attribute: e.g. 'ra impá risin Findbennach 7 go 'mmarálaid dóib assa aithle d'imbúalad . . .' (and he attacked the Findbennach and they fought together) (*TBC LL* 4889).

alienated from the concrete spatial domain, since the motion verb *tuidecht* 'come' does not trigger the interpretation of *do Choinculainn* as endpoint of a path.

(6)   gorub *agtaidhecht atuaidh do Choinculainn* domarbhasdairse Mac Bhuachalla
         (*TBC III* §10)
         at-come_VN from-the-north to Cú-Chulainn_dat.sg
         'that it was as Cú Chulainn came from the north that he killed Mac Buachall'

If we interpret action as a process involving the release of energy that is either transferred to P2 or remains undirected (or indeed self-directed, i.e. towards P1),[20] a state as a process where no energy is released (but which may be the result of such an energy release), and an experience as a process where energy is absorbed (and the source remains unspecified), then the choice of a P1 marker that describes an affected entity in conjunction with the latter type of processes makes most sense, intuitively, to the outside observer.

It is possibly on the basis of similar reasoning that Baudiš declared P1 in Irish to be 'energyless', and this may also have been the motivation for deriving the agentive use of *do* from its genitival or possessive sense, rather than from its spatial use. One might invoke diachrony again and assume that agentive *do*, as the 'original' P1 marker in VN clauses, has replaced a different marker, spreading from an already established use with experience VNs. Although this type of development is certainly a possibility, there is, as has already been pointed out, no evidence that this is what actually happened in Irish. Another solution to the dilemma of finding an, in Baudiš's terms, 'energyless' P1 with 'energetic' VNs would be to assume that the use of *do* to mark P1 is an extension of the 'affected-person' sense (as in e.g. the receiver), in which the attribute 'effect' has been neutralized to such an extent that the preposition now merely denotes a 'participant'. The problem, however, in ridding *do* of any sense of directionality is that this leaves very little to distinguish it from any preposition establishing a spatial relation.

However, it might be possible to reconcile the attribute 'effect' with the agentive use if we recall the following points: first, the use of a preposition as P1, and more specifically AG marker, does not necessarily cover all possible subtypes of AGs. Secondly, *do* in agentive function in continuous discourse (for example, narrative texts, opposed to the isolated VN clauses of the annals) tends to appear in subordinate constructions. These two points appear at first sight to have very little in common, but a link can be established.

It can be assumed that the canonical encoding of a prototypical AG, one characterized by volition, control, independence, and salience, is that of the subject of a transitive finite verb clause. The fact that there are several markers of agency is a strong indication that each of these caters for members of the category AG whose semantic characteristics are most compatible with a member of the category *do*, or

---

[20] Cf. King's (1988) more determinedly topological definition of an action as 'an event-space in which the agent produces energy'.

la, or *ó*. The very specific applicability of *ó* in early Irish has already been demonstrated. As shown above (Section 3.1.1), *do* as marker of P1 appears, on the one hand, more often with VNs requiring an AG as P1 than with those requiring an EXP, but, on the other hand, in continuous text almost exclusively in syntactically dependent VN constructions. Thus, if we look beyond the clause level, we notice that the processes presented in VN clauses with overt P1 are subordinate to the processes presented in main clauses. What happens at the point of the narrative 'now'—i.e. the current state of development with regard to the narrated progress in time and plot at the 'time' of the process related in the main clause—is controlled from within the main clause; the process (and its participants) described by the subordinate clause are, as far as the composite situation is concerned, of less salience, influence, and relevance at the current point of development. To illustrate, in the sentence 'Ficfit fornd iar tiachtain dúin' (they will fight against us when we come back) (*TBC I* 158), the complement of *do* is weaker in control than the subject of the main clause as far as the time frame of the main clause is concerned. The situation portrayed in the main clause is clearly more salient and influential for further developments than that of the subordinate VN clause; P1 of the subordinate VN clause is not necessarily 'energyless' and therefore weak in control within the context of the VN clause itself. Thus there is a gradient in control between participants in different processes, from the perspective of the complex situation portrayed by a complex syntactic construction.

An immediate challenge to the interpretation of agentive *do* sketched here would seem to come from the data in *The Annals of Ulster*. This text contains large numbers of syntactically independent VN constructions, many of which contain *do* as P1 marker (see again Section 3.2.2). As one counter-argument to this challenge, one might mention that the style employed in *The Annals of Ulster* (and other Irish annalistic texts) is a highly specialized one, which does not bear much resemblance to the continuous discourse of narrative. Indeed, where 'micro-narratives' are developed on the basis of the events related in *The Annals of Ulster*, independent VN constructions tend to form the headlines of these, and the ensuing narrative uses finite verb clauses. Thus it is quite possible that the P1-marker function of *do* as established in continuous narrative was employed, out of context, as it were, in *The Annals of Ulster* as a concise mode of presenting a situation, in a genre where economy of style was highly important. Although this is conceivable, the problem is, of course, that the argument cannot by supported by hard evidence. But even within *The Annals of Ulster*, there is some evidence that a P1 expressed by a *do*-phrase is conceptualized as lower in energy (which implies a lower potential to control a complex situation) than, for example, a subject P1 or a preposed P1 (in the construction P1+do_{VN}(+P2)).

Do occurs only relatively rarely in the construction VN+PP$_{P1}$, especially compared to its almost exclusive status as P1 marker in this construction in the narrative texts, and even rarer is its occurrence in this construction with the VN *marbad* 'kill', which could be described as the 'energy-rich' and indeed control-rich VN *par excellence*: the action carried out by the AG affects a change of state in P2 (in the terminology of King 1988, such a verb is a causative), and the affected entity is on the same level on an animacy scale as the AG, which means that the action requires a high expenditure of energy on the part of the AG.[21] The VN *marbad* occurs almost exclusively in the constructions P1+do_{VN}(+P2) and P2+do_{VN}+P1. The latter serves as a device to focus P2, which necessarily implies, in the context of occurrence, that P1 is given less prominence, rendered less salient. This lower degree in salience can be seen to be underlined by the use of the preposition *do*, which marks P1 in subordinate VN clauses in narrative texts. Of course, the attributes of control and salience cannot be equated. However, in a construction that gives prominence to the entity that is lowest in control and primarily affected by a process, the encoding of the AG as 'also affected', or indeed, simply as the 'other participant', supports the syntactic focusing of P2.

4.6. Welsh *i*: P1 as affected entity

The preposition *i* in medieval Welsh shows a range of uses similar to that of *do* in medieval Irish. This, the shared etymology,[22] and the fact that *do* in Irish is frequently found as marker of P1, possibly contributed to Evans's (1950) conclusion that *i* was at some time more prevalent in this use, but was gradually replaced by *o*.

In its spatial sense, similar to that of *do*, the preposition *i* marks the endpoint of a path (see (7a)). Its use to describe the receiver with, for example, *rodi* 'give' can be regarded as an extension of this spatial sense (see (7b)). With this, compare the use of *i* with *erchi* 'request' and *gorchymyn* 'order, command', where the complement of the preposition is not only the receiver (of a request or an order), or in other words the endpoint of an abstract path, but is also affected by the entity travelling along that path, in that a reaction (i.e. compliance with a request, or obeying an order) is expected. The attribute 'effect' is also visible in uses such as (7c), where *i* marks the person affected by the state portrayed in the clause.

(7) (a)   kyuodi a oruc, a *dyuot y Lynn Cuch*   (P. 1.9)
            come_VN to Glynn Cuch
            'he rose, and came to Glynn Cuch'

    (b)   *Mi a rodaf yt peir*   (B. 34.18)
            me PRT give_fut.1sg to-you cauldron
            'I will give you a cauldron'

---

[21] This is true if P1 is an AG acting as a single individual, without assistance. On the preposition and the 'AG in charge', see Section 4.7.

[22] Note, however, that the form **do*, which results in both Welsh *i* 'to' and Irish *do* 'to', merges in Welsh with **dē* (which underlies both Welsh *y/i* 'from' and Irish *de/di* 'from'). It is this *y/i* < **dē* that is the first element in compound prepositions such as *y am*, *y wrth*, *y gan* (see also the form *dy wrth* (*CO* 10)). According to *GMW* (§223 n. 1) 'the simple preposition *y* "from" was discarded to avoid confusion with *y* "to"'.

(c)   ac *ennein yssyd reit ymi*   (*P.* 18.11)
        bath COP-rel necessity to-me
        'and I need a bath'

Again as with Irish *do*, the attributes of direction and effect, seen in conjunction with different types of processes, would seem to make the preposition *i* as a P1 marker most compatible with VNs expressing experiences, since P1 here is an absorber of energy, rather than its source. As shown in Chapter 2, *i* is not well attested as a P1 marker in the current database, and the few examples do not invite reliable generalizations as to the specific nature of P1 as expressed by *i*. However, among four instances of syntactically independent VN+i_{p_1}, one is ambiguous as to whether the prepositional phrase describes P1 or the addressee,[23] one can be interpreted as a state affecting the person identified by the *i*-phrase (see (8*a*)), and two contain reflexive VNs, as in (8*b*), in which the energy expended in the process is directed towards the AG. Of the three attestations of VN+i_{p_1} in dependent position, two (which are lexically identical) are ambiguous in that *i* could express either P1 or the beneficiary (see (8*c*)). A clear case of *i* expressing an EXP-P1 is given in (8*d*).

(8) (*a*)   *Diwarnawd yn hely yr brenhin*   (*CO* 26)
           day PRT hunt_VN to-the king
           'One day the king was hunting' (or: on a hunt)

    (*b*)   *Emystynnu idaw ynteu yn y peir*   (*B.* 44.20)
           stretch-oneself_VN to-him PRON
           'He stretched himself out in the cauldron'

    (*c*)   *Yskithyr Yskithyrwyn . . . a uinnaf y eillaw ym*   (*CO* 639)
           PRT want_pres.1sg to shave_VN to-me
           'I want the tusk of Yskithyrwyn . . . to shave with'

    (*d*)   *heb wybot y'r Cawr*   (*CO* 812)
           without know_VN to-the giant
           'without the Giant's knowing'

The expression *heb wybot i* X, as exemplified in (8*d*), is the only construction noted by Evans (1948: 269) where an *i*-phrase following a VN marks the EXP. Even if we assume that, at some stage in medieval Welsh literary usage, *i* was ousted by *o* as P1 marker, we do not have enough data to determine how widespread its usage may have been. What we can say, however, is that the encoding of P1, which in our material is more often an AG than an EXP, in VN clauses as the source of energy (a conceptualization that is very close to a prototypical AG) is clearly dominant in the data available (and confirmed in e.g. Richards 1951 and Evans 1948). An encoding juxtaposed to this—namely, P1 as affected entity—does occur, but only rarely.

Especially where one is dealing with non-contemporary texts, cause and effect in linguistic usage are difficult to distinguish. We have seen that, in Irish narrative, VN+do_{p_1} tends to occur in dependent position—i.e. representing subordinate pro-

---

[23] *Ma.* 90.9; see the discussion in Section 2.1.2, example (8).

cesses in complex situations. This, provided the available data are representative, may favour the marking of P1 as a low-control, low-energy status. On the other hand, the Welsh texts analysed, and especially the narratives, make frequent use of independent VN constructions with overt P1 (although, as we have seen, the frequency of usage varies greatly from text to text). This in turn may favour the marking of P1 as being more agent-like—i.e. as a source of energy.

4.7. Irish *la*: the person in charge

The use of *la* as P1 marker differs from that of the other prepositions discussed thus far, in that *la* is predominantly found with the verb forms commonly labelled passive. Furthermore, a tendency was observable in *The Annals of Ulster* to use *la* where the process defined by a VN or process noun requires the effort of more than one person, but where only one person is specified: in these cases, *la* marks the AG in charge.

The spatial sense of *la* can be paraphrased as 'in the vicinity of', usually not implying any direct physical contact. There is no element of motion or directionality, as with other spatial prepositions used in P1 function. Rather, the complement of *la* in a concrete spatial sense can be visualized as being the prominent entity in a local area, and thereby defining this area. Within this area, the referendum is located on the same horizontal plane as the complement. The commonly accepted etymology of *la* (from *leth* (u,n) 'side') would suggest an even narrower definition, 'by the side of, beside'. However, although this narrow sense does occur, the more common spatial sense of *la*, roughly 'in the vicinity of', does not specify the exact relative positions of the entities involved in the relation. The complement is most often animate—i.e. human—as in (9)

(9)   Issin tšessed bliadain luid *do fóglaim gaiscid 7 chless la Scáthaig.*
       (*TBC I* 378)
       to learn_VN weapons_gen.pl and trick_gen.pl with Scáthach
       'In [his] sixth year he went to learn weaponry and fighting skills with Scáthach.'

As I have suggested in an earlier study (Müller 1992: 115), the person in whose vicinity a process takes place can be interpreted as AG if the verbal element requires an AG as P1, but where no other AG is mentioned or to be inferred from the context. This section further elaborates on this suggestion.[24] The entity defining an area in

---

[24] See also Kronasser (1968), and Radden (1985), the former on a general link between spatial-temporal proximity and causality, the latter on English causal prepositions. The agentive use of English *by* is treated by Langacker (1990: 139–40), establishing a link between the spatial sense and the use as AG marker via the attribution of responsibility for the execution of an act to the *by*-phrase in sentences such as *Bragging by officers will not be tolerated*. We are dealing, according to Langacker, with a 'more dynamic conception of the landmark *vis-à-vis* the trajector as source'. The interpretation of the landmark as source, rather than merely a spatial reference point, comes with the notion of responsibility being

which a process takes place is linked with the process in such a way that this entity is seen to provide the cause or condition for that process, or carry the responsibility for the process, provided this entity has the capability to do so—i.e. is capable of exercising control over the process in question. The example quoted in (9) may serve as an illustration of this linking process, since a case could be made for the interpretation of the *la*-phrase as marking the IAG—i.e. not a purely spatial reference point, but the person responsible for the process of the young boy's (i.e. Cú Chulainn's) learning (see also the discussion of ambiguous cases of *la* as P1 marker, Sections 3.1.1 and 3.3.3).

The causal link established between a process and the complement of *la* may be weaker or stronger, depending on the context. In an example such as (9), where there is a P1 subject characterized by volition and control, the default causal link is correspondingly weaker. It is worth noting here that where the relation marked by *la* is one of joint action or motion, the complement of *la* is usually the person in charge, whereas P1 of the verbal element identifies the accompanying person (see Müller 1990, 1995). In (10*a*), P1 has considerably less control over the process than the complement of *la*, and almost certainly does not participate voluntarily; *la* marks the IAG. Where no P1 is specified, *la* may denote the sole cause(r), or, in certain contexts, a predominantly spatial relation, as in (10*b*). This tends to be the case with phrases such as *la Connachta, la hUltu,* lit. 'with the Connachtmen/Ulstermen', where the name of the group may, rather than referring to a group of individuals, denote the territory (note, however, the discussion concerning this particular example in Section 3.3.3, and compare the editor's interpretation). One could argue that the group identifying the territory is also the group (solely) controlling the process: the muster of an army in the Connachtmen's territory is not likely to involve anyone else. On the other hand, the scope of the phrase *la Connachtu* (i.e. all inhabitants of Connacht, and thereby the territory controlled by them) is not likely to be coextensive with the group of people involved in the muster of the army.

(10) (*a*)   . . . *meni thaeth cara nó náma limm* d'f̵eraib Hérend innocht.
            (*TBC LL* 557)
            unless fall_pres.sub.3sg friend or enemy with-me
            '. . . unless a friend or enemy of the men of Ireland fall by me tonight.'

     (*b*)   *Tarcomlad slóiged mór la Connachtu*   (*TBC I* 1)
            assemble_pret.pass.sg hosting big with Connachtman_acc.pl
            'A great army was mustered by the Connachtmen' (O'Rahilly 1976: 125); or:
            'a great army was assembled in Connacht'

The fact that a causal link between a process and the complement of *la* is established by virtue of proximity (rather than any sense of directionality inherent in

present in the relation. The agentive use of Japanese *ni* is discussed in Kabata and Rice (1997). The use of the locative particle *ni* (locative 'at', as well as allative 'to') to mark the agent in certain passive constructions is interpreted as marking the 'human source' behind an activity (1997: 115).

the meaning of the preposition) makes an AG marked by *la* the person in charge of, or responsible for, a process, but not necessarily the only actant involved, even where no other person is specified. And, as we have seen, *The Annals of Ulster* shows a tendency for *la* to be used with VNs or process nouns requiring, realistically, more than one actant, but where only one is named. The agentive sense of *la* is thus one of a cause(r), and the causal link established by default on the ground of proximity may not be a sufficiently strong link to make *la* an expression of the independent, sole AG (characterized by volition and control), in control of an action. One might argue that to identify the spatially defined causer with the sole AG is the logical next step in establishing the causal link, where this is permitted by the context—i.e. where there is a process which requires an AG, but where no other AG is specified. This is certainly a possibility, and it has thus far been tacitly assumed, through our labelling of the *la*-phrase accompanying the passive as P1 marker.

In Section 3.5, the Irish 'passive' was interpreted as a 'non-personal' active with additional foregrounding properties for nominal P2s. This interpretation is highly compatible with the use of *la* as potential P1 marker, via its sense of describing the person in charge: the concept of an AG in charge is not by default equated with a sole actant, but may be so assigned if no other potential candidate for this role is present in the context. However, the link of responsibility and causation between AG in charge and process is a weaker, and less immediate one (i.e there is scope for the involvement of others) than that between process and AG as source (i.e. as the sole source of energy).

4.8. Welsh *gan* and *y gan*: P1 as the person in charge, and point of departure

Gan and *y gan* show considerable semantic overlaps in medieval Welsh, and the exact contribution of the element *y* ($< *d\bar{e}$)[25] to the compound preposition is sometimes difficult to determine. The fact that both are found with apparently the same sense in otherwise identical environments gives rise to the question whether *gan* and *y gan* are, by the Middle Welsh period, variants of the same preposition. The functional overlap is most prominent with the IAG, especially with verbs such as *cael* 'get', *kymryt* 'take', *prynu* 'buy', where *gan* or *y gan* marks the person from whom something is got, taken, or bought, with varying degrees of that person's co-operation. *Gan* has a spatial sense 'by the side of, alongside of, in the vicinity of', as in (11*a*), and, although *y gan* is attested with a sense 'from the side of, from the vicinity of', as in (11*b*), both can be used to mark accompaniment (see (11*c*) and (*d*)), and possession (examples from Williams 1948).

---

[25] Cf. Old Irish *di/de* 'from, of', and Middle Breton *digant* 'from', as opposed to *gant* 'with', which is etymologically identical to Welsh *gan* (see Hemon 1975 for an overview of the Middle Breton prepositions, and J. E. C. Williams 1948 for further discussion of *$\bar{d}e$*, and its development in Welsh).

(11) (a)   a *mynet* y orymdeith *gan lann y weilgi*   (*Ma.* 79.12)
            go_VN by/along shore the sea
            'and they went for a walk along the seashore'

     (b)   galw o Uendigeiduran y mab attaw. *Y gan Uendigeiduran y kyrchawd y mab* at
            Uanawydan   (*B.* 43.13)
            from ('from-with') Bendigeidfran PRT go_pret.3sg the boy
            'Bendigeidfran called the boy to him. From Bendigeidfran the boy went to
            Manawydan'

     (c)   a phan *aetham ni gan arthur*   (*BT* 55.6–7)
            go_pret.1pl we with Arthur
            'and when we went with Arthur'

     (d)   *dyret y gennyf*   (*ChO* 9.11)
            come_ipv.2sg with-me
            'Come with me'

A further peculiarity emerging from our data is that some texts show a strong preference for *gan* or *y gan* in otherwise identical constructions, whereas other texts have both. Again the most prominent use is the IAG with *cael*, and *Llyfr Cyfnerth* (both manuscripts) prefers *cael y gan*; *Peredur* only has *cael gan*; *Culhwch ac Olwen*, *Manawydan*, and *Math* show both. One may speculate whether this points towards a stylistic preference on the part of some authors or redactors for one form over the other, whereas others treated them as equivalent both stylistically and functionally. Linguistic development is another argument that could be used to support the hypothesis that *y gan* and *gan* are really two variants of one preposition: *y gan* disappears over time, while *gan* becomes the common marker of P1 in passive constructions (both with the *cael*-passive and with the synthetic impersonal verb form) in Modern Welsh. This should indicate that, at some stage, the form *y gan* was considered functionally not distinct enough to maintain a separate identity. However, it is doubtful whether prepositional mergers in general presuppose large-scale functional overlap before the merger takes place. For example, Old Irish *fri* and *la* merge into Modern Irish *le*, with the latter inheriting some, if not all uses of *fri* (thus, for example, an Old Irish *as-beir fri* 'says to' becomes a Modern Irish *deir le*). This particular merger was quite probably a phonological reality before the functional merger took place (witness the frequent occurrence of *re/ri* in e.g. *TBC LL* and *III* for older *fri* and *la*), and the phonological/phonetic similarity between *gan* and *y gan* may well have contributed to the demise of a distinct *y gan*, especially since the element *y* was unstressed (preceding a pre-tonic *gan*).

Although the use of *gan*, as opposed to the compound preposition, in P1 func- tion with either the *cael*-passive or the impersonal verb form, or indeed with VNs, is not a prominent feature of the data investigated here, there are a few examples that can be interpreted as such, as we have seen above (see Sections 2.1.2 and 2.3). Thus another question arises, especially in conjunction with the eventual loss of *y gan* in Modern Welsh and the exclusive use of *gan* to mark P1 in passives—namely, whether it is possible to trace an agentive sense for both prepositions, i.e. a use whereby the person marked by the prepositional phrase is most closely associated with controlling the process element of a situation. Further, the possibility that the use, especially of *y gan* with the impersonal verb form (as opposed to the *cael-*passive), was, if not modelled on, then facilitated by, the corresponding Latin structure (passive + *ab* 'from') needs to be considered.

As Lewis (1937) suspects, the key to the use of *y gan* with passives (and as IAG marker) lies in a literal reading of the compound *y gan* 'from alongside *X*', or 'from with *X*', therefore 'from the sphere of influence of *X*', but not 'out of *X*' (where *X* is not only the spatial point of origin, but the material source or originator of an entity, or the source of energy of a process). In other words, similar to the interpretation of the agentive use of Irish *la*, the person in whose vicinity (*gan*) a process takes place comes to be causally connected with the process, and the element *y* adds a sense of directionality 'from'. As with *la*, I interpret the causal link, established as default option in the absence of a more suitable candidate, between the complement of *gan* and a process as weaker than that expressed by Welsh *o* or Irish *ó*, where the preposition marks the unambiguous point of origin, or source of a process. It does not appear to be necessary to assume, as Lewis (1937) does, that the sense of directionality inherent in the compound *y gan* is vital to explain the use of *gan* to mark P1 and IAG. As we have seen, Old Irish *la* never had any sense of directionality, but the spatial sense 'in the vicinity of', in practice often 'in the territory of', is sufficient to trigger the sense of controlling AG, or AG in charge. Thus the use of *gan* as the marker of IAG, or CAUSE, or indeed P1, is relatively straightforward to reconcile with the spatial sense of the preposition, which in turn may have contributed to the demise of *y gan*, in that it is possible to arrive at the agentive use of *gan* without a necessary directional link, provided by *y gan*.

This directional element is assumed by Fife (1990) in his interpretation of Modern Welsh *gan*, to which he ascribes two basic senses, one locative, as in expressions of possession, and a path specification, usually translated 'from'. According to Fife, the agentive use of *gan* falls under the path specification, with a root in 'from *X* as the source of action'. He stresses the abstract nature of this path specification, which explains why *gan* cannot be used to express concrete, spatial notions. He appears to take Lewis's (1937) reading of the origin of the agentive use—namely, that 'the agentive use of *gan* was originally derived from the "with" sense by the addition of an overt "from" element, giving Middle Welsh *y gan*'—for granted, and the question remains whether the assumption of two basic senses for *gan*, locative and path, is necessary to account for the preposition's varied senses. What appears unnecessary is a reinterpretation of the complement of *gan* as the source of a process, rather than as marking, in the first instance, the entity defining the region in which a process takes place, and which in turn becomes associated with the process by default. Thus Fife's (1990: 515) statement that 'across languages the same sort of mix of genitive and ablative images as found in GAN are seen in agentive structures', citing, for example, Latin *ab* 'from', and German *von* 'from', appears to assume a sense of directionality for *gan* that is too strong, and not necessary, leading in turn to the suggestion of two distinct basic senses. The prime motivation for positing the path specification appears to be the use of *gan* with *cael* 'get' (which in turn forms the *cael*-passive) and with the impersonal verb form. And, while the influence (as assumed by Fife) of a Middle Welsh *y gan* 'from with' on the agentive use of *cael* cannot be excluded (see also J. E. C. Willliams 1948: 8), it does not necessarily follow that this is the actual conceptualization of agentive *gan* in Welsh usage.

In the present interpretation, the use of a *gan*-phrase with processes such as *cael* (Middle Welsh *kaffael*) 'get', *prynu* 'buy', *cymryt* (Middle Welsh *kymryt*) 'take' to denote the person giving or selling an entity works via an association of control through proximity. This type of association is not unknown in other languages; for example, in German it is perfectly possible to buy, get, or learn something *bei* 'by, at, with, apud' someone, as well as *von* 'from' someone. This appears preferable to Fife's assumption of a path specification for *gan*, which, according to Fife, involves a 'very tortuous course of calculation to eventually equate the object of GAN with the tr[ajector] of the process of SEEING' in a sentence such as 'Cafodd Gwynfor ei weld gan Ifor' (Gwynfor was seen by Ifor) (1990: 482), 'unless such a structure has been unitized and speakers equate them directly' (ibid.). Unitization cannot be excluded, but an interpretation of the agentive use of *gan*, both medieval and modern, which does not require the 'semantic acrobatics' (ibid.) of a path specification for the preposition as well as a non-directional spatial meaning, would seem to be preferable.

5   Summary and Concluding Remarks

The investigation in this book has pursued aspects of the marking of P1 in early Welsh and Irish, and of the way in which agentive constructions are employed in their contexts. It has emerged from the Welsh material that prepositional P1 marking in VN constructions is very consistent in the use of *o* 'from'; VN constructions other than $vn+o_{p1}$ are of marginal occurrence only. The semantic specification of *o* as P1 marker was analysed as that of the source of energy of a process, more specifically an action. This is supported by the character of CAUSE and INST marked by *o*: in causal function, *o* specifies an influence that results in the situation described by the clause; the CAUSE can be interpreted as the source from which the situation develops. In instrumental (or modal) function, *o* only rarely marks a concrete instrument or tool controlled by an AG, but more often marks the abstract manner, or, with a concrete complement, the material or substance out of which something is made or develops. In addition, *o* can also denote the IAG, or 'giver', with VNs such as *caffael* 'get' or *bot* (in possessive construction) 'be'/'have'. This is, however, rare, compared to the use of *gan* 'with' or *y gan* 'from (with)' in this function.

The construction $vn+o_{p1}$ occurs with considerable frequency as independent VN clause as a feature of dynamic narrative (it has, however, also emerged that this usage is, although frequent in absolute terms, not prominent in all the texts analysed here). The typical agentive VN clause in early Welsh contains a VN that represents new, and a P1 that represents given information. The use of the clause-initial VN— i.e. the positioning of the process content at the beginning of the clause, but leaving the anchoring into narrative reality up to the context—was interpreted as an indication that independent agentive VN clauses in early Welsh are used to advance the narrative by means of focusing the content of the VN.

The clause types $vn+pp_{p1}$ and $p2+do_{vn}+p1$ in Irish narrative likewise show a considerable consistency regarding the marking of P1, which is almost invariably *do* 'to', and regarding their virtual restriction to syntactically dependent positions. A feature they share with Welsh VN clauses is the givenness of P1 in the large majority of cases. The annalistic material showed a different distribution of P1 markers. This has led to the conclusion that there is a tendency to use different markers to express different types of P1, specifically different types of AG: that is, different members of the category AG find expression by members of different lexical categories—namely, *la* 'with', *do* 'to', or *ó* 'from'. The sense of *do* as P1 marker was identified as that of a person affected by the process, which can be linked to the spatial/directional sense of the preposition by way of *do* expressing the receiver with verbs of giving. The agentive use of *ó* with VNs can be explained from its use to denote the starting point of a path (concrete or abstract)—i.e. the spatial source; this latter use also explains ambiguities between spatial and agentive sense of *ó* with passive verbs of giving or sending. The comparatively frequent use of *ó* with plural complements in the annalistic material (and particularly in the collocations *ó genntaib* and *ó Gallaib* 'by the gentiles/Foreigners'—i.e. 'by the Vikings') can be interpreted as evidence, on the one hand, that *ó* tends to be used to denote the group from which a process originates (spatial source), without giving further details as to the identity of the individuals carrying out the action. On the other hand, the use of *ó* in the expressions *ó genntaib/Gallaib* may owe some of its consistency to a Latin model (*a gentibus*).

The preposition *la* as P1 marker with VNs or process nouns is widespread only in the annalistic material. In a large number of attestations, the agentive function of *la* can be identified as being that of the AG in charge—i.e. as the person under whose leadership an action is carried out, with a number of unspecified persons taking part in the action. The specific sense of *la* in agentive function, the person in charge, can be linked with the spatial sense of the preposition by way of a default establishment of a causal link between a process and the person in whose vicinity the process takes place. This interpretation of the agentive sense of *la* is supported by the fact that *la* is the dominant marker of P1 with the passive (which in turn was interpreted as an impersonal with additional focusing properties for noun phrase P2s), and by the specifics of its use to mark CAUSE and IAG. *La* marking the CAUSE tends to denote an external influence or event that has a shaping influence on a situation (rather than being the sole source of the situation described in the clause). *La* is also the most common preposition to mark the IAG, most frequently with *do-tuit* 'falls (in battle)' and with the substantive verb, where *la* expresses the giver. The derivation of the agentive use of *la* from the marking of the INST, put forward by Baudiš and others, does not find support in the data. On the whole, there is very little overlap between the marking of the INST, especially of the concrete INST (used by an AG)—i.e. a tool or weapon or the like—and that of P1 in either early Welsh or Irish. The use of Welsh *gan* with passives to denote P1 was interpreted along similar lines to the use of Irish *la*, as that of the person in charge, where the complement of the preposition defines the spatial region in which the process takes place, and which in turn becomes identified as the person responsible for the process (and note also the use of *gan* to mark the IAG and the external, contributing CAUSE). An additional element of directionality can be attributed to the element *y* in *y gan*, lit.: 'from with' or 'from alongside', as opposed to the *o* 'from' marking P1 in VN clauses. The fact that full passives are absent from the Welsh narratives, but occur regularly in *Brut y Tywysogyon* (and comparatively often correspond to Latin full passives in *Annales Cambriae* and *Cronica de Wallia*) may indicate that the development of the full passive in Welsh was supported by familiarity with Latin usage, and possibly by a desire to create a Latinate style. However, the choice of preposition (*y gan* and (later) *gan*, rather than *o*) may be a sign that the AG of a passive clause was not conceptualized as identical with the AG of a VN construction, where we overwhelmingly find *o*.

Throughout this book, little reference has been made to diachronic developments. Occasionally, especially in the Irish material, comparatively 'late' features became obvious, such as the use of the independent 'object' pronoun (*é* 'him', *iad* 'them') to mark P2 in passive clauses in *TBC LL* or *III*, or the use of *oc* 'at' to mark P1 in *TBC III*. Spatial *oc* describes a position at a point, rather than in a vicinity or region. However, a vicinity defined by a single person or persons can become a point, and the two spatial senses can overlap. This overlap would seem to have favoured the use of *oc* in P1 function, perhaps facilitated by other contexts where *oc* over time comes to adopt uses of *la*.[1] However, the diachronic development of prepositional semantics, as well as the syntax and semantics of VNs and passives (or indeed impersonals) in Celtic, awaits further study.

---

[1] Cf. e.g. the expression of (temporary) possession, where in Old Irish we find *attá* X *la* Y 'X has Y', as opposed to Modern Irish *tá* X *ag* Y. Ownership, on the other hand, is consistently marked by *le* (Modern Irish *is liom-sa an teach* 'the house is mine' is a direct continuation of Old Irish *is limm-sa a tech*).

APPENDIX 1

VN clauses with overt P1 in Middle Welsh narrative

INDEPENDENT VN CLAUSES

VN+0

CO 4; 164–5; 175; 399; 408; 413–14; 442; 459; 459–60; 461; 463; 476; 510; 558; 818; 819–20; 920; 925; 940; 990; 992; 996–7; 1036; 1038; 1040; 1050; 1145; 1167; 1179; 1182–3; 1184–5; 1187–8; 1205; 1209; 1213–14

P. 1.20; 7.19; 8.13; 8.19; 13.16; 16.28

B. 43.13–14; 44.1; 44.2; 45.15; 46.3; 47.3

MLl 50.15; 53.4; 57.26

Ma. 69.11; 72.22; 72.24; 77.17; 87.1; 88.8; 91.23

BR 6.20; 11.3; 11.27; 12.14

Per. 12.23; 14.18; 24.22; 38.24; 38.28; 39.13; 67.4

VN+i

CO 26

B. 44.20

Ma. 90.8; 90.9

VN+gan

B. 36.20

P1+i+VN

CO 584; 589–90; 627; 731; 765

Ma. 84.4

VN+GEN_{P1}

CO 3; 14; 22; 46; 384; 461; 469; 487; 786/1; 786/2; 801; 804–5; 990; 1052; 1053; 1062; 1104; 1110; 1232; 1243

P. 3.14

B. 44.19; 46.2; 46.14; 48.5–6

MLl 54.23; 55.7

Ma. 75.7

Ow. 728

Per. 26.5; 30.25/1; 30.25/2; 61.7–8

DEPENDENT VN CLAUSES

VN+0

CO 1043
P. 8.7; 8.21; 25.14
B. 41.3; 43.25; 45.25
MLl 52.13; 52.26
Ma. 68.9; 73.3; 77.3; 77.17–18; 78.28; 85.14; 92.4
CLl 4; 55–6; 62; 68; 72; 76; 130
BR 2.17–18; 3.13; 10.22–3; 21.7
Ow. 102; 276; 400–1; 426; 513; 635/1; 635/2
Per. 7.18; 7.25; 22.6; 24.23; 29.2; 39.8; 50.3; 50.13; 61.1; 65.12

VN+i

CO 639; 651–2; 812

VN+gan

Ma. 84.26–7

P1+i+VN

CO 1223–4
P. 15.16
BR 12.14–15; 12.18–19
Per. ?64.21–2

VN+GEN_{P1}

CO 3; 4; 39; 167; 414–15; 456; 457; 512; 720; 796; 970–1; 1028; 1053; 1062; 1102
P. 12.21; 13.9; 16.8; 19.26; 21.27; 23.12
B. 32.17; 33.13; 36.13; 38.21; 44.24–5
MLl 50.14; 53.2; 53.25; 55.23; 57.2; 57.25; 58.18; 64.11
Ma. 68.16–17; 76.27; 78.9–10; 78.14; 78.22; 81.13–14; 81.25–6; 84.1; 85.11; 85.27; 91.1
CLl 3; 13–14; 16; 24; 65; 76–7
BR 2.27; 3.26; 7.1; 8.23; 9.10; 10.5; 10.6; 10; 18.27; 20.9
Ow. 5; 32; 95; 218; 252–3; 307–8; 562; 796; 806
Per. 7.24; 9.22; 11.22; 12.25; 21.17; 23.2; 23.4/1; 23.4/2; 34.29–30; 40.9; 40.11; 41.7; 41.9; 46.30; 47.9; 60.23; 64.3

VN clauses with overt P1 in Middle Welsh law texts

Llyfr Cyfnerth

VN+*o*

Independent VN clauses

V 30b10, W 84a2, V 41b14, V 41b15–16, V 41b20, V 42b19, V 44a18, W 104a4

Independent VN clauses in condition chains

V 19b3, V 24b9, W 65b10, W 65b12, W 70a9, V 35a1, V 35a2, V 36a5, V 36b9, W 81b11, W 81b13–14, W 82a6, W 82a7, W 87b19, W 88b6, W 91a4, V 40b3, V 41a22, V 42b17, V 43b1, V 43b2, V 43b4, V 43b5–6, V 43b6, V 43b8, V 45b1, V 45b6, V 45b8, V 45b11, W 103a4

Dependent VN clauses (introduced by a preposition)

V 24b14, V 35a12, V 35a13, V 35a14–15, V 40b7, V 41b21

Object clauses and P2 complements

V 24b12, W 79b17, W 39a21

VN+GEN$_{P1}$

Independent VN clauses

V 3b15

Independent VN clauses in condition chains

W 81b1, W 82a7, W 82a12–13, V 45b3, V 45b7

Dependent VN clauses (introduced by a preposition)

V 13b25, V 39a6, V 39b16

Llyfr Cynghawsedd

VN+*o*

Independent VN clauses

§§10.11, 12.48, 17.3, 19.25, 22.40–1, 47.47, 51.6

Independent VN clauses in condition chains

§§1.3, 3.10, 4.12, 5.14, 6.18–19, 7.26, 8.31, 8.32, 10.5, 11.20, 13.7, 13.9, 15.34, 21.44, 24.1, 26.10, 26.11, 27.15/1, 27.15/2, 29.21, 29.21–2, 46.9, 47.45, 51.44, 51.45, 51.47–8

Dependent VN clauses (introduced by a preposition)

§§10.17, 19.26, 21.8, 22.21, 28.17, 34.39, 47.36, 49.13

Object clauses and P2 complements

§§14.17, 14.18, 14.26–7, 17.2, 17.10, 19.29–30, 22.16, 22.35–6, 22.39, 24.6, 46.20, 47.40, 48.20, 48.34, 49.5, 49.9, 49.13

Subject clauses

§§10.4, 22.14

VN+GEN$_{P1}$

Independent VN clauses

§24.5

Independent VN in condition chains

§§31.29, 51.43

Dependent VN clauses (introduced by a preposition)

§§7.28, 16.44, 17.47, 17.1(p.79), 48.14

Object clauses and P2 complements

§§13.13, 17.4, 17.8, 22.15/1, 22.15/2, 22.16, 22.26, 22.27, 33.36, 33.38

Subject clauses

§§9.35, 10.17

APPENDIX 3

Passives with overt P1 in *Brut y Tywysogyon*

Figures are dates for *BT(R)* (Jones 1973); details in parentheses concern the Peniarth 20 version (Jones 1941)

Section A. AD 823–1042

823 (*BT(P)*: active), 848 (*BT(P)*: active), 849 (*BT(P)*: active), 852 (*BT(P)*: active), 855, 871, 878, 904, 918, 920, 934, 942, 946, 949, 954/1 (*BT(P)*: no P1), 954/2, 963, 970 (*BT(P)*: active), 978 (*BT(P)*: active), 980, 983, 984, 993 (*BT(P)*: no P1), 995 (*BT(P)*: active), 999/1 (*BT(P)*: no P1), 999/2 (*BT(P)*: no P1), 1000 (*BT(P)*: active), 1012 (*BT(P)*: active), 1018 (*BT(P)*: active), 1033 (*BT(P)*: active), 1035/1, 1035/2 (*BT(P)*: active).

Section B. AD 1190–1275

1191, 1193, 1194, 1195, 1202, 1204, 1208 (no P1), 1220, 1227/1, 1227/2, 1230, 1241 (*BT(P)*: active), 1242, 1249 (*BT(P)*: active), 1255, 1256, 1275.

APPENDIX 4

IAG, CAUSE, and INST in medieval Welsh

The IAG

GAN AND Y GAN

	cael gan	*cael y gan*
CO	1193, 1199	1185
P.	7.12, 21.8, 25.2	
B.	34.10	
MLl	52.3, 53.3, 53.21, 54.19	56.6, 57.24, 58.14
Ma.	69.8, 90.22/1, 22/2, ?84.26	68.25, 79.4
BR	5.30	
Ow.	203, 767	
Per.	12.29, 16.25, 21.5, 22.15, 52.25	
WML	W 40a8, W 64b2, V 43a24, V 45b25	V 1b13,14, W 38b16, W 39a12, W 39b4, W 39b8, W 39b19, W 40a3, W 40a6, V 6a16, V 6a20, V 6b17, V 6b22, V 6b25, V 7a5, V 7a25, V 7b3, V 7b6, V 7b25, V 8a7, V 8a10,11, V 8a22, V 8b7, V 8b11,12, V8b16, V 8b18, V 9a16,17,18, V 9a19, V 9b12, V 9b25, V 10a1, V 10b12, V 10b14, V 11a18, V 11a23, V 1b10, V 1b14, V 11b16, V 11b24, V 12a2, V 12a5, V 12a14, V 12a18, V 13a11, V 15a2, V 15a17, V 17a25, V 27a21, V 33a17, V 36a4, W 80a8, W 85a17, W 90a17, V 38a8, V 38b17
Cyngh.	§8.31	
		y gan denoting the giver without *cael*:
WML		V 6b23, V 9b23
	prynu gan	*prynu y gan*
MLl	53.1, 53.3, 54.20	63.15
	kymryt gan	*kymryt y gan*
P.		17.23
MLl	54.26	53.28
Ma.		91.23, 91.26
CLl		167
Ow.	811	15

	keissaw gan		keissaw y gan
CO			1191
Ma.			85.21
Per.			14.12
WML	V 24a6		
			mynnu y gan
CO			566
Cyngh.			§49.16
	diodef gan		diodef y gan
P.			19.27
MLl	58.20		
			(cf. Per. 30.6: godef y gan)
	clybot gan		
P.	24.13		
			craessaw/annerch y gan
P.			12.15 (craessaw)
B.			41.7 (annerch)
			dyuot y gan
B.			35.3
WML			W 39a6, W 40b3, V 8a19,20,21, V 26b18, W 89a11, W 90b5
	bot yn barawt gan		
Ow.	675, 257		

Other possible IAG constructions

P.	27.1 (ac os kynghor gennyt ti hynny)		
B.	42.8 (rac llygru y wlat oed genti hitheu hynny)		
Per.			14.12 (erchi y gan 'on behalf of')
WML			V 25a12 (amot . . . ygan y perchennaƀc)
			V 45a3 (Perchennaƀc . . . a dyly dec adeu ugeint ygan y neb a llatho . . .)
Cyngh.			§8.32 (. . . am vraut e gan er ygneyt . . .)
			§16.41–2 (hep rod ac estyn y gan argluyd)

o

with *cael*, expressing the giver:
CO 41–2
WML V 14a14, V 14a15, V 14b3, V 14b17, V 15a4
expressing the giver, without a verb: WML V 27a2

bot (possessive)
Ma. 76.27

other constructions
CO 1001, 1123

The CAUSE

o

o marks an internal motivation

Experience (VN)
CO 1217
P. 19.19
B. 40.5, 38.19
BR 1.6
Ow. 457
Per. 41. 23

State/emotion/state of mind
CO 16
P. 12.25
B. ?42.2, 45.17, 46.3, 56.9
MLl 64.7, 67.19
Ma. 81.14
CLl 137
Per. ?14.5, 28.5, 68.8
WML V 41b7
Cyngh. §22.14

Action or activity
CO 640
P. 25.1
Ma. 81.3, 84.27
CLl 103
WML ?V27b16, ?V 27b17, ?V 27b25, ?W 64a9 (possibly, *o* has conditional meaning ('if') in these examples)

o marks an external motivation

Event or state, external circumstance
P. 24.20
MLl 55.15, 64.10
Per. 46.6
WML V 7b5, V 24b3, V 29b18, ?W 89b2, V 39b12 ff., ?85a12

Action or activity
P. 3.20
MLl 50.16
Ma. ?78.1, 92.12
CLl 52
Ow. 98, 462
WML ?W 89b6

O hynny: *CO* 249; *B.* 14.22; *Per.* 10.1, 21.9

A M

am marks an internal motivation

Activity or state
P. 21.18, 25.2, 25.14
B. 46.4
Ow. 749, 775
Per. 21.7, 21.9–10, 21.17, 22.15, 51.13, 61.22, 67.19

am marks an external motivation

Concrete complement
CO 483, 533
P. 20.13
B. 37.22, 47.18
Ow. 304
WML ?V 45b2, ?V 45b7

Past event, activity or experience
CO 260, 599, 1075
P. 21.13, 21.18
B. 37.21

Am hynny: *CO* 259, 278, 498, 996; *Ow.* 412; *Per.* 7.25, 16.26

R A C

rac marks an external motivation

Quality or characteristic, or external circumstance
CO 80, 226, 229, 668
P. 22.23
B. 36.19
BR 2.13, 4.13, 11.1, 21.5
Ow. 214
Per. 25.14
WML V 42a10

rac marks an internal motivation

Quality or characteristic
BR 5.1
Ow. 56
Per. 31.10

Emotional/mental state, or (quality of) experience
Ow. 199, 385
Per. 31.23, 43.2
WML W 65b11

Rac ouyn: *CO* 8; *MLl* 57.17; *Ma.* 91.3, 91.11; *CLl* 82; *WML* W 89b14

GAN

Concomitant (external) circumstance
BR 15.5, 15.6
Ow. 152, 200, 530
Per. 24.30, 30.24, 34.11

Concrete complement
Ma. 82.14
BR 2.13, 2.14
Ow. 592
WML W 85a13

TRWY

Activity (expressed or implied)
CO 4
B. 47.7
WML V 43b25, V 44a2, V 44a4
Cyngh. §§17, 19

WRTH

Quality or characteristic
MLl 56.14

Process (action, event or state)
Cyngh. §§21.8, 22.21, 22.28, 48.14

Wrth hynny: *CO* 248; *P.* 19.24; *B.* 34.26, 38.22; *MLl* 52.25; *CLl* 113; *Ow.* 299; *WML* V 33a3, V 36b15; *Cyngh.* §§22.33, 22.35, 24.3, 36.45–6, 47.7, 47.8, 48.24, 48.30, 48.48, 49.8, 49.16, 49.25, 50.32, 50.40

OTHER PREPOSITIONS

dy wrth: *CO* 10; *yr*: *B.* 34.14, *WML* V 24b3, W 85a13, *y am*: *WML* W 83a12

The INST (including instances of prepositions denoting the material from which something is made, or the mode/manner in which an action is carried out)

A(C)

Concrete complement (tool, in the widest sense)
CO 370, 668, 702, 703, 966, 974, 1188, 1226
P. 15.10, 16.24, 17.10, 20.19
B. 36.20
MLl 60.17
Ma. 75.3, 75.19, 76.6, 76.24, 86.20, 88.6, 90.15, 91.24, 91.25

BR 8.2
Ow. 131, 507, 591, 668
Per. 9.1, 14.9, 17.22, 17.26, 18.10, 19.7, 19.15, 19.19, 19.22, 19.27, 29.6, 30.1, 31.12 31.20, 40.27, 47.16, 49.7, 53.30, 60.19, 68.23
WML V 11a20, V 13a24, V 14a15, V 14b6, V 14b10, V 18b2, V 33b17, V 34b6, W 91a1, V 42a17, V 42a18, V 45b4, V 45b12

Concrete complement (material)
BR 4.5, 5.23, 13.8, 18.7, 18.8
Ow. ?639

Abstract complement
WML V 24a22, V 24a25, V 24b5

o

Abstract complement (denoting (type of) activity, or a quality)
P. 6.11, ?8.21
MLl 62.10
Ma. 68.11, 70.5, 73.15, 83.20, 86.7
CLl 161
Ow. 411, 444
Per. 7.2, 35.3, 47.13, ?57.29, 58.22
WML V 7a16, V 12b25, ?V 21a17, ?106b19

Concrete complement
P. 36.28
CLl 5
Ow. 395, 411, 444, 450
Per. 9.2
WML V 2a8, V 34b12

Concrete complement (material)
MLl 54.12, 58.12, 83.12, 83.24
Ow. 334
Per. 9.6
WML W 40b2, V 7a9, V 45a6

Abstract complement (manner)
P. 23.15
Ma. 83.24
CLl 66, ?142
Ow. ?639
WML V 2a13, V 13a2, W 64b2, V 35a12–13, V 37b1, W 89b5 (= V 38b8–9), V 38a4, V 39b20, V 43a20, V 44a6, V39b20, V 44a17
Cyngh. §§11.21, 11.25, 17.8

Holi . . . o datanhud/o ach ac etrif etc.: *WML* V 25a16; *Cyngh.* §§9.45–6, 10.1, 10.2, 11.20, 12.30, 14.16, 15.33, 16.44, 16.45, 17.46, 19.21, 19.25, 22.13, 23.39, 24.49, 46.9, 47.28, 49.43, 50.28

TRWY (MANNER AND MEANS)

Treulaw (amser) trwy digriuwch etc.: *P.* 5.6, 7.2, 11.14, 18.21; *B.* 37.5; *Ma.* 86.7

Abstract complement
P. 8.23
WML V 1a2, V 14a3, V 22a19
Cyngh. §§17.47, 19.22, ?22.32

Concrete complement (including (types of) persons in law texts)
CO 27
WML W 65a20
Cyngh. §§22.30, 48.32

OTHER PREPOSITIONS

ar: *Ma.* 69.14; *gan*: *WML* V 24b18–19, W 103b15

APPENDIX 5

VN clauses with overt P1 in *Táin Bó Cúailnge*

VN+PP~P1~

VN+do~P1~

TBC I 150, 158, 623, 649, 767, 1293, 1530, 2144, 2581, 2604, 2819, 2867, 2874, 3416, 3501, 3764, 3902, 4003, 4129

TBC LL 833–4, 838–9, 840, 863, 952–3, 1331–2, 1571, 1577, 1605–6, 1676, 1677, 1964–5, 2008, 2105, 2165–6, 2923, 3247, 3417–18, 3793, 4781

TBC III: ZCP 8: 544.33, 545.29, 549.17, 549.24, 550.28, 554.5; *RC* 14: §§10/1, 10/2, 11, 12, 13; *RC* 15: §§90, 92, 126

VN+la~P1~

TBC I 1740, 3369

VN+ó~P1~

TBC LL 3265–6
TBC III: ZCP 8: 547

VN+GEN~P1~

TBC I 153–4, 160, 161, 485, 724–5, 1031, 1079, 1225, 1247–8, 1292, 1295, 1570, 1674, 1812, 1820, 2593, 2609, 2726, 2810, 3364, 3510, 3894, 4032, 4092/1, 4092/2, 4144

TBC LL 8, 35, 365, 588, 895, 896, 987, 1477, 1565, 1721, 1725, 2107, 2626, 2627, 2723, 2929, 3238, 3239, 3240, 3290, 3291, 3361, 3672, 3892, 3914, 4032, 4583, 4599

TBC III: ZCP 8: 548.5, 550.14; *RC* 14: §§14, 62; *RC* 15: §208

P2+*do*~VN~+P1

TBC I 396, 1901, 2542, 3858
TBC LL 332–3, 1554, 2401, 2785, 2788
TBC III: ZCP 8: 539.22, 547.26; *RC* 14: §§21, 34, 61; *RC* 15: §§196, 206

P1+*do*~VN~(+P2)

TBC I 590, 1971–2, 2294–5, 2875, 2881–2, 4136–7
TBC LL 508, 776–7, 1550–1, 1717–18, 1824–5, 2302, 2457, 2730, 3147, 3380, 3824, 3848–9, 3887, 3891, 3974, 3992–3
TBC III: ZCP 8: 547.28, 553.13, 553.14, 553.31; *RC* 15: §§75, 95, 111, 157

PURPOSE CLAUSES

TBC LL 1816–17, 2535, 2610, 4164
TBC III: *ZCP* 8: 553.34; *RC* 14: §§20, 34, 60; *RC* 15: §202

Agentive VN clauses in Irish law texts

VN+PP$_{P1}$

?CG 485 (*la*)
BB §§37 (*ó*), 41 (*ó*)
UR §9 (*do*)
BCr §17 (*ó*)

VN+GEN$_{P1}$

CG 549
?UR §12
BCr §26

P1+*do*$_{VN}$(+P2)/PURPOSE CLAUSES

CG 553, 572, 584
BCr §§31/1, 31/2, 36

APPENDIX 7

VN+GEN$_{P1}$ in *The Annals of Ulster*

VERBAL NOUNS

AU 851.3 (*tetacht*), 924.1 (*derghe*), 1024.1 (*tuitim*), 1028.7 (*dul*), 1128.1 (*tuitim*)

PROCESS NOUNS

AU 434 (*brat*), 675.1 (*bellum*), 679.3 (*bellum*), 715.4 (*sloghadh*), 738.9 (*slogad*), 772.3 (*sloghadh*), 805.7 (*slogad*), 808.4 (*slogad*), 1002.2 (*slogad*), 1034.7 (*slogad*), 1051.4 (*éc*), 1120.3 (*éc*)

APPENDIX 8

VN+PP$_{P1}$, VN+LPN$_{P1}$, VN+IPN$_{P1}$ in *The Annals of Ulster*

Clauses containing VNs

Entry	P1 marker	VN	P1 type
721.8	*la*	*innred*	γ
733.7	*do*	*coscrath* (2)	γ(?)
742.2	*la*	*foirtbe*	β
752.14	*do*	*foirddbe*	β
752.15	*la*	*foirddbe*	β
754.6	*do*	*foirtbe*	β
777.6	*la*	*cumuscc*	γ
793.4/1	*la*	*sarugad*	α?
793.4/2	*la*	*guin*	β
795.3	*ó**	*loscad*	β
798.2	*do*	*innreda*	β
798.17	*la*	*sarugad*	α
794.8	*la*	*indreth*	γ
809.7	*la*	*indredh*	γ
811.2 SC	*do*	*sarugad*	β
812.12	*la*	*indred*	γ
815.7	*do*	*orgain* *guin*	β
818.8	*do*	*orggain*	γ
821.3	*ó**	*orggan*	β
822.3/1	*la*	*indred*	γ
822.3/2	*la*	*indred*	γ
822.3	*do*	*eludh*	β
824.2	*ó**	*orggain*	β
825.1	*ó**	*loscuth*	β
826.8	*la*	*loscad*	γ
827.2	*la*	*sarugad*	α, α
827.3	*do**	*orggan*	β
827.5	*la*	*coscradh*	γ
827.6	*la*	*coscrad*	γ
827.9	*do**	*coscradh*	β

Entry	P1 marker	VN	P1 type
828.4/1	ó**	guin	β
828.4/2	ó**	loscadh	β
830.4	la	loscad	γ
830.6	la	cumbe	γ
831.6	do*	indred	β
831.9	la	sarugad	α?
831.11	la	indredh	γ
832.1	ó*	orggain	β
832.3	ó*	orggain	β
823.4	ó*	ergabail	β
832.6	ó*	orggain	β
833.5	ó*	orggain	β
833.7	la	loscudh	γ
833.11	ó*	orgain	β
834.9/2	ó*	orgain	β
835.3	la	indredh	γ
835.5	ó*	orggain	β
835.11	ó*	loscadh	β
835.12	ó**	orggain	β
836.3	la	gabail	γ
837.5	ó*	loscadh	β
837.7	la	indredh	γ
837.9	la	marbad	β
839.1	ó*	loscadh	β
840.1	ó*	orggain	β
840.4	la	indredh	γ
841.2/1	la	cumsundud	α
841.2/2	la	marbad	α
842.6	ó*	orggain	β
842.7	ó*	orgain	β
842.11	ó*	orgain	β
844.4	ó*	loscad	β
845.2	ó*	orggain	β
845.7	la	orgain	α, α
846.2	do*	orggain	β
847.3	la	toghal	γ
861.1	do	indredh	γ
867.8	la	loscad	γ, γ
869.6	ó	orccain	γ
870.2	la	indred	γ
902.2	ó	indarba	γ, γ
904.2	la	sarugad	γ
914.1	ó	indred	γ

Entry	P1 marker	VN	P1 type
915.3/1	ó	frithuidecht	β
915.3/2	ó(pro)	indred	β
915.7	ó(pro)	indred	β
918.4	do(pro)*	sagaith	β
921.8/1	ó**	indred	β
921.8/2	ó(pro)**	indred	β
926.1	do**	orgain	β
927.4	ó	coscrad	α
936.2	do(pro)**	anad	β
939.1	ó**	orcain	β
970.5	la	orcain	γ
970.6	la	orcain	γ
982.4	ó	orcain	γ
999.7	la	indred	γ
1002.4	la	crechad	γ
1007.10	la	athnugudh	α[?]
1010.6	la	dalladh	γ
1028.5	la	orcain	β
1052.8 SC	ó	innarba	α
1053.1	do	marbad	α
1053.4	do	marbad	α
1108.6	la	dichennadh	β(γ?)
1125.1 SC	la	lanecor	γ
1127.2	la	dichennadh	β
1129.4	do(pro)	loscadh	γ

Clauses containing Latin process nouns

Entry	P1 marker	LPN	P1 type
454	la[H²]	cena Temhra	γ
482.1	la	bellum ^	γ
504.2	la	bellum ^	γ
558.2	la	ceana Temra	γ
565.1	la	occissio	α
569	la	occissio	α
577.4	la	iugulatio	β
590.2	la	bellum ^	γ
597.1	la	occisio	α
598.2	la	occisio	γ
600.2	la	iugulatio	α

Entry	P1 marker	LPN	P1 type
604.2	ó	*iugulatio*	α
618.2	ó	*iugulatio*	α
623.3	la	*expugnatio*	γ
628.6	la	*uastatio*	γ
634	la	*iugulatio*	α
635.1	la	*occisio*	α
654.1	la	*iugulatio*	α
676.4	la	*distructio*	γ
681.1	la	*combustio*	γ
717.6	la	*comixtio*	α
721.6	do	*uastatio*	γ, γ
741.1	la	*percutio*	γ
743.4	la	*bellum* ^	γ
744.9	la	*lex, lex* ^	γ
747.8	la	*bellum* ^	γ
753.4	la	*lex* ^	γ
753.10	la	*interfectio*	β
757.3	ó	*combustio*	β
757.9	la	*lex* ^	γ
774.7	la	*comixtio*	γ?
777.7	la	*strages*	β
778.4	la	*lex* ^	γ, γ
789.16	la	*strages*	β
790.6	la	*cedis*	β
793.2	la	*lex* ^	γ, γ
795.2	la	*occisio*	α
797.5	la	*uastatio*	γ
798.2	ó*	*combustio*	β
799.3	ó	*iugulatio*	α, α
799.9	la	*lex* ^	γ
805.8	la	*uastatio*	γ
806.5	la	*lex* ^	γ
808.5	ó	*iugulatio*	β
810.3	la	*uastatio*	γ
819.1	la	*uastatio*	γ
822.7	la	*strages*	β
823.5	la	*lex* ^	γ, γ
825.4	la	*lex* ^	γ
829.2	ó	*iugulatio*	α
833.7	la	*iugulatio* *loscudh*	γ
852.2	ó**	*uastatio*	β
903.4	ó?	*occisio*	α, α

Clauses containing Irish process nouns

Entry	P1 marker	IPN	P1 type
469	*la*	*feis Temra*	γ
470	*la*	*feis Temra*	γ
483.2	*la*	*cath*	γ(x 4)
560.1	*la*	*feis Temra*	γ
568	*la*	*fecht*	γ(+γ)
580.2	*la*	*fecht+*	γ
746.5	*la*	*ar*	γ
756.3	*la*	*slogad+*	γ
771.1	*la*	*slogad*	γ
777.3	*la*	*slogad+*	γ
779.1	*la*	*sloghadh*	γ
783.9	*la*	*forus*	α, α?
789.12	*le*	*cath+*	γ
794.6	*la*	*sloghadh*	γ
802.2	*la*	*sloghadh*	γ
812.8/1	*la*	*ar*	β
812.8/2	*la**	*ar*	β
812.9	*la*	*ar*	β
812.1	*la*	*ar*	β
812.11	*la*	*ar*	γ
813.4	*la**	*ar+*	β
814.6	*la*	*slogadh*	γ, γ
815.5	*la*	*slogad*	γ
820.2	*la*	*slogad*	γ
821.5	*la*	*slogad*	γ
822.3	*la*	*sloigedh*	γ
828.3	*ó***	*mucar(+PP)*	β
835.1	*la*	*sloghadh*	γ
836.1	*ó**	*ar+*	β
841.5	*la*	*slogadh*	γ
841.5/2	*la*	*slogad*	γ
851.3	*do*	*slat*	β
852.8	*la*	*ar*	β
855.3	*la*	*crech*	γ
859.2	*la*	*slogad*	γ, γ
860.1	*la*	*sloighedh+*	γ
874.4	*la*	*slogad*	γ
882.1	*la*	*sloghedh*	$γ(co^n β)$
889.1	*la*	*slogad*	$γ(co^n β)$
896.6	*la*	*ár*	β
896.7	*ra/la*	*ar*	β

Entry	P1 marker	IPN	P1 type
905.2	*la*	*slogad*	γ
906.3	*la*	*slogad*	γ
908.1	*la*	*slogad*	β, γ, γ
913.6	*la*	*sloghedh*	γ
914.3	*la*	*slogad*	γ
914.7	*la*	*slogad+*	γ
915.3	*la*	*slogad+*	γ
917.2	*la*	*ár*	β, β
917.3	*la*	*slogad*	γ
919.3	*le*	*cath+*	γ
924.3	*la*	*sloghadh*	γ
929.4	*la*	*sloghadh*	γ
938.6	*la*	*slogad*	γ, γ
939.4	*la*	*slogad*	γ
940.1	*la*	*slogad*	γ, γ
940.5	*la*	*crech*	γ
941.3	*la*	*slogad*	γ
947.1	*la*	*slogad*	γ
949.1	*la*	*sloghadh*	γ, γ
949.2	*la*	*crech*	γ
949.5	*la*	*slogad*	γ
955.3	*la*	*slogad*	γ
962.1	*la*	*crech*	γ
963.1	*la*	*longa*	γ
965.6	*la*	*slogad*	γ
968.3	*la*	*slogad*	γ
970.3	*la*	*slogad*	γ
971.6	*la*	*slogad*	γ
985.2/1	*la*	*slogad*	γ
985.2/1	*la*	*crech*	β
992.3	*la*	*sluagad*	γ
996.3	*la*	*crech*	β, β, β
998.1	*la*	*slogad*	γ, γ
998.5/1	*la*	*sluagad*	γ
998.5/2	*la*	*sluagad*	γ
999.5	*la*	*crech*	γ
999.8	*la*	*slogad*	γ
1000.7	*la*	*slogad*	γ
1001.5	*la*	*crech*	β
1001.6	*la*	*tochur+*	γ, γ
1002.1	*la*	*slogad*	γ
1002.8	*la*	*slogad*	γ, γ
1004.7	*la*	*slogad*	γ

Entry	P1 marker	IPN	P1 type
1005.7	la	slogad	$\gamma(co^n\,\beta)$
1006.4	la	slogad	γ
1007.6	la	slogad	γ
1007.7	la	slogad	γ
1009.1	la	crechdighail	γ
1009.6	la	crech	γ
1010.4	la	slogad	γ
1011.6	la	slogad	γ
1011.7	la	slogad	γ
1012.2/1	la	slogad	γ
1012.2/2	la	slogad	γ
1012.2/3	la	slogad	γ
1012.2/4	la	slogad	γ
1012.3	la	slogad	γ
1013.1	la	crech	γ
1013.3	la	slogad	γ
1013.6	la	slogad	γ
1013.7	la	crech	γ
1013.8	la	ár	γ
1014.2	la	sloghud	γ, γ
1014.7	la	sluagad	γ, γ
1017.7	la	ár	γ
1018.4	la	slogad	β
1021.3	la	crech	γ
1024.7	la	crech	γ
1025.4	la	sluagad	γ
1025.5/1	la	crech	γ
1025.5/2	la	crech	β
1026.1	la	slogad	γ
1026.2	la	slogad	γ
1026.3	la	slogad	γ
1026.8	la	feall	α
1027.2	la	slogad	γ
1027.6	la	crech	β
1028.8	la	crech	β
1031.4	la	slogad	γ
1031.5	la	slogad	γ
1031.6	la	slogad	γ
1031.8	la	creach	γ
1033.4	la	aenach+	γ
1041.5	la	crech	β
1041.6	la	crech	β
1044.4/1	la	crech	γ

Entry	P1 marker	IPN	P1 type
1044.4/2	*la*	*crech*	γ
1045.4	*la*	*crech*	γ
1047.6	*la*	*crechsluaighedh*	γ
1053.3	*la*	*crech*	γ, β
1056.6	*la*	*crech*	γ
1059.1	*la*	*crech*	γ
1059.4	*la*	*crech*	$\gamma(co^n \beta)$
1061.5	*la*	*sluagad*	γ
1062.4	*la*	*crech*	γ
1063.4	*la*	*coinnmedh*	γ
1067.2	*la*	*sloigedh*	γ
1073.4	*la*	*slogadh*	γ
1075.2	*la*	*slogadh*	γ, β
1076.4	*la*	*sloigedh*	γ
1077.1	*la*	*sloigedh*	γ
1083.6	*la*	*crech righ*	γ
1084.4/1	*la*	*slogadh*	γ
1084.4/2	*la*	*crech*	γ
1084.5	*la*	*slogadh*	β
1087.7	*la*	*longus*	$\gamma(\beta), \gamma$
1088.2	*la*	*slogadh*	γ
1094.2	*la*	*slogadh*	γ
1094.9	*la*	*cath+*	γ
1097.6/1	*la*	*slogadh*	γ, β
1097.6/2	*la*	*slogadh*	γ
1099.7	*la*	*slogadh*	γ, β
1099.8	*la*	*slogadh*	γ, β
1100.3	*la*	*crech*	γ
1100.4	*la*	*slogadh*	γ
1101.4	*la*	*slogadh*	γ, β
1101.5	*la*	*crech*	γ
1102.6	*la*	*slogadh*	β
1104.5	*la*	*slogadh*	γ
1104.6	*la*	*slogadh*	γ
1105.6	*la*	*sluagadh*	γ
1106.1	*la*	*crechsluaigedh*	γ
1109.4	*la*	*slogadh*	γ
1109.5	*la*	*slogadh*	$\gamma(co^n \beta)$
1110.9	*la*	*crech*	γ
1111.6	*la*	*slogadh*	β
1112.3	*la*	*crech*	γ
1113.7/1	*la*	*slogadh*	$\gamma(co^n \beta)$
1113.7/2	*la*	*slogadh*	$\gamma(co^n \beta)$

Entry	P1 marker	IPN	P1 type
1113.7/3	*la*	*slogadh*	$\gamma(co^n \beta)$
1113.8	*la*	*slogadh*	γ, β
1114.3	*la*	*sluagadh*	γ
1115.8	*la*	*crech*	γ, β
1118.6/1	*la*	*slogadh*	γ, γ, γ
1118.6/2	*la*	*slogadh*	γ
1120.1	*la*	*sloigedh*	γ
1121.4	*la*	*sluagadh*	β, β
1121.5	*la*	*crechsluagadh*	γ
1122.3	*la*	*sluaigedh*	γ
1122.5	*la*	*crech*	γ, β
1125.3	*la*	*sluagadh*	γ
1126.2	*la*	*sluagadh*	γ
1126.9	*la*	*crec*	γ
1126.12	*la*	*crechsluaghadh*	γ
1127.1	*la*	*sluagadh*	γ
1128.6	*la*	*creachsluagadh*	γ
1128.7	*la*	*creach*	γ, β
1128.8	*la*	*sluagadh*	$\gamma, \beta, \beta, \beta$
1130.5	*la*	*sluagadh*	γ, β
1131.1	*la*	*crechshluagadh*	γ, β
1131.2	*la*	*sluagadh*	γ, β

Notes: P1 type: see Section 3.2.2; *: P1=*gennti*; **: P1=*Gaill*; (pro): pronominal P1; ^ after e.g. *bellum*, *cath*: genitive phrase; + after e.g. *slogad*: genitive phrase; SC: subordinate (dependent)VN clause; PP: prepositional phrase; co^n β: P1 phrase is followed by a prepositional phrase consisting of co^n 'with' and a plural noun phrase.

APPENDIX 9

$P2+do_{VN}+P1$ in *The Annals of Ulster*

Entry	P1 marker	VN	P1 type
553.3/1	*la*	*tabairt*	α
798.2	*do*	*breith*	β
818.7	*la*	*sarugud*	β
	la	*guin*	
823.7	*la*	*denum*	γ, β
832.5	*do*	*breith**	β
836.5	*do*	*orgain**	β
837.6	*ó*	*dilgiunn**	β
842.5	*do*	*ergabhail**	β
842.9	*do*	*ergabail***	β
842.1	*ó*	*guin**	β
		loscadh	
845.1	*do*	*ergabail**	β
845.8	*la*	*ergabhail*	γ
864.1	*la*	*dalladh*	γ?
864.2	*la*	*marbad*	α
865.4	*do*	*indarbu*	β
867.5	*ó*	*orcain*	γ
874.5	*do*	*orgain***	β
879.6	*do*	*ergabhail***	β
881.3	*do*	*coscrath***	β
887.1	*ó*	*marbad*	α
891.2	*oc*	*sarugud*	α?
895.5	*ó*	*orcain***	β
896.1	*la*	*guin*	β
904.4	*la*	*marbad*	β
914.1	*la*	*sarugud*	γ
914.2	*ó*	*guin*	β
915.6	*ó*	*guin*	β
916.3	*ó*	*bas***	β
916.5	*la*	*aighe*	γ
919.2	*la*	*dalladh*	γ
920.6	*ó*	*brisiuth**	β
921.7	*do*	*dergiu*	β
921.8	*la*	*anacal*	γ?

Entry	P1 marker	VN	P1 type
925.4	*la*	*marbad*	γ?
926.4	*ó*	*marbad*	β
932.2	*la*	*marbad*	α
935.4/1	*la*	*togail*	γ
935.4/2	*do*	*togail*	γ
936.2	*ó*	*orcain***	β
938.6	*la*	*orcain*	γ
940.2	*ó*	*marbad***	β
940.3	*la*	*guin badud*	α
941.4	*do*	*marbad*	β
942.4	*do*	*arcain***	β
942.5	*do*	*marbad*	α
942.7	*do*	*indriuth**	β
943.2	*do* *la*(H¹)	*marbad**	β γ
943.2/2	*ó*	*arcain***	β
943.3	*do*	*marbad***	β
943.4	*ó*(+pos)	*marbad*	β
944.2	*do*	*marbad*	β
945.2	*la*	*marbad*	γ
945.7	*do*	*marbad*	γ & γ
946.1	*do*	*orcain***	β
948.1	*la*	*marbad*	γ
950.1	*do*(+pos)	*marbad*	β
950.4	*ó*	*marbad*	β
950.5	*do*	*marbad***	β
950.7	*do*	*loscadh***	β
951.5	*do*	*marbad*	β
953.1	*do*	*arcain*	β
953.3	*ó*	*arcain*	β
956.3	*do*	*marbad*	β
958.2	*do*	*marbad***	β
959.1	*do*	*arcain*	β
962.2	*do*	*marbad*	β
964.2	*do*	*marbad*	β
964.4	*do*	*marbad*	β
964.6	*do*	*arcain***	β
966.4	*la*	*marbad*	α
967.1	*la*	*marbad*	β
970.1	*do*	*arcain*	γ
971.1	*do*	*marbad*	β
971.2	*do*	*innarbu*	β
971.5	*do***	*marbad*	β

Entry	P1 marker	VN	P1 type
972.2	*la*	*marbad*	α
974.3	*la*	*marbad*	α
976.1	*la*	*marbad*	α?
977.1	*la*	*marbad*	γ?
977.3	*la*	*marbad*	α?
977.4	*la*	*marbad*	α?
980.8	*do*	*ergabhail***	β
982.2	*do*	*marbad*	β
986.3	*do*	*arcain*	β
988.3	*la*	*marbad*	α
989.2	*do*	*arcain***	β
989.3	*do*(+pos)	*marbad*	β
989.8	*do*	*marbad*	β
990.1	*do*	*argain*	β
993.2	*do*	*marbad*	β
993.4	*la*	*marbad*	α
994.1	*do*	*marbad*	β
994.3	*do*	*loscadh*	γ
994.7	*do*	*marbad*	α
995.2	*do*	*argain***	β, γ
997.3	*do*	*arcain***	β
997.4	*la*	*dallad*	γ
998.4	*do*	*marbad*	β
999.1	*do*	*marbad*	β
999.2	*do*	*marbad*	β
999.3	*do*	*ergabhail*	γ, γ
1000.2	*la*	*marbad*	α
1001.3	*do*	*marbad*	β
1002.3	*ó*	*marbad*	α?
1004.6	*do*	*marbad*	β
1004.8	*la*	*marbad*	α
1005.2	*ó*	*marbad*	α
1005.3	*la*	*marbad*	α
1006.7	*do*(+pos)	*marbad*	α
1007.1	*ó*	*marbad*	α
1007.3	*do*	*marbad*	β
1007.4	*do*(+art)	*marbad*	α
1007.5	*la*	*marbad*	α
1007.8	*do*	*marbad*	α
1007.12	*do*	*marbad*	α, α
1009.3	*do*	*marbad*	β
1009.4	*la*	*dallad*	γ
1011.1	*ó*	*guin*	β
1012.6	*do*	*marbad*	γ?

Entry	P1 marker	VN	P1 type
1013.1	*do*	*marbad*	β
1013.11	*do*	*denam*	γ
1013.13	*do*	*marbad***	β
1014.5	*la*	*marbad*	α
1015.1	*la*	*marbad*	α
1015.5	*ó*	*marbad*	β
1015.7	*la*	*marbad*	α
1016.6	*la*	*marbad*	α
1017.2	*ó*	*marbad*	β
1017.4	*ó*	*marbad*	β
1017.6	*la*	*marbad*	α
1018.2	*la*	*dallad*	γ
1018.3	*do*	*marbad*	β
1018.5	*do*	*arcain*	β
1018.6	*la*	*marbad*	β
1019.1	*la*	*marbad*	β
1019.8	*la*	*marbad*	β
1019.9	*do*	*tabeirt*	β
1019.1	*la*	*brisiudh*	γ
1020.2	*la*	*dalladh*	γ
1020.3/1	*la*	*marbad*	β
1020.3/2	*do*	*marbad*	β
1020.7	*do*	*marbad*	β
1021.6	*do*	*marbad*	β
1022.5	*la*	*marbad*	α
1022.7	*do*	*marbad*	α
1023.2	*ó*	*marbad*	γ?
1023.3	*do*	*gabail***	β
1023.5	*ó*	*marbad*	β
1023.6	*la*(+art)	*marbad*	β
1023.9	*do*	*marbad*	β
1023.10	*do*	*marbad*	α
1024.1/1	*la*	*gabail*	γ
1024.1/2	*do*	*marbad*	β
1024.3	*do*	*marbad*	β
1024.4	*do*	*marbad*	α
1024.5	*do*	*marbad*	β
1025.6	*do*	*arcain*	γ
1027.2	*la*	*dallad*	γ
1028.1	*do*	*marbad*	β
1029.5	*do*	*marbad*	β
1029.6	*do*	*erghabhail*	γ
1030.6	*la*	*marbad*	α
1030.9	*do*(+art)	*marbad*	α

Entry	P1 marker	VN	P1 type
1030.11	*do*	*marbad*	α
1031.2	*do***	*argain*	β
1031.7	*la*	*dallad*	γ
1031.9	*do*	*marbad*	α
1032.1	*do*	*marbad*	α
1033.7	*la*	*marbad*	α
1043.2	*do*	*marbad*	β
1035.2	*do*	*marbad*	α?
1035.5	*la*	*marbad*	α
1035.6/1	*do*	*arcain*	γ
1035.6/2	*do*	*arcain*	γ
		loscad	
1036.3	*la*	*dallad*	γ
1036.6	*la*	*dallad*	γ
1037.2	*la*	*dallad*	γ
1038.2	*la*	*marbad*	α
1038.4	*do*	*marbad*	β
1038.6	*do*	*marbad*	α
1039.5	*do*	*marbad*	β
1041.3	*do*	*marbad*	β
1041.4	*do*	*marbad*	β
1042.1/1	*la*	*loscadh*	γ
1042.1/2	*do*	*loscadh*	γ
1042.6	*do*	*marbad*	β
1043.2	*do*(+pos)	*marbad*	β
1044.1	*ó*	*marbad*	β
1044.2	*do*	*dallad*	β
1044.3	*do*	*marbad*	α, α
1045.5	*do*	*loscad*	α?
1046.1	*la*	*loscad*	γ
1046.2	*do*	*marbad*	β
1046.3	*do*	*marbad*	α
1046.4	*do*	*marbad*	α
1047.3	*do*	*marbad*	α
1047.5	*la*	*marbad*	α
1049.3	*la*	*marbad*	α
1049.4	*la*	*marbad*	α
1050.7	*ó*	*arcain*	β
1051.1	*do*	*loscad*	β
1051.2	*do*	*marbad*	α
1051.3	*la*	*dallad*	γ
1052.1	*do*	*marbad*	β
1052.6	*do*	*marbad*	α
1053.5	*do*	*marbad*	β

Entry	P1 marker	VN	P1 type
1053.6	*do*	*marbad*	β
1054.3	*do*	*marbad*	α
1054.5	*do*	*marbad*	β
1055.1	*la*	*marbad*	α
1056.4	*do*	*marbad*	β
1057.9	*la*	*marbadh*	α
1058.2	*la*	*marbadh*	α
1058.6	*la*	*marbadh*	α
1059.2	*la*	*muchadh*	α?
1061.2	*la*	*marbadh*	α
1062.1	*la*	*marbadh*	α
1062.3	*la*	*marbadh*	β
1062.5	*do*	*marbadh*	α
1062.7	*do*	*marbadh*	α
1063.5	*ó*	*gabail*	β
1064.6	*la*	*marbad*	β
1064.8	*la*	*marbad*	α
1065.5	*la*	*marbad*	α
1065.7	*ó*	*marbadh*	β
1065.8	*la*	*marbad*	α
1065.9	*do*	*marbadh*	β
1067/4	*la*	*marbadh*	β & α
1068.3	*la*	*marbadh*	β
1068.4	*do*	*guin*	β
1068.5	*d'*	*marbadh*	α
1070.6	*do*	*marbadh*	α
1070.7	*do*	*marbadh*	α
1070.11	*d'*	*argain*	γ
1070.12	*do*	*marbadh*	β
1071.1	*la*	*athrighadh*	γ, β
1072.5	*la*	*marbadh*	β
1072.6	*la*	*marbadh*	α
1072.7	*la*	*marbadh*	α
1073.2	*do*	*marbadh*	α
1075.5	*do*	*marbadh*	β
1076.2	*do*	*marbadh*	β
1076.3	*do*	*marbadh*	α
1077.2	*la*	*marbadh*	α
1077.4	*ó*	*marbadh*	β
1078.2	*la*	*marbadh*	α
1078.3	*do*	*marbadh*	β
1080.1	*do*	*marbadh*	β
1081.1	*ó*	*marbadh*	β
1081.3	*la*	*marbadh*	α

Entry	P1 marker	VN	P1 type
1082.2	*la*	*marbadh*	α
1083.5	*la*	*marbadh*	α
1084.1	*ó*	*marbadh*	β
1084.7	*do*	*marbadh*	α
1086.3	*do*	*marbadh*	β
1087.2	*do*	*marbadh*	β
1087.4	*la*	*marbadh*	β
1087.5	*la*	*marbadh*	α
1089.1	*ó*	*loscadh*	β
1089.5	*la*	*marbadh*	β
1090.2	*ó*	*marbadh*	α?
1091.3	*la*	*marbadh*	α
1092.2	*la*	*milledh*	β
1092.3	*la*	*dallud*	γ
1093.4	*la*	*dalladh*	γ
1093.5	*do*	*marbadh*	β
1094.1	*la*	*dalladh*	γ
1094.3	*la*	*cor (ár)*	β
1094.7	*ó*(+pos)	*marbadh*	β
1096.4	*do*	*marbadh*	α
1096.7	*la*	*marbadh*	β
1097.7	*do*	*marbadh*	β
1098.1	*do*	*marbadh*	β
1098.2	*do*	*slat*	β
1098.4	*do*	*marbadh*	β
1099.9	*do*	*loscudh*	β
1100.2	*la*	*gabail*	γ
1100.8	*d'*	*marbadh*	α
1101.1	*do*	*marbadh*	β
1101.3	*do*	*orcain***	β
1101.8	*la*	*fuaslucudh*	α
1102.2	*do*	*marbadh*	β
1102.3	*do*	*marbadh*	β
1102.5	*do*	*marbadh*	β
1102.7	*do*(+pro)	*denum*	β
1102.9	*do*	*marbadh*	β
1102.10	*do*	*arcain*	β
1102.11	*do*	*loscudh*	β
1103.2	*la*	*innarba*	γ
1103.4	*do*	*marbadh*	β
1104.8	*do*(+pos)	*marbadh*	β
1107.3	*do*	*marbadh*	β
1107.5	*do*	*guin*	β
1107.8	*do*	*denam*	α

Entry	P1 marker	VN	P1 type
1108.6	*do*	*gabail*	γ, γ
1108.1	*la*	*togail*	β
1109.9	*do*	*marbadh*	α
1111.8	*la*	*tinol*	β
1111.9/1	*do*(+pos)	*marbadh*	β
1111.9/2	*do*	*marbadh*	β
1113.5	*la*	*marbadh*	α
1113.6	*do*	*marbadh*	α
1113.7	*la*	*dalladh*	γ & β
1115.2	*la*	*ergabail*	γ
1115.3	*do*	*tabairt*	β
1115.5	*do*	*marbadh*	β
1115.7	*do*	*loscadh*	β
1116.6	*do*	*marbadh*	β
1117.1	*do*	*marbadh*	β
1117.3	*do*	*marbadh*	γ, β
1117.5	*la*	*cor (ár)*	β
1118.1	*do*	*marbadh*	β
1119.1	*do*	*scailedh*	β
1119.3	*do*	*marbadh*	β
1119.7	*do*	*marbadh*	β, β
1120.3	*do*	*guin*	β
1120.6	*do*	*marbadh*	β
1121.2 SC	*do*	*gabail*	β
1121.3	*do*(+pos)	*marbadh*	β
1124.6	*la*	*marbadh*	γ
1124.7	*la*	*marbadh*	β
1126.1	*do*	*marbadh*	β
1126.11	*do*	*coisecradh*	α
1127.5/2	*do*(+pro)	*dilsiugadh*	β
1127.5/3	*do*(+pro)	*aithrighadh*	β
1128.2	*do*	*marbadh*	β
1128.5	*do*	*denam*	α
1128.9	*do*	*denum*	α
1129.2	*do*	*marbadh*	β
1129.4	*do*	*gabail*	γ
1129.5	*la*	*denam*	γ
1129.7	*do*	*marbadh*	β

Notes: P1 type: see Section 3.2.2; *: P1=*gennti*; **: P1=*Gaill*; (+pos): preposition + possessive; (+art): preposition + article; (+pro): pronominal P1.

APPENDIX 10

P1+do_{VN}(+P2) in *The Annals of Ulster*

Entry	VN	P1 type	Entry	VN	P1 type
817.8	*dul*	β	926.5	*gabail*	β
818.4	*dul*	α	927.3/1	*derghiu*	β
818.5	*dul*	α	927.3/2	*derghiu*	γ
829.3	*dul*	α	928.7	*dul*	α
831.1	*tiachtain*	α	930.1	*toghail*	γ(co^n β)
831.1	*tuidecht*	γ(co^n β)	944.3	*arcain*	γ, γ
836.4	*dul*	α	945.6	*telcudh*	γ?
840.4	*innriud*	γ	951.3	*orcain*	γ(co^n β)
846.9	*tiachtain*	α	955.2	*tuitim*	α
849.6	*tiachtain*	β	967.5	*arcain*	γ
849.7	*tiachtain*	α	974.1	*dul*	γ
850.3	*frithtuidecht*	γ	985.2	*indriudh*	γ
853.2	*tuidecht*	γ	986.2	*tuidecht*	β
854.2	*dul*	γ	988.1	*comtuitim*	α, α
858.4	*tuidhecht*	γ(co^n β)	989.6	*dul*	γ
862.2	*indriudh*	γ(co^n β)	989.7	*gabail*	α
866.1	*dul*	γ(co^n β)	997.2	*ec*	α
870.2	*indrudh*	γ	1000.3	*ec*	α
871.2	*tuidecht*	γ, c	1002.7	*dul*	γ
877.3	*tuidecht*	α	1003.2	*comtuitim*	α, α
885.8	*labradh*	α	1004.1	*escor*	α
896.8	*dul martrai*	α	1007.9	*deirgiu*	α
911.4	*gabail*	α	1009.7	*escor*	α
913.8	*techt*	α	1011.2	*innredh*	γ
914.3	*tairecht*	γ	1012.1	*éc*	α
915.7	*tichtain**	β	1013.2	*torrachtain*	γ
916.6	*innriuth***	β	1015.2	*techt*	γ
917.2	*gabail*	γ(co^n β)	1016.8	*ec*	α
917.4	*tuidecht (in)*	γ?	1019.6	*ecaibh*	α
918.4	*dergiu*	β	1019.7	*techt*	γ
918.7	*dul*	γ	1021.5	*dul*	α?
920.5	*dergiu*	γ	1022.3	*ecaib*	α

Entry	VN	P1 type	Entry	VN	P1 type
1023.7	*ec*	α	1070.4	*ec*	α
1023.8	*ecaib*	α	1072.2	*ec*	α
1025.3	*ec*	α	1072.4	*tuitim*	α
1026.4	*ec*	α	1072.8	*dul*	β
1027.1	*ecaib*	α	1075.4	*ec*	α
1023.3	*ecaib*	α	1076.7	*ec*	α
1027.4	*comtuitim*	α, α	1078.1	*ecaibh*	α
1027.5	*comtuitim*	α, α	1078.4	*ecaibh*	α
1028.2	*ec*	α	1080.4	*ecaibh*	α
1028.6	*ec*	α	1080.6	*dul*	γ
1029.2	*comtuitim*	α, α	1082.3	*ec*	α
1030.3	*ec*	α	1083.6	*gabail*	α
1030.4	*dul*	α	1084.3	*ec*	α
1030.7	*ec*	α	1086.4/1	*ec*	α
1030.8	*ec*	α	1086.4/2	*ec*	α
1030.10	*brisiudh*	β	1087.1	*ec*	α
1031.1	*tiachtain*	α	1088.5	*ec*	α
1031.4	*techt*	γ	1089.4	*ec*	α
1034.5	*innredh*	γ	1089.7	*ec*	α
1035.1	*ec*	α	1091.4	*ec*	α
1035.4	*techt*	γ	1093.4	*ec*	α
1037.1	*dul*	α	1096.2	*comtuitim*	α, α, α
1043.1	*ec*	α	1099.5	*gabail*	α
1046.5	*gabail*	α	1102.7	*tuidhecht*	$\gamma(co^n\ \beta)$
1049.6/1	*gabail*	α	1103.3	*marbadh*	β
1049.6/2	*gabail*	α	1104.7	*ec*	α
1051.4	*dul*	α	1105.3	*techt*	
1052.3	*ec*	α	1105.5	*éc*	α
1052.4	*ec*	α	1107.7/1	*gabail*	α
1054.1	*ecaibh*	α	1107.7/2	*gabail*	α
1057.2	*tuitim*	α	1108.7	*ec*	α
1057.3	*tuitim*	α	1109.3	*tuitim*	β
1057.4	*dul*	α	1109.7	*techt*	γ
1057.6	*tuitim*	α	1109.8	*tuitim*	β
1060.8	*ec*	α	1110.4	*arcain*	β
1063.6	*ec*	α	1114.2	*gabail*	α
1064.4	*ec*	α	1115.6/1	*gabail*	α
1064.5	*gabail*	α	1117.5	*tuitim*	β
1064.7	*ec*	α	1118.9	*ec*	α
1065.4	*gabhail*	α	1119.5	*ec*	α
1065.1	*beth*	α	1119.8	*tuitim*	α
1070.1	*ec*	α	1120.5	*ec*	α
1070.2	*ec*	α	1121.1	*éc*	α

Entry	VN	P1 type	Entry	VN	P1 type
1122.1	*tuitim*	α	1127.5	*impodh*	β
1122.4	*éc*	α	1127.6	*tuitim*	α
1122.6	*éc*	α	1127.7	*éc*	α
1123.1	*gabail*	β	1128.1	*gabail*	β
1123.3	*éc*	α	1128.4	*éc*	α
1127.2	*gabail*	β	1130.2	*éc*	α
1127.4	*éc*	α	1130.3	*tuitim*	α, α, β

Notes: P1 type: see Section 3.2.2; co^n β: P1 phrase is followed by a prepositional phrase consisting of co^n 'with' and a plural noun phrase.

APPENDIX 11

Agentive passives in *Táin Bó Cúailnge*

PASSIVE + *LA*

TBC I 1, 399, 462, 589, 598, 1306, 1443, 1560, 1740, 1919, 2568, 3187, 3333
TBC LL 114, 589, 685/1, 685/2, 685/3, 690/1, 690/2, 904, 1186, 1465/1, 1465/2, 1831, 1934, 2887, 3821, 4708, 4765
TBC III: ZCP 8: 538.13, 538.24; *RC* 14: §§18, 54; *RC* 15: §§69, 73

PASSIVE + *Ó*

TBC I 216, 1543, 1545, 1567, 1622, 2243, 3872, 3885
TBC LL 1429, 1470, 2261, 3127, 3130, 3170, 3172, 3745
TBC III: RC 15: §§135/1, 135/2, 140

PASSIVE + *DO*

TBC I 1686, 1695
TBC LL 1302, 4872
TBC III: ZCP 8: 538.29, 545.32

PASSIVE + *RA/RE*

TBC LL 4269
TBC III: RC 15: §102

PASSIVE + *OC*

TBC LL 589, 2531, 2607, 3793, 4250
TBC III: ZCP 8: 542.18, 553.34; *RC* 14: §§18, 20, 33, 60; *RC* 15 §202

APPENDIX 12

Agentive passives in Irish laws and annals

Law texts

CG 28
BB §§33, 35

The Annals of Ulster

PASSIVE + *LA*

AU 804.8 (add. marg. H²), 850.3, 856.5, 882.1, 906.3, 908.1, 999.4, 999.8, 1013.4, 1071.1, 1126.11

PASSIVE + ó

AU 1004.5, 1128.5

APPENDIX 13

IAG, CAUSE, and INST in medieval Irish

The IAG

L A

do-tuit la

TBC I 1552, 1873, 2147, 2170, 2609, 2874, 3338, 3370, 3389

TBC LL 557, 888, 1061, 1115, 1182, 1185, 1243, 1257, 1668, 1750, 1771, 1827, 1856, 2098, 2115, 2170, 2174, 2189, 2443, 2599, 2887, 3128, 3384, 3714, 3819, 3841, 3859, 3928, 4274

TBC III: ZCP 8: 540.31, 540.35; RC 14: §11; RC 15: §§96, 99, 100, 127/1, 127/2, 129/1, 129/2, 157, 163, 166, 169, 223

AU 822.3, 924.2, 1042.4, 1057.3, 1057.6, 1067.4, 1072.4, 1082.3, 1109.3, 1109.8, 1119.8, 1122.1, 1127.6, 1128.1, 1130.3

do-tuit fri

TBC LL 1264

do-tuit re/ra

TBC LL 4583
TBC III: ZCP 8: 553.1; RC 14: §22; RC 15: §226

do-tuit oc/ag

TBC LL 2445, 3809

substantive verb + la; la denotes the giver

TBC I 1186, 1392, 1555, 1627, 1635, 2051

substantive verb + ó

TBC I 1564

Other constructions

TBC I 540, 804, 809, 993, 1013, 1054, 1238, 4007, 4111, 4019 (cf. 1054)
TBC LL 207, 776, 4715
AU 608.1, 842.9, ?896.8

F R I

TBC I 1012

O C/A G

TBC LL 600, 3265–6, 3277 ff., 4706, 4710, ?4857
TBC III: ZCP 8: 538.14, 550.24

ó

TBC I 611, 2742, 3991
TBC LL 1125, 4013, 4017, 4035, 4723
TBC III: RC 14: §45
AU 825.16, 883.4;
ó denotes the SOURCE/giver in: *CG* 58, 84, 333

T R E

TBC I 4063
AU 964.6

The CAUSE

L A

La marks an external motivation

Natural phenomenon
TBC I 311, 357, 2003 (topographical detail)

Event or activity
TBC I 211, 429, 1998

Quality or characteristic
TBC I 1721

La marks an internal motivation (emotion, degree thereof)
TBC I 3578

R E/R A

Re/ra marks an external motivation

Quality or characteristic (of external circumstance, or of person)
TBC I 2080/1, 2080/2, 2083, 2267, 2271
TBC LL 128/2, 1170, 1485/1, 1485/2, 1486, 1487, 2129/1, 2129/2, 2575, 2285, 2289, 3168, 4151, 4152
TBC III: ZCP 8: 545.32; *RC* 15: §§118/1, 118/2, 151

Re/ra marks an internal motivation

Emotion
TBC LL 2833

FRI

Fri marks an external motivation

TBC I 267, 1580
TBC LL 128/1
TBC III: ZCP 8: 540.23
CG 548

AR

Ar marks an external motivation

Quality or characteristic
TBC I 792, 2358
TBC LL 1374, 2119, 4676
TBC III: RC 15: §§175/1, 175/2

Activity or event
TBC I 3335
TBC LL 2493/1, 2493/2
UR §3

Ar marks an internal motivation

Emotion (or quality/degree thereof)
TBC I 229, 2745/2, 3333, 3365
TBC LL 1387, 1736, 1927, 3888
CG (experience) 582/1, 582/2

Quality or characteristic
TBC I 3249
TBC LL 2253, 2940/1, 2940/2
BCr §§49
UR §?23/2
CG 3, ?88, ?131

Ar omun

TBC I 2369, 2581, 2745/1, 3333
TBC LL 1388, 3183/2, 3254/2
AU 772.6

Ar úathbás

TBC I 3943, 4034

Ar ecla

TBC LL 1388, 3183/1, 3254/1

Cid ara^n . . .

CG 1, 30, 87, 152, 171, 248, 277, 328, 358, 368, 386, 417, 434, 444, 448, 457, 472

Is aire . . .

TBC I 2182, 3453
TBC LL 365, 466, 2310, 2603, 2731, 3929, 4123, 4159
AU 553.3
BCr §27

DE/DI, <DE, DO> (ANGLE BRACKETS CONTAIN FORMS OTHER THAN *DE/DI*)

Is de atá . . . (and similar structures)

TBC I 334, 540, 924, 925, 950, 976, 989, 1038, 1063, 1231, 1520, 1647, 1656, 1784, 1787, 1788, 1965,
    1981, 2029, 2035, 2463, 2482, 2487, 2546, 3293, 3300, 3319, 3340, 3365, 3513, 4132, 4148, 4150,
    4154
TBC LL 1262, 1265, 1351, 1358, 1376, 1380, 1760, 1783, 1904, 4913
TBC III: RC 15: §112

De marks an external motivation

Quality or characteristic
AU 1123.1
BCr §24 <doa>
CG 171

Activity or event
TBC I 403, 842, 1749 <dia>
TBC LL 602, 1239, 1481 <do> (natural phenomenon), 2183
AU 809.7, 1115.1 <dia>, rel.

De marks an internal motivation

Emotion, state of mind, physical state
TBC I 2087 <do>, 3952/1, 3952/3
TBC III: RC 15: §§119/1 <d>, 119/2 <do>

Activity or experience (incl. disease etc.)
TBC I 2162
TBC LL 2107 <d'>, 3360
TBC III: RC 15: §§90, 128
AU 665.3 <do>, gl. Lat. de; 974.1, 997.2 <do>, 1075.4 <do>, 1093.5 <dia>, 1107.5, 1120.3
CG 558

TRE

Tre marks an external motivation

Activity or event
TBC LL 3291
AU 1009.3, 1031.3

Quality or characteristic
AU 1123.2
CG 61

OTHER PREPOSITIONS

ó: *CG* 276,

a: *TBC* I 1511, *BCr* §56,

is uime . . .: *TBC LL* 995 (*Cid 'ma . . .*), 1916–17, 1924–5 (identical phrases); *TBC III*: *ZCP* 8: 540.23, 544.2, 544.3, 544.5, 544.10; *RC* 15: §§102, 215, 219, 228

The INST (including examples of the abstract means and manner, and material)

CO^n (CONCRETE COMPLEMENT: TOOL IN THE WIDEST SENSE)

TBC I 331, 334/1, 334/2, 350, 501, 583, 906, 1206, 1231, 1353, 1357, 1358, 1985, 2025, 2492, 3096, 3109, 3195, 4037, 4067, 419, 4130
TBC LL 633, 1798

DE

Concrete complement (the pp follows béim *'blow' etc.)*

TBC I 2236 <di>, 3sg.f, 2892 <do>, 2894 <do>, 5053 <dá>
TBC LL 632 <di> 3sg.f, 882, 1144 <do>, 1743 <dia>, 2254 <di>, 3sg.f, 3298 <dá>, 3302 <dá>, 3340, 3349, 3352, 3647, 3807 <dá>, 4866 (x2) <dá>, <dind>, 2403 <dá>
TBC III: *RC* 15: §§80 <dha>, 83 <dha>, 86 <da>, 89 <don>, 138/1, 138/2 (x3) <dá>, 195 <dá>

Concrete complement

TBC I 799–800, 2236, <dá>, poss.3sg.m. (x3)
TBC LL 308 <do>, 513 <dia>, 635, 659 <do>, 1303 <dá>, 1904, 2254 (x3; <dia> x2, <dá>), 3112
TBC III: *ZCP* 8: 552.18 <d>
AU 501.2 <da>, 964.6 <dia>

Concrete complement (material)

AU 1125 <do>

Abstract complement, incl. actions (abstract means and manner)

TBC I 1636
TBC LL 562, 630, 655 <dia>, 656 <dia>, ?806 <do>, 1118 (x3), 3097, 3292 <do>, 4247 <de>, <do>, <d'>
TBC III: *ZCP* 8: 539.16 (x2) <d>

OTHER PREPOSITIONS

tre: abstract complement (incl. actions), manner: *TBC* I 787; *AU* 915.6, 964.4 (the instances in *AU* where *tre* marks the manner/abstract means, in analogy to Lat. *per*, have not all been collected here); *UR* §§3 (x4), 23
ar: abstract complement: *TBC* I 4051
a: concrete complement (action implied) *TBC* I 1994
la: *AU* 978.5 (*daighidh*); *BDC* §30
ra: abstract complement: *TBC LL* ?2925
fri daigid: *AU* 867.5, 891.2, 901.1, 912.4 (H[1])

THE PREPOSITIONLESS DATIVE

Abstract
TBC I 331, 348, 370
BCr §§?32, ?60, ?65
CG 527, 556, 557

Concrete
BDC §§30, 33

References

Ahlqvist, A. (1976), 'On the Position of Pronouns in Irish', *Éigse*, 16: 171–6.

—— (1982) (ed.), *Papers from the 5th International Conference on Historical Linguistics* (Current Issues in Linguistic Theory 21; Amsterdam: Benjamins).

Aijmer, K. (1985), 'The Semantic Development of *will*', in Fisiak (1985), 11–21.

Andersen, P. K. (1985), 'Die grammatische Kategorie Passiv im Altindischen: Ihre Funktion', in Schlerath (1985), 47–57.

—— (1990), 'Review Article: Typological Approaches to the Passive', review of Shibatani (1988), *Journal of Linguistics*, 26/1: 189–202.

—— (1991), *A New Look at the Passive* (Duisburger Arbeiten zur Sprach- und Kultur-wissenschaft, vol. 11; Frankfurt: Peter Lang).

Awbery, G. (1976), *The Syntax of Welsh* (Cambridge: Cambridge University Press).

Ball, M. J., and Müller, N. (1992), *Mutation in Welsh* (London: Routledge).

Baudiš, J. (1913), 'Zum Gebrauch der Verbalnomina im Irischen', *Zeitschrift für Celtische Philologie*, 9: 380–417.

Bergin, O., and Marstrander, C. (1912) (eds.), *Miscellany Presented to Kuno Meyer* (Halle: Niemeyer).

Best, R. I., and Bergin, O. (1929) (eds.), *Lebor na Huidre: The Book of the Dun Cow* (Dublin: Hodges, Figgis & Co. (for the Royal Irish Academy)).

—— —— O'Brien, M. A., and O'Sullivan, A. (1954–83) (eds.), *The Book of Leinster* (6 vols.; Dublin: Dublin Institute for Advanced Studies).

Binchy, D. A. (1938), 'Bretha Crólige', *Ériu*, 12: 1–77.

—— (1941), *Críth Gablach* (Medieval and Modern Irish Series, vol. 11; Dublin: Dublin Institute for Advanced Studies (repr. 1979)).

—— (1966), 'Bretha Déin Checht', *Ériu*, 20: 1–66.

Bolinger, D. (1952), 'Linear Modification', *Proceedings of the Modern Language Association of America*, 67: 117–44.

Bolkestein, A. M., De Groot, C., and Mackenzie, J. L. (1985) (eds.), *Syntax and Pragmatics in Functional Grammar* (Dordrecht: Foris).

Breatnach, L. (1987), *Uraicecht na Ríar: The Poetic Grades in Early Irish Law* (Early Irish Law Series, vol. 2; Dublin: Dublin Institute for Advanced Studies).

Bromwich, R., and Evans, D. S. (1988) (eds.), *Culhwch ac Olwen* (Caerdydd: Gwasg Prifysgol Cymru).

—— Jarman, A. O. H., and Roberts, B. F. (1991) (eds.), *The Arthur of the Welsh: The Arthurian Legend in Medieval Welsh Literature* (Cardiff: University of Wales Press).

Brown, G., and Yule, G. (1983), *Discourse Analysis* (Cambridge: Cambridge University Press).

Brugman, C. (1981), 'The Story of OVER', MA thesis, University of California, Berkeley (distributed by the Indiana University Linguistics Club).

Chafe, W. (1976), 'Givenness, Contrastiveness, Definiteness, Subjects, Topics and Point of View', in Li (1976).

Charles-Edwards, T. M. O. (1980), 'Review Article: The Corpus Iuris Hibernici', *Studia Hibernica*, 20: 141–62.

—— (1986), 'Cynghawsedd: Counting and Pleading in Medieval Welsh Law', *Bulletin of the Board of Celtic Studies*, 33: 188–98.

—— (1989), *The Welsh Laws* (Writers of Wales Series; Cardiff: University of Wales Press).

—— and Kelly, F. (1983) (eds.), *Bechbretha: An Old Irish Law-Tract on Bee-Keeping* (Early Irish Law Series, vol. 1; Dublin: Dublin Institute for Advanced Studies).

Cole, P. (1981) (ed.), *Radical Pragmatics* (New York: Academic Press).

Cuyckens, H. (1995), 'Family Resemblance in the Dutch Spatial Prepositions *door* and *langs*', *Cognitive Linguistics*, 6: 183–207.

Davies, S. (1992), 'Storytelling in Medieval Wales', *Oral Tradition*, 7/2: 231–57.

—— (1996), *Crefft y Cyfarwydd* (Caerdydd: Gwasg Prifysgol Cymru).

Dik, S. C. (1989), *The Theory of Functional Grammar. Part I: The Structure of the Clause* (Functional Grammar Series 9; Dordrecht: Foris).

Disterheft, D. (1980), *The Syntactic Development of the Infinitive in Indo-European* (Columbus: Slavica).

—— (1981), 'Remarks on the History of the Indo-European Infinitive', *Folia Linguistica Historica*, 2: 3–34.

—— (1982), 'Subject Raising in Old Irish', in Ahlqvist (1982).

—— (1984), 'Irish Complementation: A Case Study in Two Types of Syntactic Change', in Fisiak (1984).

—— (1985), 'Purpose and Consecutive in Irish', *Ériu*, 36: 107–23.

Dottin, G. (1913), *Manuel de l'Irlandais Moyen. I. Grammaire* (Paris: Honoré Champion).

Dressler, W. (1968), *Studien zur Verbalen Pluralität. Iterativum, Distributivum, Durativum, Intensivum, in der Allgemeinen Grammatik, im Lateinischen und Hethitischen* (Sitzungsberichte der Österreichischen Akademie der Wissenschaften 259/1. Vienna/Graz/Cologne: Böhlau).

Dumville, D. (1976), '*Scéla Lái Brátha* and the Collation of *Leabhar na hUidhre*', *Éigse*, 16: 24–8.

—— (1982), 'Latin and Irish in the Annals of Ulster, A.D. 431–1050', in Whitelock *et al.* (1982).

Edel, D. (1989), 'Die inselkeltische Erzähltradition zwischen Mündlichkeit und Schriftlichkeit', in Tranter and Tristram (1989), 99–124.

Eska, J. F., Gruffydd, R. G., and Jacobs, N. (1995) (eds.), *Hispano-Gallo-Brittonica: Essays in Honour of Professor D. Ellis Evans on the Occasion of his 65th Birthday* (Cardiff: University of Wales Press).

Evans, D. E., Griffith, J. G., and Jope, E. M. (1986) (eds.), *Proceedings of the 7th International Congress of Celtic Studies, Oxford, 10–15 July 1983* (Oxford: D. Ellis Evans).

Evans, D. S. (1948), 'Astudiaeth Fanwl o Gystrawen Testunau Rhyddiaith Cymraeg Canol a Gyhoeddwyd yn y BBCS', MA dissertation, University of Wales.

—— (1950), 'Nodiadau cystrawennol: I. y berfenw', *Bulletin of the Board of Celtic Studies*, 13: 188–90.

—— (1964), *A Grammar of Middle Welsh* (Dublin: Dublin Institute for Advanced Studies (repr. 1976)).

—— (1985), 'Culhwch ac Olwen. Tystiolaeth yr iaith', *Ysgrifau Beirniadol*, 13: 101–13.

Fife, J. (1985), 'The Impersonal Verbs in Welsh', *Bulletin of the Board of Celtic Studies*, 32: 92–126.

—— (1986), 'The Semantics of *gwneud* Inversions', *Bulletin of the Board of Celtic Studies*, 33: 133–44.

—— (1988), *Functional Syntax: A Case Study in Middle Welsh* (Lublin: Catholic University).

—— (1990), *The Semantics of the Welsh Verb: A Cognitive Approach* (Cardiff: University of Wales Press).

—— and King, G. (1991), 'Focus and the Welsh "Abnormal Sentence": A Cross-Linguistic Perspective', in Fife and Poppe (1991), 81–153.

—— and Poppe, E. (1991) (eds.), *Studies in Brythonic Word Order* (Amsterdam: Benjamins).

Fisiak, J. (1984) (ed.), *Historical Syntax* (Berlin: Mouton).

—— (1985) (ed.), *Historical Semantics—Historical Word-Formation* (Berlin: Mouton).

Foley, W. A., and Van Valin, R. D. (1985), 'Information Packaging in the Clause', in Shopen (1985), i. 282–364.

Fox, B., and Hopper, P. J. (1993) (eds.), *Voice: Form and Function* (Amsterdam: Benjamins).

Fraser, J. (1912*a*), 'A Use of the Verbal Noun in Irish', in Bergin and Marstrander (1912), 216–26.

—— (1912*b*), 'The Prepositions in the Würzburg Glosses', *Zeitschrift für Celtische Philologie*, 8: 1–63.

Gagnepain, J. (1963), *La Syntaxe du nom verbal dans les langues Celtiques I: Irlandais* (Paris: Klincksieck).

Genee, I. (1994), 'Pragmatic Aspects of Verbal Noun Complements in Early Irish: *do*+VN in the Würzburg Glosses', *Journal of Celtic Linguistics*, 3: 41–73.

—— (1996), 'Between Noun and Verb: On the Expression of Verbal Noun Arguments in Old and Middle Irish Texts', *Belfast Working Papers in Language and Linguistics*, 13: 141–60.

—— (1998), *Sentential Complementation in a Functional Grammar of Irish* (Academisch Proefschrift, Faculteit der Geesteswetenschappen, Universiteit van Amsterdam; The Hague: Holland Academic Graphics).

Geeraerts, D. (1989), 'Introduction: Prospects and Problems of Prototype Theory', *Linguistics*, 27: 587–612.

—— (1993), 'Vagueness's Puzzles, Polysemy's Vagaries', *Cognitive Linguistics*, 4: 223–72.

Givón, T. (1979), *On Understanding Grammar* (New York: Academic Press).

—— (1984), *Syntax: A Functional Typological Introduction*, vol. i (Amsterdam: Benjamins).

Goetinck, G. (1975), *Peredur: A Study of Welsh Tradition in the Grail Legends* (Cardiff: University of Wales Press).

—— (1976) (ed.), *Historia Peredur vab Efrawc* (Caerdydd: Gwasg Prifysgol Cymru).

Gonda, J. (1956), Review of Hartmann (1954), *Lingua*, 5: 428–43.

Gray, E. A. (1982) (ed.), *Cath Maige Tuired* (Irish Texts Society, vol. 52; London: Irish Texts Society).

Graur, J. (1933), 'AB, AD, APUD et CUM en Latin de Gaule', *Bulletin de la Société de Linguistique*, 89–100: 225–98.

Greene, D. (1967), 'Old Irish *is . . . dom* "I am" ', in Meid (1967), 171–3.

Halliday, M. A. K. (1967), 'Notes on Transitivity and Theme in English: Part 2', *Journal of Linguistics*, 3: 199–244.

—— (1985), *An Introduction to Functional Grammar* (London: Edward Arnold; 2nd edn., 1994).

Hannay, M. (1985), *English Existentials in Functional Grammar* (Functional Grammar Series 3; Dordrecht: Foris).

Hartmann, H. (1954), *Das Passiv* (Heidelberg: Carl Winter).

Havers, W. (1911), *Untersuchungen zur Kasussyntax der Indogermanischen Sprachen* (Straßburg).

Hawkins, B. (1984), 'The Semantics of English Spatial Prepositions', Ph.D. dissertation, University of California, San Diego.

—— (1988), 'The Natural Category MEDIUM: An Alternative to Selection Restriction and Similar Constructs', in Rudzka-Ostyn (1988), 231–70.

Hemon, R. (1975), *A Historical Morphology and Syntax of Breton* (Dublin: Dublin Institute for Advanced Studies).

Hughes, K. (1972), *Early Christian Ireland: Introduction to the Sources* (London: The Sources of History Ltd.).

Huws, D. (1991), 'Llyfr Gwyn Rhydderch', *Cambridge Medieval Celtic Studies*, 21: 1–37.

Jamison, S. T. (1979*a*), 'The Case of the Agent in Indo-European', *Sprache*, 25: 129–43.

—— (1979*b*), 'Remarks on the Expression of Agency with the Passive in Vedic and Indo-European', *Zeitschrift für Vergleichende Sprachforschung*, 93: 196–219.

Jarman, A. O. H. (1982) (ed.), *Llyfr Du Caerfyrddin* (Caerdydd: Gwasg Prifysgol Cymru).

—— and Hughes, G. R. (1976) (eds.), *A Guide to Welsh Literature, vol. I* (Swansea: Christopher Davies).

Jeffers, R. (1978), 'Old Irish Verbal Nouns', *Ériu*, 29: 1–12.

Jones, E. D. (1982), 'Rhagymadrodd', in Jarman (1982).

Jones, G., and Jones, T. (1989), *The Mabinogion* (London: Everyman; 1st edn., 1949; rev. edn., 1974; rev. edn., 1989).

Jones, R. M. (1986), 'Narrative Structure in Medieval Welsh Prose Tales', in Evans *et al.* (1986), 171–298.

Jones, T. (1941) (ed.), *Brut y Tywysogyon. Peniarth Ms 20* (Cardiff: University of Wales Press).

—— (1946), 'Cronica de Wallia and other Documents from Exeter Cathedral Library MS 3514', *Bulletin of the Board of Celtic Studies*, 12/1–2: 27–44.

—— (1973), *Brut y Tywysogyon or the Chronicle of the Princes. Red Book of Hergest Version* (2nd edn., Cardiff: University of Wales Press).

Kabata, K., and Rice, S. (1997), 'Japanese *ni*: The Particulars of a Somewhat Contradictory Particle', in Verspoor *et al.* (1997), 109–27.

Keenan, E. L. (1985), 'Passive in the World's Languages', in Shopen (1985), i. 243–81.

Kelleher, J. V. (1963), 'Early Irish History and Pseudo-History', *Studia Hibernica*, 3: 113–27.

—— (1971), 'The Táin and the Annals', *Ériu*, 22: 107–27.

Kelly, F. (1988), *A Guide to Early Irish Law* (Dublin: Dublin Insitute for Advanced Studies).

King, R. T. (1988), 'Spatial Metaphors in German Causative Constructions', in Rudzka-Ostyn (1988).

Kronasser, H. (1968), *Handbuch der Semasiologie* (Heidelberg: Carl Winter).

Kuryłowicz, J. (1964), *The Inflectional Categories of Indo-European* (Heidelberg: Carl Winter).

Lakoff, G. (1987), *Women, Fire and Dangerous Things: What Categories Reveal about the Mind* (Chicago: University of Chicago Press).

Langacker, R. (1987), *Foundations of Cognitive Grammar*, i. *Theoretical Prerequisites* (Stanford: Stanford University Press).

—— (1990), *Concept, Image and Symbol: The Cognitive Basis of Grammar* (Cognitive Linguistics Research, vol. 1; Berlin: Mouton de Gruyter).

—— (1991), *Foundations of Cognitive Grammar. II, Descriptive Application* (Stanford: Stanford University Press).

—— and Munro, P. (1975), 'Passives and their Meaning', *Language*, 51: 789–830.

Leumann, M., Hofmann, J. B., and Szantyr, A. (1965), *Lateinische Grammatik*, ii. *Lateinische Syntax und Stilistik* (Munich: C. H. Beck).

Lewis, H. (1928), 'Y berfenw', *Bulletin of the Board of Celtic Studies*, 4: 179–89.

—— (1937), 'Some Mediæval Welsh Prepositions', in *Mélanges Linguistiques Offerts à H. Pedersen* (Copenhagen: Levin & Munksgaard), 293–300.

—— (1941), 'Nodiadau cymysg: Goddrych y berfenw', *Bulletin of the Board of Celtic Studies*, 10: 297–303.

Li, C. N. (1976) (ed.), *Subject and Topic* (New York: Academic Press).

Lindner, S. (1981), 'A Lexico-Semantic Analysis of English Verb-Particle Constructions with UP and OUT', Ph.D. thesis, University of California, San Diego.

Lloyd-Morgan, C. (1991), 'Breuddwyd Rhonabwy and Later Arthurian Literature', in Bromwich *et al.* (1991), 183–208.

Lovecy, I. (1991), 'Historia Peredur ab Efrawg', in Bromwich *et al.* (1991), 171–82.

Mac Airt, S. (1944), *The Annals of Inisfallen* (Dublin: Dublin Institute for Advanced Studies; repr. 1988).

—— and Mac Niocaill, G. (1983) (eds.), *The Annals of Ulster (to A.D. 1131)*, Part I: *Text and Translation* (Dublin: Dublin Institute for Advanced Studies).

Mac Cana, P. (1992), *The Mabinogi* (Cardiff: University of Wales Press).

McCloskey, J. (1980), 'Is there Raising in Modern Irish?', *Ériu*, 31: 59–99.

Mac Eoin, G. (1982), 'The Dating of Middle Irish Texts', Sir John Rhys Memorial Lecture 1981, *Proceedings of the British Academy*, 68: 109–37.

—— (1994), 'The Interpolator H in *Lebor na Huidre*', in Mallory and Stockman (1994), 39–46.

Mac Gearailt, U. (1989), 'Zum Irischen des 12. Jahrhunderts', *Zeitschrift für Celtische Philologie*, 43: 11–52.

—— (1992), 'The Language of Some Late Middle Irish Texts in the Book of Leinster', *Studia Hibernica*, 26: 167–216.

—— (1994), 'The Relationship of Recensions II and III of the *Táin*', in Mallory and Stockman (1994), 55–70.

—— (1997), 'Infixed and Independent Pronouns in the LL Text of *Táin Bó Cúailnge*', *Zeitschrift für Celtische Philologie*, 49–50: 494–515.

Mac Néill, E. (1923), 'Ancient Irish Law: The Law of Status and Franchise', *Proceedings of the Royal Irish Academy*, 36 C: 256–316.

Mallory, J., and Stockman, G. (1994) (eds.), *Ulidia. Proceedings of the First International Conference on the Ulster Cycle of Tales* (Belfast: December Publications).

Meid, W. (1967) (ed.), *Beiträge zur Indogermanistik und Keltologie. J. Pokorny zum 80. Geburtstag gewidmet* (Innsbrucker Beiträge zur Sprachwissenschaft, vol. 13; Innsbruck: Institut für Sprachwissenschaft der Universität).

—— (1970) (ed.), *Die Romanze von Froech und Findabair. Táin Bó Froích* (Innsbrucker Beiträge zur Kulturwissenschaft, Sonderheft 30; Innsbruck: Institut für Sprachwissenschaft der Universität Innsbruck).

Morgan, T. J. (1938), 'Braslun o gystrawen y berfenw', *Bulletin of the Board of Celtic Studies*, 9: 195–215.

Müller, N. (1988), *Die Präposition la im Altirischen* (Magisterarbeit, Universität Bonn).

—— (1990), 'Zur altirischen Präposition *la*', in Tristram (1990), 115–23.

—— (1992), 'Die Präposition *la* im Altirischen', *Zeitschrift für Celtische Philologie*, 45: 102–31.

—— (1994), 'Passive and Discourse in *Táin Bó Cúailnge*', in Mallory and Stockman (1994), 193–200.

—— (1995), '*With*-Relations and Suffixed Pronouns in Early Irish', *Journal of Celtic Linguistics*, 4: 89–97.

Nettlau, M. (1893), 'The Fragment of the Tain Bó Cuailnge in MS Egerton 93', *Revue Celtique*, 14: 254–66.

—— (1894), 'The Fragment of the Tain Bó Cuailnge in MS Egerton 93', *Revue Celtique*, 15: 62–78, 198–208.

Ó hAodha, D. (1978), *Bethu Brigte* (Dublin: Dublin Institute for Advanced Studies).

Ó Béarra, F. (1994), '*Táin Bó Cuailnge* III: abach aimrid?', in Mallory and Stockman (1994), 71–6.

Ó Concheanainn, T. (1974), 'The Reviser of Leabhar na hUidhre', *Éigse*, 15: 277–88.

—— (1976), '*Aided Nath Í* and the Scribes of Leabhar na hUidhre', *Éigse*, 16: 146–62.

—— (1983), 'The Source of the YBL Text of TBC', *Ériu*, 34: 175–84.

—— (1984), 'LL and the Date of the Reviser of LU', *Éigse*, 20: 212–25.

—— (1986), 'The Manuscript Tradition of Two Middle Irish Leinster Tales', *Celtica*, 18: 13–33.

—— (1987), 'The Manuscript Tradition of *Mesca Ulad*', *Celtica* 19: 13–30.

—— (1991), '*Aided Nath Í* and Uí Fhiachrach Genealogies', *Éigse*, 26: 1–27.

Ó Máille, T. (1910), *The Language of the Annals of Ulster* (Manchester: University Press).

O'Rahilly, C. (1961), *The Stowe Version of Táin Bó Cuailnge* (Dublin: Dublin Institute for Advanced Studies).

—— (1967), *Táin Bó Cúalnge from the Book of Leinster* (Dublin: Dublin Institute for Advanced Studies; repr. 1984).

—— (1976), *Táin Bó Cúailnge Recension I* (Dublin: Dublin Institute for Advanced Studies).

Ó Sé, D. (1992), 'The Perfect in Modern Irish', *Ériu*, 43: 39–67.

Ó Siadhail, M. (1989), *Modern Irish. Grammatical Structure and Dialectal Variation* (Cambridge: Cambridge University Press).

O'Sullivan, W. (1966), 'Notes on the Scripts and Make-up of the Book of Leinster', *Celtica*, 7: 1–31.

Pape-Müller, S. (1980), *Textfunktionen des Passivs* (Tübingen: Niemeyer).

Paprotté, W., and Dirven, R. (1985) (eds.), *The Ubiquity of Metaphor* (Amsterdam: Benjamins).

Parry, T. (1953), *Hanes Llenyddiaeth Gymraeg hyd 1900* (3ydd argraffiad; Caerdydd: Gwasg Prifysgol Cymru).

Pedersen, H. (1909, 1913), *Vergleichende Grammatik der Keltischen Sprachen*, i. *Lautlehre*; ii. *Bedeutungslehre (Wortlehre)* (Göttingen: Vandenhoeck & Ruprecht).

Pinkster, H. (1985), 'The Discourse Function of the Passive', in Bolkestein *et al.* (1985), 107–18.

Poppe, E. (1988), *Untersuchungen zu Stellung und Funktion Temporaler Adverbialausdrücke in Mittelkymrischen und Alt/mittelirischen Narrativen Prosatexten* (Habilitation, Universität Marburg).

—— (1991), 'Word Order in *Cyfranc Lludd a Llefelys*: Notes on the Pragmatics of Constituent Ordering in MW Narrative Prose', in Fife and Poppe (1991), 155–204.

—— (1995), 'Notes on the Narrative Present in Middle Welsh', in Eska *et al.* (1995), 138–50.

Prince, E. F. (1981), 'Toward a Taxonomy of Given-New Information', in Cole (1981).

Pütz, M., and Dirven, R. (1996) (eds.), *The Construal of Space in Language and Thought* (Berlin: Mouton de Gruyter).

Radden, G. (1985), 'Spatial Metaphors Underlying Prepositions of Causality', in Paprotté and Dirven (1985), 177–207.

Ramat, A. G., Carruba, O., and Besmini, G. (1987) (eds.), *Papers from the Seventh International Conference on Historical Linguistics* (Amsterdam: Benjamins).

Rees, M. (1935), 'Cystrawen Arddodiaid ym Mhedair Cainc y Mabinogi', unpublished MA dissertation, University of Wales.

Richards, M. (1948) (ed.), *Breudwyt Ronabwy* (Caerdydd: Gwasg Prifysgol Cymru).

—— (1951), 'The Subject of the Verb Noun in Welsh', *Études Celtiques*, 5: 51–81, 293–313.

Rice, S. (1996), 'Prepositional Prototypes', in Pütz and Dirven (1996), 135–65.

Roberts, B. F. (1971), *Brut y Brenhinedd* (Dublin: Dublin Institute for Advanced Studies).

—— (1975) (ed.), *Cyfranc Lludd a Llefelys* (Dublin: Dublin Institute for Advanced Studies).

—— (1976), 'Tales and Romances', in Jarman and Hughes (1976), 203–43.

—— (1991), 'Culhwch ac Olwen, The Triads, Saints' Lives', in Bromwich *et al.* (1991), 73–95.

Rosch, E. (1978), 'Principles of Categorization', in Rosch and Lloyd (1978), 27–48.

—— and Lloyd, B. B. (1978) (eds.), *Cognition and Categorization* (Hillsdale, NJ: Lawrence Erlbaum).

—— and Mervis, C. B. (1975), 'Family Resemblances: Studies in the Internal Structure of Categories', *Cognitive Psychology*, 7: 573–605.

Rudzka-Ostyn, B. (1988) (ed.), *Topics in Cognitive Linguistics* (Amsterdam: Benjamins).

Russell, P. (1995), *An Introduction to the Celtic Languages* (London: Longman).

Sandra, D., and Rice, S. (1995), 'Network Analyses of Prepositional Meaning: Mirroring whose Mind—the Linguist's or the Language User's?', *Cognitive Linguistics*, 6: 89–130.

Schlerath, B. (1985) (ed.), *Grammatische Kategorien. Akten der VII. Fachtagung der Indogermanischen Gesellschaft* (Wiesbaden: Dr. Ludwig Reichert Verlag).

Schoenthal, G. (1976), *Das Passiv in der Deutschen Standardsprache* (Munich: Hueber).

Schwyzer, E. (1943), *Zum Persönlichen Agens beim Passiv, besonders im Griechischen* (Abhandlungen der Preußischen Akademie der Wissenschaften Jahrgang 1942, phil.-hist. Klasse Nr. 10; Berlin: Akademie der Wissenschaften (in Kommission bei Walter de Gruyter u. Co.)).

Shibatani, M. (1985), 'Passives and Related Constructions: A Prototype Analysis', *Language*, 61: 821–48.

—— (1988) (ed.), *Passive and Voice* (Typological Studies in Language 16; Amsterdam: John Benjamins).

Shopen, T. (1985) (ed.), *Language Typology and Syntactic Description* (3 vols.; Cambridge: Cambridge University Press).

Siewierska, A. (1984), *The Passive: A Comparative Linguistic Analysis* (London: Croom Helm).

Stokes, W., and Strachan, J. (1901–3) (eds.), *Thesaurus Palaeohibernicus* (2 vols.; Dublin: Dublin Institute for Advanced Studies; repr. 1975).

Strachan, J. (1904), 'The Infixed Pronoun in Middle Irish', *Ériu*, 1: 153–79.

Taylor, J. R. (1988), 'Contrasting Prepositional Categories: English and Italian', in Rudzka-Ostyn (1988), 299–326.

—— (1995), *Linguistic Categorization: Prototypes in Linguistic Theory* (2nd edn., Oxford: Oxford University Press).

Thomas, P. W. (1996), *Gramadeg y Gymraeg* (Caerdydd: Gwasg Prifysgol Cymru).

Thomson, R. L. (1968) (ed.), *Owein, or Chwedyl Iarlles y Ffynnawn* (Dublin: Dublin Institute for Advanced Studies; repr. 1975).

—— (1991), 'Owein: Chwedl Iarlles y Ffynon', in Bromwich *et al.* (1991), 159–69.

Thurneysen, R. (1912), 'Táin Bó Cúailghni nach H. 2.17.', *Zeitschrift für Celtische Philologie*, 8: 525–54.

—— (1921), *Die Irische Helden- und Königssage bis zum Siebzehnten Jahrhundert.* (Halle: Niemeyer; repr. 1980 Hildesheim: Olms).

—— (1935) (ed.), *Scéla Mucce Meic Dathó* (Medieval and Modern Irish Series, vol. 6; Dublin: Dublin Institute for Advanced Studies; repr. 1975).

—— (1946), *A Grammar of Old Irish* (Dublin: Dublin Institute for Advanced Studies; repr. 1980).

Tranter, S., and Tristram, H. L. C. (1989) (eds.), *Early Irish Literature: Media and Communication/Mündlichkeit und Schriftlichkeit in der Frühen Irischen Literatur* (Scriptoralia 10; Tübingen: Gunter Narr).

Tristram, H. L. C. (1990) (ed.), *Deutsche, Kelten und Iren. 150 Jahre Deutsche Keltologie. Gearóid Mac Eoin zum 60. Geburtstag Gewidmet* (Hamburg: Buske).

—— (1993) (ed.), *Studien zur Táin Bó Cúailnge* (Tübingen: Gunter Narr).

—— (1994) (ed.), *Text und Zeittiefe* (Tübingen: Gunter Narr).

—— (1997), 'Latin and Latin Learning in the *Táin Bó Cúailnge*', *Zeitschrift für Celtische Philologie*, 49–50: 847–77.

Tuggy, D. (1993), 'Ambiguity, Polysemy and Vagueness', *Cognitive Linguistics*, 4: 273–90.

Ungerer, F., and Schmid, H. J. (1996), *An Introduction to Cognitive Linguistics* (London: Longman).

Van Oosten, J. (1984), 'The Nature of Subjects, Topics and Agents: A Cognitive Explanation', Ph.D. dissertation, University of California, San Diego.

Vandeloise, C. (1994), 'Methodology and Analyses of the Preposition *in*', *Cognitive Linguistics*, 5: 157–84.

Verspoor, M., Lee, K. D., and Sweetser, E. (eds.) (1997), *Lexical and Syntactical Constructions and the Construction of Meaning* (Amsterdam: John Benjamins).

Vendryes, J. (1956), 'Sur l'emploi impersonnel du verbe', *Celtica*, 3: 185–97.

Wade-Evans, A. W. (1909), *Welsh Medieval Law* (Oxford: Clarendon Press).

Wagner, H. (1956), 'Rezension von Hartmann: *Das Passiv*', *Zeitschrift für Celtische Philologie*, 25: 141–5.

—— (1959), *Das Verbum in den Sprachen der Britischen Inseln* (Tübingen: Niemeyer).

West, M. (1990), 'Leabhar na hUidhre's Position in the Manuscript History of *Togail Bruidne Dá Derga* and *Orgain Brudne Uí Dergae*', *Cambridge Medieval Celtic Studies*, 20: 61–98.

Whitelock, D., McKitterick, R., and Dumville, D. (1982) (eds.), *Ireland in Early Mediaeval Europe. Studies in Memory of Kathleen Hughes* (Cambridge: Cambridge University Press).

Wierzbicka, A. (1996), *Semantics: Primes and Universals* (Oxford: Oxford University Press).

Wiliam, A. Rhys (1988), 'Llyfr Cynghawsedd', *Bulletin of the Board of Celtic Studies*, 35: 73–85.

Williams, I. (1927), *Breuddwyd Maxen* (Bangor: Jarvis & Foster).

—— (1930), *Pedeir Keinc y Mabinogi* (Caerdydd: Gwasg Prifysgol Cymru).

Williams, J. E. C. (1948), '*Dē* yn y Gymraeg', *Bulletin of the Board of Celtic Studies*, 13: 1–10.

—— (1954), 'The Preposition *ar* in Irish', *Celtica*, 2: 305–24.

—— (1956), 'On the Uses of Old Irish *fri* and its Cognates', *Celtica*, 3: 126–48.

—— and Ford, P. K. (1992), *The Irish Literary Tradition* (Cardiff: University of Wales Press).

—— and Ní Mhuiríosa, M. (1987), *Traidisiún Liteartha na nGael* (Baile Átha Cliath: An Clóchomhar).

Williams ab Ithel, J. (1860), *Annales Cambriae* (London: Longman, Green, Longman & Roberts).

Williams, S. J. (1980), *A Welsh Grammar* (Cardiff: University of Wales Press).

Windisch, E. (1877), 'Zum irischen Infinitiv', *Beiträge zur Kunde der Indogermanischen Sprachen*, 2: 72–86.

—— (1905) (ed.), *Die altirische Heldensage Táin Bó Cúalnge nach dem Buch von Leinster* (Leipzig: Hirzel).

Winters, M. (1987), 'Syntactic and Semantic Space: The Development of the French Subjunctive', in Ramat *et al.* (1987), 607–18.

Wittgenstein, L. (1953), *Philosophical Investigations* (Oxford: Basil Blackwell).

Wodtko, D. (1987), *Die Verbalnomina des Altirischen und deren Indogermanische Grundlagen* (Magisterarbeit, Universität Köln).

Zimmer, H. (1890), 'Keltische Studien 8: Über das italo-keltische passivum und deponens', *Zeitschrift für Vergleichende Sprachforschung*, 30: 224–89.

Index

abnormal sentence 59
agent (AG) 4–5, 35, 40, 43, 93, 99–100, 106, 132,
 186, 191–2, 194
 in charge 123, 138, 194–7, 202
 sole 123
 type α 124, 127–9
 type β 124, 125, 127–9
 type γ 124, 125–6, 127–30
Ahlqvist, A. 19 n., 150
Aijmer, K. 25 n.
Andersen, P. K. 15–16, 166

backgrounding 167
Ball, M. J. 16 n.
Baudiš, J. 8 n., 14, 16 n., 21 n., 91, 96, 99 n., 118,
 134–5, 138, 182, 183, 184, 185, 190, 191
beneficiary 144, 194
Bergin, O. 29 n.
Best, R. I. 29 n.
Binchy, D. A. 31, 32, 115, 160, 189 n.
Bolinger, D. 60
bot 43, 45, 186
Breatnach, L. 32
Bromwich, R. 27
Brown, G. 6 n.
Brugman, C. 22 n.
buith 86, 93

causative 192
CAUSE 5, 74, 76–80, 173–6, 199, 200
 Irish markers:
 ar 174
 de 175–6
 do 175–6
 fri 173–4
 la 173–4, 202
 ó 176
 re/ra 173
 tre 176
 Welsh markers:
 am 77–8
 gan 79, 202
 o 76–8, 201
 rac 79
 trwy 79

Chafe, W. 6 n., 59
Charles-Edwards, T. M. O. 29, 31, 66
circumstantial elements 21
cleft sentence 89
code switching 32
cognitive grammar 1
 see also cognitive linguistics
cognitive linguistics 1, 2, 22
co^n-clause 163–4
condition chain 63, 66, 68
continuity 7, 51–3, 73, 110–11, 138, 154–7, 164, 166,
 169
control 4, 75, 77–8, 186, 187, 188, 191, 192, 196
coreferentiality 110, 136–8, 156–7
Cuyckens, H. 22 n., 23 n.

dativus commodi 182
Davies, S. 26, 27 n., 28 n.
diachronic analysis 179–80
dialogue, *see* direct speech
Dik, S. C. 1, 4 n., 15, 135
direct speech 39, 46, 47, 56, 59, 87, 94–5, 100, 106,
 147–8, 159, 160
Disterheft, D. 10 n., 14, 110
Dottin, G. 104 n.
Dressler, W. 62
Dumville, D. 29 n., 32

Edel, D. 30 n.
ergative 183
etymology 179, 184, 193, 195
evaluation 112, 113, 114
Evans, D. S. 8 n., 27, 181, 188
Existentialsatz 134
experiencer (EXP) 4, 5, 35, 43, 93, 100, 106, 131,
 186, 192

family resemblance 22–3
Fife, J. 15, 16 n., 17, 58, 59, 60, 99 n., 135 n., 181,
 199
focus 59, 60, 61, 133, 193, 201
Foley, W. A. 167
Ford, P. K. 30 n.
foregrounding 167–8, 197
Fox, B. 16 n.

Fraser, J. 99 n., 104 n., 133, 135, 174, 182, 184, 185
function:
    pragmatic 135
    presentative 135, 138
    semantic 4, 154
    syntactic 4, 154
functional grammar 1, 15
    systemic 1
functional linguistics 2

Gagnepain, J. 10 n., 14, 110 n., 115, 118 n., 133, 135 n., 182, 183, 185
Geeraerts, D. 23 n., 24 n.
Genee, I. 8 n., 99 n., 110
genidol:
    cyfrannol 180
    goddrychol 181
    normal 180
Givon, T. 25 n., 166
Goetinck, G. 28
Gonda, J. 20 n.
Gray, J. 159
Greene, D. 183, 185
gwneuthur-inversion 58–61, 110

Halliday, M. A. K. 1, 5 n., 6 n.
Hannay, M. 135
Hartman, H. 20, 184
Havers, B. 183
Hawkins, B. 22 n.
Hemon, R. 197
historical infinitive 62, 135 n.
historical present 62
    see also narrative present
Hofman, J. B. 62
Hopper, P. J. 16 n.
Hughes, K. 32 n., 33
Huws, D. 27, 170–3

impersonal 16–22, 68, 140
indirect agent (IAG) 5, 74–6, 77, 142, 196, 197–8, 200
    Irish markers:
        fri 171–2
        la 202
        la/ra 170–2
        ó 172
        oc 170, 172
        tre 172–3
    Welsh markers:
        gan 75–6, 202
        o 75, 200
        y gan 75–6
infinitive 8, 13–14, 62
    do-infinitive 92
    Infinitiv 181

information:
    given 6, 7, 48–50, 58, 59, 60, 61, 63, 72–3, 106–8, 150–1, 159, 161, 164–5, 166–8, 169
    inferable 6, 7, 48–9, 150–3
    mainstream 53, 56, 58, 59, 157
    new 6, 7, 48–50, 60, 61, 72–3, 107–8, 110, 150–2, 160, 164, 166, 169
    packaging 6, 48–51, 106–10, 150–4
    resumption of 7, 52, 136–8, 156, 164
    sideline 53, 157
    structure 72, 134–40
instrument (INST) 5, 74, 80–2, 176–8, 201
    Irish markers:
        co^n 176–7, 184
        de 176–7
        la 177
        tre 177
    prepositionless dative markers 177–8
    Welsh markers:
        a(c) 80
        o 80, 201
        trwy 81

Jamison, S. T. 166
Jeffers, R. 8 n.
Jones, E. D. 28 n.
Jones, R. M. 26 n., 27 n.
Jones, T. 29, 69

Kabata, K. 196 n.
Keenan, E. L. 16 n., 167
Kelleher, J. V. 32 n.
Kelly, F. 31, 32
King, G. 25, 59 n., 193
King, R. T. 187
Kronasser, H. 195 n.
Kuryłowicz, J. 20 n.

Lakoff, G. 22 n.
Langacker, R. 1, 16 n., 195 n.
Latin influence 26, 72–3, 122, 123, 183, 202
Leuman, M. 62
Lewis, H. 8 n., 180 n., 181, 199
Lindner, S. 22 n.
literary tradition 26
Lloyd, B. B. 23 n.
Lloyd-Morgan, C. 28 n.
Lovecy, I. 28 n.

mabinogion 27–8
Mac Airt, S. 32
Mac Cana, P. 30
McCloskey, J. 105 n.
Mac Eoin, G. 27 n., 29 n., 30
Mac Gearailt, U. 145–6
Mac Néill, E. 160
Mac Niocaill, G. 32

Mallory, J. 30 n.
Meid, W. 159
Mervis, C. B. 23 n.
metaphor 183
Morgan, T. J. 8 n., 9, 47 n., 180, 181, 186
Müller, N. 16 n., 21 n., 22 n., 167 n., 174 n., 177 n.,
    195, 196
Munro, P. 16 n.

narrative 39, 46, 47, 66, 87, 94–5, 106, 147–8, 159,
    162, 192, 200
narrative present 62
    see also historical present
Nettlau, M. 29
network models 23–4
Ní Mhuiríosa, M. 30 n.
nom d'action 118
nom verbal 14, 85, 99, 115

Ó Béarra, F. 30 n.
Ó Concheanainn, T. 29 n.
Ó Máille, T. 19 n.
O'Rahilly, C. 29, 30 n., 31, 140, 142
oral tradition 26
origin 76, 143, 187, 188–9, 202
Ó Sé, D. 20 n.
Ó Siadhail, M. 20 n., 150
O'Sullivan, W. 29 n.

P₁ 2
    definiteness 38–9, 46, 47, 86, 94, 99–100, 106,
        148, 159, 161, 165, 167
    genitive as 12, 48–7, 119, 180, 185–7
    indefinite 39, 46, 97
    markers 21–3, 25
        German: *von* 199
        Irish: *do* 84, 99, 115, 118, 120–1, 124, 125–30,
            144–6, 182, 187, 190–9, 201; *la* 84, 115–16,
            118, 120–1, 122, 124, 126–30, 140–2, 159, 160,
            183, 192, 194–7, 201, 202; *ó* 84–5, 115, 118,
            120–1, 122–3, 124–30, 142–3, 151, 160, 162,
            164, 183, 185, 188–9, 192, 199, 201, 202; *oc*
            126–7, 143–4, 159, 161; *ra/re* 146
        Latin: *ab* 183, 199; *apud* 162
        Welsh: *gan* 34, 39–41, 69, 180, 197–200, 202;
            i 34, 39–43, 180, 193–5; *o* 34–9, 69, 180–1,
            187–8, 199, 200; *y gan* 69, 71, 180, 197–200,
            202
    noun phrase 39, 96
    pronominal 38–9, 94
P₂ 2
    clause as 154, 159
    definiteness 38–9, 87, 99–100
    indefinite 39, 160
    noun phrase 39, 149–50, 154, 159, 160, 168–9,
        197
    pronominal 39, 149–50, 154, 159

Pape-Müller, S. 166 n.
Parry, T. 28 n.
participants 2, 62
passive 3, 14–22, 197
    agentive 17, 21–2, 68–74, 150–70, 202
        in German 166–7
        in Latin 166–7, 202
        in Vedic Sanskrit 166–7
    cael-passive 17, 181 n., 198
    clusters 157
    full, *see* agentive
Pedersen, H. 9, 20
Pinkster, H. 166
pivot 167–70
polysemy 22, 23, 179
Poppe, E. 59, 60 n., 61, 62
preposition:
    local sense 144, 184, 187, 190
        see also spatial sense
    locative function, *see* local sense
    merger 198
    sociative sense 184
    spatial sense 24, 25, 140, 179, 188, 195, 197
        see also local sense
    temporal sense 190
Prince, E. F. 6 n.
process 2, 62, 91, 96, 97
process noun 118, 119, 138
    Irish (IPN) 121, 125, 129–30, 136
    Latin (LPN) 122–3, 129, 136
prototype 22, 23, 24, 169, 179, 191, 194
    categories 23, 25
purpose clause 65, 104–5, 117

Radden, G. 22 n., 25, 195 n.
receiver 143
Rees, M. 77 n., 80 n.
Rice, S. 22 n., 24, 25, 196 n.
Richards, M. 8 n., 28, 37, 186 n.
Roberts, B. F. 27, 28 n.
Rosch, E. 23
Russell, P. 8 n., 9 n., 17, 18 n.

salience 133, 139–40, 169–70, 191
Sandra, D. 24, 25 n.
saorbhriathar (autonomous verb form) 19
Schmid, H. J. 23 n.
Schoenthal, G. 166 n.
Schwyzer, E. 21 n.
sef-construction 58–9
Shibatani, M. 15
Siewierska, A. 14, 16 n., 166
source (SOURCE) 75, 76, 85, 142, 143, 172, 194, 199,
    200, 202
    Welsh markers 75
Stockman, G. 80 n.
Strachan, J. 150

Szantyr, A. 62

Taylor, J. R. 2 n., 22 n., 23 n.
temporal organization:
  anterior 112, 159, 160
  hypothetical 111, 113
  linear 56, 112–13, 158, 160, 164
  posterior 111, 158, 160
texts:
  annals:
    Irish 32, 118–40, 161–5
    Welsh 29, 68–74
  compilatory nature of 26, 30
  dating 27–33
  law:
    Irish 31, 115–17, 160–1
    Welsh 28–9, 63–8
  narrative:
    Irish 21–31, 140–60
    Welsh 27–8
theme (Thema) 135, 136
Thomas, P. W. 13 n.
Thurneysen, R. 19, 30, 159
topic 59, 135 n., 166, 169
  New Topic 135, 169
Tristram, H. L. C. 26, 30
Tuggy, D. 23 n.

Ungerer, F. 23 n.
unit status 200

vagueness 23
Vandeloise, C. 22 n.
Van Oosten, J. 25 n., 166
Van Valin, R. D. 167
Vendryes, J. 20, 21 n.
verbal noun (VN) 3, 8–11
  clause:
    dependent 35, 37, 39, 43, 45, 49, 50, 52
    independent 35, 39, 43, 48–9, 50, 52, 57, 58,
      60, 62, 73, 88, 94–5, 100, 102, 134–5, 192, 201

clusters 54–5, 58
construction types 12–14
  $dyuot$+GEN$_{P1}$+$a(c)$+VN 50–1, 60, 119
  i_{P1}+VN 12, 42–3
  P1+do_{VN}(+P2) 83, 99–105, 107–8, 110, 113–15,
    117, 139, 181, 192–3
  P1+i_{VN}(+P2) 13–14, 42, 131–4, 181
  P2+do_{VN}+P1 13–14, 83, 99–105, 107, 110, 113,
    113–15, 122, 126–30, 133, 138–9, 182, 192, 201
  VN+GEN$_{P1}$ 12–13, 43–7, 50–1, 52, 53–5, 63–5,
    83, 92–8, 107, 108, 113, 114–15, 116, 119–20,
    185–7
  VN+PP$_{P1}$ 12, 33–43, 45, 48, 51–2, 53–5, 57,
    63–5, 83, 84–92, 106–7, 110, 112–15, 118,
    120–6, 129, 136, 138, 182, 186, 194, 201
  intransitive 37–8, 43, 86, 92, 106, 113, 114, 131–2,
    186
  narrative 62
  nominal characteristics 9, 11
  transitive 3, 37–8, 86, 106, 113, 114, 131–2, 186
  verbal characteristics 9–11
verbum dicendi 92
volition 4, 77, 191, 196
Vorgangsnomen 91–2, 96, 118

Wade-Evans, A. W. 28
Wagner, H. 20 n.
West, M. 29 n.
Wierzbicka, A. 23 n.
Wiliam, A. Rhys 29
Williams, I. 29
Williams, J. E. C. 30 n., 79 n., 174 n., 181, 197, 200
Williams, S. J. 13 n., 16 n., 42 n.
Windisch, E. 29 n., 31 n., 142, 145, 182, 183
Winters, M. 25 n.
Wittgenstein, L. 23 n.
Wodtko, D. 8 n.

Yule, G. 6 n.

Zimmer, H. 20 n.